Hear Me Talkin' to Ya

HEAR ME

The Story of Jazz
as Told by the Men Who Made It

TALKIN' TO YA

EDITED BY

Nat Shapiro & Nat Hentoff

DOVER PUBLICATIONS, INC.
New York

Published in Canada by General Publishing Company, Ltd., 30 Lesmill Road, Don Mills, Toronto, Ontario.

This Dover edition, first published in 1966, is a reprint of the work originally published by Rinehart and Company, Inc., in 1955. This edition contains the complete text of the original work except for a three-page discography which was deleted because it was no longer current.

This edition is published by special arrangement with Holt, Rinehart and Winston, Inc.

International Standard Book Number: 0-486-21726-4
Library of Congress Catalog Card Number: 66-28271

Manufactured in the United States of America
Dover Publications, Inc.
180 Varick Street
New York, N. Y. 10014

Acknowledgments

For arrangements made with various publishers, magazines, organizations and individuals whereby certain copyrighted material was permitted to be reprinted, and for the courtesy extended by them, the following acknowledgments are gratefully made:

Doubleday & Company, Inc. · for an excerpt from *His Eye Is on the Sparrow* by Ethel Waters and Charles Samuels. Copyright 1950, 1951 by Ethel Waters and Charles Samuels, reprinted by permission of Doubleday & Company, Inc.

Down Beat · for articles or portions of articles by or about, and portions of interviews with, the following: Wingy Manone, Nat Towles, Bunk Johnson, George Baquet, Louis Armstrong, Jack Weber, Preston Jackson, Lil Armstrong, George Wettling, Tony Catalano, Paul Mares, Ben Pollack, Wayne H. Rohlf, George Johnson, Jimmy McPartland, Frank Trumbauer, Russ Morgan, Jelly Roll Morton, Joe Oliver, Cuba Austin, Billie Holiday, Fletcher Henderson, John Hammond, Irving Mills, Ned E. Williams, Billy Strayhorn, T-Bone Walker, W. C. Handy, Maurice Waller, Joe Venuti, Red Nichols, Miff Mole, Count Basie, Lester Young, Gene Krupa, Artie Shaw, Roy Eldridge, Lena Horne, Charlie Parker, Stan Getz, Anita O'Day, Stan Kenton, Dave Brubeck, Woody Herman, Paul Desmond, Andre Previn. The material is reprinted by special permission of Down Beat, Inc. and Norman Weiser. Copyright 1938, 1939, 1940, 1941, 1942, 1943, 1944, 1945, 1946, 1947, 1948, 1949, 1950, 1951, 1952, 1953, 1954.

Duell, Sloan & Pearce, Inc. · for excerpts from *Mr. Jelly Roll* by Alan Lomax, by permission of Duell, Sloan & Pearce, Inc.

Ebony · for permission to use an excerpt from an article entitled "How Gangsters Run the Band Business" by Earl Hines which appeared in *Ebony* magazine.

v

Esquire · for excerpts from articles by Louis Armstrong, Count Basie, and Rex Stewart which originally appeared in the *Esquire 1947 Jazz Book.*

Farrar, Straus & Giroux, Inc. · for permission to use an excerpt from *The Trouble with Cinderella* by Artie Shaw, published by Farrar, Straus & Giroux, Inc. Copyright 1952.

Fawcett Publications · for excerpts from an article by Louis Armstrong which appeared in *True, The Man's Magazine,* November 1947.

Jazz · its editor, Bob Thiele, and Frederic Ramsey, Jr., for excerpts from *Chicago Documentary* by Frederic Ramsey, Jr. which first appeared in *Jazz* magazine.

Jazz Journal · and to Sinclair Traill for permission to use excerpts from articles appearing in *Jazz Journal* by John Provenzano, (May 1950); Armand Hug, (December 1950); Cecil and Lloyd Scott, (January 1954); Mezz Mezzrow, (May 1953); Count Basie, (May 1950); and Fats Waller, (May 1952).

Jazz Music · and to Max Jones for permission to use excerpts from articles appearing in *Jazz Music* about Mutt Carey and Albert Nicholas.

Jazz Record · and its editor Art Hodes for permission to use excerpts from articles that appeared in *Jazz Record* magazine by or about Carl Van Vechten and Muggsy Spanier.

Le Jazz Hot · and Charles Delauney for permission to use excerpts from articles that appeared in *Le Jazz Hot* by Preston Jackson, Tommy Brookins, and Kaiser Marshall.

Melody Maker · the weekly music newspaper published in London, England, and its editors, for permission to reprint excerpts from articles by and interviews with Ralph Berton, Jimmy McPartland, Joe Turner, Mary Lou Williams, Billie Holiday, Billy Ternent, W. T. Ed Kirkeby, Billy Eckstine, and Mary Ann McCall.

Metronome · for permission to use directly quoted material from interviews that appeared in *Metronome,* with Rex Stewart, Gene Krupa and Teddy Hill.

New Orleans Jazz Club · for permission to use excerpts from the feature, "Libretto," appearing in its publication, *The Second Line,* April 1951 and January 1951.

Random House · for permission to use excerpts from *Really the Blues* by Mezz Mezzrow and Bernard Wolfe. Reprinted by permission of Random House, Inc. Copyright 1946 by Random House, Inc.

RCA Victor Records · for permission to use excerpts from the notes written by W. T. Ed Kirkeby for the RCA Victor Album, *"Fats"* (LPT—6001).

The Record Changer · and its editors, Bill Grauer and Orrin Keepnews, for their cooperation and for permission to reprint excerpts from articles appearing in *The Record Changer* by or about Kid Ory, Bud Scott, Sidney Bechet, Ed Allen, Baby Dodds, Louis Armstrong, and Cuba Austin.

Hoagy Carmichael · for permission to reprint material from *The Stardust Road*. Copyright 1946 by Hoagland Carmichael.

The Stackpole Company · for permission to use an excerpt from *The Kingdom of Swing* by Benny Goodman and Irving Kolodin, published by Stackpole Sons, 1939.

Duke Ellington · and his publicity representative, Joe Morgan, for permission to use excerpts from a series of articles by Duke Ellington that appeared in *Swing* magazine, 1940.

Leonard Feather · for information from his *Encyclopedia of Jazz*, which was graciously made available to the editors prior to the publication of Mr. Feather's invaluable work.

Contributors

Ed Allen · Ferdinand Arbelo · Lil Armstrong · Louis Armstrong · Gus Arnheim · Cuba Austin · Buster Bailey · George Baquet · Danny Barker · Count Basie · Ray Bauduc · Sidney Bechet · Parker Berry · Ralph Berton · Wellman Braud · Tommy Brookins · Dave Brubeck · Mutt Carey · Hoagy Carmichael · Tony Catalano · Dick Clark · Kenny Clarke · Buck Clayton · Eddie Condon · Ray Conniff · Paul Desmond · Buddy De Franco · Baby Dodds · Billy Eckstine · Roy Eldridge · Duke Ellington · Pops Foster · Bud Freeman · Charlie Gaines · Erroll Garner · Stan Getz · Dizzy Gillespie · Joe Glaser · Albert Gleny · Benny Goodman · John Graase · Norman Granz · Benny Green · Freddie Greene · Johnny Guarnieri · Bobby Hackett · Edmond Hall · Fred "Tubby" Hall · John Hammond · W. C. Handy · Coleman Hawkins · Fletcher Henderson · Leora Henderson · Woody Herman · Teddy Hill · Earl Hines · Milt Hinton · Billie Holiday · Lena Horne · Armand Hug · Alberta Hunter · Preston Jackson · Bunk Johnson · George Johnson · James P. Johnson · Lonnie Johnson · May Johnson · Jo Jones · Richard M. Jones · Stan Kenton · W. T. Ed Kirkeby · Lee Konitz · Gene Krupa · Don Lamond · George Lewis · Arnold Loyacono · Wingy Manone · Paul Mares · Joe Marsala · Marty Marsala · Kaiser Marshall · Mary Ann McCall · Jimmy McPartland · Carmen McRae · Louis Metcalf · Mezz Mezzrow · Lizzie Miles · Irving Mills · Miff Mole · Russ Morgan · Jelly Roll Morton · Snub Mosely · Turk Murphy · Joe Newman · Albert Nicholas · Red Nichols · Anita O'Day · Joe

"King" Oliver · Kid Ory · Hot Lips Page · Tony Parenti · Tiny Parham · Charlie Parker · Oscar Peterson · Alphonse Picou · Ben Pollack · Andre Previn · Sam Price · John A. Provenzano · Popsie Randolph · Jim Robinson · Wayne H. Rohlf · Wally Rose · Pee Wee Russell · Bud Scott · Cecil Scott · Lloyd Scott · Tony Scott · Gene Sedric · Artie Shaw · Omer Simeon · Zutty Singleton · Willie "The Lion" Smith · Muggsy Spanier · Johnny St. Cyr · Johnny Stein · Rex Stewart · Billy Strayhorn · Joe Sullivan · Billy Taylor · Jack Teagarden · Billy Ternent · Nat Towles · Lennie Tristano · Frank Trumbauer · Bobby Tucker · Joe Turner · Carl Van Vechten · Joe Venuti · Frank Walker · T-Bone Walker · Fats Waller · Maurice Waller · Ethel Waters · Jack Weber · George Wettling · Paul White-man · Ernie Wilkins · Clarence Williams · Mary Lou Williams · Ned E. Williams · Spencer Williams · Lester Young.

Introduction

This is the story of jazz, as told by the musicians whose lives *are* that story. This book, therefore, is not an attempt to duplicate any of the formal histories of jazz that have appeared or are now in preparation. The academic histories are written by non-participants. This is the story—and the stories—that musicians tell.

From the remembrances of the musicians whose book this is, there emerges a portrait of the jazzman. This portrait is one of a skilled artist who takes his music seriously at the same time that he feels it joyously. This portrait, happily, is not anything like the caricatures of jazzmen too often found in the movies, daily press, and even in many otherwise accurate magazines and books. As you will hear in the voices to come, the musicians of jazz are citizens of a strong and original creativity, with deeply felt traditions of expression and a richly experienced way of life.

Our part in this book was solely to give these men and women their first collective opportunity to tell their story their own way. To do this, we talked to scores of jazzmen, from members of New Orleans brass bands to San Francisco polytonalists. The conversations took place in night clubs and bars, in offices, on the sidewalk between sets, and in homes. There were also letters, tape recordings, and telephone conversations. There were scrapbooks that have been saved for years by the families of musicians. Generous musicians even allowed us to look into material for books they themselves had been writing, or hoping, for a long time, to write.

We also looked through magazines and newspapers to find first-person accounts by jazz musicians that had been lost as the magazines went out of business and as newspapers settled into bound volumes in libraries. There were also articles that had appeared in specialized magazines that most readers would not ordinarily come by. And there were other articles and interviews in English and French publications to which even American jazz specialists do not often have access.

This book is told directly and in many voices. You will, therefore, find in it candor, conceit, warmth, contradictions, bitterness, nostalgia, fulfillment, and frustration. There are many incidents and personalities in these pages that cannot be found in the formal histories, for much comes out in informal conversation that does not usually get into the history books. Most of the material is used here with no editorial or grammatical interference. For example, Louis Armstrong's colorful reminiscences of Storyville are set down virtually as Louis himself typed them.

We do not pretend that, even in its informal way, this volume is entirely comprehensive. The world of jazz is multi-layered and complex. To tell the really complete story of jazz—and some of it has already been lost with the deaths of musicians—would require many more volumes than this one. And we hope that those volumes will eventually come into being, perhaps through grants-in-aid to researchers from foundations, perhaps through the continually valuable work of the Institute of Jazz Studies in New York, a non-profit organization of which Professor Marshall Stearns of Hunter College is Executive Director.

We did not, and could not, talk with all the jazz musicians now alive nor utilize all first-person accounts of jazzmen in print. We did not, and could not, try in one book to cover fully all periods and all aspects of jazz. We preferred to indicate the perspective of jazz evolution, as seen by the musicians themselves. We did, however, attempt to fill in several important and misunderstood areas of jazz in particularly complete detail.

This book, for example, tells the actual story—so far as it can be comprehended as a whole—of Bix Beiderbecke. And you will find here, too, a detailed account of the dissonant background and restless beginnings of modern jazz, as well as first-person descriptions of the way life was enjoyed in New Orleans at the start of the century, when jazz began to come of age there. There is a chapter on Kansas City that describes, as no previous book has, the extraordinary jazz spirit that pulsated through that city in the late 'twenties and early 'thirties.

But there are parts of the jazz story that are not covered in full detail. There are the blues. The blues weave through this work—as they inevitably must in any expression of jazz—but the blues deserve and need their own book. There are several large bands of the swing era, some of the earlier musicians, the boogie-woogie pianists, and several of the modern jazzmen whom we did not have space to include. There are the beginning and the development of jazz in the Southeast and the Southwest. There is the story of the pre-jazz spirituals, work songs, and play songs.

The people to whom we owe thanks number in the hundreds. They include all the musicians who gave their time and their memories. They include the many magazine editors who allowed us to reprint valuable material that might otherwise never have been collected in more permanent form. We are particularly grateful to Norman Weiser, publisher of *Down Beat* magazine, who opened the twenty-year files of that publication to us.

But finally, of course, we come back to the musicians themselves, for this is the book they wrote. Danny Barker, for example, whose career parallels the evolution of jazz. Danny is one of the musicians who is writing his own book and has interviewed and collected data from scores of the major jazzmen of the early nineteen hundreds who are still alive. He is one of the jazz researchers who deserves aid.

We should also like to thank particularly "the man who plays like the wind," Jo Jones, who helped make Kansas City come alive in these pages. And, together with the long list of other musicians who contributed to this book, we would like to acknowledge the aid and support of Joe Glaser, John Hammond, Bob Maltz, Frank Walker, Willard Alexander, and Leonard Feather, Sinclair Traill, of *Jazz Journal*; Orrin Keepnews and Bill Grauer, of *The Record Changer*; Mike Nevard and Max Jones, of *The Melody Maker*; George Simon, of *Metronome*; Art Hodes and Bob Thiele, of the late-lamented *Jazz Record* and *Jazz*, respectively; Charles Delauney, of *Le Jazz Hot;* Dr. Edmond Souchon, of the New Orleans Jazz Club; and Carl Haverlin, Russell Sanjek, and Theodora Zavin, of Broadcast Music, Inc. We would also like to thank especially Lillian Ross, of *The New Yorker,* for her advice and encouragement, and Mrs. Nat Shapiro (Dr. Vera Miller), for her astute editorial judgment, patience, and black coffee.

Contents

III. *"Travelin' Light"*

IV. *"Undecided"*

PART I

"Way Down Yonder in New Orleans"

1

It was always a musical town—especially The District—Storyville.

DANNY BARKER

One of my pleasantest memories as a kid growing up in New Orleans was how a bunch of us kids, playing, would suddenly hear sounds. It was like a phenomenon, like the Aurora Borealis—maybe. The sounds of men playing would be so clear, but we wouldn't be sure where they were coming from. So we'd start trotting, start running—"It's this way!" "It's that way!"—And, sometimes, after running for a while, you'd find you'd be nowhere near that music. But that music could come on you any time like that. The city was full of the sounds of music. . . .

CLARENCE WILLIAMS

Yes, New Orleans was always a musical town—a happy town. Why, on Mardi Gras and Christmas all the houses were open and there were dances all over. It was "open house" everywhere, and you could walk in almost any door and have a drink and eat and join the party.

DANNY BARKER

There were countless places of enjoyment that employed musicians, not including private affairs, balls, soirees, banquets, marriages, deaths, christenings, Catholic communions, confirmations, picnics at the lake front, country hay rides, and advertisements of business concerns. During the carnival season (Mardi Gras) any little insignificant affair was sure to have some kind of music and each section would engage their neighborhood favorite. It might be Joe Oliver, who lived around the corner; or Cheeky Sherman, on somebody's piano; or Sandpaper George; or Hudson, on toilet pipe, now called the bazooka; or Picou, on the kazoo, a kazoo inserted into an old E-flat clarinet, which he fingered as he blew.

The colored and white bands battled (or bucked), frequently from opposite lake-front camps. It was the custom to have picnics and family outings on Sundays during the summer at places like Spanish Fort, West End, Milenberg, Birch Town, and Seabrook.

The city was split by Canal Street, with one part of the people uptown and the Creoles downtown. When people would come into New Orleans, like gamblers and workers from Memphis, and they'd say "Let's go down to Frenchtown," that meant you went below Canal Street. Storyville was below Canal Street on the outer part.

But the people I knew called all that was in Storyville "The District." I never heard it called Storyville. It got called that when somebody up here in the North read about it. It was never Storyville to me. It was always The District—the red light district.

LOUIS ARMSTRONG

There was so much good music that was played in Storyville—they talked about it and its musicians so much until the word District being used so much wouldn't sound so good . . . Storyville has been discussed in colleges and some of the largest universities in the world . . . If not all over the world . . . I'll bet right now most of the youngsters and hot club fans who hear the name Storyville hasn't the least idea that it consisted of some of the biggest prostitutes in the world . . . Standing in their doorways nightly in their fine and beautiful negligees—faintly calling to the boys as they passed their cribs.

Storyville was kind of divided—I'd say—about middle ways of the City of New Orleans . . . Canal Street was the dividing line

4

between the uptown and the downtown section . . . And right behind Canal Street was Storyville . . . And right off Canal Street was the famous Basin Street which was also connected with Storyville . . . And somewheres in or near Storyville was a famous gambling joint called Twenty-Five . . . That was the place where all the big-time pimps and hustlers would congregate and play "Cotch" (that's a game they played with three cards shuffled and dealt from the bottom of the deck) . . . And you could win or lose a whole gang of money . . . These pimps and hustlers, et cetera, would spend most of their time at Twenty-Five until their girls would finish turning tricks in their cribs . . . Then they would meet them and check up on the night's take . . . Lot of the prostitutes lived in different sections of the city and would come down to Storyville just like they had a job . . . There were different shifts for them . . . Sometime—two prostitutes would share the rent in the same crib together . . . One would work in the day and the other would beat out that night shift . . . And business was so good in those days with the fleet of sailors and the crews from those big ships that come in the Mississippi River from all over the world—kept them very very busy.

ALPHONSE PICOU

Those were happy days, man, happy days. Buy a keg of beer for one dollar and a bag full of food for another and have a *cowein*. These boys don't have fun nowadays. Talking 'bout wild and wooly! There were two thousand registered girls and must have been ten thousand unregistered. And all crazy about clarinet-blowers!

DANNY BARKER

New Orleans, until the 'twenties, was the safest haven in the Americas for the world's most vicious characters. There was a charge, that a person could be arrested for, called "D and S" (dangerous and suspicious) whereby the police had the power to arrest anyone who could not walk to the 'phone booth to call his or her employer and prove that they earned an honest livelihood, or anyone who looked crafty, slick, or sinister.

5

Most arrests were Negroes who frequented barrooms and gambling joints during working hours.

As for the big sporting houses in The District, they were for whites. It was before my time, but they tell me that a mulatto passing for white could get in. And there were farmers and sugar men and riverboat men all through Louisiana who were mulattoes. So, if you looked white or Spanish, you went in. Lulu White and the Countess Willie Piazza were themselves reputed to be Creole.

JELLY ROLL MORTON

So, in the year of 1902, when I was about seventeen years old, I happened to invade one of the sections where the birth of jazz originated from.

The Tenderloin District in New Orleans was considered second to France, meaning the second greatest in the world, with extensions for blocks and blocks on the north side of Canal Street.

Every place in New Orleans had a gambling house, and I don't know of any time that the racetracks were ever closed—a hundred days of races at City Park, then they would be at the Fair Grounds for another hundred days—and so they would go on continuously for three hundred and sixty-five days a year.

I'm telling you this Tenderloin District was like something that nobody has ever seen before or since. The doors were taken off the saloons there from one year to the next. Hundreds of men were passing through the streets day and night. The chippies in their little-girl dresses were standing in the crib doors singing the blues.

The streets were crowded with men. Police were always in sight, never less than two together, which guaranteed the safety of all concerned. Lights of all colors were glittering and glaring. Music was pouring into the streets from every house. . . .

Some very happy, some very sad, some with the desire to end it all by poison, some planning a big outing, a dance, or some other kind of enjoyment. Some were real ladies in spite of their downfall and some were habitual drunkards and some were dope fiends as follows: opium, heroin, cocaine, laudanum, morphine, et cetera. I was personally sent to Chinatown many times with a sealed note and a small amount of money and would bring back several cards of

6

hop. There was no slipping and dodging. All you had to do was walk in to be served.

They had everything in The District from the highest class to the lowest—creep joints where they'd put the feelers on a guy's clothes, cribs that rented for about five dollars a day and had just about room enough for a bed, small-time houses where the price was from fifty cents to a dollar and they put on naked dances, circuses, and jive. Then, of course, we had the mansions where everything was of the highest class. These houses were filled up with the most expensive furniture and paintings. Three of them had mirror parlors where you couldn't find the door for the mirrors, the one at Lulu White's costing thirty thousand dollars. Mirrors stood at the foot and head of all the beds. It was in these mansions that the best of the piano players worked.

SPENCER WILLIAMS

All along this street of pleasure there were the dance halls, honky-tonks, and cabarets, and each one had its music. My old friend, Tony Jackson, who composed *Pretty Baby* and *Some Sweet Day*, used to play piano at a house run by Miss Antonia Gonzales, who sang and played the cornet. The largest of the cabarets on Basin Street was the Mahogany Hall, owned by my aunt, Miss Lulu White, and when my mother died, I went to live with her and became her adopted son. I'd go to sleep to the sound of the mechanical piano playing ragtime tunes, and when I woke up in the morning it would still be playing. The saloons in those days never had the doors closed, and the hinges were all rusty and dusty. Little boys and grownups would walk along the avenues, swaying and whistling jazz tunes.

BUNK JOHNSON

That was the Crescent City in them days, full of bars, honky-tonks, and barrel houses. A barrel house was just a piano in a hall. There was always a piano player working. When I was a kid, I'd go into a barrel house and play 'long with them piano players 'til early in the mornin'. We used to play nuthin' but the blues.

I knew Mamie Desdoumes real well. Played many a concert with

7

her singing those same blues. She was pretty good-looking, quite fair, with a *nice* head of hair. She was a hustlin' woman. A blues-singing poor gal. Used to play pretty passable piano around them dance halls on Perdido Street.

When Hattie Rogers or Lulu White would put it out that Mamie was going to be singing in their place, the white men would turn out in bunches and them whores would clean up.

LOUIS ARMSTRONG

Lulu White was a famous woman of the sporting world in Story-ville . . . She had a big house on Basin Street called Mahogany Hall . . . The song was written after her house had gotten so famous. . . . Rich men came there from all parts of the world to dig those beautiful Creole prostitutes . . . And pay big money . . . Lulu White was colored. . . . Around the corner from Lulu White was the famous Cabaret of Tom Anderson . . . All the race-horse men went there during their stay and the racing season in New Orleans . . . In those days a band who played for those places didn't need to worry about salaries . . . Their tips were so great until they did not even have to touch their nightly gappings . . . Most of the places paid off the musicians every night after the job was over instead of the weekly deal . . . That was because those places were threatened to be closed any minute. So the musicians and the performers didn't take any chances.

MAHOGANY HALL
"SOUVENIR" BOOKLET

The NEW Mahogany Hall

A picture of which appears on the cover of this souvenir was erected specially for Miss Lulu White at a cost of $40,000. The house is built of marble and is four story; containing five parlors, all handsomely furnished, and fif-teen bedrooms. Each room has a bath with hot and cold water and extension closets.

The elevator, which was built for two, is of the latest style. The entire house is steam heated and is the handsomest house of its kind. It is the only one where you can get three shots for your money—

> The shot upstairs,
> The shot downstairs,
> And the shot in the room. . . .

This famous West Indian octoroon first saw the light of day thirty-one years ago. Arriving in this country at a rather tender age, and having been fortunately gifted with a good education it did not take long for her to find out what the other sex was in search of.

In describing Miss Lulu, as she is most familiarly called, it would not be amiss to say that besides possessing an elegant form she has beautiful black hair and blue eyes, which have justly gained for her the title of the "Queen of the Demi-Monde."

Her establishment, which is situated in the central part of the city, is unquestionably the most elaborately furnished house in the city of New Orleans, and without a doubt one of the most elegant places in this or any other country.

She has made a feature of boarding none but the fairest of girls—those gifted with nature's best charms, and would, under no circumstances, have any but that class in her house.

As an entertainer Miss Lulu stands foremost, having made a life-long study of music and literature. She is well read and one that can interest anybody and make a visit to her place a continued round of pleasure.

ADVERTISEMENT
NEW ORLEANS BLUE BOOK

COUNTESS WILLIE PIAZZA

Is one place in the Tenderloin District you can't very well afford to miss. The Countess Piazza has made it a study to try to make everyone jovial who visits her house. If you have the "blues," the Countess and her girls can cure them. She has, without a doubt, the most handsome and intelligent octoroons in the United States. You should see them; they are all entertainers.

If there is anything new in the singing and dancing line that you would like to see while in Storyville, Piazza's is the place to visit, especially when one is out hopping with friends—the women in particular.

The Countess wishes it to be known that while her mansion is peerless in every respect, she only serves the "amber fluid."

"Just ask for Willie Piazza."
PHONE 4832 MAIN
317 N. Basin

DANNY BARKER

There were all kinds of characters and all kinds of places in The District. I've been keeping a scrapbook, based on what I remember and on what other musicians have told me. Here are some of the things from my book:

Definitions of Different Types of Joints

Whore house—managed by a larceny-hearted landlady, *strictly* business.

Brothel—juice joint with rooms, and a bunk or a cot near.

Sporting house—lots of stimulants, women, music. An old queer or cripple serves.

Crib—Two or three stars venture for themselves, future landladies.

House of assignation—women pull shifts and report where they are needed.

Clip joint—While one jives you, another creeps or crawls in and rifles your pockets.

And here are some sporting women and the nicknames of a few well-known Crescent City characters:

Albertine McKay, former sweetheart of Lee Collins. She marched him around with a .38 special loaded with dum-dum bullets.

Daisy Parker, Louis Armstrong's moll, who greeted him with a brickbat.

Kidneyfoot Rella, who is said to have spit in Black Benny's face as he lay dead in his coffin.

Also—Flamin' Mamie, Crying Emma, Bucktown Bessie, Dirty Dog, Steel Arm Johnny, Mary Meathouse, Gold Tooth Gussie, Big Butt Annie, Naked Mouf Mattie, Bird Leg Nora, Bang Zang, Boxcar Shorty, Sneaky Pete, Titanic, Coke Eye Laura, Yellow Gal, Black Sis, Boar Hog, Yard Dog, Bodidily, Roody Doody, Big Bull Cora, Piggy, Big Piggy, Stingaree, Bull Frog Sonny, Toot Nan, Knock on the Wall, Sore Dick, Sugar Pie, Cherry Red, Buck Tooth Rena, Bad Blood, Copper Wire, Snaggle Mouf Mary, Linker-Top, Topsy, Scratch, Joe the Pimp, Onery Bob, Tee Tee, Tee Nome, Tee Share, Tee Boy, Raw Head, Smoke Stack, Stack O Dollars, Pupsy, Boogers, Copper Cent, Street Rabbit, Boo Boo, Big Boo Boo, Fast Black, Eight Ball, Lily the Crip, Tenderloin Thelma, Three Finger Annie, Charlie Bow Wow, Good Lord the Lifter, Peachanno, Cold Blooded Carrie, Miss Thing, Jack the Bear.

CLARENCE WILLIAMS

Those places were really something to see—those sportin' houses. They had the *most* beautiful parlors, with cut glass, and draperies, and rugs, and expensive furniture. They were just like millionaires' houses. And the girls would come down dressed in the finest of evening gowns, just like they were going to the opera. They were just beautiful. Their hair-dos were just so, and I'm telling you that Ziegfeld didn't have any more beautiful women than those. Some of them looked Spanish, and some were Creoles, some brown-skins, some chocolate-brown. But they all had to have that figure.

Places like that were for rich people, mostly white. Oh, once in a while a sailor might come, but generally only the wealthiest would come. Why, do you know that a bottle of beer was a dollar? The customers would buy champagne mostly and would always insist on giving the musicians money. When the piano player would get tired, there would be a player piano that you put a quarter in and we'd make money then too. Those houses hired nothing but the best, but only piano players, and maybe a girl to sing. And there was no loud playin' either. It was sweet, just like a hotel.

Of course, those houses were so impressive that lots of people would be scared to go in. But, in the other part of the section, there were cabarets and dance halls and lots of hustlers. There were places like the Red Onion, the Keystone, and Spanola's, which was one of the roughest. Spanola's was on Basin Street, a place where the roustabouts and the lowest of people went. There a man could meet a gal, then do his business without any fuss at all.

Talk about those jam sessions you have today! Why, you should have seen the sessions we had then. 'Round about four A.M., the girls would get through work and would meet their P.I.'s (that's what we called pimps) at the wine rooms. Pete Lala's was the head-quarters, the place where all the bands would come when they got off work, and where the girls would come to meet their main man. It was a place where they would come to drink and play and have breakfast and then go home to bed.

Most of the P.I.'s were gamblers and pianists. The reason so many of them were pianists was because whenever they were down on their luck, they could always get a job and be close to their girls —play while the girls worked.

Some of the P.I.'s would wear diamonds the size of dimes. And do you know that you could buy all of the cocaine, morphine, heroin, and hop you wanted in the section, almost right out in the open? But I never knew hardly any musicians that took dope. It was mostly the girls who were out to destroy themselves if their man left them or something like that. And in those days there were no teen-agers or anything like that takin' dope. Of course, there were lots of young girls workin' in the sportin' houses, but that was different. Another thing about the section, there was never a holdup or robbery that I could remember. You could drink and never be afraid that anybody'd take your money.

Well, at Pete Lala's, everybody would gather every night and there'd be singin' and playin' all night long. The piano players from all over the South would be there, in for the races, and everybody would take a turn until daylight.

2

For every occasion—dances, funerals, parties, and pa-rades—there was a band and there were some mighty battles.

LOUIS ARMSTRONG

As many bands as you heard, that's how many bands you heard playing right.

I thought I was in Heaven playing second trumpet in the Tuxedo Brass Band—and they had some funeral marches that would just touch your heart, they were so beautiful.

DANNY BARKER

My grandfather worked for Emile Labat, the Creole section's most successful burial establishment. Emile Labat owned two famous horses—the most beautiful in New Orleans. They always pulled the hearse, which was driven by a very old, dark, very solemn man who never smiled. His name was Joe Never Smile. On occasions, if the widow of the deceased person was sincere in her sorrow, the under-taker would suggest that the horses be draped with a beautiful lace covering. If the deceased was grown, the covering was black. If a child, white. The fee for that was fifteen or twenty dollars extra, and it gave the funeral procession a very solemn look. In fact, the spectators felt extra sad and would say, "They sure putting so-and-so away in fine style."

Now getting back to Joe Never Smile and the two horses. It was known throughout New Orleans and vicinity that these two horses cried on certain occasions. That is if the deceased person were going upward and not below. It was a mystery to everybody, and, on one of my trips to New Orleans, I casually asked Grandfather what was the gimmick. He said Joe Never Smile was a very slick character. Joe always kept a quart wine bottle full of onion juice, and, in Joe's spare moments, he would buy a sack of onions and squeeze the juice in the bottle. Just before leaving for a funeral, he would pour the juice on a cloth and wipe the horses' eyes while no one was around.

Emile Labat would have raised hell as he was kind to his animals and a humanitarian. . . .

As this observer recalls, in the days before they closed The District (which was 1917), the most exciting form of musical entertainment (aggregation) was not the jazz bands but the brass bands. The bass beat on the bass drum, beautifully executed by Black Benny, would suddenly silence a crowd of some seven or eight thousand loud and boisterous pleasure-seekers. All ears perked up for maybe a minute anxiously awaiting the lead trumpet to blow the three double-eighth notes, *ta-ta*, *ta-ta*, *ta-ta*, signaling the band members who were scattered nearby, having wandered among the crowd. Characters like Bunk Johnson, Buddy Petit, Kid Rena, Frankie Duson, Chris Kelly, would be in the nearest barroom drinking—jiving some sporting women and drinking to everybody's health, and ruining his own. The bandmen who didn't indulge would be coralled by groups of admirers and answering questions on the merits and playing abilities of the stars.

It was the greatest thrill of a kid to hold and watch a musician's instrument whom he idolized. The most miserable feeling a youngster in New Orleans can experience is to be in a classroom in school, studying, and hear a brass band approaching, swinging like crazy, then pass the school, and fade off in the distance. You will witness a lot of sad expressions in that room. Now if it happens to be lunch hour, recess twelve to one, when the bell rings at one P.M., a lot of seats will be vacant. That is in schools in the barrel-house section. Now that's an honest fact, as this observer was guilty three or four times himself. The music would excite and move you to such an extent that when you would realize it, you had "second-lined" maybe ten or twenty blocks from school. . . .

There were many funerals that had three or four bands of music.

It was not rare to see funerals which had three or four brass bands in the procession, because a member probably was active in eight to twelve organizations—Masons, Odd Fellows, Tulane Club or Zulu Club, the Vidalia, Veterans, Charity, and a few more.

It was more than likely his request to be buried as he lived, among a crowd and lots of music. As in the case of Giles, the greatest of them all, the Excelsior Brass Band's bass drummer—and Black Benny. Every musician in New Orleans offered their services.

On both occasions it was a sad sight to see their silent bass drums draped in mourning, carried by a close friend behind the hearse.

The money earned (three or four dollars) for playing a funeral was and is still called "fun money" and is usually quickly spent for drinks after the musicians disband.

WINGY MANONE

On the way to the graveyard, they all walked slowly, following the cornet player. The cornet player was the boss. Sometimes it took them four hours to get to the cemetery. All the way they just swayed to the music and moaned. At the graveside they chanted questions, such as "Did he ramble?" "Did he gamble?" or "Did he lead a good life until the police shot him down on St. James Street?" Then after the body was buried, they'd go back to town and all the way they'd swing. They just pulled the instruments apart. They played the hottest music in the world.

NAT TOWLES

Yeah, that's just the way it was in those days. You'd march to the graveyard playing very solemn and very slow, then on the way back all hell would break loose! No music, you understand, we didn't know what a sheet of music was. Just six or seven pieces, half a dozen men pounding it out all together, each in his own way and yet somehow fitting in all right with the others. It had to be right, and it was, because it came from the right place.

16

Oh, the brass bands might have had more men, two clarinets maybe, or two cornets. Bolden used Bunk on second, but I never heard that outfit. Oliver called Louis north to Chicago, but that was an exception. Usually there were six musicians in a band: a clarinetist, trombonist, banjo player, drummer, bassman, and trumpeter, who was almost always the leader. Once in a while a pianist might be added, but never a saxman! One of the Hall boys, not Edmond and not Robert, tried to make a go of the saxophone. He didn't get many jobs.

KID ORY

And during Mardi Gras—man! That's when we really had fun. All day and night bands marched up and down the streets playing their heads off. We played sometimes for a local colored fraternity and marched in front of their parade.

The whites had an idea of a real king—he came in on Canal Street. The colored people had the King of the Zulus and he came in on Basin Street—dressed in funny feathers and straw—boy, that was something.

ZUTTY SINGLETON

There were so many bands in New Orleans. But most of the musicians had day jobs, you know—trades. They were bricklayers and carpenters and cigar makers and plasterers. Some had little businesses of their own—coal and wood and vegetable stores. Some worked on the cotton exchange and some were porters. They *had* to work at other trades 'cause there were so many musicians, so many bands. It was just about the most musical town in the country. Most all the kids took music lessons of some kind, and I got my inspiration from my uncle, Willie Bontemps, who played bass and guitar in Jack Carey's band. I played my first jobs with Steve Lewis—house parties and such.

We played for society kids on Saturday afternoons—that was with Papa Celestin and the Tuxedo Band. We also played at the New Orleans Country Club and the Louisiana Restaurant, which was a fine, high-class place.

DANNY BARKER

Being a musician was not usually a full-time job in New Orleans. The musicians had trades and professions. They were skilled craftsmen—master bricklayers, plasterers, roofers, excellent carpenters, cigar makers, pavers, et cetera. For example, there'd be a whole family, all of whom were slaters. And another, all of whom were plasterers. They would become apprenticed to their grandfathers and learn the family craft.

Some of the families were half-French and half-African. And numerous families were cigar makers, which shows the Spanish influence.

So, if you were a musician, you had a regular trade, and on week ends, or on some nights, you played music.

ALPHONSE PICOU

I was born in the year 1879. My father was a cigar maker and my mother was a housewife.

As a boy, the first jazz I heard was a jazz band at the corner of St. Phillips and Claiborne. It was called the Excelsior Band. The only musician I remember from that band was Fice Quiyrit, the trumpet player. It was a long time ago.

Was it ragtime? No, no, it was nothing but marches they was playing—brass marches—parade music. I think the first ragtime jazz band I ever heard was Boo Boo Fortunea. He was the only man at that time who played the slide trombone. It was approximately— well, before 1900. I was still fifteen or sixteen years old then.

He played the trombone and he was a barber at that time. He was living right around the corner from where I lived and he heard me practicing my instrument and he came up to my house and knocked on the door. My mother went to the door and she asked him what he wanted. He said, "I would like to see that young man who is playing that instrument." So she said, "That's my son." He said, "Will you call him to the door?" And I went to the door and he says to me, "Were you the one that was playing the clarinet?" I says, "Yes." He says, "Well, I'd like for you to come to my shop around the corner because I want to talk to you."

So I went to the shop and we had a talk and he said to me, "Will you come here tonight and I would like to have you play with me in my band." I told him, "Of course. Okay." He told me to be there at eight. It was the first time that I ever played with a band. I was sixteen.

I had been taking lessons before that. I took lessons for about eighteen months. My teacher's name was Mr. Morand. He was a Creole.

Now let me finish telling you about the band. So I was invited down to the rehearsal that night and I went to the place and I said to him, "What do you want me to do?" I said, "Do you want me to play my instrument? Is there any music?" He said, "Music? You don't need none." I said, "How am I going to play?" He said, "You're going to come in on the choruses." I said, "All right," and then I tuned up; we all tuned up our instruments. He said that when I couldn't come in, to stay out and listen until I could come in. I did just what he told me and we got into it, and through with it, and the whole band shook my hand and told me I was great.

That was on a Thursday night, the rehearsal, and on the Saturday night following they had an engagement to play a ball (at that time the dances were called balls) on Liberty Street. So I went there and I got there at about eight. The hall was jam-packed. I was not really satisfied about their not having any music but I thought I would try anyway. I went and took a few drinks and the first thing you know I was playing more than them!

Every number we played the people just clapped their hands. We had to play them two or three times and that's the way I started with a band.

That particular style of playing without music was very new to me. I think it was impossible to me! It seemed a sort of style of playing without notes.

I remember when we got a new piece of music we would get the music and play the tunes with the music, then, after that we didn't need that music no more. We'd go "out of the way" with it. That was ragtime.

JOHNNY ST. CYR

A jazz musician have to be a working class of man, out in the open all the time, healthy and strong. That's what's wrong today; these new guys haven't got the force. They don't *like* to play all night; they don't think they *can* play unless they're loaded. But a working man have the *power* to play hot, whiskey or no whiskey. You see, the average working man is very musical. Playing music for him is just relaxing. He gets as much kick out of playing as other folks get out of dancing. The more enthusiastic his audience is, why, the more spirit the working man's got to play. And with your natural feelings that way, you never make the same thing twice. Every time you play a tune, new ideas come to mind and you slip that on in.

DANNY BARKER

There was a variety of prices. In my day, you'd get about three dollars for a parade or funeral. It was according to the hours. If the parade lasted from nine A.M. to six P.M.—an all-day parade—you'd probably get eight or nine dollars.

Everything in New Orleans was competitive. People would always be betting on who was the best and greatest in everything. That's where the battles of music came in.

Lots of the bands couldn't read too much music. So they used a fiddle to play the lead—a fiddle player could read—and that was to give them some protection. The banjo then was strictly a rhythm instrument. Buddy Bolden would say, "Simmer down, let me hear the sound of them feet." The New Orleans bands, you see, didn't play with a flat sound. They'd shade the music. After the band had played with the two or three horns blowing, they'd let the rhythm have it. That's what Buddy Bolden meant when he said that. The rhythm then often would play that mixture of African and Spanish syncopation—with a beat—and with just the rhythm going. They'd let the people use their imagination for the other sounds.

The marching brass bands used more instruments than the dance bands. And those brass bands could play legitimate marches, the same marches the Army Band of the United States would

20

play for the President if he died. They could play beautiful hymns and marches, like *Nearer My God to Thee* and *Maryland, My Maryland*. But when they came back from the funeral—and the band, by the way, never went into the cemetery when the band played for a funeral—well, on the way back, they'd put their music in their pockets and everybody started wailing.

I remember the Onward Brass Band had to play the marches for the Masonics or the Odd Fellows. They hired one band during the day—a big military band—that would play all the marches and that would introduce each dignitary of the organization with military music. But the band was sitting. And between those introductions and the marching and the drilling, they would play some dance music, so they would swing.

They played the shuffle beat on the snare drum and mostly two beats on the bass drums. At first, in the bands, the snare drums and the bass drums were played by different men like in the marching bands. But there was one particular guy in New Orleans who put the two drums together and played both himself, and that's where the foot pedal was invented.

EDMOND HALL

As for why New Orleans was such a musical city and had so many bands, I think one reason had to do with the clubs. There were a lot of private clubs, organizations, in New Orleans. Two or three guys would get together, you know, and make up the club and it would grow. So, when a member of the club died, they would hire a band for his funeral, and if the club had some part in a parade, they would have a band for that too. All the clubs tried to outdo each other. Like I remember what used to happen when different clubs would go to their camps out on the water by the lake front. There would be one band playing at the camp of one club and another band at the camp of another, and each band would try to outplay the other. You could hear music real well over the water, you know.

One thing about funerals, by the way, that isn't made clear in some of the stories. The bands themselves never went into the cemeteries. . . .

You could always make a living in New Orleans just playing gigs like that—funerals, lawn parties, parades, et cetera. Buddy Petit, for example, never did take a steady job. He didn't have to, and that's true of a lot of men who are good musicians, and who, by the way, have never been written about. Now, Buddy Petit used to carry a book with him listing the dates he had in advance. He was his own contractor. Buddy could tell you one year from the day he spoke to you where you were playing if he had a job for you—he was booked that far in advance; and Buddy always got a deposit on a job in advance. Even if the job was a year away. What finally killed Buddy's reputation as a contractor was that he often had two or three jobs a night. He couldn't play each one so he'd have other bands out and the people who hired him never knew whether his band was the one that was going to be there or not.

Louis Armstrong and Buddy played a lot of funerals together, by the way. Buddy is a man they've never written much about. He kind of what you call set a pace around New Orleans. He was a real leader and he set the pace for a lot of the other bands. I mean these other bands would hear Buddy play something and they would all want to play it. So far as I know he only left New Orleans once to go out to California with Jelly Roll Morton —to Los Angeles. I don't know what happened but he didn't stay out there. If Buddy had left New Orleans to go to Chicago when a lot of the other men left, I'm positive he would have had a reputation equal to what the others got. . . .

In the very early days of brass bands, in the 'nineties and even before, the music was mostly written—I mean in the kind of band my father played in. As time went on, there was more improvising.

I started on guitar, not clarinet, in 1917, when I was seventeen. My father was a musician. His name was Edward Hall. As a matter of fact, he was a member of the Onward Brass Band that came to New York from New Orleans in 1891. Some booking agent brought the band to New York that year. I'm not sure though what the occasion was. I remember my father telling me they were in New York eighteen days. The last member of the band who was living, by the way, died a few months ago. He was the tuba player and he was about eighty-three years old when he died.

The band came all the way from New Orleans just for that New York event. As I remember the story, every state sent a band. It was a kind of festival, and that New Orleans band my father was in won first prize. . . .

In the brass band, on my own instrument they used to have four different clarinets: an E-flat clarinet, a C clarinet, an A clarinet, and a B-flat clarinet—and a musician had to know all four. The reason for that was when there was something to play in the key of E-flat we would pick up the E-flat clarinet, and the same thing when there was something in the key of A, et cetera. That shows you how much music advances. Today you can take one clarinet and play everything on it. But the fact is that when we had to know all four the standards of musicianship in the brass bands were pretty high. . . .

There were five of us in my family, and when we got to a certain age my father would pass out clarinets. The first four of us each got a different kind of clarinet; the fifth was too young but he picked it up later. He is Herbert Hall, who has the band at the Cinderella Club in Greenwich Village now. . . .

High Society was one of the testing pieces for a clarinet player who wanted to play in a band in New Orleans. The Picou chorus was the accepted one. It was first a piccolo solo in a brass band but Picou was actually the first to play it on the clarinet. Anyway, that's the story I heard. Of course, everybody played their own way on the chorus. Nobody played it note for note. Each man used different ideas, like I remember Barney Bigard's way of playing it. But the Picou chorus was the basic one, the first four bars especially.

ALPHONSE PICOU

I composed so many tunes. How did I happen to play *High Society*, the famous chorus? Well, I was seventeen at the time. I was playing at that time with John Robichaux, and before that I was playing with the Manuel Perez band, and he used to get all that old-time music—what they're asking for right now.

He bought that *High Society* for me. It was a march tune. We

23

were at Mahogany Hall then. I took the piccolo part and transposed it to my instrument. It made a wonderful hit. So the next night we had to play at another hall where they had all the Creole meetings. At that time they didn't allow a dark man to come in. If you were dark you had to stay out. I was there, and Manuel Perez liked the way I played *High Society* and he says, "Come on in"—when a crowd was there—"Come on and play *High Society*," and they let me play that solo by myself. I made a wonderful hit—Lord! They played *High Society* all night. . . .

I played parades with Manuel Perez and the Onward Brass Band, also with Joe Oliver and Kid Rena. I played funerals too.

KID ORY

I had a brass band too. When I got a job I'd supply any number of men they wanted. If I didn't have them, I could pick them up. I had a sign on my house, "ORCHESTRA AND BRASS BAND." You couldn't miss it. At that time they used to advertise dances and picnics by hiring a wagon with a big sign on the side with the band playing in the wagon. I decided I'd try a new idea and advertise my band that way. I rented a furniture wagon and told a fellow to make signs, "KID ORY," with address and telephone number. After that I began to get lots of calls for jobs and got real well known. . . .

They used to have "cutting contests" every time you'd get on the streets. Freddie Keppard's band whipped us good because he was a stronger trumpet player than we had at first. Then we started whipping everybody. The public was on my side. When the other band was finished, they'd tie the wagons together. The crowd tied them to keep them from running away from us.

I used to say, "I'll let you go when I think you should go." Mutt Carey's brother played trombone. I liked him but he didn't like me. He was kind of jealous because Mutt came to play with me. I gave him a spanking in a contest. He stopped me afterward on the corner and said, "He can beat me playing trombone, but he can't whip me!" I threw my arms around him and said, "I just love you, Jack." He turned out to be a preacher before he passed.

GEORGE LEWIS

We used to come to work or go on parades in big horse-drawn trucks, and when two trucks met, there would be a "cutting contest." One day we caught Buddy (Petit) drunk, and our band really wore them out. The following Sunday we drove up and we saw Buddy sitting there with his head hanging down and his hands flopping, so we got set to go after them again. And then somebody sneaked around and chained the wheel of our truck to theirs so we couldn't get away, and Buddy jumped to his feet, and that day they really wore *us* out!

WINGY MANONE

Down the street, in an old sideboard wagon, would come the jazz band from one ballroom. And up the street, in another sideboard wagon, would come the band from another ballroom, which had announced a dance for the same night at the same price. And those musicians played for all their worth, because the band that pleased the crowd more would be the one the whole crowd would go to hear, and dance to, at its ballroom later that night.

At the back of the wagon were the trombone players, because the only way they could handle their slides was over the end of the wagon. And that's how they got the name "tailgate" trombonists. They all played a Dixieland "vamp" style, because there weren't any room in the wagon for fancy stuff.

BUNK JOHNSON

Bands in those days fighting all the time. One band get a job in the Love and Charity Hall, another band move right over there and play better through the windows. During Mardi Gras and parades, bands got taken around in wagons, and they'd back them, tailgate to tailgate, and play each other down.

MUTT CAREY

If you couldn't blow a man down with your horn, at least you could use it to hit him alongside the head.

25

3

The kids were poor and they often improvised their instruments as well as their music.

DANNY BARKER

It was gay New Orleans, the city of pleasure. For the least significant occasion, there would be some music. That's why so many kids in New Orleans took up music. They heard it all the time. It's like later kids would idolize Babe Ruth, and today Willie Mays. Well, in New Orleans, gambling, race horses, being a pimp, or playing music were the sports. The city didn't appropriate any money to give the kids places and equipment to play other sports, so they turned to what they saw and knew. Or if they were thick in the head, they'd end up doing stevedore work on the levee in the hot sun.

MUTT CAREY

In New Orleans, all the boys came up the hard way. The musicianship was a little poor. You see, the average boy tried to learn by himself because there were either no teachers or they couldn't afford music lessons.

BABY DODDS

I tried hard to play that tin flute I bought but I finally had to turn it over to Johnny. He played it fine and I backed him up with homemade drums made by punching holes in a tin can and using chair rounds for sticks. Those were my first drums and Johnny and I had a lot of fun playing together at home . . . Johnny was already playing a clarinet before I got my first set of drums. Dad wouldn't buy them for me because he said there was too much noise in the house. I finally got a rope bass drum and picked up a snare, and after a while had a full set—all from pawnshops—and it only cost me four or five dollars.

When I was only fourteen, I had a swelled head, big ideas to play with big brother Johnny's band—he was twelve years my senior, you know. So on my fourteenth birthday I went out and got a bottle of gin and swilled the lot, then smoked a whole packet of cigarettes. Then up to brother Johnny to demand to be put in his band.

I'd played since I was a toddler and thought I was good.

But Johnny's reply was, "Run along, Sonny, and learn to play those drums first and don't bother me until you can." So, I took his advice and went to music school—school I called it—four long years and soon realized that I had been drumming all wrong. I had to start all over again, disregard the beats that I'd learned in the past, and get myself a foundation of the rudiments of drumming.

So, at nineteen, I was a pretty competent man, skilled in all forms of drum technique. I went right back to my brother Johnny for a job and he got me my first professional engagement—with King Joe in the famous King Oliver band, in which Johnny was the clarinetist. Perhaps I should put the fans right on the point about my brother. Johnny had a fine regard for good music and good musicians and he detested musicians who tried to make jazz out of bad music. . . .

I learned in the streets, first learning to beat the big drum correctly so as to know just where to put a particular beat and make it fit with the music. Later I graduated to side drum. We were a brass band then and used a couple of piccolos and clarinets. Why, even Johnny played in that band and they were all good men.

Boy, you had to be good on side drum, 'cause if you weren't

—and put the other musicians out—they'd just push you off the sidewalk.

GEORGE LEWIS

When I was seven years old, my mother gave me twenty-five cents to go to the store and buy a toy violin. When I got there, they had sold out all the violins, so I bought the fife. I learned to play on that; I never had a music lesson in my life, and still can't read music. When I was sixteen years old, I got a real clarinet. I bought it with my own earnings and paid four dollars for it.

KID ORY

My first instrument was a cigar-box banjo that I made myself. When I was a little better than ten years old, my father bought me a real banjo from New Orleans. We used to go out on the bridge and practice. When I was thirteen, I formed a band where I lived then, in Laplace, Louisiana, about twenty-nine miles from New Orleans. We had a homemade violin, bass viol, guitar, banjo —played on a chair for drums. We saved all the money we made, except for fifteen cents a piece for carfare, so we could buy good instruments later. We used to go 'round crowds and hustle.

We saved the money and I decided to give picnics with beer, salad—fifteen cents to come in and dance. We played the same numbers we are playing now, like *Pallet on the Floor*, besides some waltzes. We used to go down to New Orleans week ends to hear the different bands that played in the parks. They play a tune once, that's all I want to hear so we could play it too. Take two and make one out of it if we couldn't get all of it.

Bolden was one I heard and Edward Clem who had four or five pieces. He played something like Bolden—just passed through sometimes on an excursion. I used to go down to the railroad station and sometimes I'd see him on the train passing through.

I talked to Bolden once when I was in New Orleans visiting at my sister's house. I had just come from the music store where I bought a trombone and was trying it out. He was on the sidewalk and heard me playing and knocked at the door. I answered the door and he said, "Hello, young fellow, was that you blowing the horn?" I said, "I just bought it." He said, "It's good. I'm looking for a trombone. How would you like to come and play with me?" I said I'd have to ask my sister, so he asked her and she said I was too young. I had to go back home. I was about fourteen then, the year before I moved to New Orleans.

JELLY ROLL MORTON

My first instrument was made up of two chair-rounds and a tin pan. This combination sounded like a symphony to me, because in those days all I heard was classical selections. The next instrument tried was the harmonica at the time I was five years old. After trying to play the harmonica for two years, I discovered I was the world's worst and changed to the jew's-harp, although this instrument sounded more like a bee humming than like music. When I mastered this instrument, I set out to whip the world and conquer all instruments.

We always had some kinds of musical instruments in the house, including guitar, drums, piano, trombone, and so forth and so on. We had lots of them and everybody always played for their pleasure, whatever one desired to play. We always had ample time that was given us in periods to rehearse our lessons, anyone that was desirous of accepting lessons. At the age of six, I gave up the jew's-harp and took my first lessons on the guitar with a Spanish gentleman in the neighborhood.

At the age of seven, I was considered among the best guitarists around, and sometimes I played in the string bands that were common at the time. These little three-piece combinations, consisting of bass, mandolin, and guitar, used to play serenades at late hours, from twelve to two, at the houses of friends. Naturally, the folks would welcome us when they heard those old tunes like *Hot Time in the Old Town Tonight, Wearing My Heart for You, Old Oaken Bucket, Bird in a Gilded Cage, Mr. Johnson, Turn Me Loose,* as well as different little blues and ragtime numbers we knew. There was plenty of liquor in those old-time New Orleans homes and they were liberal about entertaining us musicians. Soon the family would be up, all the friends would be informed, and a festival would be on.

Of course, folks never had the idea they wanted a musician in the family. They always had it in their minds that a musician was a tramp, trying to duck work, with the exception of the French opera house players which they patronized. As a matter of fact, I, myself, was inspired to play piano by going to a recital at the French opera house. There was a gentleman who rendered a selection at the piano, very marvelous music that made me want to play the piano very, very much. The only trouble was that this gentleman had long bushy hair, and, because the piano was known in our circle as an instrument for a lady, this confirmed me in my idea that if I played piano I would be misunderstood.

ALBERT NICHOLAS
Sid Bechet and I didn't have any musical education at the time. We'd just sit on the curbs and experiment with different melodies. Lorenzo Tio, who had made a name with John Robichaux, the Olympia, Tuxedo, and other bands, was my idol then. When I was thirteen, I was taking lessons from him; that man really knew his music and taught me all the rudiments, and he could teach as well as he could play. I also took lessons from Big Eye Louis, another favorite of mine.

I was just like the rest of the kids—wanted to know all about that new music called jazz. I was a "second-line" kid. That meant I'd follow the big bands down the streets, and, man, what a thrill when Tio or George Baquet would let me carry their cases while they played! I'd walk alongside them feeling just as important as could be.

I played my first street parade with Manuel Perez and his Onward Band, and that was one of my greatest thrills. All my life I'd wanted to participate in one of those parades.

BUNK JOHNSON
First thing is where I was born. I was born in dear old New Orleans some years ago, on December the 27th, 1879. I was born uptown on Laurel Street between Peters Avenue and Octavia

Street. So, now all of you know just where my home is. When I was seven years old, I started to taking music lessons. I took music lessons for about one year or a little better. I was doing so good in that short time, Professor Wallace he then told me to tell my mother to come over to the school because he would like very much to have a good talk with her about me. I did just what he told me to do, and my mother went over to the school and seen him. She had a good talk with him, and he then told her just what he really could do with me. Said I really had a good head for music and that he could make a real cornetist out of me if she would get me a cornet just good enough to take lessons on, and when I became good on the old one, then she could get me a real cheap brass cornet. Now, me and my old cornet, when my mother got it, night and day I puffed on it, and when I did get the slite of it, oh boy, I really went. Then my mother saw just what headway I was making with the old cornet. Then she told me, "Son, Mama saw a cheap cornet and a new one, and as you doing so good, I got to get it for you, if you will be a good boy." Now, I was that and my dear mother got it for me.

My prof told me that I had a long way to go and a short time to make it in. Boy, I got busy and I really made the grade. When I became the age of fifteen years old, I was good to go and I really have been going ever since. Now, for faking and playing by head I was hard to beat. Any band I played with, it was all right with me by music or head.

The first band I played with was Adam Olivier's, and it played by music; that was in the year of 1894. My friend, Tony Jackson, started playing with Olivier's band. I stayed with them about one year until I got a good chance to get with King Bolden. Bolden heard me play with Olivier's band. Then he wanted me to jump Olivier's band and come with him because he had the most work and the biggest name in New Orleans. It was the town's talk, King Bolden's band.

CLARENCE WILLIAMS

I came to New Orleans in 1906, when I was fourteen years old. It was after I heard Buddy Bolden, when he came through my home town, Plaquemine, Louisiana, on an excursion, and his trum-

pet playin' excited me so that I said, "I'm goin' to New Orleans."
I had never heard anything like that before in my whole life.

From the time I was six years old in Plaquemine, I had been
brought up by the people that had the Silver Brothers Hotel, and
I learned to do just about everything around a hotel—cooking
and all. I could mix drinks and would sing to the guests between
meals. I was also singin' with a little band there. We called it
serenadin'. We'd go around the streets and play, and my part
would be singin' and passin' the hat. (I could only play oom-pah
music on the piano at that time.)

I shined some shoes when I got to New Orleans and made good
money, enough to get myself a house and some furniture. My first
musical job was singin' and playin' the piano at a spaghetti place,
but before that I was goin' around to all the joints, stayin' up all
night playin' for nothing, or for drinks—whatever they'd give me.
At that time piano players would come in from all over the South
for the races, and all the local piano players would listen to 'em
to catch ideas. I'd stay up all night and then go to work the next
day. All the while, I kept figurin' ways to get some money where
I didn't have to make time. So I went to all the hotels and res-
taurants and cabarets where the colored musicians would be
workin' and told them, "Want to get your suits cleaned? Just
give 'em to me and pay me on payday." They didn't want to
keep runnin' to the tailor all the time, so I made a lot of money
that way.

But one day the porter that worked at this spaghetti place came
over to my house and said, "Do you know where I can find a
good piano player?" "You're talkin' to him," I said. "I'll go down."
And that's how I started. You know, I couldn't play but five or
six pieces, and when somebody would ask me to play a waltz,
I'd just play *Some of These Days*, or one of the other tunes I
knew, in three-quarter time.

Pretty soon I was way ahead of all the other piano players—
introducing all the new songs. When Sophie Tucker came to
New Orleans in about 1910 or 1911, they would have a ballyhoo
truck. (There was always a big to-do about shows and dances,
and the bands would get on those trucks and wagons and ride

32

all over town.) Sophie Tucker and the Avon Four, who were playin' at the Orpheum Theatre, were on one of those trucks, and I followed them around all day. At that time, she was singin' *Some of These Days, Alexander's Ragtime Band*, and other new songs, and after hearin' her sing them, I'd go home and play them over until I got them under control. Then at night I'd be able to sing and play them and make some real heavy tips. There'd be money all over the top of the piano.

I was also the first to write away to the North for professional copies of all the latest songs, like *Chinatown* and *That's A Plenty*. I made those songs famous in New Orleans. I had also begun to take piano lessons from the woman who used to demonstrate songs in the music store where I would go to listen to the new tunes. She would charge me fifty cents a lesson and, while I was there, invite all the other teachers over to watch me play. They were all amazed. I took about eight lessons all told, and just lived piano—all day and all night. I would spend only fifteen minutes on dinner so that I could use the rest of the time practicin'.

BUD SCOTT

I was first taken to guitar when four years of age. I had a cousin who had a guitar, who roomed at our house. When he was through with it at night, he put it under his bed. My mother went to the store one day, and I was left alone in the house. I had the idea to go under the bed and get that guitar. I picked it up, fooled with it a little bit, and started with *Home, Sweet Home*, a melody in three chords.

I had forgotten about my mother and everybody else; all of a sudden she came home and I made a dive to put the guitar under the bed. She told me this was all right, asked me to play again, and called in one or two of the neighbors next door. They marveled at it. My father came home and I played for him. He liked it so well that, without changing his work clothes, he went to Rampart Street and bought me an old guitar for a dollar and fifty cents. I was up early the next morning at five A.M. and that was my start. I still didn't know anything about music at that time, just what I heard.

33

4

*Bunk Johnson, King Oliver, Louis Armstrong, Kid
Ory, Freddie Keppard, Buddy Petit, Manuel Perez,
Clarence Williams, Chris Kelly, Buddy Bolden—they
all called the children home.*

DANNY BARKER

When I was growing up, Jelly Roll was a legend and the same
with Bechet. You'd hear of Jelly Roll, how he'd left and how
he'd set the pace. Somebody would see him in Chicago and bring
back the news of how successful he was there. And he was often
importing some New Orleans musicians.

It was Jelly Roll who brought Buddy Petit to California, but
Buddy didn't like it and came back to New Orleans.

A dozen books should have been written about Buddy Petit.
The way people rave over Dempsey, Joe Louis, or Ben Hogan
today, that's how great Petit was when he played. The kids would
come up and say, "Can I shake your hand, Mr. Petit?" And on
parades, they'd be ten deep around Buddy as he walked along
blowing. He was a little, Indian-looking sort of guy. He talked
broken patois.

It's this country's fault that he didn't record. They were recording Caruso at that time, but this country didn't want to accept
its heritage in the music of men like Buddy Petit. But those rich
millionaires—the Fords and those people—will go over to Paris
and buy a Cézanne or a Goya, pay fifty thousand dollars for it,

and put it in a museum. But we've got our own cultural heritage here and we ignore it.

Or like the guy in Philadelphia who has that fabulous art collection and just lets certain people come to see it. You dig what I'm talking about? When here, in jazz, is something you can hear and enjoy right here, right now.

Papa Celestin should take weeks and weeks and tell about his career in detail from day to day, as much as he remembers. And there's a whole story, Picou tells me, about the Negro symphony that used to be in New Orleans. It's not too late to get some of the older men to tell their stories.

The story of jazz should be in all the schools, so the children would know where their music comes from. They should give money so that people could go out West and study and record cowboys and Western folklore. The kids in the schools today think their country has nothing.

You take CBS and NBC and them kind of people. They have hours and hours of putting Tyrone Power and Ingrid Bergman to portraying some French story that happened years ago, while right here they have John Henry, Stack O'Lee, Casey Jones, and all them kings of fabulous stories that American kids know nothing about. So they spend millions of dollars for all that other kind of foolishness.

You remember that movie, NEW ORLEANS, that had Louis Armstrong and Billie Holiday? Well, them people took pictures of every segment of New Orleans. They made their pictures as authentic as they could get them, but they didn't put any of it in the movie, any of the authentic stuff, because they wanted the movie commercial. They showed the leading man posing for fifteen minutes, fixing his tie, while they should have been showing the people, the real thing.

MUTT CAREY

When you come right down to it, the man who started the big noise in jazz was Buddy Bolden. Yes, he was a powerful trumpet player and a good one too. I guess he deserves credit for starting it all.

BUNK JOHNSON

King Buddy Bolden was the first man that began playing jazz in the city of New Orleans, and his band had the whole of New Orleans real crazy and running wild behind it. Now that was all you could hear in New Orleans, that King Bolden's Band, and I was with him. That was between 1895 and 1896, and we did not have any "Dixieland Jazz Band" in those days. Now here is the thing that made King Bolden's Band the first band to play jazz. It was because they could not read at all. I could fake like five hundred myself, so you tell them that Bunk and King Bolden's Band were the first ones that started jazz in that city or anyplace else.

I went with Adam Olivier's band, my first band, played with them just a short while, and I had the opportunity of hearin' King Bolden's Band at Lincoln Park. And I got crazy to play with Bolden and Bolden played my style of music. I liked to read, but I played that head music better—more jazz to it. I liked to read, and I could read good, but Bolden played pretty much by ear. And made up his own tunes; but everything that he played, I could whistle, I could play. And I jumped Olivier's band and went with Bolden. That was in 1895.

I was crazy to play blues. Bolden was playing blues of all kinds, so when I got with Bolden, we helped to make more blues. *Make Me a Pallet on the Floor*, that was played in 1894 by King Bolden. And quadrilles, I was crazy to play quadrilles. This quadrille, the first eight bars of what the bands are usin' today, *Tiger Rag*, that's King Bolden's first eight bars we would play to get your partner ready for quadrille. And, in later years, 'twas taken and turned into *Tiger Rag* by musicians that could read. Had Bolden knew music, probably Bolden would have made *Tiger Rag*. So we played *Tiger Rag* before we had any Dixieland Jazz Band. The Dixieland Jazz Band is the one that taken *Tiger Rag*, the first eight bars, and turned it into the dance number what we dancin' today we call *Tiger Rag*.

And King Bolden was one fine-lookin' brown-skin man, tall and slender and a terror with the ladies. He was the greatest

36

ragtime cornet player, with a round keen tone. He could execute like hell and play in any key. He had a *head*, Buddy did!

BUD SCOTT

I joined John Robichaux in 1904. There were seven men in the band (no piano): guitar, violin, Jim Williams on trumpet (he used to use a mute), cornet, Battice Dellile on trombone, Dee Dee Chandler on drums, and the greatest bass player I ever heard in my life—Henry Kimball. They played for the elite and had the town sewed up. In about 1908, Robichaux had a contest with Bolden in Lincoln Park and Robichaux won. For the contest, Robichaux added Manuel Perez. Bolden got hot-headed that night, as Robichaux really had his gang out. On other occasions, when Robichaux was playing in Lincoln Park and Bolden in Johnson Park, about a block away, Bolden would strip Lincoln Park of all the people by slipping his horn through the knothole in the fence and calling the children home.

Each Sunday, Bolden went to church and that's where he got his idea of jazz music. They would keep perfect rhythm there by clapping their hands. I think I am the first one who started four-beat for guitar, and that's where I heard it (all down-strokes —four straight down). Bolden was still a great man for the blues —no two questions about that. The closest thing to it was Oliver and he was better than Oliver. He was a great man for what we call "dirt music." Let me tell you, he was plenty powerful. Even with all that power, the trumpet players of that day would have their notes covered, and they would not hurt the ear the way rebop does now. You could hear every instrument in these bands —every instrument. The drummer had his drums tuned—he would tune those drums like they were a piano.

GEORGE BAQUET

I was out celebrating with some of my friends, when we went to a ball at the Odd Fellows' Hall, where Buddy Bolden worked. I remember thinking it was a funny place, nobody took their hats off. It was plenty tough. You paid fifteen cents and walked in.

When we came in, we saw the band, six of them, on a low stand. They had their hats on, too, and were resting—pretty sleepy.

We stood behind a column. All of a sudden, Buddy stomps, knocks on the floor with his trumpet to give the beat, and they all sit up straight, wide awake. Buddy held up his cornet, paused to be sure of his embouchure, then they played *Make Me a Pallet on the Floor*. Everybody got up quick, the whole place rose and yelled out, "Oh, Mr. Bolden, play it for us, Buddy, play it!"

I'd never heard anything like that before. I'd played "legitimate" stuff. But this! It was somethin' that pulled me! They got me up on the stand that night, and I was playin' with 'em. After that, I didn't play "legitimate" so much.

ALPHONSE PICOU
Buddy Bolden was more of a ragtime cornet player at that time than Manuel Perez. He didn't use music. Manuel did use music. Buddy was very big and had a loud tone. You could hear him for a block. Sure, Buddy was louder than Armstrong. The loudest there ever was, because you could hear Buddy's cornet as loud as what Louis Armstrong played through the mike.

KID ORY
I used to hear Bolden play every chance I got. I'd go out to the park where he was playing, and there wouldn't be a soul around. Then, when it was time to start the dance, he'd say, "Let's call the children home." And he'd put his horn out the window and blow, and everyone would come running.

DANNY BARKER
They talk about Buddy Bolden—how, on some night, you could hear his horn ten miles away. Well, it could have happened, because the city of New Orleans has a different kind of acoustics from other cities. There is water all around the city. There is also water all under the city, which is one of the reasons why they would bury people overground—in tombs, mounds, et cetera—because if you dug over three feet deep, you would come up with water.

38

Adding to this dampness, there was the heat and humidity of the swamps, of the bayous all around New Orleans. From the meeting of the dampness and the heat, a mist, a vapor comes up into the air there, and there are continuously changing air currents. And, because of all this, because sound travels better across water, and because of all those moving air currents, when you blew your horn in New Orleans—especially on a clear night—when guys like Bolden would blow their beautiful brass trumpets, the sound carried.

ALBERT GLENY

When I first met Bolden, he came at my house. He asked me if I was playing regular. I told him no. He asked me to be a member of his band. So I played in his band for four or five years.

Bolden was a strong trumpet player. You couldn't help from playing good with Bolden. He was crazy for wine and women and vice versa. Sometimes he would have to run away from the women. I used to take his horn away from him sometimes and bring him to my house. When he went mad, he would walk up and down the street talking to the wrong people—foolish—about this gal and that gal.

LOUIS ARMSTRONG

Buddy got drinking too much . . . staying up two or three nights a week without sleep and going right on to work like so many hot musicians. They get low in their minds and drink some more. People thought he was plumb crazy the way he used to toss that horn. The sad part is Buddy actually did go crazy a few years later and was put away in an insane asylum in Jackson, Mississippi. He was just a one-man genius that was ahead of 'em all . . . too good for his time.

Now Bunk, he's another man they ought to talk about. What a man! Just to hear him talk sends me. I used to hear him in Frankie Duson's Eagle Band in 1911. Did that band swing! How I used to follow him around. He could play funeral marches that made me cry.

MUTT CAREY

Of course, Bunk Johnson deserves credit for what he used to do. He had marvelous ideas and I used to like to hear him play. He wasn't quite the drive man that Joe (Oliver) and Freddie Keppard were, however. He always stayed behind the beat instead of getting out there in the lead like those other men. Bunk was good, and he was solid when he was playing. Bunk had plenty of competition on his way up and he never was the king down there.

PRESTON JACKSON

Most everybody has heard of Joe Oliver and Louis Armstrong but few ever heard of Mutt Carey in his prime. Mutt Carey, in his day, was equal to Joe Oliver. Mutt is the first trumpet player or cornetist that choked his horn. He used a drinking glass in the bell of his horn, and how he did swing! Mutt wasn't a high-note player; he wasn't as strong as Louis Armstrong or Joe Oliver. Muggsy reminds me a lot of Mutt. Mutt hardly ever played as high as B-flat or high C; that was out of his range. Mutt had a very mellow tone and a terrific swing. The softer the band played, the better Mutt played. The drummer used sandpaper, there being no wire brushes at that time. You could hear every instrument. They seemed to blend better than the average band nowadays. Whenever the band became noisy, Mutt would look back and sideways and say, "Sh, sh," meaning get down softer. That didn't stop them from swinging. Some cats can't swing soft. Mutt could make many pretty runs and changes. He was strictly gutbucket or barrelhouse. Nothing technical about his playing. Just swinging all the time, pretty diminished chords. He choked his cornet and made it moan just like Joe Oliver did later. I never will forget Mutt Carey.

MUTT CAREY

I was the youngest of seventeen children in my family. You know, my brother Jack had the Crescent Band in those days and was a pretty good trombone player, as was my brother John and my brother Milton. Pete and myself played the trumpet.

I was twenty-two when I started playing the trumpet. Lots of boys had a head start on me because they began playing earlier, but I caught up with them. You see, I first learned the drums but got tired of packing those drums around, so I switched over to the trumpet. My brother, Pete, gave me my first lessons on the horn. Later, John taught me also.

I got my first job with Jack's Crescent Band in 1912. They had a lot of good bands in those days and a lot of fine musicians playing with them. I played with almost all of them during my years in New Orleans.

There was Frankie Duson's Eagle Band. I played with them. Baby Ridgley had the Tuxedo Band, which I also played with. I played with Kid Ory's Band too. Jimmy Brown had the Superior Band, and I also played with them. I played with Joe Oliver in a brass band too. Old Joe could really play his horn.

In my brother Jack's band, Sidney Bechet was playing the clarinet and Jim Johnson was on bass. Charles Moore was the guitarist and Ernest Rodgers played drums. Then there was my brother Jack and I.

My first job was in Billy Phillips' place. We played anything we pleased in that joint; you see, there was no class in those places. All they wanted was continuous music. Man, they had some rough places in Storyville in those days. A guy would see everything in those joints and it was all dirty. It was really a hell of a place to work.

PRESTON JACKSON

Mutt never could play high, but he made Joe Oliver throw his trumpet away once. There was a big parade in New Orleans and Mutt was with the Tuxedo Brass Band, while Joe was with the Onward Brass Band. His outfit was a few feet in front of the Tuxedo Band in the parade, and Mutt was playing some grand stuff. Joe couldn't take it long. He just threw his horn away and went into a pawnshop and bought another.

Later on, about 1914 I should say, Joe began to improve a lot. He used to practice very hard. I remember he once told me that it took him ten years to get a tone on his instrument. He used a half-cocked mute, and how he could make it talk! He played the variation style too; running chords I mean. His ear was wonderful —that helped a lot.

One of the best numbers I ever heard Joe play was *Eccentric*. He took all the breaks, imitating a rooster and a baby. He was a riot in those days, his band from 1915 or '16 to 1918 being the best in New Orleans. The La Rocca boys of the Dixieland Jazz Band used to hang around and got a lot of ideas from his gang. The boys playing with Joe then were Johnny Dodds, clarinet; Edward Ory, trombone; Ed Garland, bass viol; Henry Zeno, drums; Eddie Polla, violin; and a guitar player whose name I have forgotten. He didn't use a piano. How those boys could swing, and it was jazz they played, too, not ragtime music.

MUTT CAREY

Joe Oliver had a few numbers that were on sheets of music, but he got away from it as quickly as he could. You see, Joe was no great reader. Joe Oliver was very strong. He was the greatest freak trumpet player I ever knew. He did most of his playing with cups, glasses, buckets, and mutes. He was the best gut-bucket man I ever heard. I called him freak because the sounds he made were not made by the valves but through these artificial devices. In contrast, Louis played everything through the horn.

Joe and I were the first ones to introduce these mutes and things. We were both freak trumpet men. Some writers claimed I was the first one to use mutes and buckets, but it wasn't so. I got to give Joe Oliver credit for introducing them. Joe could make his horn sound like a holy-roller meeting; God, what that man could do with his horn! Joe's band followed me into San Francisco, and it didn't go over because I had come there first with cups and buckets, and the people thought Joe was imitating me. Joe and I used to get a kick out of that whenever we talked about it. He sure got his laughs from it.

I'll tell you something about Joe's records. I haven't heard a single one that comes close to sounding like Joe's playing in person. I don't know what it was, but I'll tell you the truth, I don't believe that it is Joe playing on the records sometimes. It never sounded to me much like Joe.

LOUIS ARMSTRONG

Storyville had a lot of different characters . . . People from all over the world made special trips to see what it looked like . . . There were amusement for any type of person . . . Regardless of some of the biggest pimps who lived there at that time Story-ville had its nice spots also . . . There were night clubs with all of that good music that came from the horns of the great King Joe Oliver (my my whatta man) . . . How he used to blow that cornet of his down in Storyville for Pete Lala . . . I was just a youngster who loved that horn of King Oliver's . . . I would delight delivering an order of stone coal to the prostitute who used to hustle in her crib right next to Pete Lala's cabaret . . . Just so's I could hear King Oliver play . . . I was too young to go into Pete Lala's at the time . . . And I'd just stand there in that lady's crib listening to King Oliver . . . And I'm all in a daze . . . That was the only way we kids could go into The District—I mean Storyville . . . I'd stand there listening to King Oliver beat out one of those good ol good-ones like *Panama* or *High Society* . . . My, whatta punch that man had . . . And could he shout a tune . . . Ump . . . All of a sudden it would dawn on the lady that I was still in her crib very silent while she hustle those tricks —and she'd say—"What's the matter with you, boy? . . . Why are you still there standing so quiet?" And there I'd have to ex-plain to her that I was being inspired by *the* King Oliver and his orchestra . . . And then she handed me a cute one by saying— "Well, this is no place to daydream . . . I've got my work to do." So I'd go home very pleased and happy that I did at least hear my idol blow at least a couple of numbers that really *gassed* me no end . . .

King Oliver was full of jokes in those days . . . Also the days before he passed away (bless his heart). He had a good heart.

Whatta band he had at Pete Lala's . . . Oh that music sounded so good . . . In that band he had Buddy Christian on the piano

43

—Professor Nicholson on the clarinet—Zue Robertson on the trombone—himself on cornet and Henry Zeno on drums . . . ahh —there was a drummer for ya . . . He had a press roll that one very seldom hear nowadays . . . And was he popular . . . With everyone . . . With all the prostitutes—pimps—gamblers— hustlers and everybody . . . Of course they called gamblers "hustlers" in those days . . . Most of the pimps were good gamblers also . . . And Henry Zeno was in there with them . . . He even had several prostitutes on his staff working for him . . . By that he would handle more cash than the average musician . . . And he was a little short dark sharp cat—and knew all the answers . . . He even was great in a street parade . . . He also played in the Onward Brass Band which was made up of the top-notched musicians and featuring on the cornets Manuel Perez and King Oliver . . . And you never heard a brass band swing in your whole life like those boys . . . Ump Ump Ump . . . I'll never be able to explain how they would swing like mad—coming from the cemetery—after playing funeral marches to the cemetery with the body and after the Preacher sez—ashes to ashes and dust—et cetera—Henry Zeno would take his handkerchief off of the snare under the bottom of his snare drum so's every member could get in his place and get ready to march back to the hall with some of the finest swing music pushing them . . . And with Black Benny on the bass drum and Henry Zeno laying that press roll on the cats (the second line) that was a musical treat in itself . . . P.S. the second line (cats) was consisted of raggidy guys who hung around poolrooms and et cetera.

Henry Zeno died a natural death . . . He lived up in Carrolton —a section of the city that's miles away from Storyville . . . Yet —still—when he died everybody all over the city including Story- ville were very sad . . . The day of his funeral—there were so many people that gathered from all sections of the town until you couldn't get within ten blocks of the house where Henry Zeno was laid out . . . There were as many white people there to pay their last respect for a great drummer man and his comrades, and the people who just loves to go to funerals no matter who dies . . . Although I was only a youngster—I was right in there amongst them . . . I had the advantage of the other kids—by meeting great men as Henry Zeno and King Oliver, et cetera . . . So it broke my heart too. . . .

MUTT CAREY

Now, at one time, Freddie Keppard had New Orleans all sewed up. He was the king—yes, he wore the crown. Then Louis got in and killed the whole bunch of them. Freddie really used to play good. He could have been as big as Louis, since he had the first chance to make records, but he didn't want to do it because he was afraid that other musicians would steal his stuff.

Keppard was the first man I ran into in a hand battle, and it was just my hard luck to run into the king. We had a big audience on the street. It was on Howard and Villare Streets in New Orleans. The crowd knew I was a younger musician and they gave me a big hand mostly to encourage me. It certainly was an experience for me I'll never forget. Freddie had a lot of ideas and a big tone too. When he hit a note you knew it was hit. I mean he had a beautiful tone and he played with so much feeling too. Yes, he had everything; he was ready in every respect. Keppard could play any kind of song good. Technique, attack, tone, and ideas were all there. He didn't have very much formal musical education, but he sure was a natural musician. All you had to do was play a number for him once and he had it—he was a natural! When Freddie got to playing, he'd get devilish sometimes and he'd neigh on the trumpet like a horse, but he was no freak man like Joe Oliver. Freddie was a trumpet player any way you'd grab him. He could play sweet and then he could play hot. He'd play sweet sometimes and then turn around and knock the socks off you with something hot.

RICHARD M. JONES

Freddie Keppard was playin' in a spot across the street and was drawin' all the crowds. I was sittin' at the piano, and Joe Oliver came over to me and commanded in a nervous harsh voice, "Get in B-flat." He didn't even mention a tune, just said, "Get in B-flat." I did, and Joe walked out on the sidewalk, lifted his horn to his lips, and blew the most beautiful stuff I have ever heard. People started pouring out of the other spots along the street to see who was blowing all that horn. Before long, our place was full and Joe came in, smiling, and said, "Now, that _____ won't bother me no more."

From then on, our place was full every night.

MUTT CAREY

Who was the greatest trumpet player in jazz? Louis Armstrong— there's no question there! Louis played from his heart and soul, and he did that for everything. You see, he tried to make a picture out of every number he was playing to show just what it meant. He had ideas, enough technique to bring out what he wanted to say, and a terrific lip. You know, when the ideas struck him, he had the technique to bring them out right there on the horn.

When I left New Orleans, Louis was just a beginner. He had just gotten out of the Waifs' Home, and he was a coming trumpet man then.

I remember once when Louis came out to Lincoln Park in New Orleans to listen to the Kid Ory Band. I was playing trumpet with the Kid then and I let Louis sit in on my chair. Now, at that time, I was the "Blues King" of New Orleans, and when Louis played that day he played more blues than I ever heard in my life. It never did strike my mind that blues could be interpreted so many different ways. Every time he played a chorus it was different and you knew it was the blues—yes, it was all blues, what I mean.

When he got through playing the blues, I kidded him a little. I told him, "Louis, you keep playing that horn and some day you'll be a great man." I always admired him from the start.

I give Freddie Keppard and Joe Oliver credit too. They were great boys but there's no one who ever came close to Louis. No, Louis was ahead by a mile! Louis makes you feel the number and that's what counts. A man who does something from the heart, and makes you feel it, is great. You see, Louis does that for everything. And one thing, Louis never rehearsed a blues number;

46

he played them just as he felt at the time he was up there on the stand.

Louis sings just like he plays. I think Louis proves the idea and theory which holds that if you can't sing it, you can't play it. When I'm improvising, I'm singing in my mind. I sing what I feel and then try to reproduce it on the horn.

Then Louis' tone is so big and he fills all those notes—there is no splitting them when he plays. There's nothing freakish about Louis' horn. He fingers what he wants to play, and there are no accidents in the notes he brings out. You know, it's a pleasure just to hear Louis tune up. Why, just warming up, he blows such a variety of things that it is a wonder to the ears, and a real pleasure. Louis set the pace for the whole world for trumpet players. Joe and Freddie did their bits but they never could touch Louis. God knows, both of them were good but, what the heck, man, they never could touch Louis.

BUNK JOHNSON

When I would be playing with brass bands in the uptown section (of New Orleans), Louis would steal off from home and follow me. During that time Louis started after me to show him how to blow my cornet. When the band would not be playing, I would let him carry it to please him. How he wanted me to teach him how to play the blues and *Ball the Jack* and *Animal Ball, Circus Day, Take It Away*, and *Salty Dog* and *Didn't He Ramble?*, and out of all those pieces he liked the blues the best.

I took a job playing in a tonk for Dago Tony on Perdido and Franklin Street and Louis used to slip in there and get on the music stand behind the piano. He would fool around with my cornet every chance he got. I showed him just how to hold it and place it to his mouth, and he did so, and it wasn't long before he began getting a good tone out of my horn. Then I began showing him just how to start the blues, and little by little he began to understand.

Now here is the year Louis started. It was in the latter part of 1911, as close as I can think. Louis was about eleven years old.

47

Now, I've said a lot about my boy Louis and just how he started playing cornet. He started playing it by head.

ZUTTY SINGLETON

The first time I ever saw Louis was when he was about twelve, thirteen years old. He was singing with three other kids in an amateur show at Bill and Mary Mack's tent show in New Orleans. Louis was singing tenor then, and they broke it up that night. The other three boys were Red Happy, Little Mack, and a guy by the name of Clarence. This happened just before Louis got sent to the Waifs' Home, and so I didn't see him again for a while. But I heard about him at the Home. Some of the fellows that were sent there would come back and say how fine this Louis Armstrong was playing.

Then I saw Louis playing in a band at a picnic. He was marching along with the band, so we got up real close to him to see if he was actually playing those notes. We didn't believe he could learn to play in that short time. I can still remember he was playing *Maryland, My Maryland*. And he sure was swingin' out that melody.

KID ORY

The first time I remember seeing Louis Armstrong, he was a little boy playing cornet with the Waifs' Home band in a street parade. Even then he stood out. In those days I had a brass band I used for funerals, parades, and picnics. Benny, the drummer of my brass band, had taken Louis under his wing.

One evening, Benny brought Louis, who had just been released from the Waifs' Home, to National Park, where I was playing a picnic. Benny asked me if I would let Louis sit in with my band. I remembered the kid from the street parade and I gladly agreed.

Louis came up and played *Ole Miss'* and the blues, and everyone in the park went wild over this boy in knee trousers who could play so great. I liked Louis' playing so much that I asked him to come and sit in with my band any time he could.

Louis came several times to different places where I worked

and we really got to know each other. He always came accompanied by Benny, the drummer. In the crowded places, Benny would handcuff Louis to himself with a handkerchief so Louis wouldn't get lost.

In my dance band at that time—around 1917—Joe (King) Oliver was my trumpet player. I received an offer to take my band to Chicago, but I was doing too well in New Orleans to leave. Joe, however, along with Jimmie Noone, who was my clarinetist, decided to go up to Chicago. Joe told me before he left that he could recommend someone to take his place. I told him I appreciated his thought but that I had already picked out his replacement.

There were many good, experienced trumpet players in town, but none of them had young Louis' possibilities. I went to see him and told him that if he got himself a pair of long trousers I'd give him a job. Within two hours, Louis came to my house and said, "Here I am. I'll be glad when eight o'clock comes. I'm ready to go."

I was doing one-nighters all over New Orleans in yacht clubs, country clubs, and promoting my own dances at Pete Lala's hall Sundays and Cooperative Hall Mondays. These were the top jobs in New Orleans. After he joined me, Louis improved so fast it was amazing. He had a wonderful ear and a wonderful memory. All you had to do was to hum or whistle a new tune to him and he'd know it right away. And if he played a tune once, he never forgot it. Within six months, everybody in New Orleans knew about him.

DANNY BARKER

There are some trumpet players who died that you never hear about. Now, Chris Kelly was a master and played more blues than Louis Armstrong, Bunk, and anybody you ever knew. Manuel Perez was different. He was a military man, played on a Sousa kick. He was a great street-parade trumpet player. Perez had a reddish complexion. He was on a Spanish kick, his father and his grandfather Spanish and his mother colored. And he had a beautiful head of hair. He had a stocky build, like a middleweight or light-heavy, could blow, blow real loud—*High Society, Panama*. Nobody could top him in the street parades because he could hit those high notes. He always had a stomach full of food, while most of them fellows who played the street parades were full of whiskey. About two hours later, they pooped out, but Manuel Perez didn't; he had eaten two pots of gumbo before he left.

New Orleans, through the years, had some thirty-odd halls, each one incorporated, and most of them are active and standing today. Each of these halls had a different class distinction based on color, family standing, money, and religion. The most exclusive was the Jean Ami, which very few jazzmen ever entered—down to the Animal Hall, where even a washboard band was welcome if they could play the blues.

So, Chris Kelly, who was dark of color, low on finance, Baptist from birth, and cultured in the canebrakes, never gave a thought to ever blowing his blues in the Jean Ami Hall and a dozen other amusement places.

Chris could play slow, lowdown gut-struts until all the dancers were exhausted and dripping wet. His masterpiece was *Careless Love*, preached slow and softly with a plunger. He always played it at twelve o'clock, just before intermission. He'd blow a few bars before knocking off, and his fans would rush about, seeking their loves because that dance meant close embracing, cheek-to-cheek whisperings of love, kissing, and belly-rubbing.

The dance would always end in a fight by some jealous lover who was dodged or couldn't be found at Chris' signal. The moment the fisticuffs started, he would knock off a fast stomp that sounded like *Dippermouth Blues*.

Now, there was a caste system in New Orleans that's died out now. Each one of those caste systems had its own trumpet player, and Chris Kelly played for those blues, cotton-picking Negroes, what they called in the old days, "yard and field" Negroes. They were real primitive people who worked in the fields, worked hard. They wore those box-backed suits and hats with two-colored bands on them, shoes with diamonds in the toe, or a two-dollar gold piece in the toe. Shoes cost them around twenty dollars, and the shoemakers put that in the toe. And they put that silver stuff on when they shined the shoes. When the sun was shining, it would light you up. Chris Kelly played for those people. They would give a ball at the New Hall, which was the young men's charity hall, and every time they gave something there, the undertaker would be glad because there were three or four bodies, and sometimes women's titties would be chopped off. They featured that in New Orleans. They had special instruments for doctoring breasts and would come up with a razor to do that. Chris Kelly played for people like that. He looked like Sidney de Paris, but lighter, and he always had three or four stooges with him. They idolized him and he would never have to touch his horn. You see, Cootie Williams, that style he plays, he got that style from Chris Kelly. Chris used to go to Mobile, where they had the same caste system as New Orleans. He played a dicty dance there one night and played nothing but barrelhouse with that plunger. He was the first one I saw play with the plunger. Although New Orleans never featured it, he could play with it. And he also played church music, especially *Swing Low, Sweet Chariot*. He really moved the people. He should have been a preacher. But he preached so melodiously with his horn that it was like somebody singing a song, and he would go into the blues from there. When he went to Mobile and did that, nobody else could go to Mobile any more. They only wanted Kelly.

Chris would come on the job with a tuxedo, a red-striped shirt, a black tie, a brown derby, and a tan shoe and a black shoe. Whatever he picked up in the house before he left, that's what he wore. And nobody said anything to him because they wanted to see *him*.

He just played for a certain element in New Orleans and couldn't play for the people that Piron played for, and he couldn't play the cabarets, but he played for those people. He worked all the little towns and worked every night and always made the job. He talked a real, broken patois, African almost. The Creoles couldn't understand him. They didn't like him and they didn't want to see him in the street, because he played for what was supposed to be the bad element. When he would play a street parade, mostly advertising, all the kitchen mechanics would come out on the street corner, shaking. The Creoles would hate to see that. I wanted to work with that man so badly, but he would never hire me. I used to hang around him and try to sit in his band, but he would look at me with a frown, because he knew my uncle was Paul Barbarin and he knew my grandfather. And the cats in his band would say, "He shouldn't play with us. He's from another caste." But I loved him. Also, everywhere he played they had to fry fish and have gumbo, especially for him. He wouldn't eat it because he was suspicious and he'd bring red beans and rice or chicken in his bucket. King Oliver was suspicious too. They wouldn't eat anybody's food, but they had to feed their bands. That was in the contract. Musicians like Chris Kelly were very temperamental, and if they weren't taken care of, there was no telling what would happen.

Everybody acknowledged the cornet player as leader because he carried the lead, and everybody improvised around him. But they had some wonderful trombone players, too. Kid Ory had a wonderful band, and Jack Carey, who used *Tiger Rag* as a theme. He'd play it all the day in the street to announce his coming— "Jack Ca—rey! Jack Ca—rey!" Zue Robertson was a hell of a trombone player, but he wasn't a leader. He played in the circuses and carnivals, too, like a lot of the New Orleans musicians. There was Honore Dutrey, too.

And then there was Black Benny, the drummer—six foot six— nothing but muscle. He was handsome in a sort of African way. He was all man, physically. He feared nobody. He was raised in the Third Ward—Perdido and Bolivar Streets—that was called "the battleground." It was one of the toughest neighborhoods in New Orleans other than the "Irish Channel." Black Benny was a great drummer. He had an African beat. He was something to see on the street with his bass drum that looked like a snare drum in front. You'd have to ask all the drummers how he did it, but he could move a whole band with just that bass drum. All the drummers could do it, but he had the reputation for being best at it. Everybody in New Orleans—for it was a very competitive city—had the reputation for doing something best. Benny was also a ladies' man, a bouncer, and a prizefighter. He was a man who didn't like to see anybody take advantage of an underdog. He would also win the battle royals.

The battle royals were when they'd put five men in the ring, one in the center, and blindfold them. The bell would be hit, and everybody would start punching. Whoever stayed the longest won the prize—five or ten dollars. These were men. Those five cats in the ring—just before the bell was hit—would look to see in what position each other was, and then, after the blindfolds were on and the bell sounded, they'd be punching like mules kicking. You'd have to be an awful brave man to get in that ring. And Black Benny won them all.

JELLY ROLL MORTON

A lot of bad bands, that we used to call "spasm" bands, played any jobs they could get in the streets. They did a lot of "ad-libbing" in ragtime style with different solos in succession, not in a regular routine, but just as one guy would get tired and let another musician have the lead.

None of these men made much money—maybe a dollar a night or a couple of bucks for a funeral, but still, they didn't like to leave New Orleans. They used to say, "This is the best town in the world. What's the use for me to go any other place?" So, the town was full of the best musicians you ever heard. Even the rags-bottles-and-bones men would advertise their trade by playing the blues on the wooden mouthpieces of Christmas horns—yes sir, play more low-down dirty blues on those Kress horns than the rest of the country ever thought of.

New Orleans was the stomping grounds for all the greatest pianists in the country. We had Spanish, we had colored, we had white, we had Frenchmens, we had Americans, we had them from all parts of the world, because there were more jobs for pianists than any other ten places in the world. The sporting houses needed professors, and we had so many different styles that whenever you came to New Orleans, it wouldn't make any difference that you just came from Paris or any part of England, Europe, or anyplace—whatever your tunes were over there, we played them in New Orleans.

I might mention some of our pianists—Sammy Davis, one of the greatest manipulators of the keyboard I guess I have ever seen in the history of the world; Alfred Wilson and Albert Cahill, they were both great pianists and both of them were colored. Poor Alfred Wilson, the girls taken to him and showed him a point where he didn't have to work. He finally came to be a dope fiend and smoked so much dope till he died. Albert Cahill didn't smoke dope, but he ruined his eyes staying up all night, gambling. Albert was known as the greatest show player in existence as I can remember. Then there was Kid Ross, a white boy and one of the outstanding hot players of the country.

All these men were hard to beat, but when Tony Jackson walked in, any one of them would get up from the piano stool. If he didn't, somebody was liable to say, "Get up from that piano. You hurting its feelings. Let Tony play." Tony was real dark and not a bit good-looking, but he had a beautiful disposition. He was the outstanding favorite of New Orleans, and I have never known any pianists to come from any section of the world that could leave New Orleans victorious.

Kid Ross was the steady player at Lulu White's. Tony Jackson played at Gypsy Schaeffer's, one of the most notoriety women I've ever seen, in a high-class way. She was the notoriety kind that everybody liked. She didn't hesitate about spending her money and her main drink was champagne, and, if you couldn't buy it, she'd buy it for you in abundance. Walk into Gypsy Schaeffer's and, right away, the bell would ring upstairs and all the girls would walk into the parlor, dressed in their fine evening gowns and ask the customer if he would care to drink wine. They would call for "the professor" and, while champagne was being served all around, Tony would play a couple numbers.

If a naked dance was desired, Tony would dig up one of his fast speed tunes, and one of the girls would dance on a little narrow stage, completely nude. Yes, they danced absolutely stripped, but in New Orleans the naked dance was a real art.

54

CLARENCE WILLIAMS

At that time, everybody followed the great Tony Jackson. We all copied him. He was *so* original and a great instrumentalist. I know *I* copied Tony, and Jelly Roll too, but Jelly was more influenced by Albert Cahill. Yes, Tony Jackson was certainly the greatest piano player and singer in New Orleans. He was on the order of how King Cole is now, only much better. About Tony, you know he was an effeminate man—you know.

He was of a brown complexion, with very thick lips. Tony was a sensible dresser, not too flashy, except when he went on drinkin' sprees. He went up to Chicago, and I remember when I got there that he worked at an after-hours place where all the big actors and show folks would come to see him. Tony was the best—and the most popular song he wrote was *Pretty Baby*.

Tony played all the best places in The District, Lulu White's and Countess Willie Piazza's. In fact, I followed Tony into Willie Piazza's.

BUNK JOHNSON

Jelly was one of the best in 1902 and, after that, noted more so than Tony Jackson and Albert Cahill because he played the music the whores liked. Tony was dicty. But Jelly would sit there and play that barrelhouse music all night—blues and such as that. I *know* because I played with him in Hattie Rogers' sporting house in 1903. She had a whole lot of light-colored women in there, best-looking women you ever want to see. Well, I was playing with Frankie Duson's Eagle Band on Perdido Street and sometimes after I'd knock off at four in the morning, Jelly would ask me to come and play with him—he'd play and sing the blues till way up in the day.

CLARENCE WILLIAMS

I became manager of a cabaret in 1913, a place on Rampart Street right across from Union Station, a very rough place where the railroad fellows would hang out. The kind of a place where, from time to time, they would break it up when there was a fight. The man who owned the place came to me and asked me to run it. He told me, "I'll furnish the liquor, and you furnish the entertainment and the girls."

Well, I put my brother in charge and hired a floorwalker six feet tall and carrying a police stick. I had the place cleaned and scrubbed and painted and made a strict rule. Nobody was allowed in 'less they would wear a coat and a collar. It turned out to be a respectable place, and if anybody got rough, the floorwalker would knock those fellows out and throw 'em outside.

I made more than fifteen hundred that Mardi Gras week. I had different musicians, all top-notchers, and girls to sing, Creole girls. I would give them fifty per cent on all the drinks they sold. They were cocktails, only the girl's drink would be some soda with a cherry in it. Of course, the guys would get the real thing. Some of those girls made as high as twelve or fifteen dollars a night.

A lot of the best musicians worked for me there, among them King Oliver, Sidney Bechet, and young Louis Armstrong, who was about twelve or thirteen years old, a happy kid, just like he is today, and workin' on a coal cart. Most all the musicians in New Orleans worked with me. Do you know that I took Bunk Johnson away from home, and he played with me in a sportin' house in Alexandria? And I took Bechet when he was in knee pants. We went all over Texas. Joe Oliver came with me, too, in my own show. About those fellows that "discovered" Bunk a few years ago. They came to me and I told them, "Listen, there's one boy you forgot about," and I told them where to find Bunk. I gave the man his address in New Iberia.

SIDNEY BECHET

Clarence Williams and I toured through Texas with Louis Wade. Louis played piano, I played clarinet, and Clarence sang. Much of the time, we plugged early numbers that Clarence had written, numbers that everyone knows today. We played every kind of date—dances, shows, and one-night stands. We even played in ten-cent stores to sell sheet music.

CLARENCE WILLIAMS

You might say that I was the first Negro music publisher in New Orleans, and I went into partnership with A. J. Piron. Piron, at that time, was what you might call the Paul Whiteman of New Orleans, his having one of the best orchestras in the city, playin' at the best hotels. Piron was important to me because he could write the songs down for me.

LOUIS ARMSTRONG

When I was young and very green, I wrote that tune, *Sister Kate*, and someone said that's fine, let me publish it for you. I'll give you fifty dollars. I didn't know nothing about papers and business, and I sold it outright.

CLARENCE WILLIAMS

Well, in 1916 I was sittin' in the studio one day by myself and somebody sticks a long envelope under the door. It was a check from the Columbia Record people for sixteen hundred dollars! Up until then, we had gotten royalty checks, oh fifteen or twenty dollars for piano rolls, at the most. I looked at that check and actually thought it was for sixteen dollars. It was for a song called *Brown Skin, Who You For?* and the Columbia people had sent a representative down and they recorded it on a dictaphone and sent it up to New York. A band recorded it there and the next thing I knew, I got this check. I believe it was the most money anybody ever made on a song in New Orleans. After that, everybody was writing songs down there. The news got around and, in the Mardi Gras, all the bands were playin' *Brown Skin, Who You For?* Canal Street was decorated with brown-skin leather, and all the children were singin' it. Walkin' down Rampart Street, it was the biggest day of my life. You ask George Brunies about it. He was a youngster then, but he was at the head of the parade in one of the hottest bands down there, playin' my song.

Another thing, I was the first to use the word, "jazz," on a song. On both *Brown Skin, Who You For?* and *Mama's Baby*

Boy, I used the words, "jazz song," on the sheet music. I don't exactly remember where the words came from, but I remember I heard a woman say it to me when we were playin' some music. "Oh, jazz me, baby," she said.

I didn't bother none with music stores then. They would always be tellin' you, "We don't have any calls for it." Instead, I would go from door to door with my music. I'd knock on a door and say, "I've got a new song. It's only ten cents." And they'd say, "Come on in." I'd sit down at the piano and play and sing, and pretty soon the neighbors would be in and I'd be sellin' plenty of copies. I'd also go around from park to park and to all the dance halls pluggin' my songs, and sometimes Lizzie Miles would go around with me to sing.

ARNOLD LOYACANO

Can't truthfully say who had the first white jazz band in New Orleans. Don't know. But I do know Jack Laine had the most popular band at that time. He was more in demand, around 1900, and he developed fellows like Nick La Rocca, Tom Brown, Raymond Lopez. They all played with him. In Laine's own words, he put a horn in their hands! He had two or three bands at that time, so popular that he couldn't fill all the dates. Many times, Bud, my brother, and I subbed for him. Bud is seventy-two now, and he played often with Laine. He remembers, too.

We were playing on a tailgate wagon here. They plastered signs on the sides and we'd stand in the wagon and play while it crept down the streets. We'd been playing as a group for about ten years, I guess.

JACK WEBER

It was in a saloon that Leon Rappolo first picked up a clarinet. Leon's father owned a Negro saloon, and every now and then a colored band would drop in to play a chorus as ballyhoo for a colored dance coming up or a prize fight. Late at night, they'd serenade the saloon for free drinks. And once in a while these musicians would stop off and shoot a game or two of pool. Rappolo's kid would tease the clarinet players in these bands to

58

teach him some licks. *And they did.* Later on, playing with Eddie Shields at Toro's Cabaret, he'd learn from Eddie the things Eddie's brother, Larry, had shown him.

Those clarinetists who gave Rappolo tips on clarinet playing were fakers, every one of them. Some of them thought that if they learned how to read, it would ruin their ability to improvise! There were just two classes of musicians in New Orleans in those days—high-class musicians, who read music and who played in the opera house and similar spots, and dance musicians. The dance musicians played in honky-tonks or took one-night jobs when they could. The best men in the dance bands were fakers, playing ragtime.

Their tunes came from a million sources. Many of them were stolen from old marches (*High Society*, for instance) and were the leader's interpretation of the old marches. Because he couldn't read, the band played it differently from the original. Other band leaders stole it in turn, and, because they couldn't read either, the tune was played with many variations. After the leader had shown the trumpet man the melody (or what he *thought* was the melody), the trumpeter would play it for the band, and the men would come in, making a complete arrangement. It was "every man for himself," with the trumpeter taking the lead and everyone else filling in the best he could. The order, "Don't take down," was a signal to everyone in the band to play all the time—no laying down the horn for a minute.

There was another difference between the "high-class" musician and the dance musician. The latter was proud of his status and didn't want to sound like an opera-house tooter, so he tried to get as honky-tonk a tone as possible to avoid a "legit" tone. They built up the honky-tonk tone with mutes, of which they had an endless variety. Sharkey Bonano, when he traveled north to New York, astounded Manhattan natives by showing them the New Orleans trick of putting the bell of the trumpet into a bucket of water! They had endless gadgets in those bands—kazoos, plunger mutes, half-cocoanut shells at the bell—as well as the regular theater mute.

I remember talking with an old circus trumpeter in New

Orleans back in 1915 on a dance date, a fellow named Sam Rickey. He told me that they had been playing ragtime down there for thirty years. New Orleans, too, was the spot where bands first started off a tune with two warning beats.

The riverboats on the Mississippi played ragtime numbers almost exclusively, except for numbers the Original Dixieland Band had published. We used numbers like *Raggin' the Scale, Maple Leaf Rag, Tiger Rag, Sensation,* and *Eccentric.* But they didn't have the same names then. *Tiger Rag* was called *No. 2,* and *Sensation* was known by the name, *Meatballs.*

Different bands had different names for the same tune, but they used variations and played the tunes in different keys. Blues they made up or stole from the Negro bands. A number like *No. 2* (*Tiger Rag*) was played in different keys and had only two parts until the Original Dixieland Band added parts for dance dates and recordings.

Their instrumentation was different, too. Most bands used two trumpet players, not for first and second parts, but because a job would last from nine A.M. to four A.M. It took two good men, taking turns, to hold up under the strain of playing melody that many hours. The general instrumentation was first and second trumpet, trombone, clarinet, guitar, bass fiddle, and drums. Piano was added only in night clubs, as the budget never included anything extra for moving a piano in for a job.

Before the World War, there were several orks playing New Orleans cabarets. Jimmy Brown, pianist, and his ork were at the Oasis; Louis Armstrong was at Anderson's cabaret; Leon Rappolo and a band without a name at Toro's—Leon's dad placed him there to keep him out of mischief—with Eddie Shields at the piano and Santo Pecora on trombone.

Down on one side of Lambert Street was Basin Street (now known as Saratoga), where all classes of people congregated in cabarets—even respectable citizens, although the majority were anything but that! Many of the musicians in these cabarets played left-handed. Nick La Rocca played left-handed trumpet, for instance, and Jack Loyacano played left-handed trombone.

But outside the cabarets, the jazz bands were playing too.

Negro funeral bands went down the streets, and white musicians gathered on the sidewalk to listen. Colored bands played dance dates, and white boys watched from outside and "sweat" the band to get ideas—they never went inside. And when white bands played a dance, the Negroes listened outside and danced in the street.

As late as 1923, the bands in New Orleans were playing the same as they had before the war. The trumpeter would more or less make up a tune, the others would ask, "What key?" and they would start. If it sounded good and was worth a repeat (judging by the applause) they *couldn't* repeat—because they didn't remember how they had played it. Repeating was especially tough on blues. We used to play four-change blues like *Beale Street*, but we would be careful not to use the original melody. It was the same way with pop tunes; they were played differently than they were written. They called these variations "obligatos."

Many of these tunes were published and copyrighted by the Original Dixieland Jazz Band, and some of the songs were specifically their own. *Blueing the Blues*, for instance, was written by Ragas; *Clarinet Marmalade*, by Shields; *Fidgety Feet*—which includes part of Liszt's *Hungarian Rhapsody*—as it was played by Edwards.

Edwards, incidentally, was the only reading musician of that band. In 1921, when I heard them in New York, Edwards had to play the melody first so that La Rocca could learn the lead on *Rose of Washington Square!* The personnel of the band, at the beginning, included Ragas, fake piano player; Larry Shields, clarinet; Nick La Rocca, trumpet; Eddie Edwards; and Tony Sbabaro.

One of the odd things about the New Orleans ragtime musicians was their tendency to influence their brothers and sons to be musicians. Or maybe they were born that way—who knows? Anyhow, there were a lot of brother teams tooting horns in those days. The Brunies family, for instance. George, trombone, began his musical career with an upright alto which he bought for three dollars in a hock shop. Henry, his brother, played trombone. Abbie, another brother, played trombone. Merritt, the fourth brother, played cornet for some time; he's now police chief in Biloxi, Mississippi. Their uncle or cousin was Iron Lip (Richard) Brunies. And another uncle, called "Double-Head," played bass fiddle when he wasn't working in a New Orleans brewery.

The Shields are a great family of musicians. I used to live across the street from Larry Shields, and I remember hearing his clarinet playing along with the music of an older brother, Jim, the only music reader in the family. Larry has other brothers— Pat, Lawrence, and Eddie, all musicians.

Another brother set was Tom "Red" Brown, trombone, and Steve Brown, bass. Red's band was known as Brown's Ragtime Band. It was he who brought the first band to Chicago for Harry James of Schiller's Cafe, who had gone to New Orleans to get an orchestra. That band included Red, trombone; Raymond Lopez, cornet; Lambert, drums; Arnold (Jack's brother) Loyacano, bass; and Larry Shields, clarinet. They went to Chicago in 1915, or possibly 1916, and played at another spot before going into the Schiller. But it was at the Schiller that the sign, "JAZZ MUSIC," was set up for the first time.

5

Then the Navy closed Storyville down. But jazz went on in New Orleans—and it's still going on.

OFFICIAL STATEMENT BY MAYOR MARTIN BEHRMAN OF NEW ORLEANS

Preterpermitting the pros and cons of legislative recognition of prostitution as a necessary evil in a seaport the size of New Orleans, our city government has believed that the situation could be administered more easily and satisfactorily by confining it within a prescribed area. Our experience has taught us that the reasons for this are unanswerable, but the Navy Department of the Federal Government has decided otherwise.

JOHN A. PROVENZANO

Then, in 1917, came the death march of the famous Red Light District, played by the order of the Secretary of the Navy, Daniels.

The scene was pitiful. Basin Street, Franklin, Iberville, Bienville, and St. Louis became a veritable shambles of Negro and white prostitutes moving out. With all they had in the world reposing in two-wheel carts or on wheelbarrows, pushed by

Negro boys or old men, the once Red Light Queens were making their way out of Storyville to the strains of *Nearer My God to Thee*, played by a massed combination of all the Negro jazzmen of the Red Light dance halls.

By nightfall, the once notorious Red Light District was only a ghost—mere rows of empty cribs. Ugly little Chippy, who could beg more dimes for her Sweet Lucy, was gone; beautiful blonde Helen Smith, from the Storm, would be missed by many an admirer. The saloons and the old familiar wagons, with their weiners and hot hamburgers, remained for a time. Now and then a Negro organ-grinder came out to give one of Old Man Giorlando's untuned organs an airing, but the green shutters were closed forever. The old Red Light District of New Orleans became history.

LOUIS ARMSTRONG

Before they clamped down on Storyville there were an awful lot of killings going on . . . Mysterious ones too . . . Several sailors were all messed up—robbed and killed . . . That's one of the main reasons for the closing of Storyville . . . Those prostitutes commenced to having their pimps—hide somewheres around and either rob—or bash their brains in—anything to get that money —That's when the United States Navy commenced to getting warm . . . And brother when they became warm—that meant trouble and more trouble. Not only for the vice displayers but for all the poor working people who made their living in Storyville such as cooks—waiters—maids—musicians—butlers—dishwashers—and lots of people whom were in different vocations . . . I'm telling you—it was a sad sad situation for anybody to witness . . . I was only fifteen years old . . . But at that age— being around from a real young age delivering stone coal in those cribs—hanging around the pimps, Cotch players, et cetera, I really knew what it was all about . . . So I had to feel sorry just like the rest of them . . . The law commenced to arresting all the prostitutes they caught standing in the doors . . . And send them over to Isolation Hospital to be examined . . . And if they had the least thing wrong with them—or they're blood-bad—

they'd be sent away for a long long time . . . And believe me, they were lots of the prostitutes who had to be sent away for treatment . . . And of course reports from those cases help the Navy to have a strong alibi to close her down . . . Tch Tch. . . .

Ever since I was a little boy selling newspapers—my mother and father (when they were living together) would tell me lots about Storyville . . . Of course, that was to kind of frighten me from spending my few newspaper nickles down there.

After Storyville closed down—the people of that section spreaded out all over the city . . . So we turned out nice and reformed. Some went into other neighborhoods kinda bootlegging the same thing (that jive) savvy? Especially the neighborhoods which was lively and jumped just a wee bit . . . In the Third Ward where I was *raised*—there were always a lot of honky-tonks—gambling, prostitutes, pimps going on . . . But all on a small scale . . . Very very small at that . . . A case of—from sugar to (S) salt . . . Where it would cost you from three to five dollars to see a woman in Storyville—it didn't cost but fifty to seventy-five cents to see and be with a woman in the Third Ward . . . There were no whites up this way at all. They were all colored. Right *amongst* all this vice—I still went to Fisk School right in the heart of it all. At Franklin and Perdido Streets . . . Every corner had a saloon and honky-tonk in the rear . . . They call them lounges up North. Of course, those honky-tonks weren't as elaborate either . . . But I'm just trying to give a fast picture of how a lounge would look in the rough without all of that swell ta doo stuff they put in nowadays. Decorately speaking——

They weren't any standing in the doors either . . . Because after Storyville closed—that one situation wasn't supposed to ever happen in New Orleans again . . . And it didn't. Now after Storyville shut down, the girls couldn't just call out the door for beer. But the wrinkle was—they could catch a "john" (a sucker) and call down to whatever saloon they'd like to trade with and say these words—"Oh Bell Boy—Oh Bell Boy"—and when the bell boy from that particular saloon answers—this Chic will say to him—"BRING ME A HALF A CAN" . . .

Which means a nickle of beer . . . And he'll say O.K. and go into the saloon and repeat the same thing—and less than a few minutes he'll be on his way over to this small-time whore's house with this half a can (nickle of beer) . . . She meets him at the door with her bucket or pitcher—he pours it in and collects the "Tack" (I mean the nickle) and returns to the saloon and sits outside on a beer barrel and waits for another order . . . He gets a salary just delivering drinks . . . If they desire a whole can—that's a dime of beer . . . Quite naturally you get lots more . . . So if you have more than two in the party—it's very wise to order a whole can . . . It wasn't anywhere near as handy for the girls as it was in the old days.

DANNY BARKER
This is what it was like in New Orleans around 1925. It is not true that nothing happened after Storyville closed. There were always, in New Orleans, both before and after Storyville closed, there were always so many musicians, so many great cats all the way down the line. Part of it was due to the fact that in New Orleans we had more access to instruments where other parts of the South didn't. After the Spanish-American War, most of the Army bands disbanded in New Orleans, and so the pawnshops were loaded with instruments. For any occasion in New Orleans, you had music. There were cats like Buddy Petit, Kid Rena, Sidney Desvigne, Sam Morgan, Hippolyte Charles, Punch Miller, Walter Blue, Maurice Durand, Leslie Dimes, and all these guys were playing in the 'twenties. These people didn't care to play for regular jobs in the cabarets because they were too confining. The point I want to make is that there were still a lot of jazz musicians around in the 'twenties. A lot of them would play road-houses and vaudeville shows and circuses and riverboats and lake-boats, like at Lake Pontchartrain. And also—this was during the 'twenties, too, as well as before—there were so many halls in New Orleans, fifteen or twenty. And each one would have some kind of an affair going on. There was also always some kind of lawn party or parades going on.

So you never had to figure on getting work in The District, so it wasn't so important when it closed. Piron had some of the best jobs on the lake front. His first name was Armand. And there were other good bands on the lake front. So those tonks in Storyville weren't too important. And, as a matter of fact, some of the clubs were going in the 'twenties. They would have a closing and then a quick opening, under cover, in The District. Also, bands like Lee Collins' would be based in New Orleans but would be on the road for a while and play towns outside of New Orleans. Little towns in states like Mississippi, Alabama, Georgia, Florida, and Louisiana. Men like Buddy Petit, Sam Morgan, Leslie Dimes, Baptiste Brown, and Victor Spencer were some of the New Orleans musicians who would take these road trips. New Orleans, you see, was the center of bands, and, as way back as I can remember, people in that area would get their bands from New Orleans, and, in fact, they still do. They would go out on the road a week or two weeks, and people in these small towns would keep you on option, according to the business you did and according to how you acted. New Orleans had always been looked on as a city for musicians and New Orleans' being an entertainment center—all the great shows played in that city, like in the Lyric Theatre. And all the big circuses would come through New Orleans. And if they needed a musician, they knew they could pick one up in New Orleans.

All the minstrel shows, like the Rabbit Foot Minstrels and Silas Green and the Georgia Minstrels, used New Orleans musicians year in and year out. You would see a cat disappear, you would wonder where he was, and finally somebody would say that he'd left for one of the shows, that they had sent for him. During the 'twenties, as before, the town had so much night life. Even now, the bars stay open twenty-four hours a day. And then there are musicians who didn't want to leave New Orleans to go up North. Even though they had offers. Some cat would meet a pretty Creole girl, and she'd say she didn't want him to go on the road. So, he'd settle down in New Orleans because there were enough gigs. A lot of out-of-town musicians settled there, too, because there was always some kind of work, good food, and a carefree life.

When department stores had openings or sales, they would always use a band, and that too went on in the 'twenties. Anything in New Orleans pertaining to drawing a crowd, you would use somebody's band, and they still do. We in New Orleans, in the 'twenties, were aware of what was happening in jazz. We'd hear records by other bands and folks would buy them. We'd pass a house and hear a piano roll and things like that. But the records didn't particularly have the best of the music you heard around New Orleans. Then, when the King Oliver and Clarence Williams records started coming out and those terrific Louis Armstrong Okehs, those other records that had come before seemed like there was something in them empty. They didn't have that kind of beat, and they didn't have all the improvisation that was going on in Oliver's and Louis'. And we would hear blues records by Bessie or Clara Smith, Ma Rainey, Sara Martin, et cetera. But the backgrounds on most of those records didn't do them justice. They should have had more of the musicians like Oliver and Louis behind them.

CLARENCE WILLIAMS
Do you remember back before the war, about 1938 or 1939, when those record collectors wrote those letters to Bunk Johnson? Well, it was me that told them where he was working and living —down in New Iberia, Louisiana.

LETTERS FROM BUNK JOHNSON
TO FREDERIC RAMSEY, JR., 1939, 1940

Dear Friend,

I am here, only making out now. For work, we have work only when rice harvest is in, and, that over, things go real dead until cane harvest. I drive a truck and trailer and that only pays me $1.75 a day and that do not last very long. So you all know for sure how much money that I make now. I made up my mind to work hard until I die as I have no one to tell my troubles to, and my children cannot help me out in this case. I have been real down for about five years. My teeth went bad in 1934, so that was my finish playing music. I am just about to give it up. Now I haven't got no other way to go but put my shoulder to the wheel and my nose to the grinding stone and put my music down.

Now for the taking of the picture of mine, you can have one or six. Now six will cost five dollars, and if you care to pay for the six, I will be glad because Armstrong wants one. I would like to give Williams one, Foster one, Bechet one, and I would like to keep one, which would be the six. Now, if you only want me to take one, I will do so. So, you can send me what you think about it, for one or six. Now, if there is some things you would want to know about music, please let me know when you answer.

Willie Bunk Johnson

My dear kind friends,

Only a few words I want to say to you about my delay in sending you these pictures and these letters. Now, I'm pretty sure that you all know just how everything is down South with the poor colored man. The service here is really poor for colored people. We have no colored studios. This is a Cajun town and, in these little country towns, you don't have a chance like the white man, so you just have to stand back and wait until your turn come. That is just the way here. So please do not think hard of me. You think hard of the other fellow.

You all do your very best for me and try and get me on my feet once more in life. Now, here is just what I mean when I say the word, "on my feet." I mean this: I wants to become able to play trumpet once more, as I know I can really stomp trumpet yet. Now, here is what it takes to stomp trumpet, that is a real good set of teeth. And that is just what I am in deep need for. Teeth and a good trumpet and old Bunk can really go. Now, my friends, the shape that I am in at the present time I cannot help myself, so you all can judge that. Now, as I said before, that this town is very dead and it is real tough on a poor man when he do get in the shape I am in. Now, I have the very best of health and nothing but good clothes. Old Bunk is only in need for a set of teeth and a good job. Now, I truly thank you for the treat of the money. They come in need time. I did not have a penny in my house or no place else. Do tell my dear old pal, Clarence Williams, to write me and to send a few late numbers of his. Now, I cannot play them but I can think them. O Boy, that will make me feel good anyway. If I have not got no teeth I can have something to look at when I get to thinking about the shape I am in and have no good way to go but work, just as I could get it, some weeks nothing at all. Now, you tell Louis to please send me a trumpet, as he told me that he would, and you all do your best for me. From a good old, kind friend, as ever, and will always be so, so answer me at once.

Willie Bunk Johnson

BUNK JOHNSON

When I came back to music and was out in San Francisco in 1943, Harry James was playin' at the Civics Auditorium. I knew his papa, a fine man, bandmaster in the circus.

Young Harry says to me, "Pops, I don't have to tell you. You and Louis, only men that can play this horn." That was real nice of young Harry, but he play real good trumpet himself. I told him so. Never catch a real good musician knock a musician.

Take my boy Louis. Anybody in this world knows any more about playin' that trumpet than Louis Armstrong—show him to me. And I'll show the doubter! I'll run 'im! And if I can't run 'im —Man, I'll sure talk him down!

You should see some of those old fellows down in New Orleans

I grew up with. My, they're old! Shuffling along, can't remember nothin'. Couldn't play a chorus to save their life. Whiskey got some of them. Whiskey heads are all dead! Bunk is still here!

When I look back over the objects in my life, why I can remember back to when there was no discrimination in Louisiana. When I was a boy you got on a mule car in New Orleans and walk up and put your nickle in the bandbox and sat down. Discrimination came in 1889. Too much prejudice in the South since then. And I've played music for white people all over the world and many of my best friends are white. But there's always somebody who'll come up and say to you, "Hey, nigger, play this."

JOHN A. PROVENZANO

Today the spotlight in New Orleans night life is Bourbon Street, known as the Vieux Carre section of old New Orleans. Casually strolling in a nightery on Bourbon Street, with its elaborate front, well-stocked bar, and clean, roomy dancing floors, one finds it difficult to understand the music. In this particular outfit, the drummer appears to be the leader. He wants to play a piece all by himself, and does. How the patrons of the place stand the racket is more than I can explain. No one is able to understand what the band is trying to play; but that doesn't seem to worry the boys much; they think Hollywood is their next port of call.

Memories go back to the days of the loud jazz bands of the early 'nineties, when we were just starting out with patch-up cornets and trombones, leaky valves on clarinets which were usually minus a key or two, and homemade bass fiddles, and warped guitars. We must have sounded just as lousy to the professional element, but by constant plugging night and day for days, months, and even years, some went to fame and fortune (also ruin).

In another club on Bourbon, Oscar "Papa" Celestin, now well on his way to his seventies, has the jazz world on its toes. Believe it or not, but Papa Celestin today is just the same great trouper that he was in the early 'nineties, when jazz fans couldn't agree as to which of the two between himself and the immortal Manuel

Perez produced the better tone on the cornet. Perez has gone to his Maker, but the other representative of the real New Orleans jazz music is fortunately still with us.

Papa Celestin has set an example that the present young generation of bottle-man horn tooters would do well to follow. The fact that he and that illustrious master, Alphonse Picou, the dean of all clarinetists, still have their flags flying high in the jazz world gives one hope for the future.

PART II

"Up a Lazy River"

6

*Many of the jazzmen worked their way North in
Fate Marable's riverboat bands.*

DANNY BARKER

One of the most beautiful sounds in the city of New Orleans was
Fate Marable playing his steam calliope about seven in the evening
every night. Those calliope concerts from the riverboats *J. S.* and
Bald Eagle started in the first couple of years after the boats started
using music—around 1916 and '17, I'd say. Well, Fate would play
the calliope in the evening to let the people know the boats were
going to cut out on excursions. All over that river, Fate Marable
had a fabulous reputation.

This is how the riverboats got music on them. Those boats had
roustabouts on them, and half of those roustabouts played guitar,
and nearly all sang. Well, when those boats went up the river,
the roustabouts were on the lower deck and the passengers, the
gamblers, et cetera, stayed up on the upper deck. But when the
people on the upper deck heard the singing and playing of
the roustabouts, they would come downstairs, and that gave Strekfus, the owner of the boats, the idea of putting music on the boats.

TONY CATALANO

In 1907, Fate (Marable) came out of Paducah, Kentucky, and
started to work with me on the steamer, *J. S.* (That boat burned

75

some time ago.) The Strekfus Lines now have another boat by the same name. Those boats were responsible for the start of many a famous musician as Fate, Louis Armstrong, Joe (King) Oliver, the Dodds brothers, Jules Buffano, Wayne King, Emil Flint, and others.

About 1919, Fate dropped in at a dance in New Orleans at the Cooperative Hall and heard Kid Ory's band playing *Honky-Tonky Town* by Chris Smith. Fate asked who was playing the trumpet, and it turned out to be Louis Armstrong. Bob Lyons was managing the band and playing bass. Fate went up to Lyons and asked if he could use the trumpet man the nights Lyons didn't use him. So Fate did use him, and that's how Louie got his start to get out and go North, as Fate gave him steady work on the *Capitol* of the Strekfus Lines.

ZUTTY SINGLETON

There was a saying in New Orleans. When some musician would get a job on the riverboats with Fate Marable, they'd say, "Well you're going to the conservatory." That's because Fate was such a fine musician and the men who worked with him had to be really good.

You know, Fate had a white band on the riverboats before he had his colored band. The boats would spend the winter in New Orleans and then, around April, go up to St. Louis, stoppin' at Natchez and other places for a night or two. The way it worked on the boats was Monday night the dances were for colored. Every night the boats would travel up and down the river for a while and then come back.

The riverboat bands played dance music mostly. But Fate had things like Jelly Roll's tunes in the book. Numbers like *The Pearls* and *Jelly Roll Blues*. And he had songs like *Frankie and Johnny*. As a matter of fact, *Frankie and Johnny*, with Fate's band, was the first record I was ever on. At that time they brought the machines along with them and we made the record for Okeh in New Orleans. The other side was *Piano Flight*.

I remember when Baby Dodds, who was in the band that Louis was in on the *Capitol* steamboat, somehow got me on the stand so

I could listen to Louis. It was bitterly against the rules but somehow Baby did it.

The bands on the boats then were made up of two trumpets, one trombone, mellophone, violin, banjo, drums, and bass.

POPS FOSTER

The boat would stop every night in a different town. . . . big back-wheel boats. They advertised, like one-nighters, but still you were on the boat. There was a pretty big dance floor, with soda fountains—and a place to sleep. We started playing about eight. The boat left at nine. Everybody was down there by then. We had to play fourteen numbers by eleven thirty. Those fourteen numbers just had to be up there. There were two intermissions, one ten-minute, one fifteen-minute. The day rides would take you a long ways. Then, the band would also get off the boat and go into the sugar cane.

BUSTER BAILEY

We were playing in Memphis at the same time they were playing in Storyville in New Orleans. The difference was that the New Orleans bands did more improvising. Ours were more the note variety. We played from the sheets.

Ours were just dance bands. Fellows that played the circus were the top musicians of the day and, during the off season, a lot of them would play in the local bands like those led by Handy, George Bynum, Stewart, et cetera. There was also King Phillips, one of the first jazz clarinet players I ever heard.

I had started playing the clarinet when I was thirteen. I was born in Memphis. I remember, as a matter of fact, the first time W. C. Handy played *Memphis Blues*, around 1916. The first time he played it was in the Clay Street School, back of my house. There was a little concert. I was going to the school at the time.

One of the ways we'd get new popular tunes in Memphis was through the magazine, *Etude*. Every month they'd publish two new numbers and we'd learn them—but with a beat.

In 1917, we began to improvise after hearing recordings of *Livery Stable Blues* and stuff like that. Also some of the boys had drifted up from New Orleans. There was George Williams, around 1912 and 1913, a great trombone player and a very good musician, composer, and arranger who also improvised. He played with Handy's reading band.

So the first I heard of the New Orleans style was on records. The next I heard were Wilbur Sweatman's records on Columbia. Also there was the winter of 1917 when I made a tour down to New Orleans and heard the New Orleans music in the city itself. We only stayed a week. I was in high school at the time. I heard Johnny Dodds at Tom Anderson's. And I heard Piron, Mutt Carey, Clarence Williams. We stopped by Williams' place; he had a publishing house.

That trip to New Orleans, by the way, made it easier for me to adapt to the New Orleans musicians when I went on to Chicago later on. After that trip, I came home and started jazzing it up in Memphis. One of the jobs our band had, for example, was to accompany the draftees to the station in 1917 and '18. We played *Draftin' Blues*, *Preparedness Blues*, and I jazzed them up. Everybody would follow me. I was the center of attraction. They were playing the straight lead, but I—as the principal of my school said—was embellishing around the melody. At that time, I wouldn't have known what they meant by improvisation. But embellishment was a phrase I understood. And that was what they were doing in New Orleans—embellishment. In my day in Memphis, if a guy played with a good, swinging beat, he was a good ballroom man. Before 1917, the word jazz didn't exist—not around my city anyway.

Well, I went to Chicago in 1919. I had two more weeks of high school to finish, but I wanted to go to Chicago. All my friends were going. There was better money there, I thought, and there was a little girl who had gone there that I wanted to follow. At that time, everybody from New Orleans and many people east of the Mississippi and as far west as Arkansas were migrating North. The word was there was lots of money in Chicago.

I was sixteen when I got there, and I was hired by Erskine Tate who was about to bring a band into the Vendome Theatre.

That Tate band in Chicago was composed of all legitimate

musicians, and I was regarded as a legitimate musician, too. In Chicago, I started studying with Franz Schoeppe, first clarinetist with the Chicago Symphony. That was in 1919. Benny Goodman started studying with him two or three years later.

There were many of the New Orleans group in Chicago then —King Oliver, Freddie Keppard, Sidney Bechet, Preston Jackson, Jimmie Noone, Manuel Perez, et cetera—twenty or thirty of them. There were also Ed Garland, Honore Dutrey, Eddie Atkins, Jim Robinson, a lot of them. I was working at the theater and they all used to come in to hear "the young kid, a hell of a clarinet player, playing all the overtures." At night, I'd sit in at places like the Panama Cafe, Royal Gardens, Dreamland, Elite Cafe No. 1 and Elite Cafe No. 2. As I said, it wasn't difficult for me to adapt to the New Orleans musicians' styles after I'd made that trip down there.

I thought I'd start in with lots of money in Chicago, but I started at twenty-four dollars a week. I was making more than that by that time around home.

*Downtown was the Original Dixieland Jazz Band;
and on Chicago's South Side you could rock to the
music of Keppard, Oliver, Armstrong, Ory, Johnny
and Baby Dodds, Preston Jackson, Jimmie Noone,
Lil Armstrong, and many more.*

PRESTON JACKSON

Man, I had a right to be scared when I played my first gig in Chicago, and, believe me, I was. Those were the days of tough competition in solid cats like Roy Palmer and Kid Ory on trombone and Joe Oliver, Tig Chambers, and Sugar Johnny on trumpet—competition that would scare the good notes out of anybody, and I was no exception.

I remember I was taking lessons from Roy Palmer when the gig came up. Roy was trombonist with Doc Watson who had all the gigs in town sewed up. Doc had some fine men in his outfit like Roy and William Hightower and Horace Eubanks. After hearing them play so much, I was really scared when Richard Jones asked me to sit in with his band here in Chicago.

Jones was a wonderful pianist, who knew Buddy Bolden and came to Chicago with King Oliver long before Lil Hardin became known as the wizard of the keys. Besides Jones, Tig Chambers was also in the band. I'd seen him years before when I was a kid in New Orleans and he was pioneering hot rhythms at Cole's Pavilion. It was probably the thrill of sitting in with Tig that made me accept the gig down on Thirty-ninth and Rhodes.

I'll never know how I got through that first hour, I was so choked up, but I finally came around because musicians like that inspire you—especially on your first gig. "Blow it, kid. Sock it out." Tig and Jones kept shouting until I finally loosened up and did tricks with that slide that I probably never did before or since.

ARNOLD LOYACANO

I was in Tom Brown's band, which was the first white band to ever go to Chicago and play jazz. This is the story. In 1915, Myrtle Howard was a vaudeville dancer at West End, in New Orleans, and her manager, Joe Gohrum, heard us playing and asked if we'd like to go up to Lamb's Cafe, in Chicago.

No one knew we were leaving because if we didn't make good and had to come back, that'd look pretty bad. So we kept it a secret. When we got to Chicago it was snowing and very cold. We stayed at the first hotel we saw, the Commercial, on Wabash and Harrison Streets. We didn't even have an audition. We began playing at eight o'clock that night.

Now just remember that there had been a string ensemble playing there, and WE had been playing on the back of a wagon. We couldn't play soft. Didn't know what soft was!! Here we come in with a trombone, clarinet, and cornet. People held their ears and yelled, "*Too loud.*" Well, why not? We'd followed strings! And there was a tile floor in the place, and what looked like a tin ceiling.

The first piece we played was *No. 2*. It was popular here but no one knew the name of it. We just called it *No. 2*. They paid us twenty-five dollars a week in Chicago—the salary was the big thing. We'd been making a dollar a night down in New Orleans.

That's when people started calling our music "jazz." The way the Northern people figured it out, our music was loud, clangy, boisterous, like you'd say, "Where did you get that jazzy suit?" meaning loud or fancy. Some people called it "jass." Later, when the name stuck, it was spelled with a "z," "jazz."

About 1921, the Rhythm Kings came along. They induced me

to play bass with them. They needed a bass man, none were around but me, so I was forced into it.

That was the original outfit. Paul Mares, on trumpet; George Brunies, on trombone; Leon Rappolo, on clarinet; Jack Pettis, on sax; Elmer Schoebel, on piano; Frankie Snyder, on drums; and me, on bass. In my estimation, this was the starting of a new jazz era, because jazz had died down, and this band had what the previous bands didn't have. They had more men, more drive, and had more harmony.

Farewell Blues was originated because these guys were fishing for harmony, and the notes sounded like a train whistle. I was a good reader and so was Elmer, and we sort of helped the others when they needed it. But the hours were just too long; from eight at night until six or eight in the morning. We were at the Friar's Inn, and we played as long as the customers were there. We used to have fellows throw us hundred dollar bills to keep us playing, in Chicago!!

JOHNNY STEIN

Whenever I have got into a jive session on New Orleans and the history of jazz, it seems that the talk always turns to Nick La Rocca and how he originated the Dixieland Jazz Band. It is now time that the *true* version be known of how this band was originated.

I, Johnny Stein, and not Nick La Rocca, organized and brought this band to Chicago in March, 1916, which was called "Stein's Original Dixieland Jazz Band." The band consisted of the late Alcide "Yellow" Nunez, clarinet; Eddie Edwards, trombone; the late Henry Ragas, piano; Nick La Rocca, cornet; and I, Johnny Stein, as drummer who had been working at the Pup Cafe in New Orleans, my first and only professional engagement in New Orleans. The Pup Cafe was then the mecca for show people and was considered one of the hottest spots in town.

One night an actor named Gus Chandler asked me if I would like to go to Chicago with a hot band. Mr. Chandler got in touch with the manager of the Schiller Cafe and with Mr. Sam Hare, who was the proprietor.

We all left for Chicago to start our engagement at the Schiller

Cafe, as "Stein's Original Dixieland Jazz Band." We were an over-night sensation in Chicago. The Chicagoans came, stared, and listened, and then they started dancing.

We were billed as "Stein's Original Dixieland Jazz Band," and we might have added "Jam Band," because our tunes were all original, such as *Livery Stable Blues, Skeleton Jangle, High Society*, and *Dixieland One Step*.

We were getting along fine at the Schiller, with the crowds increasing nightly. Then, without warning, the four men left me holding the bag. They then reorganized, calling themselves "The Original Dixieland Jazz Band," omitting Stein, and went to work in the old Belvedere Hotel in the Loop in Chicago. From there, they went to Bert Kelly's Stables, across the bridge on Clark Street, then to New York, and later to London. I got four New Orleans musicians, who were in Chicago at the time, to finish my contract engagement at the Schiller. They were Larry Shields, clarinet; Ernie Erdman, piano; Doc Berenson, cornet; and Jules Cassard, trombone.

When the Schiller engagement was over, I left for New York to go into the Alamo Cafe on 125th Street, located in a basement beneath a burlesque house.

This band, which I organized, went by the name of the "Original New Orleans Jazz Band," and included Archille Baquet, clarinet; Frank Lotak, trombone; Frank Christian, trumpet; and Jimmy Durante, piano.

My band played in and around New York City from 1917 to 1925, with Jimmy Durante continuing with us. We worked in places such as the College Inn in Coney Island, the Nightingale, and George Gutrie's summer place in Upper New York State, coming back to the Alamo off and on for several years.

Since then, I have been around New York, playing club dates, and recently wound up an engagement at the Top Hat in Union City, New Jersey's leading night club, with my four-piece swing band, known as "Johnny Stein and His Swingaroos." However, I have never forgotten my first date in the North at the Schiller Cafe, when I introduced jazz to the Chicagoans, and what a sight we must have been in our dusters—the only uniform we had—

throwing in a straw hat once in a while for more class. I also want to give credit to Tom Brown, as he took a band, which he called "Tom Brown's Ragtime Band," to Chicago two or three years prior to my engagement there. I think they played the Lamb's Cafe, which was located in the Loop.

In those days, bands were called "Ragtime and Syncopated," and I lay claim to being the first to use the word, "Jazz," in connection with a band.

RALPH BERTON

Around 1919 the best units were those of King Oliver and of the New Orleans Rhythm Kings. But, believe me, there were many orchestras of value whose names are forever effaced from our memories. Imagine that for one reason or another Jelly Morton had not had the chance to record the numerous records that he made. I am convinced that if he had not had the chance to make those records his name today would be totally unknown to the followers of jazz.

So certain good musicians of that time who did not have the chance to record will remain forever unknown. Have you ever heard anyone talk about Frankie Quartell? He was the first trumpet player I ever heard use a glass as a mute. Do you know the name of Arnold Johnson, an excellent pianist of that time?

TOMMY BROOKINS

Among the great pianists of Chicago was a man named Glover Compton, who always played with a big cigar in his mouth. He was at the Dreamland and his favorite song was *Dearest, I Love You*, which he played in his own style—that is to say, the ragtime tradition.

Glover remained later for a long time in Europe and especially played in Paris, a little before the last World War. There are no records by him.

And before Louis Armstrong and the orchestra of Carroll Dickerson played at the Sunset, at the corner of Thirty-fifth Street and Calumet, the Sunset had a remarkable band headed by Sammy

Stewart. For many years it remained one of the best in Chicago. Sammy Stewart had gathered together only musicians of class and he played arrangements in a style that was sophisticated for that era. This pianist also played classical works magnificently.

FRED "TUBBY" HALL

I came to Chicago in March, 1917—was there long before Oliver, although I didn't have a real job for several months. In May, I got a job with a New Orleans jazz band—Keppard's brother on guitar, with Sugar Johnny, Lawrence Duhe, Roy Palmer, and Ed Garland, who was later replaced by Wellman Braud.

WELLMAN BRAUD

I did not leave New Orleans with the Creole Band, but joined them in Chicago in 1917. That is when I took up strong bass. Lil Hardin was with us then. They played swing music then, same as today, but more drive. People would shout in their chairs. We opened the Pekin, 1917. Played at Dreamland until one o'clock and then played at the Pekin till six in the morning. There were turn-out houses nightly in both places. But Bill Bottoms of the Dreamland said he didn't like the idea of a "jazz" band in his cabaret. Then Izzy Shaw booked us at the De Luxe and the "jazz band" nearly ran Bottoms out of business. We opened at eight nightly and at ten o'clock we didn't have standing room. I would come down the street and the people would say, "That's the bass picker from the jazz band!"

ALBERTA HUNTER

You probably won't believe this because it sounds just like a fairy tale, but, believe me, it's God's honest truth. I ran away from home when I was eleven years old and got to Chicago when I was eleven years and two days old with a nickel and a dime—just fifteen cents—in my pocket.

I had told my mother I was going to stay overnight with a friend, Irma White, and got my school teacher, Miss Florida Cummings Edgerton, to take me to Chicago instead of some other little girl who couldn't make it. I still remember that train trip and the conductor looking at my pass. I was wearing red shoes and stockings and a blue dress.

The only person I knew of in Chicago was a girl named Ellen Winston, who was my mother's chum's daughter. Now, I didn't know anything at all about Chicago except that the streets ran in numbers and I honestly didn't know where Ellen Winston lived or where I was goin'.

Well, here's the thing that was so amazing. After we got to Chicago, I recall getting off a streetcar and waving goodbye to my teacher and then I just looked around me and walked up to the first house I saw. Inside, there was a door open and inside was a woman washing clothes.

I stood there a bit and she says, "Come in, child, who're you lookin' for?" I asked her if she knew an Ellen Winston, and she said, "Why, there's a *Helen* Winston lives here. She'll be home around five o'clock. Why don't you wait for her?"

Well, it *was* my mother's chum's daughter, and when she came in that door and saw me, she screamed and hugged me, and both of us cried.

She was workin' in service and that night she called the lady she worked for and asked if she needed extra help. The lady told her "yes," and the very next day I started as a second cook at six dollars a week and room and board. My new friend dressed me in her old clothes to make me look older than I was, and, at the end of my first week, I sent my mother two dollars.

About a year or two later, I heard stories about girls making as much as ten dollars a week in night clubs and so I went looking for one of those jobs. I was scared and afraid they'd all run me out because I looked so bad and was so little.

The very first place I worked was Dago Frank's on Archer and State Street. That was a place where the sportin' girls hung out. The boss heard me and said, "Get her outta here, she's terrible!" But the piano player who was real nice (he was a terrible piano player, though) told the boss, "Aw, let her stay, she's only a kid."

Well, I worked there for a year and ten months, learnin' all the new songs off piano rolls and getting experience. But the police got on the place and it was closed down.

Next, I went to Hugh Hoskins' club on Thirty-second and State, and it was there I started going to town. I just packed that place singin' the blues. In fact, all the stars from downtown started comin' in to hear me. I was getting big.

Then I went over to the Panama, on Thirty-sixth and State, and there I was makin' seventeen-fifty a week—and that was money! The Panama had an "upstairs" and a "downstairs"—five girls and a piano player downstairs and another five girls and a piano player upstairs.

And do you know who was workin' downstairs all at the same time? There was "Bricktop," Cora Green, Florence Mills, Mattie Hite (a fine singer), and Nettie Compton. And don't leave out Glover Compton who played piano. Everybody knew Glover Compton. He was doing the stuff that Willie "The Lion" Smith did later on, you know, the big fat cigar hangin' out of the corner of his mouth and sittin' sideways at the piano talking to the people. Glover was great.

Now the downstairs at the Panama was more of a quiet reserved type of entertainment. But upstairs it was rougher. Upstairs, we had Mamie Carter, a dancer, the "shake" kind, and Twinkle Davis who danced and sang. (She couldn't sing much but it made no difference 'cause she had the most beautiful legs and that's what people came to see.) Then there was Nellie Carr who sang and did splits, Goldie Crosby, and myself. There, I would really lay the blues on. In fact, it was at the Panama that I introduced the *St. Louis Blues*. Oh yes, I was there a long time and people like Bert Williams and Al Jolson would come to hear me sing *St. Louis Blues*, *Mammy's Little Coal Black Rose*, and other blues and popular numbers. But then there was some trouble downstairs and the place was closed down.

But it was at the Dreamland that I really went to town. It was there that I introduced *Loveless Love*, which W. C. Handy brought to me on a little piece of paper—not even on manuscript. It was at the Dreamland that I also introduced *A Good Man Is Hard To Find*, *Someday Sweetheart*, and an Irving Berlin song that never really got too popular, *Come on Home*. Sophie Tucker heard about *A Good Man Is Hard To Find* and sent over her maid to tell me that she wanted to see me. I knew she wanted the song, and so I didn't go. So do you know how she got it? She sent over her piano player, Ted Shapiro, to listen to it and learn it, and got somebody to take down the words. But when she sang the song she always gave me credit.

That Dreamland was some place. It was *big* and always packed. And you had to be a singer then—there were no microphones and those bands were marvelous. King Oliver's band was there when I started (Louis wasn't with him yet), and, I'm telling you, you could sing one chorus or fifty or sixty choruses and that band would never be a beat away. And they'd always end on the same note and at the same time the singer did.

Singers then would go around from table to table singin' to each table, hustlin' dollars in tips. But nobody at the other tables would get mad when they couldn't hear you. I made a lot of money that way.

I was under contract to Paramount Records then, but I recorded *Everybody Loves My Baby* for Gennett for Clarence Williams. I used my sister's name, Josephine Beatty, and they called the band the Red Onion Jazz Band. Bechet was in it, Wellman Braud, and Baby Dodds, I remember.

Another thing about the Dreamland. Each entertainer had what was called an "up," when they would go out and perform. And, believe me, there was always something going on. There were no such things as intermissions and there was never a quiet moment. When you worked at the Dreamland, you worked from about seven thirty in the evening to three or four in the morning—and you didn't move out of there.

Everybody would go to hear Tony Jackson after hours. Tony was just marvelous—a fine musician, spectacular, but still soft. He could write a song in two minutes and was one of the greatest accompanists I've ever listened to. Tony was always jolly, but he had bad teeth, just terrible! He had mixed grey hair and always had a drink on the piano—always! It was only beer, but he drank plenty of that. Tony wrote *Pretty Baby*, which he dedicated to a tall skinny fellow, and another song that everybody sang at that time, *When Your Troubles Will Be Mine.*

Yes, Tony Jackson was a prince of a fellow, and he would always pack them in. There would be so many people around that piano trying to learn his style that sometimes he could hardly move his hands—and he never played any song the same way twice.

Another musician who was playing in Chicago then was Freddie Keppard. He played at the De Luxe, at Thirty-sixth and State, upstairs. The De Luxe was much smaller than the Dreamland, more intimate, you might say. You know, he doesn't get the credit he should get. In fact, I often wonder why people don't mention him more often. And he was really a fine fellow, easy to get along with. I never saw him drunk either. Yes, he was a prince of a fellow and always givin' youngsters pointers about music.

Freddie was about medium height, a shade lighter than I am, and always clean-shaven. He always played in his shirt sleeves, rolled up—yes, a very fine fellow.

TOMMY BROOKINS
The first time that I heard Freddie Keppard was in the course of a Breakfast Dance given by the Eighth Infantry Regiment at the corner of Thirty-fifth Street and Giles Avenue. The place could hold six to seven thousand people. I was astonished by the power of this musician. He played with assurance and more strongly than any other trumpet player I have ever heard. He was a great trumpet player, possessing a lot of rhythm and an exceptional quality of execution. His style was very different from that of Armstrong. It was more lyrical.

With his orchestra of eight musicians, Keppard succeeded in carrying everyone away. He made as much noise as the military brass band that opened the proceedings.

PRESTON JACKSON
Keppard? Well, compare him to Perez, who was the best teacher. *He* read very well. Keppard was just the opposite, all barrelhouse. He played two or three notes a bar and was called King Keppard. He was tops. He didn't have a lot of execution. Liquor killed Kep-

pard, finally. He used to carry a water bottle full of liquor under his arm. One time a fellow said, "We don't allow liquor on the job." Keppard picked up the bottle and got ready to go. The guy told him to stay.

JELLY ROLL MORTON

The Freddie Keppard Creole Band was tremendous. They really played jazz. The reason Baquet, the clarinet, played straight, more or less, was because he was the only one who could read and they had him play the lead for that reason. He played it rather straight, down low. I never heard a man that could beat Keppard—his reach was so exceptional, both high and low, with all degrees of power, great imagination, and more tone than anybody. Any little place in the music that didn't have any notes on, he would fill right up. He really couldn't read a note. Liked to hear the tune first, because he didn't want to admit he couldn't read. He frequently found excuses; he would be having valve trouble, fingering the valves, shaking the instrument, spitting it out; all the while he would be listening. Somebody would bawl him out and he would say, "Go ahead, I'll play my part!" Next time, he would pick up his horn and play right through the number.

RICHARD M. JONES

Music was different in New Orleans because many were too blamed ignorant to read, not like New York or Chicago musicians. Keppard and others practiced at the 25 Club, in New Orleans. They would all go down there after they got through with their jobs, late at night. I would play over the new pieces because I could read. Then some other pianist would get up and try to play it; perhaps he could play it a little better. But they would forget it before they got through and would have to fill in with a break and other stuff. That's where the improvisation came from. They had nothing to do all day but play checkers; so they couldn't help learning their instruments. There were no schools; if they wanted to take up an instrument, they had all the time in the world to perfect their playing.

90

BUSTER BAILEY

Freddie Keppard was playing then too. He was one of the greatest, but you never hear much about it. The difference between him and Joe Oliver is that Joe didn't drink, at least not that much. Freddie was the original man to come out of New Orleans to New York. He had a chance to make the first jazz records—before the Original Dixieland Jazz Band—but he was afraid people would steal his tunes and arrangements so he didn't record them.

Freddie could play as soft and as loud, as sweet and as rough, as you would want. He loved to play *Pagliacci*, too. Freddie and the other musicians had no idea that the music they were playing was unusual. Manuel Perez was another who was very good. As for the crowds, they came in to drink, to dance, to hear the jazz music. All of those clubs carried shows and there were singers that went from table to table.

I doubled from the Vendome to the Lorraine Gardens where I worked for Freddie Keppard. Lil Hardin was in the band and so was Jimmie Bertrand, who later taught Lionel Hampton and started him on vibes. Lil Hardin is from my home town. She caused me to want to go to Chicago. We had been neighbors. She left around 1914–15 and went to Chicago where she worked at the Dreamland and the Pekin Gardens. She was making a hundred-fifty a week salary. That was like five hundred at that time, and the news got back to Memphis. I was in such demand in Memphis during the time I was going to school that I was working all the time, but I only got paid two-sixty a night for dances and five dollars out of town for expenses. So I wanted to go to Chicago to get some of that money. So I left even before I finished those last two weeks of high school.

LIL ARMSTRONG

In the summer of 1918, my folks moved from Memphis to Chicago, and I made it my business to go out for a daily stroll and look this "heaven" over. Chicago meant just that to me—its beautiful brick and stone buildings, excitement, people moving swiftly, and things happening. On one of these strolls, I came to a music store on

91

South State Street (Jones' Music Store). I stopped and gazed at all the sheet music in the window display, wishing I had every one of them, but, knowing how impossible that was, I decided to go in and buy one that I had heard so many people whistling on the street.

I hummed it over to the salesman (Frank Clemons), and he sat down and played it over for me. Well, he didn't play it well, so I asked him if I might try it over. He readily consented and was very surprised that I played at sight as well as adding something to it. When I finished, he had me try out other numbers and then asked if I'd like the job of demonstrating music. I told him I'd go home to get my mother's consent and return later to see the boss.

I didn't *stroll*, I *ran* all the way home to break the news to Mother. Oh, but was Mother indignant. "The very idea, work! And above all things, for only three dollars a week! I should say not, young lady," she said.

Well, in no time at all I sold her the idea, just to learn all the music and have something to do until time to return to school. Off I went to work the next morning, thrilled beyond words over my first job.

As soon as I got to the music store, I got busy playing all the music on the counter, and by two P.M. the place was packed with people listening to the "Jazz Wonder Child." I played on and on, all the music there, all my classics. My, what a thrill. No wonder the people called me child, I looked to be about ten years old in my middy blouse and eighty-five pounds.

Mrs. Jones ran an employment and booking agency at the store, so all the musicians and entertainers hung out there. They'd rehearse, sit around, and gossip for hours. Almost every day there was a jam session and I took charge of every piano player that dared to come in.

But one day the great Jelly Roll Morton from New Orleans came in and I was in for a little trouble. I had never heard such music before, they were all his original tunes. Jelly Roll sat down, the piano rocked, the floor shivered, the people swayed while he ferociously attacked the keyboard with his long skinny fingers, beating out a double rhythm with his feet on the loud pedal. I was thrilled, amazed, and scared. Well, he finally got up from the piano, grinned, and looked at me as if to say, "Let this be a lesson to you."

It was indeed a lesson because from then on when I played, all eighty-five pounds of me played. But do you think the people were satisfied? No, they wanted Jelly Roll to hear me play. . . . Well, I'm really in for it, and, suddenly remembering that he had played nothing classical, I sat down to the piano very confidently, played some Bach, Chopin, and the *Witches' Dance*, which they especially liked. The session ended with me still the winner.

The following week the New Orleans Creole Jazz Band came in town and gave an audition for Mrs. Jones. When they started out on the *Livery Stable Blues* I nearly had a fit. I had never heard a band like that; they made goose pimples break out all over me. I'm telling you they played loud and long and got the biggest kick out of the fits I was having over their music. Mrs. Jones booked them at a Chinese restaurant on the North Side immediately.

The band consisted of violin, clarinet, cornet, trombone, bass, and drums, so they had to add a piano player to accompany the girl singer. Mrs. Jones sent several men pianists but none proved satisfactory, so Frank Clemons suggested that she send me over just for one night to see what would happen. She argued that I was a minor and would not be allowed to play in a cabaret, but she took a chance anyway, and off I went thrilled again.

When I sat down to play I asked for the music and were they surprised! They politely told me they didn't have any music and furthermore never used any. I then asked what key would the first number be in. I must have been speaking another language because the leader said, "When you hear two knocks, just start playing."

It all seemed very strange to me, but I got all set, and when I heard those two knocks I hit the piano so loud and hard they all turned around to look at me. It took only a second for me to feel what they were playing and I was off. The New Orleans Creole Jazz Band hired me, and I never got back to the music store—never got back to Fisk University.

Four weeks later we were playing at the De Luxe Cafe (Thirty-fifth and State) and I was making the unheard of salary of twenty-seven fifty weekly besides twenty dollars a night in tips.

The members of this band were Sugar Johnny (cornet), a long, lanky, dark man with deep little holes in his skinny face. He never had too much to say and I wondered about that, but how was I to know he was dying on his feet with T.B.? Couldn't tell by his playing. Lawrence Dewey (clarinet), he was skinny, too, but much lighter in color and always smiling. Roy Palmer (trombone), was the darkest one, but jolly and happy-go-lucky. Violinist Jimmie Palao (a decided Creole with his olive complexion and straight hair) was skinny and coughed all the time. He died with T.B. also. The bassist was Eddie Garland, who was the healthiest of the skinny ones. Tubby Hall (drums) was as fat as the others were skinny, and the youngest of the band that left New Orleans to make jazz history.

The band was a sensation from the first night at the De Luxe Cafe, so much so that there were no available seats after nine P.M. and a line waiting outside that kept King Jones yelling to the high heavens to tell them that soon there would be seats.

Sugar Johnny played a growling cornet style, using cups and old hats to make all kinds of funny noises. Dewey's clarinet squeaked and rasped with his uneven scales and trills. Roy was sliding back and forth on the trombone, making a growling accompaniment to Sugar Johnny's breaks. Jimmie's violin sighed and wheezed while he scratched the strings with his bow. To top all this, Montudi Tubby and I beat out a background rhythm that put the Bechuana tribes of Africa to shame.

But this was New Orleans jazz, and the people ate it up. Ah, what fun! Everybody in town falling in to dig us. No dancing, just listen and be sent. De Luxe Cafe . . . deluxe business. . . . deluxe jazz by the New Orleans Creole Jazz Band.

ZUTTY SINGLETON

I first met Jelly Roll in Chicago. He was livin' high then. You know, Jelly was a travelin' cat, sharp and good lookin' and always bragging about he wrote this and that and the other thing—in fact, everything! And let me tell you this—no one ever won an argument with Jelly either!

Once I was walkin' somewhere with Louis and Lil Armstrong (they were together then), and Lil had got herself a brand new baby grand piano. We all went to Louis' place and Jelly sat down at that piano and really gave us a serenade. He played and played, and after each number he'd turn around on that stool and tell us how he wrote each number and where it came from. It was a real lecture, just for the benefit of me and Lil and Louis.

PRESTON JACKSON

I feel that if it wasn't for Lil, Louis would not be where he is today. She inspired him to do bigger and better things. Lil is the cause of Louis leaving Joe Oliver's band, where he was playing second trumpet, and going out for himself, and thereby gaining a little recognition. At that time, Lil and Louis were pianist and cornetist, respectively, with Joe Oliver.

Now I will tell you of my first experience with Lil. I first saw her demonstrating music at Jones Music Store in Chicago. Lil was just a young miss then but how she could swing, yes, I mean swing, no ragtime. Lot of people think that Benny Goodman was first to play swing music, but we all know that Benny studied under Jimmie Noone, the master. Getting back to Lil, she only received three dollars a week on her first job, but I knew she wouldn't be there long, no, man, not with all that piano she was swinging. One month later she joined the New Orleans Creole Band with such men as Freddie Keppard, Ed Garland, Paul Barbarin, Jimmie Noone, and Eddie Vincent. She received fifty-five dollars per week, what a difference in salary. Man, Lil didn't know how much she could swing.

Later Lil had her own band at Dreamland Cafe, 3520 State Street, and was there five years. Joe Oliver came there from New Orleans, heard Lil play, and paid her more money than she had ever earned to join his band. That was in 1921. Joe had been there since 1918. Every band that could play anything was from New

Orleans. Sidney Bechet was with the New Orleans Creole Band; Johnny Dodds was with Joe Oliver's band and mentioned Lil being responsible for Louis leaving Joe.

POPS FOSTER

Yes, I remember King Oliver. He was a happy-go-lucky guy. He liked to play pool all day long, and baseball. He would eat a lot. We would order one or two hamburger sandwiches, and he would eat a dozen at a time, and a quart of milk. He got along fine with the fellows—always playing, and kidding.

RICHARD M. JONES

Joe had been afraid of Keppard and Perez in New Orleans—he didn't have much confidence. He worked as a butler. Practically overnight, he woke up and started playing. He was a good reader and a good technician. Anything you'd stick up, he'd wipe it right off.

JELLY ROLL MORTON

Yes, "now you'll get a chance to see my red underwear!" that's what Joe used to say when he got going, with his stiff shirt bustin' on the stand, blowing for all he had, and his red undershirt showing. . . .

BUSTER BAILEY

Joe King Oliver was an important figure at that time. He was an eating guy for sure. He was also a good guy, sort of sensitive in a way. He liked to joke a lot; he liked to play the "dozens" (talk about your parents and all in a joking way—it was a way of trying to get each other's goat). King Oliver was a great musician with a mute. With an ordinary tin mute, he could make the horn talk.

Joe was a jealous guy. He knew what some of the musicians who came to listen were after, and so he wouldn't play certain numbers. But they'd come in and sneak in and steal the riffs. They'd write down the solos, steal like mad, and then those ideas would come out on *their* records. When Joe would see them coming, he'd play something different, but they'd steal everything.

Some guys would come in to sit in with you and learn what you were doing. We'd call them alligators. That was our tip-off word, because they were guys who came up to swallow everything we had to learn.

PRESTON JACKSON

There were a lot of keen youngsters around Chicago in those days. Buster Bailey was a kid just beginning, while Tommy Ladnier was only just starting out. I didn't play anything then, but was thinking of taking the clarinet. I used to sit on the bandstand all night, listening.

At that time we used to hang around Joe Oliver's band on off nights. Joe was at Royal Gardens then and coaching Louis Panico, Isham Jones' cornetist. Joe's band was probably at its peak then with Johnny Dodds on clary; brother Baby Dodds drumming; Honore Dutrey, trombone; Bill Johnson, bass; little Lil Hardin on the ivory.

I used to sit behind Dutrey every night and watch him play cello parts all night long because cello parts were easier to get than trombone music. Other musicians were considered out of the ordinary if they could play just one cello part. Dutrey was wonderful about showing me fine points on the horn. I learned lots from him.

That band just went mad when they played. Usually fast stuff, the Garden was a turmoil and a tumult from the start of the evening until the last note died away. Why! I thought they'd blow the roof off the place for dead sure, especially after Louis Armstrong joined the band.

I'll never forget the day he came into town (about 1920 or 1921). He wore a brown box-back coat, straw hat, and tan shoes. We called him Dippermouth. Satchmo was unheard of then. Well, Louis played a horn like nobody had ever heard. He and Joe were wonderful together. I had heard Louis play before in 1915 at a playground dedication when the Jones Waif Band featured Louis and Henry Rena. Louis was terrific even then. I was going to the school where the playground was. That's how I happened to hear him.

TOMMY BROOKINS

Toward 1923, I was still a little kid and I was in school in Chicago where the kids were talking about Joe Oliver and his Creole Jazz Band. That was when I went for the first time to the Royal Gardens. But I was still too young and I was wearing short pants so I had to borrow a pair of pants long enough to have some hope of getting in, and, with those long pants and the help of the doorman, I did. To remain inconspicuous, I went up to the balcony.

The place was always packed. People belonging to all classes of society attended (doctors, lawyers, students, entertainment people, musicians, people of all colors were found there).

It's necessary to point out that in this era Chicago was without doubt the leading city in the world in terms of nocturnal activity. This was the time of Prohibition.

The Royal Gardens could contain a thousand people. If business there was excellent it was also due to the fact that besides an orchestra without rival the Royal Gardens presented sensational attractions. There was a half-dozen acts of unusual class, acts like Ethel Waters and Bodidily, the singer who created *Someday Sweetheart*. No one could sing like he could. The review included at least sixty people: chorus girls, Creole dancers, et cetera.

Although he didn't have what is usually called a "personality," Joe Oliver impressed me from the first time I saw him. He was a tranquil man and it was surprising to see him blow such joyous music.

In this era, Louis Armstrong played in the ensemble and Oliver took the majority of the solos. He had a real "gutbucket tone" and really moved. Armstrong was only rarely heard playing solo. It was necessary to wait till Joe Oliver was sick to have a real idea of the talent of Louis. On that evening when he was sick, Oliver played as a member of the ensemble but let Louis solo and, believe me, Louis really played, showing everyone present all he knew, all his tricks, and he received after each song tremendous acclamations.

One can say that from that time on there was a question only of Louis. The school kids began to imitate the acts of "Satchmo."

Hearing Louis after Oliver it seemed that Louis was more powerful.

One of the things that struck me most at the Royal Gardens was the smile of Baby Dodds. When he played drums he had the most patched-up material for a drum set that I'd ever seen in my life, but he had a rhythm entirely his own, and I feel that as a drummer he has more personality than any other specialist on any other instrument. He was a man of natural playfulness, possessed by rhythm. Just to see him smile and to hear his beat would make you happy.

As for Johnny Dodds, his brother, I sincerely believe that he was the greatest clarinetist that ever lived and I've never heard any clarinetist play like he did in the lower register of his instrument.

There was no other orchestra during that time that could play like Joe Oliver and his Creole Jazz Band.

PRESTON JACKSON

After a while, Joe Oliver went to the Lincoln Gardens, and that is where he really hit his stride. The New Orleans Rhythm Kings were there every night too. It was common to see musicians writing on their cuffs in those days. Rappolo, the Rhythm Kings' clarinetist, was always writing—and his numbers are still played today.

Yes, in those days the King was really *King* and the boys tore the tops off their music so that no one else could see what they were playing.

GEORGE WETTLING

There was a painted canvas sign about two by four feet square hanging outside the best-looking building that housed the Lincoln Gardens Cafe, a sign that read "KING OLIVER AND HIS CREOLE JAZZ BAND." From the looks of the place on the outside one would never guess that on the inside was the hottest band ever to sit on a bandstand. But once you got through the crowded hallway into the cafe proper it was a sight to behold.

The thing that hit your eye once you got into the hall was a big crystal ball that was made of small pieces of reflecting glass and hung over the center of the dance floor. A couple of spotlights shone on the big ball as it turned and threw reflected spots of light all over the room and the dancers. Usually they'd dance the Bunny Hug to a slow blues like *London Blues* or some other tune in a like slow blues tempo, and how the dancers would grind away. The ceiling of the place was made lower than it actually was by chicken wire that was stretched out and over the wire were spread great bunches of artificial maple leaves. I'll guarantee that chicken wire was the only artificial thing in the place.

If anyone ever looked good in front of a band it was Joe Oliver. He had a way of standing in front of Louie, Johnny and Baby Dodds, and the other cats, that was too much. I think one of the greatest thrills I ever got was hearing Joe play *Dippermouth Blues*. He and Louie Armstrong had some breaks they played together that I've never heard played since. I don't know how they knew what was coming up next, but they would play those breaks and never miss. Joe would stand there fingering his horn with his right hand and working his mute with his left, and how he would rock the place. Unless you were lucky enough to hear that band in the flesh you can't imagine how they played and what swing they got. After they would knock everybody out with about forty minutes of *High Society*, Joe would look down at me and wink and then say, "Hotter than a forty-five."

They always had a water pail on the stand with a big piece of ice in it and a dipper. Anyone who got thirsty would just go over to the bucket and help himself to a drink. Usually this was after they had played for about an hour. The place was informal and if the boys in the band wanted to take their coats off and really get comfortable they did.

TOMMY BROOKINS

I still remember the arrival of Louis Armstrong in Chicago. The news spread like wildfire among the musicians who hurried that same evening to Lincoln Gardens. It wasn't that Louis' name was then known, but the musicians were aware of the fact that a young trumpet player had just arrived from New Orleans and was playing with Oliver. King Oliver at that time was playing very well. He was very nice to Louis whom he had taken under his protection and who he lodged at his house. He let him play frequently and he gave him a lot of advice.

Opposite the young Louis, who was already prodigious, Oliver's style rapidly appeared to us to date a little and it was frequent to hear musicians among themselves talk of the "old style." Let's say, rather, that Joe's style was a little rougher than that of his young rival.

LIL ARMSTRONG

I was playing at the Dreamland and Joe Oliver was at the Royal Garden and Joe brought Louis over one night. We had had some pictures taken, and Joe had sent them to Louis in New Orleans. Louis wrote to him to "tell Miss Lil I like her." Well, naturally, I was interested in what he was like.

They had called him "Little Louis." When he came into the Dreamland that night he weighed two twenty-six. I was surprised. He didn't stay long, and he didn't play. I didn't have any romantic ideas at all at that time.

A couple of months later I went back with Joe's band. A chance remark Joe had made about Louis' playing interested me, and I listened. Joe and Louis were playing duets, and though Joe Oliver was Louis' idol and he wanted to play like Joe, that wasn't his style. He tried to play some of Joe's solos, but they sounded different. Joe always played with a mute, you know, and Louis played clear and straight.

My first marriage wasn't doing so good and we started going together. We were married for thirteen years, and lived together for eight.

I thought the main thing to do was to get him away from Joe. I encouraged him to develop himself, which was all he needed. He's a fellow who didn't have much confidence in himself to begin with. He didn't believe in himself.

So I was sort of standing at the bottom of the ladder holding it, and watching him climb. My feelings for him haven't changed, in spite of all the marriages.

PRESTON JACKSON

I give Lil credit, because Louis was not nationally known. He was only known around Chicago and the South, but when he left Joe and joined Fletcher Henderson, he became known here and abroad. Joe seldom featured Louis, knowing that Louis could show him up. Therefore, Louis would have never been as famous as he is, had he continued to play second trumpet to Joe Oliver.

Lil never was a flash. She is a fine soloist and can lay those chords four beats to a measure and solid just like the doctor ordered.

Lil did most of Joe's recording and helped him arrange his band. Joe wasn't using any arrangements, in fact, hardly any bands were using them then. They were swinging at the Lincoln Gardens, featuring such numbers as *Royal Garden Blues, Someday Sweetheart, Panama, High Society*, and a lot of fine tunes that are featured today. Joe's band stayed there five years. After that, they went to San Francisco, playing at the Pergola Ballroom for six months. Speaking of Joe Oliver, you cats should have heard Joe at that time. He never had to call the number he was to play. He would play two or three bars of whatever number he was going to play, stomp twice, and then everybody would start playing the same tune as if they had been told.

Getting back to Lil, most of the tunes Louis composed, Lil wrote the music to. Louis would play the melody and Lil would write it down as fast as Louis played.

When playing some of Louis Armstrong's records recorded by the Hot Five, notice the foundation. It will speak for itself.

BUSTER BAILEY

When Louis first came to Chicago, I was at the Sunset with Carroll Dickerson and he came in to join Oliver, who had come back from San Francisco. Louis upset Chicago. All the musicians from Isham Jones' big band, for example, came to Lincoln Gardens to hear the band Joe had, and especially to hear Louis.

What made Louis upset Chicago so? His execution, for one thing, and his ideas, his drive. Well, they didn't call it drive, they called it "attack" at that time. Yes, that's what it was, man. They got crazy for his feeling.

King Oliver and Louis were the greatest two trumpeters I ever heard together. You want to know how they'd get those unison breaks to go together that went over so well with the crowd? Well, the tunes always break in the middle. What Joe was going to make in the middle break, he'd make in the first ending. Louis would listen and remember; then when the middle came, Oliver and Louis would both take that same break together.

PRESTON JACKSON

Oh Boy! Did those two team together? When you saw Joe lean over towards Louis at the first ending you would know they were going to make a break in the middle of the next chorus. And what breaks they made. Louis never knew what Joe was going to play, but he would always follow him perfectly. Louis was, and is, as good a second trumpet as he is a first; he never missed. They played together for three or four years and wrote some numbers together. One of them was *Dippermouth Blues*, later called *Sugar Foot Stomp*. (They used to call him Louis Dippermouth.)

LOUIS ARMSTRONG

In 1922, when King Joe Oliver, the trumpet man of those days, sent for me to leave New Orleans and join him at the Lincoln Gardens to play second trumpet to his first trumpet, I jumped sky-high with joy. The day I received the telegram from Papa Joe, that's what I called him, I was playing a funeral in New Orleans and all the members in the Tuxedo Brass Band told me not to go because Joe Oliver and his boys were having some kind of union trouble.

When the Tuxedo Brass Band boys told me that King Oliver and his band were scabbing, I told them the King had sent for me, it didn't matter with me what he was doing. I was going to him just the same. So I went.

I arrived in Chicago about eleven o'clock the night of July 8th, 1922, I'll never forget it, at the Illinois Central Station at Twelfth and Michigan Avenue. The King was already at work. I had no one to meet me. I took a cab and went directly to the Gardens.

When I was getting out of the cab and paying the driver, I could hear the King's band playing some kind of a real jump number. Believe me, they were really jumpin' in fine fashion. I said to myself, "My Gawd, I wonder if I'm good enough to play in that band." I hesitated about going inside right away, but finally I did.

When I got inside and near the bandstand, King Oliver spied me. He immediately stopped the band to greet me, saying, "Boy, where have you been? I've been waiting and waiting for you." Well, I did miss the train that the King thought I should have been on. They went into another hot number. In that band were King Oliver, trumpet; Johnny Dodds, clarinet; Honore Dutrey, trombone; Baby Dodds, drums; Bill Johnson, bass; Lillian Hardin, piano, of course she became Mrs. "Satchmo" Louis Armstrong later, (tee hee).

When I joined the band on second trumpet I made the seventh member. Those were some thrilling days of my life I shall never forget. I came to work the next night. During my first night on the job, while things were going down in order, King and I stumbled upon a little something that no other two trumpeters together ever thought of. While the band was just swinging, the King would lean over to me, moving his valves on his trumpet, make notes, the notes that he was going to make when the break in the tune came. I'd listen, and at the same time, I'd be figuring out my second to his lead. When the break would come, I'd have my part to blend right along with his. The crowd would go mad over it!

King Oliver and I got so popular blending that jive together that pretty soon all the white musicians from downtown Chicago would all come there after their work and stay until the place closed. Sometimes they would sit in with us to get their kicks. Lillian was doubling from the Lincoln Gardens to the Edelweiss Gardens, an after-hours place. After our work I would go out there with her. Doing this, she and I became regular running buddies, and we would go to all the other places when we had the time. She knew Chicago like a book. I'll never forget the first time Lil took me to the Dreamland Cabaret on Thirty-fifth and State Streets to hear Ollie Powers and Mae Alix sing. Ollie had one of those high, sweet singing voices, and when he would sing

songs like *What'll I Do?* he would really rock the whole house.
Mae Alix had one of those fine, strong voices that everyone would
also want to hear. Then she would go into her splits, and the
customers would throw paper dollars on the floor, and she would
make one of those running splits, picking them up one at a time.

I asked Lil if it was all right to give Ollie and Mae a dollar each
to sing a song for me. She said sure, it was perfectly all right.
She called them over and introduced them to me as the new
trumpet man in King Oliver's band. Gee whiz! I really thought
I was somebody meeting those fine stars. I followed Ollie Powers
everywhere he sang, until the day he died. At his funeral I played
a trumpet solo in the church where they had his body laying out
for the last time. Ump, what a sad day that was. Mae Alix is still
a singing barmaid and as popular as ever.

Speaking of the Lincoln Gardens, I had been playing there
about two or three months, when one night, just as we were getting ready to hit the show, we all noticed a real stout lady, with
bundles in her hands, cutting across the dance floor. To my surprise it was my mother, May Ann. The funny thing about it is
that King Oliver had been kidding me that he was my stepfather,
for years and years. When he saw May Ann (tee hee) he didn't
know her. We kind of stalled the show so I could greet my dear
mother, with a great big kiss, of course. Then I said to her,
"Mamma, what on earth are you doing up here in Chicago?" May
Ann said, "Lawd, chile, somebody came to New Orleans and told
me that you were up here in this North awfully low sick and
starving to death." I told mother, "Aw, Mamma, how could I
starve when I'm eating at King Oliver's house every day, and
you know how Mrs. Stella Oliver (King's wonderful wife) piles
up King's plate, full of red beans and rice. Well, she fills mine the
same way. Now, how could I starve?" May Ann said when she
asked this man who told her the false bad news, "Why in the
world didn't my son come back home to New Orleans when
things began to break so bad for him?" this guy told her all I
could do was to hang my head and cry. Tch, tch, such lies. I was
fat as a butterball.

I took my mother to the house where I was rooming and then

went out and bought her a lot of fine vines, a wardrobe with nothing but the finest—from head to foot. Oh, she was sharp! . . .

Chicago was really jumping around that time (1923). The Dreamland was in full bloom. The Lincoln Gardens, of course, was still in there. The Plantation was another hot spot at that time. But the Sunset, my boss' place, was the sharpest of them all, believe that. A lot of after-hour spots were real groovy, too. There was the Apex, where Jimmie Noone and that great piano man, Hines, started all this fine stuff your 'yars listen to nowadays. They made history right there in the Apex. The tune, *Sweet Lorraine*, used to gas everybody there nightly. I was one of the everybodies.

They had a place on State Street called the Fiume where they had a small ofay band, right in the heart of the South Side. They were really fine. All the musicians, nightlifers, and everybody plunged in there in the wee hours of the morning and had a grand time. I used to meet a lot of the boys there after we would finish at the Lincoln Gardens. That's where I first met Darnell Howard, former sax man with "Fatha" Hines. He was playing the violin at that time with Charles Elgar's orchestra over on the West Side at Harmon's Dreamland Ballroom. Darnell was weighing one hundred and sixty-five pounds then. Of course, he has accumulated a little breadbasket since then, but still sharp.

King Oliver received an offer to go on the road and make some one-night stands at real good money. Ump! That got it. The band almost busted up. Half of the boys just wouldn't go, that's all. The same situation hits bandleaders square in the face these days, the same as then. The King replaced every man that wouldn't go. As for me, anything King did was all right with me. My heart was out for him at all times—until the day he died and even now. The tour was great. We had lots of fun and made lots of money.

At the Dreamland, in 1925, we had some fine moments. Some real jumping acts. There was the team of Brown and McGraw. They did a jazz dance that just wouldn't quit. I'd blow for their act, and every step they made, I put the notes to it. They liked the idea so well they had it arranged. Benny and Harry Goodman used to come out and set in and tear up the joint when they were real young. P.S., the boys have been hep for a long time. While at the Dreamland, Professor Erskine Tate asked me (ahem) to join his Symphony Orchestra. I wouldn't take a million for that experience. The Professor's Orchestra played hot music as well as overtures.

TOMMY BROOKINS

During this time, we never missed going every Sunday to the Vendome Theatre to hear the orchestra of Erskine Tate. It was the pit orchestra of the Vendome Theatre. Erskine was an absolutely extraordinary leader. He directed symphonic works like Toscanini would, and I'm convinced that if he had wanted to leave Chicago for New York, he would have rapidly acquired world-wide recognition.

Tate's orchestra not only accompanied the acts, but played its own selections, going from classical music to jazz. He had collected the best musicians and was able to interpret to perfection any kind of music. I remember that when we saw the oboist, all of us young kids couldn't keep from laughing, but when we realized how he interpreted the classical works we considered him from that time on with the greatest respect. His name was Fernandez. To recall for you some of the members of the orchestra, there was Jimmy Bertrand who must be considered as one of the greatest hit drummers who ever lived. He also played xylophone and washboard. It was with him that Wallace Bishop learned drums and later studied xylophone under his direction. There was also an alto saxophonist, Stomp Evans, that was considered at that time as the best, but who died young, without having recorded much.

The pianist was Teddy Weatherford. At the time of which I'm talking, he was twenty years old and he was ahead of all pianists contemporary to him. He was truly sensational then and all the pianists, Earl Hines included, copied him.

JOE GLASER

They all worked for me. I owned and managed the Sunset and a couple of other places on the South Side. The Sunset was the biggest black-and-tan club west of New York. Joe Oliver never worked for me at the Sunset, though. He worked at the Dreamland which wasn't as high-class.

The Sunset had the cream of the black-and-tan shows, and there wasn't a big name in colored show business that didn't work for me at one time or another. I spent more money for my shows than the Cotton Club. Why, I once hired a band out of Columbus, Ohio—Sammy Stewart—for thirty-six hundred a week. But Sammy was a bad boy. He would've been one of the biggest names in the business today if he didn't go wrong. Hell, Cab Calloway started for me at thirty-five a week while his sister Blanche was making two or three hundred. Ethel Waters, the Nicholas Brothers, and everybody else you could mention worked for me too.

The musicians were talking about Louis Armstrong, so I had Joe Oliver send for him—I gave him the money. Later on, I was the first one to put a sign out front "LOUIS ARMSTRONG—THE WORLD'S GREATEST TRUMPET PLAYER!" Louis worked for a while in the pit of the Vendome Theatre in Erskine Tate's band, but he was featured, mind you. He worked in Carroll Dickerson's band, but I threw Dickerson out and made Louis the leader.

He played the shows at the Sunset with a sixteen- or seventeen-piece band. We never had any small groups there. Besides the band we had twelve chorus girls, twelve show girls, and big name acts. The place sat about six hundred people and we had a high-class trade—not like some of the other joints—the best people. There were lines for every show and, mind you, we charged admission just to get in—from a dollar twenty to two-fifty or so—depending on how business was.

About those records—nine times out of ten Louis would leave the club at three, four, five A.M. to make those records for Jack Kapp or Eli Oberstein—I forget which. All of them records were made from about six to nine in the mornings. And it's true about the scat-singing story. That's really the way it started. Louis forgot the words and just sang sounds. That's the way it really started.

KID ORY

I don't know who got the idea for the Hot Five records. It may have been Richard M. Jones, who worked for the Okeh company at that time. He worked for them in Chicago, as a pianist for different blues singers and writing and selecting tunes, and it may have been through him that the Okeh company approached Louis.

The idea was that we would have a regular band at Dreamland, and then that five of us from the band would make records together. I got to Chicago a few weeks before Louis, and played around at different clubs. Then Louis got there, and we rehearsed the band for a few days before we opened at the Dreamland. We had Johnny Dodds, Johnny St. Cyr, and Lil with us.

We made our first records in Chicago at the Okeh studios, and, of course, when we made them we didn't have any expectation that they would be as successful as they became. The time was something like today, with people crazy about jazz and the Charleston, and our kind of music went over very well. Times were good, and people had money to buy records. One thing that helped the sale was the fact for a while the Okeh people gave away a picture of Louis to everyone that bought one of the records. When they did that, the sales went way up, because Louis was so popular. . . .

The only one of the Hot Five I hadn't played with was Lil, but that made no difference. She was a fine piano player, and from the first we all worked together very easily. . . .

Even though we were working in different clubs, we kept the Hot Five going. The records were very successful, and *Heebie Jeebies* was what today would be called a hit record. That was the record where Louis forgot the lyrics and started scattin'. We had all we could do to keep from laughing. Of course, Louis said he forgot the words, but I don't know if he intended it that way or not. It made the record, though.

The Hot Five never played together as a band outside of a few benefits. We'd all take a short time off from the regular jobs we had and play for a half hour or so at some affair. We always would break it up, and then go back to our jobs.

Our recording sessions would start this way: The Okeh people would call up Louis and say they wanted so many sides. They never told him what numbers they wanted or how they wanted them. Then Louis would give us the date, and sometimes he'd call me and say I'm short of a number for this next session. Do you think you can get one together? I'd say all right, and that's the way *Savoy Blues* came to be composed, two days before we recorded.

We would get to the studio at nine or ten in the morning. We didn't have to make records at night, with the lights out, or get drunk like some musicians think they have to do before they can play. In the beginning we made records acoustically, and there was a separate horn for each man. The recording engineer would motion us if we were playing too loud or too soft, and then we'd know to move back or to move in closer. Then later, of course, we made records electrically.

When we'd get in the studio, if we were going to do a new number, we'd run over it a couple of times before we recorded it. We were a very fast recording band. In fact, the records I made with the Hot Fives were the easiest I ever made. We spoiled very few records, only sometimes when one of us would forget the routine or the frame-up, and didn't come in when he was supposed to. Even then, we'd try to cover up. After we'd make a side, Louis would say, "Was that all right?" And if one of us thought we could do it over and do it better, why Louis would tell them we wanted to do it again, and so we would do it over.

I think one reason those records came out so well was that the Okeh people left us alone, and didn't try to expert us. Another reason was we all knew each other's musical styles so well from years of working together. And then, of course, there was Louis, himself. You couldn't go wrong with Louis. I always liked his style the best. That's not to take anything away from Oliver, but I always thought Louis was the greatest, and I still think so.

LOUIS ARMSTRONG

Things were jumping so around Chicago at that time, there was more work than a cat could shake a stick at. I was doubling from the Dreamland for awhile. Then I stayed at the Vendome for only a year before I decided to double again.

Then came Carroll Dickerson, the leader who had that fine band at the Sunset Cafe, owned by my boss, Mr. Joe Glaser. He hired me to double from the Vendome Theatre. After the theater I'd go over to the Sunset, at Thirty-fifth and Calumet Streets, and swing there with them until the wee hours of the morning. 'Twas great, I'll tell you. In that band there were *the* Earl Hines, Darnell Howard, Tubby Hall, Honore Dutrey, and Boyd Atkins, who wrote the tune called *Heebie Jeebies*.

The Sunset had Charleston contests on Friday night, and you couldn't get in the place unless you got there early. We had a great show in those days with Buck 'n' Bubbles, Rector and Cooper, Edith Spencer and Mae Alix, my favorite entertainer, and a gang of now famous stars. We had a finale that just wouldn't quit.

The Charleston was popular at that time (1926) until Percy Venable, the producer of the show, staged a finale with four of us band boys closing the show doing the Charleston. That was really something. There was Earl Hines, as tall as he is; Tubby Hall, as fat as he was; little Joe Walker, as short as he is; and myself, as fat as I was at that time. We would stretch out across that floor doing the Charleston as fast as the music would play it. Boy, oh boy, you talking about four cats picking them up and laying them down—that was us. We stayed there until old boss man got tired of looking at us. Ha, ha.

Things moved out further on the South Side of Chicago. The Metropolitan Theatre was running in full bloom with Sammy Stewart's orchestra out of Columbus, Ohio, holding sway. After Sammy, came Clarence Jones' orchestra. That's where I came in again.

On the drums in this orchestra was my boy, Zutty Singleton. We would play an overture and then run into a hot tune. Sometimes Zutty and I would do a specialty number together. It was a scream. Zutty, he's funny anyway, would dress up as one of those real loud and rough gals, with a short skirt, and a pillow in back of him. I was dressed in old rags, the beak of my cap turned around like a tough guy, and he, or she (Zutty) was my gal. As he would come down the aisle, interrupting my song, the people would just scream with laughter. Zutty and I played together pretty nearly all our lives. Chicago and New Orleans. We have seen some pretty tough days right there in Chicago. Also my other boy, Earl Hines. But, we kept our heads up, believe that.

The time the Savoy opened (1927), Earl Hines, Zutty, and myself had leased the Warwick Hall on Forty-seventh Street, just around the corner from the Savoy. They had such an opening that we never did get a chance to open our place. Ump! There we were with a year's lease on our hands and no place to get the rent. We decided to hustle. We gave a dance on the West Side of Chicago. The dance turned out to be a success. After all, the three of us were rather popular. With the three of us playing in those famous bands such as Erskine Tate, Dave Payton, and Clarence Jones in those theaters, the folks came to hear us dish that mess out.

Earl went back to the Apex and Zutty and I joined Carroll Dickerson again. This time Carroll had the job at the Savoy Ballroom which had just opened. The place was jumping, and we three paid off the lease at the Warwick Hall. The real estate people gave us a break and threw the whole thing out for a hundred and fifty dollars. Then we could breathe again. . . .

All in all, the 'twenties in Chicago were some of my finest days. From 1922 to 1929, I spent my youngest and best days there. I married Lillian and Alpha there. Of course, my first wife was Daisy. We stepped off into that deep water in New Orleans, way back there in 1918. Lil, my second, and Alpha, my third, we did the thing (married) in Chicago. My fourth madam, Lucille, and I were married at Velma Middleton's mother's house in St. Louis, Missouri. Looks like this is it. She's still on the mound and holding things down. Oh, but she is.

TOMMY BROOKINS

There was another place that had its hour of celebrity. They called it the Dusty Bottom. It was a rendezvous of all the young people, who came there every Sunday afternoon from three to seven, at the corner of Thirty-third Street and Wabash Avenue.

There was a dance that took place there under a large tent, in the middle of which was placed a wooden floor, but around this floor there was only the earth, and there was such an amount of dust kicked up that, by the end of the afternoon, the feet and the bottoms of the pants of the dancers were covered with dust. And that is why the place was called the Dusty Bottom.

Albert Ammons led the orchestra there, and every Sunday many pianists came because they had the chance, from time to time, to take a solo. That was a way for a musician with talent to get himself known. Nonetheless, Albert Ammons was at that time sensational. He was what we call a "loud pianist" (a powerful pianist) which was indispensable for a place in the open air like the Dusty Bottom. The Dusty Bottom wasn't only known throughout Chicago, but its reputation spread equally all through the Middle West.

LIZZIE MILES

Did Clarence Williams tell you about the time in Chi when some very big organization gave their annual affair at White City? All Chicago publishers were invited to plug their songs. He took me on account of my powerful voice. It was the largest crowd I ever sang to, and we were the only two colored out there. When our turn came, that crowd frightened him so he forgot what key I sang *Royal Garden Blues* in—after playing it for me gangs of times. Well, I went on singing and he was scrambling trying to find my key and sweating. I kept singing. Just before I got to the chorus, he caught me, and the audience knew so well what was happening that when he caught up with me, they applauded like mad. And they kept us singing for some time.

TOMMY BROOKINS

It was at Kelly's Stables on the North Side that I really got to know Johnny Dodds. He was leading a group of four musicians. No one had a fixed salary but the tips were such that they used to make between a hundred and twenty-five and a hundred and seventy a week. I ought to say that the place was frequented by gangsters and that they had easy money.

After having worked for a year at Kelly's, I was hired at the Eldorado Club at the corner of Fifty-fifth Street and Garfield Boulevard. The Eldorado was in a cellar and Jimmie Noone had the orchestra there. Many musicians and visitors from many countries came to hear his little orchestra at the Eldorado.

Jimmie Noone was the "sweetest" clarinetist who ever existed. He knew it and he often confined himself to the style to which he owed his success. But when Noone let himself go, using the high register of his instrument, his tone lost nothing of its beauty. Jimmie Noone was a calm man. His voice was gentle but he wasn't any the less energetic.

8

Chicago had its "second line" too—the Austin High Gang, Muggsy Spanier, George Wettling, and Benny Goodman. They listened and learned.

JOE GLASER
All the young musicians in town would come to hear Louis—Benny Goodman, Muggsy Spanier, and the rest. I used to let them in free. Hell, they were kids and never had any money.

BUSTER BAILEY
All the places then were black and tan—unless you went on to the Loop. But in terms of race, everything on the South Side was all right.

LIL ARMSTRONG
And they'd line up ten deep at the Dreamland. Muggsy sat in. Mostly white fellows would line up in front of that stand—Hoagy, Art Kassel, Dave Tough, and George Wettling. Like they all used to do, to start the band Oliver would toot a couple of notes real soft, turn around to the band, and instantly they knew what piece it was. At eleven o'clock the place would just be rocking. Joe never had much to say, but he had a lot of fun.

MUGGSY SPANIER

I knew the owner of the Dreamland and was allowed to sit in a dark corner of the balcony to listen to the music. I was only fourteen then, still not old enough to be allowed in a public dance hall. But as long as I heard the music, the conditions didn't matter. The band played from about nine thirty to one A.M. and after-hours they played the Pekin Cafe, one of the worst gangster hang-outs in Chicago, which has now been turned into a police station. In the summer the Pekin kept its windows open, so I'd sneak from home just about every night and sit outside on a curbstone listening to the music. Sometimes the goings-on would get rough inside, the music would stop and you'd hear the flash of forty-five caliber revolvers trying to fire with a beat. Before I knew it, I'd be running home as fast as my feet could take me. But the next night would always find me sitting on the same curbstone. I thought the music well worth running the risk of getting shot by a stray bullet.

As a kid (and Louis always called me Kid Muggsy, inscribing my prized pictures of him that way), I would go down to the South Side and listen hour after hour to those two great trumpeters, Joe King Oliver and Louis. That's when they were at the old Lincoln Gardens. It got so that I knew every phrase and intonation they played, just from listening, so that, in spite of myself, I was doing the same things—as nearly as possible, of course.

You can imagine the thrill it was the first time they let me sit in with them and play. I even remember the first tune—it was *Bugle Blues*, an original Joe Oliver tune. Gosh, I wish I could describe the way those two used to play those pretty breaks! Nothing in the world was like it.

After Louis left King Oliver and started to play at the Sunset Cafe across the street from Joe, I'd go to see Joe first and then right over to Louis in order to "keep peace in the family." Joe would send word over: "Close those windows or I'll blow you off Thirty-fifth Street!" It was a friendly, happy thing and I was completely steeped in their kind of music—which I've been playing ever since, because I love it.

Another of the thrills in my life was when Louis asked (or

allowed me, I should say) to sit in and play *Big Butter and Egg Man*. Well, just no one in the world can play it like Louis, and no one in the world can improve on the way he plays it, so I'm frank to say that as nearly as possible (because I heard him play it so much and listened so intently) I've always tried to do those famous breaks as Louis did them.

Well, if you know Louis and his inimitable and indescribable belly laugh and enthusiasm, you can imagine what encouragement it was for a young fledgling, especially at the end, when I had to hit that C-sharp and the rest of the fellows in the band joined Louis in the prodding. That in itself was an inspiration.

I mean, after all, how can you help loving a guy that makes the world smile and a happy place like Louis does? If he couldn't blow or sing a note, he'd still be worth his weight in laughs.

GEORGE WETTLING

I was in my first year of high school when King Joe and the Creole Band played in the Lincoln Gardens. A pal of mine named Gootch and I would usually go to a downtown movie. After the show we would grab a Cottage Grove streetcar and get off at Thirty-first Street. Gootch, who was in his last year of school and not a musician, would pay the admission charge and get the table nearest the band on the left side. That was where Baby Dodds sat and where I first met Baby. We have been great friends ever since.

It was about this time that Eddie Condon, Johnny Forton, Floyd O'Brien, and other hep kids were also hanging around to hear Joe and Louie. One night we saw a P.I. (one who lives and makes money from women) stabbed for making too much noise and annoying the girls at the table next to us.

I only wish I were able to live those days over again and hear the great Joe and his Creole Jazz Band play some of my favorite tunes like *New Orleans Stomp*, or *Weather Bird Rag*, or maybe *Canal Street*. I certainly am thankful that I have most of the original records Joe Oliver made and can live those old days again, if only for a while.

One of the best summers I ever had was when Louis was at the Savoy Ballroom in Chicago. Muggsy and I were working with

Floyd Town that summer, and Jess Stacy and Teschemacher were also in our band, but Muggsy and I had a standing date for every Sunday afternoon at the Savoy.

When Louis started blowing the introduction to *West End Blues* (man, was it mellifluous), everybody in the ballroom started screaming and whistling, and then Louis lowered the boom and everybody got real groovy when he went into the first strains of *West End*.

Muggsy and I always got there about twenty minutes before the first number, because Louis would always be warming up and Zutty would be on hand, too, so we would stand outside Louis' dressing room getting a little air and jiving each other. Now Louis used to call everybody Satchmouth, Dippermouth, Shadmouth, et cetera, and Zutty called everybody Face, Rivermouth, and various names and everybody got a big kick out of the different names the guys would come up with.

One of the cats that stood around with us thought he would pull one on Louis, so when Louis came walking up this guy says, "Well, what do you say, Real Estate Jaws?" Well, that broke everybody up and Louis nearly passed out laughing so hard.

JIMMY McPARTLAND

I suppose everyone who has read about the jazz of the 'twenties knows the name, Austin High School Gang. I was one of that group of youngsters who took up jazz very seriously at Austin, a school situated near Washington Boulevard and Central Avenue in Chicago.

It was lucky for me I got in with that gang, because as a boy down there on the West Side, I might easily have been mixed up with a different kind of mob.

So for me, and perhaps other Austin guys that got the music bug, jazz supplied the excitement we might otherwise have looked for among the illegal activities which flourished then in the neighborhood.

I'll tell you how I got in with the Austin mob, and how we became interested in jazz in the first place.

Every day after school, Frank Teschemacher and Bud Freeman, Jim Lannigan, my brother Dick, myself, and a few others used to go to a little place called the Spoon and Straw. It was just an ice-cream parlor where you'd get a malted milk, soda, shakes, and all that stuff.

But they had a Victrola there, and we used to sit around listening to the bunch of records laid on the table. They were Paul Whiteman and Art Hickman records, and so forth. And Ted Lewis—he was supposed to be the hot thing, but he didn't do anything to us somehow.

This went along for two or three months; we'd go in there every day, and one day they had some new Gennett records on the table, and we put them on.

They were by the New Orleans Rhythm Kings, and I believe the first tune we played was *Farewell Blues*. Boy, when we heard that—I'll tell you we went out of our minds. Everybody flipped. It was wonderful. So we put the others on—*Tiger Rag, Discontented, Tin Roof Blues, Bugle Call,* and such titles.

We stayed there from about three in the afternoon until eight at night, just listening to those records one after another, over and over again. Right then and there we decided we would get a band and try to play like these guys.

So we all picked out our instruments. Tesch said he was going to buy a clarinet, Freeman plumped for a saxophone, Lannigan picked the bass tuba, my brother said he'd play the banjo, and I chose cornet, the loudest instrument. Anything loud—that's for me!

For the next week, we scrambled around finding money to buy them. My brother and I were lucky because my father was a music teacher. He gave Richard a banjo and I got a cornet. Then he sold Bud Freeman a C melody sax. Of course, Bud didn't pay him for a long time. We were all short of dough then, and Bud's a rough man with a buck.

One way and another we all got instruments, and that was the nucleus of the Austin band. Every day we used to go to one of our houses or apartments, a different one each day because people got tired of us in a hurry. I mean, we had to change flats, otherwise the people downstairs did.

What we used to do was put the record on—one of the Rhythm Kings', naturally—play a few bars, and then all get our notes. We'd have to tune our instruments up to the record machine, to the pitch, and go ahead with a few notes. Then stop! A few more bars of the record, each guy would pick out his notes and boom! we would go on and play it. Two bars, or four bars, or eight— we would get in on each phrase and then all play it.

But you can imagine it was hard at first. Just starting, as most of us were, we'd make so many mistakes that it was horrible on people's ears. So, as I say, we had to move around because the neighbors couldn't stand it too long.

It was a funny way to learn, but in three or four weeks we could finally play one tune all the way through—*Farewell Blues.* Boy, that was our tune. After getting that one down straight, we worked on another, and so on. Within a few months, we could play nine or ten tunes creditably.

Thinking of it after all these years, it seems surprising to me how fast we did pick it up. One reason for that was the enthusiasm —it couldn't have been any better—and another was that most of us had some musical training.

My brother and I had learned violin from my father since we were five; Tesch was a violinist, too. And Jim Lannigan was the most accomplished violinist of us all. Bud Freeman was the only guy that had *not* had any training, consequently he was slow picking up the music. In fact, it was murder those first weeks. Tesch used to get disgusted with him and say, "Let's throw that bum out." But I said, "No, no, no, don't. He's coming on, he's playing."

There was one thing I could recognize in Bud then—he had a terrific beat. He still has. He began by just playing rhythm, getting on one note and holding it; I mean swinging on it, just that one note. He didn't change the harmony or anything, and we used to get so mad at him, you know. We'd yell at him, "Change the note." Still, as I remember, he played with a great beat.

So, in this way, we built up our repertoire. Now, when we finished at Austin High around three, we would go on to a jam session up until dinnertime, have dinner, and go to somebody else's home and play from, say, eight thirty till eleven or twelve at night. Every day we'd do that.

So naturally that was our practice and our tuition. We all built our embouchures, built for tone, developed our ears. The method stayed the same—play a few bars of the record, then everybody would grab his notes and build up the tune. The New Orleans Rhythm Kings, that was our model.

It finally got that we would go and play at charity meetings and different fraternities around high school, until one time we played at a social in the gymnasium at Austin. Somebody said there was a kid there who could play drums. He was from Oak Park High School, which was just the next suburb, and the kid's name was Davey Tough.

He got some drums from somewhere and came in, and, man, that was it! He just was great. That beat, he had it right then. He told us he patterned himself on Baby Dodds, who used to be with the King Oliver Band at Lincoln Gardens.

And that was the Austin High School Gang. Oh yes, plus a guy named Dave North. I guess few people ever heard of him, because he didn't record. But he used to play piano, and he stayed with us quite a while. Me being the loudest and all that, it fell in that I was the leader. So I used to stomp off.

Of course, we had to give the band a name, the Blue Friars. It was my brother's idea and he got it from the Friar's Inn, downtown, in the Loop, where the NORK were playing. On records, they called the Rhythm Kings the Friars Society Orchestra. What a society orchestra! Hello! Gone!

We were too young to get into Friar's Inn, so the only way we could hear the Rhythm Kings was to go down and stand in the doorway and listen. It was great when someone opened the door and we could hear it louder.

PAUL MARES

The New Orleans Rhythm Kings have taken a rotten shoving around as the story of the birth of jazz is told.

Well, maybe we were a bunch of kids in knee pants playing around the corner from a red light, but just show me a band today that can play Dixieland like the Rhythm Kings. There aren't any—and I know. I was in the NORK and I'm still kicking around. But I'm not hearing Dixieland.

When the Original Dixieland Band left Chicago for New York, the people in the "section" in Chicago yelled for a substitution. And I don't wonder that they did either. Chicago had a style of its own—all its own (no one else would have it).

Anyhow, the people who had heard the La Rocca band wanted that type of music again. Well, there was no place but New Orleans to find music like that. There still isn't. Abbie Brunies got a telegram asking him to come to Chicago to work in a new Dixieland band. Abbie figured that the cab business was a better deal, so he gave me the telegram, I packed my horn and suitcase and came up to take the job. I played around up here principally at Camel Gardens with Tom Brown but also in a lot of other places.

Then came the job at Friar's Inn for a Dixieland band. I had gotten Leon Rappolo up here and I sent for George Brunies to take the trombone chair. George had to have train fare and a new overcoat before he could leave New Orleans so I sent those to him and he came to join the band. The rest of the band was composed of Jack Pettis, C melody saxophone; Arnold (Deacon) Loyacano, bass; Louis Black, banjo; Elmer Schoebel, piano; Frank Snyder, drums; and—well, there was a guy by the name of Paul Mares on cornet.

Yeah, I organized the band, I suppose, but it was just because I knew the boys who could really fill that bill. The band never went under my name. I just helped get it together. If Abbie had come up as scheduled, he would have had the honor of forming the first "initial" band, the NORK.

Friar's Inn was in a basement. It was cabaret style, with tables and a dance floor. There was a post on one side of the bandstand, and Rapp used to play with his clarinet against it for tone. He used to like to play into a corner, too.

Something happened every night at Friar's. There was always lots of fun and lots of clowning in the band. I remember we used to put oil of mustard on each other's chairs on the stand. Fritzl

122

could never figure out what all the confusion was about at the beginning of a set. Jack Pettis would always go to sleep on the stand during the floorshow, and we'd wake him up by holding the oil of mustard to his nose.

We knew all our customers. Friar's was a hangout of the big money guys. Al Capone and Dion O'Bannion used to come in.

Nobody drank much at Friar's. We were all too young.

The band had lots of other offers for better money, but no one wanted to leave Friar's. Sam Levin wanted us for the New York Roseland, and they tried to get us for Ford's Arcadia in St. Louis, but nobody would leave.

We used to try to hold rehearsals, but no one would show up. So we did our rehearsing on the job. The crowd never knew the difference. Elmer Schoebel was the only man in the band who could read, and he made arrangements for us, which we'd try out on the stand. We'd kid Elmer and play it all wrong, with lots of bad notes, the first time, just to make him sore. Elmer wrote and arranged *Nobody's Sweetheart*, which we introduced.

One night Ted Fio Rito brought in his tune, *Toot Toot Tootsie, Goodbye*. He handed it to Schoebel, who played it over once. Then I picked up the lead, and the rest of the boys fell in, and we played it on the spot. That amazed Fio Rito.

We used to play *Farewell Blues* a lot; Rapp wrote that one, you know. Also we played *Bugle Call Rag* and *Tin Roof*. Bix—he was in school at Lake Forest Academy then—used to sneak down and pester us to play *Angry* so he could sit in. At the time, it was the only tune he knew.

In 1922, we went down to Richmond, Indiana, on a couple of different week ends to make records for Gennett.

We were so anxious to record that we took the first offer to come along and beat all the rest of the bands. We could have made a fortune with that band if we had played our cards right, but we didn't. We rushed into everything like we did that recording deal. Actually, the band was playing good music. We had only two tempos, slow drag and the two-four one-step. We did our best to copy the colored music we'd heard at home. We did the best we could, but naturally we couldn't play real colored style.

Lots of people think that the Rhythm Kings first played in New Orleans. They never did as a unit. A lot of us played together in bands like Abbie Brunies' outfit, but the NORK was really founded in Chicago for the Friar's Inn. The men were born into the music and came to Chicago to play it commercially. It's still true, too. The only boys who can play that music are fellows like Eddie Miller, Jess Stacy, Ray Bauduc . . . those boys who were born in New Orleans. No one else even knows what our music's about.

JIMMY McPARTLAND

Paul Mares, and the Rhythm Kings, then, were our earliest inspiration. But we listened to everything we could. We sometimes went down to a Chinese restaurant, the Golden Pheasant, where there was a band by the name of Al Haid. They played pretty good, a semi-commercial brand of jazz, so we used to go down and eat chop suey and listen to this orchestra. It wasn't as good as the NORK—but we listened.

The musicians used to come over and talk to us, and one night I heard them ask Tesch if he knew of a cornet player.

Said Frank, "There's Jimmy there plays cornet fine." They asked me if I would sit in and audition for a job, and I said, "Surely."

Next night, I came in with my cornet and sat in. All the guys were there to hear me audition. Of course, Haid had to play the tunes that I knew, and I naturally picked *Farewell Blues*, *Tin Roof*, and others I had down pat.

Everything went fine, and I got the job—thirty-five dollars a week, room and board. This would have been 1923, and I was sixteen. All that summer I worked up at Fox Lake with the Haid band. To me, it was a big deal.

The next thing I recall was a couple of weeks on the excursion boats from Chicago to Benton Harbor, just across Lake Michigan.

As soon as I started, I was told about a band playing on another boat, which had Bix Beiderbecke on cornet and a youngster named Benny Goodman on clarinet.

Everyone was saying how terrific the music was on this other boat, and rumor had it that Beiderbecke was the greatest yet. As a matter of fact, I had heard *of* the newcomer from Davenport but hadn't heard him play. And I didn't get to hear him now, because he only worked with his band for five or six days—and when we were going across the lake, they were coming back!

As for Goodman, I had never heard of his name at that time. I first met him when I was working for Frisco Hasse. After the boat job, I went back to Austin High School in the fall, and for a bit we continued our gang sessions.

Then I picked up a steady job at a place called Eddie Tancil's, in Cicero, Illinois. The band was Hasse's and the job was good. It paid sixty-five dollars a week, good money for a kid turning sixteen, seventeen, in those days, or any others.

Frisco was a drummer, and he played in this night club. It was during prohibition, and he used to sell liquor on the side. So I went to work there at Tancil's, and the guy says, "I got a little kid clarinet player coming out tomorrow night to sit in with the band. He's too young to hire."

Well, it developed that the kid was Benny Goodman—aged fifteen at most. And I thought to myself, "This little punk play clarinet? He's too small to blow it."

The little punk climbed up on the stand and got his horn ready. Then he played *Rose of the Rio Grande*, which is a hard tune— I mean the changes for those days were difficult. This little monkey played about sixteen choruses of *Rose* and I just sat there with my mouth open.

Benny blew the hell out of that clarinet, and I almost died hearing him do it. So I latched on to him immediately, and said, "You gotta come to our sessions over at Austin High." He was most happy to. He said, "Glad, sure!"

And he came out there and sat in with the Austin gang.

BUD FREEMAN

Teschemacher was a great creative artist who had not developed enough before he died to make any great records. Before he was killed in an automobile accident, he had been steadily improving, but he was a temperamental sort of guy and would work with anyone rather than be out of work. As a result, he worked with some pretty awful bands.

As for Benny Goodman, well, in those days, he really didn't know what he wanted. He thought that there never was any money in jazz until much later when John Hammond came along and showed him.

BEN POLLACK

The first time I heard Benny Goodman was in Chicago when he was a kid of eight or nine, and he was doing an imitation of Ted Lewis, who, of course, was then the king. Later, at fifteen or sixteen, and just before I brought him to the Coast to work with me at the Venice Ballroom, he was playing a mixture of Jimmie Noone, Leon Rappolo, Buster Bailey, and other great clarinet players.

He always had a terrific gift for handling his instrument, that combination of technique and tone, plus the one thing every musician seeks—a style that can be identified before his name is announced. That style is his own and he developed it himself.

JIMMY McPARTLAND

Benny and I worked around for a while and did quite well. Guys from the University of Chicago and Northwestern University would call up one of us for a band, and we came to be quite a team, around those different dances in Chicago. Both Benny and I would earn from eighty to a hundred dollars a week and still go to school. They paid good money, those college boys.

And while we were going with those university students, they used to take Benny and me over to hear Louis Armstrong, Lil Hardin, and the Dodds brothers playing with King Oliver. This was just one thrill on top of another, hearing Louis and King and those New Orleans guys.

JOE MARSALA

I started playing around 1924. Never could afford to go in, but would listen outside the Friar's Inn. Then at Columbia Hall, where Muggsy played, Johnny Lane was clarinet and had an orchestra there. I liked that kind of music. The others would go to dance, but my brother, Marty, and I used to listen to the band, and hear them jam.

I also learned a lot just from hanging around the Clark Street cabarets; that was the Fifty-second Street of Chicago around 1924–25. Sure, I heard Jimmie Noone, and Benny Goodman used to come around listening to Noone too. Then just around the corner at the Vogue was the new piano sensation—Irene Edie, the girl who was Teddy Wilson's first wife later on.

I had to do a lot of other work before I could make a living out of music. Had a job shoveling cinders off a freight car, worked in an office, worked as city buyer for a shoe company at fifteen bucks a week, worked in a rubber ball factory, in a brass foundry. But I just couldn't hold those jobs. I'd start out in the morning with the best of intentions, then by noon I'd be sick of it. I'd walk outside in the sunshine and get that open air urge and run off without even waiting for my pay.

One time I worked for a mail order house and I was sent over to the music department. I started fooling around with a saxophone, and the boss came in and chased me out. Another time I worked as a truck driver's assistant. One day the driver hit a streetcar and I flew right through the windshield—that's how I got these scars on my face. Another time while we were carrying eleven thousand dollars' worth of shoes in the truck some guy came up and said, "Get the hell off of there," and pulled out a big gun. Then two men took the truck away from us and another two grabbed the driver and me and rode us around for hours, six-seven hours, so we wouldn't be able to report to the cops.

Most of the playing I did in those days was for nothing—I just stayed up all night and did so much sitting in, they didn't have to pay me. I got to know about the different styles—Rappolo was the first clarinetist I heard on records; never heard him in person, he was working in some high-class joint that I couldn't afford. Teschemacher I was crazy about, but he never made any records that did him justice. He had a good tone and terrific technique. But Noone was the man who gave me the biggest kicks —holding the horn over that great belly of his and playing just like it was nothing.

9

*Jam sessions, gangsters, speakeasies, recording sessions,
more musicians, and then—the Chicago decline.*

MEZZ MEZZROW

There was a ginmill that became the hangout for all of Chicago's
hot men. The address was 222 North State Street, and after we
hung out there awhile we named it the Three Deuces, parodying
the name of the Four Deuces, one of the biggest syndicate whore-
houses in town. Whenever we musicians wanted to get together
with each other we'd say "Meet you at The Deuces tonight."
Years later, after Prohibition was repealed, the name was officially
adopted and hung up on a sign outside, and the spot turned into
a legit hot-music center.

I think the term "jam session" originated right in that cellar.
Long before that, of course, the colored boys used to get together and play for kicks, but those were mostly private sessions,
strictly for professional musicians, and the idea was usually to
try and cut each other, each one trying to outdo the others and
prove himself best. These impromptu concerts of theirs were
generally known as "cuttin' contests." Our idea, when we got
going at The Deuces, was to play together, to make our improvisation really collective, using an organ background behind the one
taking a solo, to see could we fit together and arrive at a climax

all at once. Down in that basement concert hall, somebody was always yelling over at me, "Hey, Jelly, what you gonna do?"—they gave me that nickname, or sometimes called me Roll, because I always wanted to play Clarence Williams' classic, *Jelly Roll*—and almost every time I'd cap them with, "Jelly's gonna jam some now," just as a kind of play on words. We always used the word "session" a lot, and I think the expression "jam session" grew up out of this playful yelling back and forth. At least I don't rightly remember ever hearing it before those sessions at The Deuces.

JIMMY McPARTLAND

Then there were the gangsters who came into the place we worked, Tancil's. Eddie Tancil himself used to be a boxer and was a tough guy. He was what you'd call a roughneck—and needed to be! Al Capone and his mob were just moving into Cicero, and naturally they wanted to clean out all this rough element so they could take over.

Of course, I didn't realize it at the time, or I'd have been less happy there. One night a bunch of tough guys came in and started turning tables over to introduce themselves. Then they picked up bottles and began hitting the bartenders with them, also with blackjacks and brass knuckles. It was just terrible.

To us they said, "You boys keep playing if you don't want to get hurt. That's all." And you know who kept playing.

The thugs tore the place apart, beat up all the waiters and barmen and Tancil, too. Eddie was fighting them and he was good, could beat the heck out of any two of those strong-arms. But when they brought out the "billies," he was outclassed.

All over the place people were gashed and bleeding. The mobsters would break a bottle over some guy's head, then jab it in his face, then maybe kick him. They made mincemeat of people. I never saw such a horrible thing in my life. But we kept playing —period.

A couple more nights of work and they came and did it again, much worse. That was the finish. Tancil got rid of the band, and two days later we found out he had been shot dead. That was the beginning of the mobs' moving in on night-club business.

GEORGE WETTLING

We would see those rods come up—and duck. At the Triangle Club, the boss was shot in the stomach one night, but we kept working. After that he walked sort of bent over.

MARTY MARSALA

Yes, there was plenty of rough stuff at one hall I remember. Two bands were there, one on the stage and one on the balcony. There were real battles of music, and plenty of roughhouse—worst roughhouse I've ever seen. I was about eighteen years old. I remember once when the guys were kidding around, and everybody was spitting on the stand around the trumpet player's chair. He got mad. He was very excitable. He says, "The next guy that spits is gonna get hit!" Someone spit and he thought it was the banjo player, although it was someone else, because I was standing there and saw it. The trumpeter hit the banjo player on the head with his horn and split the guy's head open. The dance was going on, too. They took him out and doctored him up, both of them mad as hell. They wound up the best of friends.

And at one place we worked, Capone would come in with about seven or eight guys. They closed the door as soon as he came in. Nobody could come in or out. Then he gets a couple of hundred dollar bills changed and passes them around to the entertainers and waiters. His bodyguards did the passing. We got five or ten bucks just for playing his favorite numbers, sentimental things.

EARL HINES

A frequent visitor to the Grand Terrace was the big man himself, Al Capone, who went around town in a seven-ton armored limousine. He liked to come into a club with his henchmen, order all the doors closed, and have the band play his requests. He was free with hundred dollar tips.

"Scarface" got along well with musicians. Only one I ever heard of who had a run-in with the Mr. Big of the syndicates was Mezz Mezzrow, who was working in a night spot in suburban Burnham. It seems Al's youngest brother, Mitzi, went for one of the good-looking entertainers with Mezz's outfit, and Scarface ordered her fired. Mezz argued back while a half dozen of Al's henchmen stood around laughing at the nerve of this musician arguing with Mr. Six-Shooter. Finally Al started laughing too and said, "The kid's got plenty of guts."

Another band leader who had considerable contact with the Capone group in those days was Lucky Millinder, who worked for Ralph Capone in a spot controlled by the syndicate in Cicero, headquarters of the Capone gang. Others who held jobs in Capone-controlled clubs were the late Tiny Parham and the late Jimmie Noone, one of the greatest of all jazz clarinetists.

Louis Armstrong once changed managers and was threatened with gangster violence. After that he hired two bodyguards who protected him on and off the job for many months.

JIMMY McPARTLAND

I had no job for my band. But Art Kassel—the saxophone player—had a job up in Detroit, Michigan, and he wanted to take over the band intact. His offer was pretty good, so we let him.

Under Kassel's name, and augmented with a couple of instruments, we opened at the Graystone Ballroom in Detroit. There we played opposite Fletcher Henderson's orchestra, which had Coleman Hawkins, Rex Stewart, Joe Smith, and Buster Bailey. That's where I first met Buster.

We used to go out on jam sessions with Fletcher's guys and really had a good time. Bud Freeman was knocked over by Coleman Hawkins, while I was particularly impressed by Joe Smith. He was a lovely trumpet player, and exceptionally good with the plunger mute.

Anyway, when we got to Detroit we found that Kassel wanted to play real commercial music; he had some horrible commercial tunes for us to play. It was no good, we couldn't stand that. So during the course of the evening he called some corny tune, *Jingle Bells* or some stupid thing, and the guys looked at me as much as to say, "Impossible, can't do it."

I told Art, "Sorry, Art, can't play the tune." Then Dave Tough muttered, "Come on, *Shim-Me-Sha-Wobble*." And I started off

131

. . . "One, two . . ." and we went into *Shim-Me-Sha*. Well, we kept that up, and had a lot of fun. We played more or less what we wanted to play, and Art would stand there and make a face, as if to say, "What can I do with these guys?"

The job finished and we came back to Chicago, and everyone started splitting up. Together with bassist Lannigan, I was offered work down at Friar's Inn with Bill Paley's band—a hundred fifteen bucks a week, as I recall. We took it; Jim Lannigan by this time had a bass fiddle as well as tuba, and he played both.

Now Friar's Inn was the place where the gangsters used to hang out, the big boys. One night, real late, there were only a few customers left. They were these tough blokes, as you say. I knew the gang it was, the North Side mob, which later on did the St. Valentine massacre—when they slaughtered all those monkeys against a wall.

So it was late this night, and we were off the bandstand and sitting in the back, when all of a sudden—*bang, boom, bang!* Somebody was shooting a gun.

Mike Fritzl was the boss there, and Mike says, "Play, play, fellers." We weren't all that keen, but the shooting had ceased so we got up on the stand to play, and there was the bass fiddle all shot to pieces. One of these guys had shot it into splinters just for target practice!

Jim Lannigan was sore, but he was the retiring type, and I wasn't. I said: "What the hell is the idea, Mike, this guy busting up my brother-in-law's bass?" Mike said not to worry about it, the guy would make good the damage, and I said, "That's a different thing—if he'll pay for it."

Mike asked how much Jim had paid for the bass. I happened to know he had laid down two hundred and twenty-five for it, but I said eight hundred and fifty. Believe it or not, in five minutes Mike came over with eight hundred and fifty in cash. The torpedo just peeled it off a roll; you know, these Prohibition guys were loaded with loot.

So Jim got eight hundred and fifty bucks, and he'd never said a word! With the dough he bought himself a new instrument, a beautiful thing. And he kept the remains and had them fixed up, then sold the old bass.

Jim and I stayed at the Inn about four or five months; after that, back to Kassel. Benny Pollack was leaving the Southmoor Hotel in Chicago, and Art had been booked in his place. He wanted Lannigan and me to rejoin him. This time we asked first what kind of music he was going to play.

"The kind you want to play," Art answered. He also said he would pay a hundred and forty each a week. So we let him hire us. It was big money, and in those days there was no tax, nothing like that. But a clause in the contract said that we would play so much jazz. I wouldn't take the job otherwise.

During these months with Kassel, some interesting events took place. The Mound City Blue Blowers came to town, and one night Red McKenzie came into the Southmoor saying that his guitarist had quit him. I said, "Well, get my brother on guitar." So Red hired him right off the bat, and Richard went into the Blue Blowers on guitar (by this time he was playing guitar instead of banjo).

While I was still with Kassel, McKenzie got together with Eddie Condon and they secured a recording date from Tommy Rockwell of Okeh. These were the records, put out as by McKenzie and Condon's Chicagoans, which created something of a stir in the Windy City in 1927–28. I'll tell you how we made them.

Red and Condon got together some of the Austin High School Gang to talk about the date, and a rehearsal was fixed. The four tunes were decided, and Teschemacher agreed to write out a few introductions and interludes and so on, which he did. He got up three-part harmonies for us; you can tell which are the parts on the records.

The day before the recording, we ran through them and got them for timing. Then the next day we went down and recorded. All the guys were there—Mezzrow and all the hang-arounds—and the band consisted of me, Tesch, Freeman, Lannigan, Condon, Joe Sullivan, and Gene Krupa.

As you know, Tough was our drummer; and a lot of the ideas we used were his. The reason he was not on these records is that he had recently left for Europe to join up with Danny Polo. I do not know where Wettling was. He was the next drummer, but he couldn't have been around. So they got Krupa for the date.

Gene was really the comer. Tough and Wettling were already

established, but Krupa was a couple of years younger. And in those days it made a lot of difference. This was, in fact, the first time I ever played with Krupa. *And it was the first recording session on which any of our guys had seen a bass drum used.*

We came into the studio there, and Gene set up his bass drum, tom-toms—the whole set. Then we made a take to see how it sounded, and immediately the recording manager, Mr. Ring, ran out saying, "You can't use all those drums; throw those drums out; just use sticks, cymbals, wood blocks, and so forth."

After some protests, they finally worked the thing out by laying down rugs that took up the vibration. The vibration was the thing they worried about mostly. So they let Gene play the drums, and he beat the heck out of them all the way through the set, which was fine for us, because it gave us a good, solid background.

They say that we got our particular style down well on that session. Of course, we didn't have a name for it or anything; it was simply the way we used to play.

We had names for certain devices, though, like the "explosion."

That was in the middle of a chorus. We would build up to an explosion, then go down soft; 'way down, we would say. Like, for instance, that final chorus in *Nobody's Sweetheart*. Then, at the end, the last eight or sixteen bars, we used to break out and ride. We called that the "ride out." These things were largely Davey Tough's ideas.

China Boy features something similar. *Sugar* and *Liza* were the quieter tunes. Very few people know this particular *Liza*, which was written by a guy named George Rubens. He was just a guy that liked jazz, and he was a friend of Condon's.

Another thing happened on that date; we had a vocal trio. The trio was Condon, Freeman, and myself, and we had rehearsed a couple of songs before the date. One was *Mean To Me*. I know that. And I know we recorded it, but not until the end of the date.

And by the end of that date, everyone was so knocked out—or shall I say intoxicated?—from all the stuff, that singing became a thing of chance.

Mercifully, that side was not put out!

But all the rest came out and were a big hit overnight. For their

134

time, they sold very well. And I guess they helped to bring renewed offers from Ben Pollack, the Chicago drummer.

Soon after Benny formed his band at the Southmoor, I had been invited to join. Now he was at the Blackhawk restaurant, and he and Gil Rodin and Benny Goodman came out to the hotel one night to persuade me.

I said I wouldn't leave unless it was okay with Kassel. Art said, "All right," and Pollack said he'd also want to take Bud Freeman. This made it better for me, because Bud was my pal from the Austin High mob.

So we decided "Fine," and went with Pollack to the Blackhawk.

MILT HINTON

I came up in Chicago in the era where we were coming along behind King Oliver, and people like that. When I came up these people—some of them—were on their decline. Like I played one night with Freddie Keppard and he was on his decline. He was blowing loud but not very good. Earl Hines had the only big band that was taking over. The nature of the clubs was changing too. The clubs were becoming tavern-like things.

In the early 'thirties in Chicago, there was a decline of popular interest in jazz. Chicago just went down. It was a meager period and it was pretty bad for musicians. There was the depression also. Al Capone ran the Cotton Club and the only other place was run by Ralph Capone. Boyd Atkins had a band there. It was on the North Side. My first job was with Atkins. It was my first chance to play with a big band, my first professional job. I went with Tiny Parham after that. I joined the band around 1930.

I was with Atkins only a couple of weeks and Parham a month but my first big job was when Louis left Chicago on his first big tour with a group, and we went into the club where he was playing. He had been broadcasting from there. They were looking for a trumpet player to take Louis' place and they got Jabbo Smith. Jabbo was as good as Louis then. He was the Dizzy Gillespie of that era. He played rapid-fire passages while Louis was melodic and beautiful. He played anything with a cup mouthpiece—trombone and bass trumpet, as well as trumpet. He could play soft and he could play fast but he never made it. He got hung up in Newark.

It was a wonderful band. A man named Cass Simpson, he was the end on piano. He lost his mind. Last I heard he was in an insane asylum in Illinois. He was almost fanatical. He played incessantly all day. He had terrific technique and was a fine pianist and arranger. He also had a mania for naming all of his tunes after some food. Like he had tunes called *Stringbeans and Rice, Chittlins and Greens.* He was a stout man.

Floyd Campbell was on drums. He came up to Chicago up the river with Fate Marable. Scoville Brown was on clarinet; he's now playing in a band in Greenwich Village. And Othello Tinsley was on guitar. He's with the *Chicago Defender* newspaper now. That was a band that was never written up but it was really swinging. There was also Jerome Pascale on alto. He had been with Fletcher and had studied in Boston at the Conservatory. We stayed together through the whole season. Three or four months I guess. But Jabbo goofed. He was kind of uncontrollable. We played the second season with Cass Simpson as leader.

Unfortunately, we never recorded. We were big enough at that time however to play the Regal Theatre. Cass, however, began to deteriorate; if he hadn't, he'd be blowing the end now.

Jabbo, like I said, was on a par with Louis. He was just as exciting although he wasn't playing the same kind of thing. There was a lot of talk about him in Milwaukee and Chicago. His attitude hurt him. He had delusions of grandeur and he'd always get mixed up with women. He was a nice-looking guy.

There was a kind of a trend in those days. There were some guys who were the greatest but would come in the latest. They were due at eleven and they would show up at two and then only after we'd called them. A guy like Jabbo, if he made enough for drinks and chicks in any small town like Des Moines or Milwaukee, that would suffice. That's why he was never heard on engagements in New York. I did see him in the late 'forties in Newark—that's where he got hung up.

There was another man I hear was very great—Joe Suttler. He was a trumpet player around Chicago in the late 'twenties and early 'thirties. He often could play three or four jobs at the same time and he used to make seven hundred dollars a week, which was like seven thousand dollars is now. He deteriorated mentally. He'd been in an institution and had been released but his lip finally went.

When I was coming up there was already almost no demand for the bass horn. Most of the older bass players at that time were former bass horn players. Even John Kirby was a former bass horn player and was better on that instrument. But Kirby and Billy Taylor were most successful in making the transition.

One of the great trumpet players from New Orleans around Chicago was Guy Kelly. He made that record with Albert Ammons many years ago for Decca called *Early Mornin' Blues*. Guy got on the booze quite a lot. You see, he was one of those who lived in the shadow of Louis. He didn't play like Louis but there were so many all from the same school, and Louis reached the top first. Louis had the overall greatness.

But some of the men from that same school had a few things that they did even better than Louis, but Louis had it as a whole. They all came from Louisiana, and those that didn't make it as big as Louis were a little hurt. A fellow like Guy, for example, who came from Baton Rouge, but had been playing around New Orleans. Guy had power and a big sound, in fact, he had a bigger tone than Louis. When he hit an F, it sounded like something altissimo. He was a very creative soloist. He always was a very creative soloist. He always said something.

Musicians like Guy who were in the shadow of Louis were also hurt because they felt they had had more respect in Louisiana. Punch Miller was another one. Even to this day these older musicians from Louisiana are like a cult unto themselves.

A man like Zutty Singleton, for another example, he's always been considered the senior of the Louisiana musicians. Even over Louis. Even to this day Louis looks up to Zutty and Zutty looks down to Louis. Even though Zutty isn't doing very well.

I remember a big party one night that was held a couple of years ago when Zutty had just come back from Paris. Mischa Resnikoff, the painter, threw this "welcome home" party, and Louis and Bobby Hackett and a lot of the musicians were there.

137

Zutty came in late and completely ignored Louis. Everybody was terribly embarrassed. Why did he? I think he feels that as the senior member of the jazz group (money or public recognition hasn't anything to do with it) but that, as senior member, I think maybe Zutty felt he should be the drummer in Louis' band.

Louis' success hurt quite a few of his colleagues from Louisiana. They did feel he merited his success musically but they felt like Tony Spargo said once, "Everybody seems to think Louis is the only thing from New Orleans." You see, they feel they're all responsible for the music. His trumpet represents it but they all made it. They feel most people think Louis is it, but Red Allen, Wingy Manone, Punch Miller, and Guy Kelly all play the same type of thing and they're not copying Louis. They all play New Orleans but each has his own style. It's true that Louis was the greatest soloist.

Yes, that New Orleans society is quite a clannish thing, even though they don't hire one another. Like Pops Foster, the bass player. He feels too, I think, that he should be in Louis' band. Since I'm out of Chicago they don't even recognize me. What's even worse, I came originally from Mississippi and yet that's only a stone's throw away from Louisiana. To that New Orleans society there's no such thing as a Mississippi musician or a Georgia musician. There are only Louisiana musicians. They still think that the best jazz musicians come from Louisiana but you know there was jazz played all over the South.

I know that some people in the East used to say there was a Western style of playing jazz. Well, we didn't know what it was. We were in Chicago and the Midwest and we didn't think it was any different. In fact, I didn't know there was such a label as Chicago jazz until I came to New York and heard the phrase. Fletcher Henderson came to Chicago, and, if he took a man and brought him back to New York, I'm told that they said the man played Western style but we didn't think it was anything different.

Anyway, I came up later so I guess I'm not considered Chicago jazz anyway. I don't know what the sense in labeling is to begin with. Sure, environment has a great bearing on you but labeling music that way doesn't make sense. Like they say "West Coast jazz" now. Now, how can you tell what coast it is? We just played and listened and played what we felt.

PEE WEE RUSSELL

People who use terms like the "Chicagoans" or "New Orleans Style"—I despise that stuff. Listen, write out a list of guys who are supposed to play Chicago style. And I'd like to know when did so and so leave Chicago. When was he ever there? Where was he born? Or when was he ever in New Orleans if they say he plays "New Orleans Style"? Go down the whole list. I'll grant you a few exceptions as to people who left and played in those cities, but the whole idea of labels is insipid. Most of the so-called Chicagoans did not get their music education there and many didn't even get to Chicago during the period when there was something to hear.

Bix was from Davenport; I was from Oklahoma and St. Louis. A few of us were fortunate to hear Louis but not necessarily in Chicago. The music that was played in Chicago surely had an influence on the kids around Chicago. Like Freeman and McPartland. They could hear people like Jimmie Noone—they were fortunate to be there. But Bix for one had heard Louis even before that time.

What I'm trying to say is it doesn't matter what city you hear it in. I get so disgusted with the idea that you have to be from one particular part of the country to be able to play good jazz. Take Jack Teagarden. He's from Kansas. He drifted to Texas. I was the first to get him out of there. I brought him to St. Louis. I had been down to Texas playing with Peck Kelly and it was there I heard Teagarden. And certainly Jack plays good jazz no matter where he came from.

The first real city Jack hit was St. Louis, because Houston wasn't anything then like it is now. Jack was going to work with Trumbauer but the union wouldn't let him—some six-month rule or something. Even though Trumbauer pulled all the strings. He came out to my house and he left town the next day for Indiana. That was the nearest thing he could get. He'd always loved things like Louis and all that sort of thing. And he didn't come from Chicago.

139

10

"In a Mist"—the legendary Bix.

JIMMY McPARTLAND
To me, Bix—well, that was it. What beautiful tone, sense of melody, great drive, poise, everything! He just played lovely jazz.

HOAGY CARMICHAEL
I was interrupted by the arrival of a slight, extremely young kid who had just come in.

"Hoagy, meet Bix Beiderbecke."

"Hello," Bix said through slightly reddened lips. He didn't pay much attention, though his eyes and silly little mouth fascinated me.

When he had gone, George leaned over to me. "You ought to hear that kid play; he's going to be tops some day. He's got ideas, but his lip is still weak."

"Where's he from?"

"Davenport, Iowa. He's up here now going to Lake Forest Academy. He says he's liable to get kicked out any day, but not because he comes to town every night to listen to jazz bands."

"He's nuts about Ravel and Debussy's stuff."

"Sounds like a goof."

"He is. He used to go on the boats and play the steam calliope. Then he heard a couple of guys named Louis Armstrong and King

Oliver." George stopped. "His folks wanted him to be a concert pianist. And has that kid got an ear! He can tell you the pitch of a belch!"

WAYNE H. ROHLF

First, I would like to state that I attended the same high school in Davenport, Iowa, that Bix did. I have played in bands with him and was one of his personal friends, as well as a friend of his brother, and tried to act as a kindly adviser to young Bix. Bix played pretty knocked-out piano when he was in high school, although he couldn't read a note. In fact, I don't believe he ever learned to read piano music.

It was while in high school that Bix took a fancy to the cornet. He asked his uncle, Al Petersen, a local band leader, if he would give him lessons if he bought a cornet. His uncle failed to give him much encouragement, figuring that it was just a young boy's passing fancy. The next time Al visited the Beiderbecke home, young Bix was taking choruses on the favorite tunes of the day.

Bix would sit in with all of the local bands and played on a truck with a high school jazz band at football games. He also played with the orchestra at Iowa University and Lake Forest Academy and then joined the Wolverines and eventually joined Jean Goldkette's ork. It was while Bix was with Goldkette that he learned to read music, and his teacher was none other than the famous Freddy Farrar, and, as far as I know of, Freddy is the only real teacher that Bix ever had.

HOAGY CARMICHAEL

It's the summer of 1923. We took two quarts of bathtub gin, a package of muggles, and headed for the black-and-tan joint where King Oliver's band was playing. The King featured two trumpets, piano, a bass fiddle, and a clarinet. As I sat down to light my first muggle, Bix gave the sign to a big black fellow, playing second trumpet for Oliver, and he slashed into *Bugle Call Rag*.

I dropped my cigarette and gulped my drink. Bix was on his feet, his eyes popping. For taking the first chorus was that second trumpet, Louis Armstrong. Louis was taking it fast. Bob Gillette slid off his chair and under the table. He was excitable that way.

"Why," I moaned, "why isn't everybody in the world here to hear that?" I meant it. Something as unutterably stirring as that deserved to be heard by the world.

Then the muggles took effect and my body got light. Every note Louis hit was perfection. I ran to the piano and took the place of Louis' wife. They swung into *Royal Garden Blues*. I had never heard the tune before, but somehow I knew every note. I couldn't miss. I was floating in a strange, deep-blue whirlpool of jazz.

It wasn't marijuana. The muggles and the gin were, in a way, stage props. It was the music. The music took me and had me and it made me right.

Louis Armstrong was Bix Beiderbecke's idol, and when we went out the next night to crash an S.A.E. dance where Bix was playing with the Wolverines, I learned that Bix was no imitation of Armstrong. The Wolverines sounded better to me than the New Orleans Rhythm Kings. Theirs was a stronger rhythm and the licks that Jimmy Hartwell, George Johnson, and Bix played were precise and beautiful.

Bix's breaks were not as wild as Armstrong's, but they were hot and he selected each note with musical care. He showed me that jazz could be musical and beautiful as well as hot. He showed me that tempo doesn't mean fast. His music affected me in a different way. Can't tell you how—like licorice, you have to eat some.

RALPH BERTON

My brother had already heard people talk about an orchestra of young musicians which was playing in Indiana—the Wolverines —and he became their manager. In fact, apart from Bix, the other musicians in the orchestra were rather mediocre. I heard them for the first time at the Gary Municipal Beach Pavilion at Miller Beach in Indiana. It was in 1924. Their first records at that time were just beginning to make themselves known.

HOAGY CARMICHAEL

It was nearing the Christmas holidays. Bix blew into Indianapolis and asked me to go down to Richmond with him to hear him make some records. He phoned me at my house and I hurried down to pick him up, in my new Ford, a Christmas present to myself.

When I found him he told me that he was on his way to make some records for Gennett, the same outfit that had made our record in the fall. I was delighted to go.

Remembering my own nerve-wracking experience, I thought it would be doubly pleasant to be there with no worries of my own. I asked Bix who was going to be with him on the date.

"We're going to make some records in 'slow-drag' style," Bix said, "and I've got some guys who can really go. Tommy Dorsey, Howdy Quicksell, Don Murray, Paul Mertz, and Tommy Gargano. They are going to drive from Detroit and meet me."

"Boy," I exclaimed, "that's really gonna be somethin'. What are you gonna make?"

"Hell, I don't know. Just make some up, I guess."

"How about me driving you over tonight?"

"That'll be swell," Bix said. "The guys are bringing three quarts. . . ."

We got to the studio and sat around for a while and the bottles got lighter and finally Bix started doodling on his horn. Finally, he seemed to find a strain that suited him but by that time everybody had taken a hand in composing the melody, though as the bottles got still lighter nobody seemed to have a definite understanding of what that melody was.

I have a photo of that group on that day. Bix is leaning against the piano, his legs crossed, and you see him in half profile. He looks so young, like a little boy, like Little Boy Blue—and he blew. Tommy Dorsey, beside him, bespectacled even at that early age, is slumped in a chair, his trombone at his mouth. The rest of them are in various negligent poses, waiting.

As far as I could see, they didn't have any arrangement worked out, or tune either for that matter, but when the technician came in and gave them the high sign, they took off. Away they went. Away down.

They named the piece *Davenport Blues* in honor of Bix's home town. It was done in lazy "jig style" and, as the dead soldiers were racked up, their music grew screwier and screwier.

Toddlin' Blues was the next number, and, by the time it was finished, they were having a little trouble staying in front of their horns. But the effect was wonderful. They used the "I'se a-comin' " strain from *Old Black Joe* and there were among them those who were soon "a-comin'." A few years later three of those six boys who got together to blow jazz were gone. Little Joes, all.

JIMMY McPARTLAND

Bix Beiderbecke—he had just about everything that I looked for in a musician. And when he came up on those Wolverines records, why, me and the rest of the gang—we just wore the records out.

We copied off the little arrangements, and what was going on in the ensembles. One thing was definite that we would never do—copy any solo exactly.

We didn't believe in copying anything outside of the arrangement. An introduction, ending, a first ending or an interlude, we would copy those, naturally. But never a solo. For instance, if Bix would take a solo, I wouldn't copy that. I would just play the way I felt.

But I was tremendously influenced by Bix, and hearing the Wolverines was a step forward for all of the gang. We got their numbers off, and added them to our repertoire.

My brother had found a job for the band, with Tesch, Bud, Lannigan, Dave North and no cornet, at radio station WGN. They called the band the Blue Flyers, and they were doing great.

I was going to join the Flyers when I received a wire one fateful day from Dick Voynow, pianist and manager of the Wolverines. It read: CAN YOU JOIN WOLVERINES IN NEW YORK REPLACING BIX BEIDERBECKE AT SALARY OF EIGHTY-SEVEN DOLLARS FIFTY PER WEEK QUERYMARK STOP ANSWER IMMEDIATELY STOP.

I learned later that Bix had received an offer from Goldkette.

Of course, I showed this wire to everybody. Though I patted myself on the back, I was feeling doubtful. Was it a gag? Was someone playing a joke on me?

All the guys said, "No, you're crazy! Sure, it's real. Take it; it's the greatest honor in the world." So I said I would. They advised me to wire right back, and I did: SEND TRANSPORTATION STOP I ACCEPT THE JOB STOP. McPARTLAND.

The rail fare was thirty-two fifty from Chicago to New York; that was third-class coach, no Pullman or anything. And that was exactly the sum Voynow sent me. Dick Voynow was handling all their business, and he said to leave immediately.

Well, I left that same night—with just my bag and my little beaten-up cornet. It *was* beat-up, too, and getting worse and worse. As I pressed the valves it would go clank, clank, clank. Gee! A noisy affair!

Taking Bix's place was the biggest thing that had happened to me. The Wolverines were *the* jazz band in the country, so far as we were concerned. And Bix—as I say, I had never met him, but just hearing him play was enough.

I've heard many great trumpeters since those days, but I haven't heard another like Bix. Somehow or other his style, the cleanliness and feeling, was lovely.

Let's call him the master and leave it at that.

I finally got into New York about six in the morning. It was the first time I'd been there in my life, and a beautiful hour to arrive. From the station I called up Dick Voynow, who said, "Hop in a cab and come to the Somerset Hotel." I got over there and started talking to Voynow. He 'phoned Bix, who was just coming in, pretty high.

So I met Bix.

The Wolverines were rehearsing that afternoon, and by the time I got there I was very nervous. Of course, I had memorized all the arrangements from the band's records, and when Dick asked what I wanted to play, I said: "Anything. *Jazz Me Blues, Farewell, Riverboat Shuffle, Big Boy*. Anything."

They said, "Do you know all those tunes?"

I said, "Sure."

So Voynow said, "Okay, let's go!" And he beat off and I just started right in. I knew all Bix's lead parts—so BOOM! I must have surprised those guys; their chins dropped, and everything else.

I played their routine, took my solo where Bix used to take his. And when the number was finished they patted me on the back and said, "Great, kid," and all that stuff. It made me feel good; I was no more nervous—got my cockiness back.

We went through some more tunes and I was in, right then and there.

Now Bix, from the first, had been very reticent. He didn't say anything until the rehearsal was over. Then he came over. "Kid," he said, "I'll tell you what you do. You'll move in with me. I like you."

That was what he said. So I moved in with Bix.

As we roomed together, he was able to show me the different tunes and arrangements the band had, coach me in certain little figures he used in his playing. Then, at night, we would go to the job—the Wolverines were working at the Cinderella Ballroom on Forty-eighth and Broadway—and play the tunes together.

Yes, for about five nights we both played in the band. First Bix would take the lead, then he'd play second in with me to break me in. He was an enormous help and encouragement, and I got to admire the man as much as the musician.

I must tell you about his generosity to me, a complete stranger to him until I took his place in the Wolverines. After a few days he asked me, "How can you blow a horn like that? It's a terrible thing."

I've told you that my cornet was beat, had leaks in it and everything. But I had not realized how horrible it was until Bix took me over. At that time, he was using a horn called the Conn Victor cornet—a long model cornet and a beautiful thing. He had me blow it and it sounded great.

Said Bix, "You need a horn like this, Jimmy, come on out with me." Out we went to see Voynow, who gave Beiderbecke some dough. Then we went over to the Conn company, where Bix picked up four or five horns and tried them out. Finally he said, "This is the one, Jim, for you."

He just gave me the cornet—period. So that I would have a good instrument to play. I remember him saying, "I like you, kid,

146

because you sound like I do but you don't copy me. You play your own stuff; you're a good guy."

That was nice, you know, coming from him. I had patterned my playing after his, but had tried to develop my own self at the same time. That was what we believed, in the Austin gang in Chicago: play the way you feel, yourself!

GEORGE JOHNSON

The Wolverines' records had become generally known, by musicians particularly. Vic Berton, who had just finished playing with a Chicago theater orchestra, came down to Indianapolis with an offer to engage the band—for the month of August. This offer filled in the time until our engagement at the Cinderella Ballroom.

The Cinderella was one of the finest dance halls in New York, located at Forty-eighth and Broadway, in the heart of all that is worth-while in the amusement line in that city. Opposite us, playing alternately, was Willie Creager's orchestra, the first of four orchestras that played opposite us during the four months we played there.

It was only natural that we in the band looked forward with great pride and no little doubt to our next job at the Cinderella. Pride, because in less than a year as a definite organization, we were to play in a first-rate spot on Broadway, an achievement rarely attained by any orchestra; doubt, because all our playing had been to audiences decidedly different in the matter of musical appreciation. This, in spite of the fact that Red Nichols, Miff Mole, Jimmy and Tommy Dorsey, Frank Trumbauer, and others were playing with different orchestras in the New York district.

There were a few Dixieland combinations in the smaller dance halls and cafes but no combination similar to ours, nor any with a similar style, and for this reason we all looked forward with great anxiety to our opening.

The day before we opened, several of us attended the Hippodrome Theatre, where Ray Miller's orchestra was playing a short booking before their opening at the Arcadia Ballroom, just two blocks from the Cinderella.

Miff Mole, Ruby Bloom (whom I had met the year previous in

Chicago), and Frank Trumbauer, my personal choice for saxophone royalty, were with Ray. It was our first opportunity to hear them in person. You will understand our enthusiasm when I mention that we all let out a yell that all but drowned out the band when Miff took his first break, and were all summarily ejected from the theater. We went around backstage, where I asked for Ruby and where we were introduced to Frank and Miff. The latter was very surprised to learn that we were the cause of all the noise in the theater. He had thought someone was giving him the bird.

From then on, during our stay in New York, we rarely missed the opportunity of hearing Miller's band on the nights when we started and finished early and they played late, and they came to the Cinderella as frequently.

At that time, Ray Miller's orchestra was the first of the large bands to mix a little hot music with the general run of heavy orchestrations, and their hot music would have been a great hit at the present time.

Our contract at the Cinderella was for thirty days, with two options of ninety days and one year. From the very start we were well received, and the word got around Broadway that the Wolverines at the Cinderella were something new and different.

Famous musicians came to listen and were eager to sit in, just as we had been in the days of Friar's Inn in Chicago. Most frequent of these was Red Nichols, who at that time was just coming under the influence of Bix's genius. Red probably will not like this statement, but it is my personal opinion that much of Red's playing today is the direct result of the absorption of ideas gained from listening to and playing next to Bix, together with the learning, note for note, of Bix's recordings. Even before we had landed in New York, we had heard a recording of Red's called *You'll Never Get To Heaven With Those Eyes,* in which he used Bix's chorus in *Jazz Me Blues* note for note.

Bix was a fountain of ideas that were spontaneous, as unexpected to himself as they were to us, while Red's playing has ever been methodical and carefully thought out, with each note planned ahead. Each was an artist, but Bix had the natural flow of ideas

148

which, once played, were discarded and never used again. There were too many as yet unplayed to bother with repeating.

Our first month was replete with new experiences, being the first trip to New York for any of us. Well received, our option was taken up and we knew we were set until January first. We rehearsed new numbers and made our first New York recordings, *Big Boy*, on which Bix played a piano chorus for the first time on record, and *Tia Juana*, about which the less said the better.

Bix spent most of his time after working hours sitting in with some of the Dixieland combinations in town. He always claimed that the five-piece combination was the ideal one.

When we had been in New York a month, Bix gave his notice and joined Frank Trumbauer in St. Louis.

JIMMY McPARTLAND

The next time I saw Bix was when I'd become the leader of the Wolverines and the group was now composed mainly of the Austin High gang. It was quite a combo, and everybody came around to hear us, especially Louis Armstrong.

Louis was playing then over at the Sunset Cafe, which started later than us and went on till four A.M. or so. He came over two or three evenings a week and sat in back of the band, listening to us and chuckling all over the place. He was about twenty-five then.

Pee Wee Russell, Bix, and Frankie Trumbauer were working down at Hudson Lake, about eighty miles south in Indiana. Every Monday, their night off, they would come up to hear us. When we got finished, we would all go off together and catch Louis or Jimmie Noone—another of our favorites. Sometimes we sat in with Louis at the Sunset, or with Noone at the Apex. The Apex Club was one of the regular stops.

Bix also made a point of taking me to hear Ethel Waters. It was 1927, I think, and she was in a show called MISS CALICO. She sang, man, she really sang. We were enthralled with her. We liked Bessie Smith very much, too, but Waters had more polish, I guess you'd say. She phrased so wonderfully, the natural quality of her voice was so fine, and she sang the way she felt—that knocked us out always with any artist.

FRANK TRUMBAUER

I had the band at the Arcadia Ballroom in St. Louis in 1926. Bix and Pee Wee Russell were with me. That was the stopping-off place for all the musicians who passed through. Needless to say, the band was just a little over the heads of the public in general at that time.

Charley Horvath made me an offer to conduct the Goldkette at Detroit, and when I mentioned bringing Bix with me, he wasn't sold on the idea, as he explained that Bix was around Detroit for some time and nothing happened. I refused the offer unless Bix could come along; so Charley reconsidered and told me I would have to be responsible for him, as he did not think it would work.

He didn't know what Bix and I had been doing. Bix could not read very well when we started. We taught him all that was possible in the time we had. Bix thought and played in concert, even on a B-flat instrument. We started him on violin parts—then taught him to transpose the violin parts to trumpet—and at last we gave him trumpet parts alone, and he was doing pretty well with them. At least he was in there trying. He was saving his money, had plenty of clothes, and was playing golf and looked wonderful.

We had a fine understanding and could anticipate what the other was about to do on his instrument. We sat at the piano for hours and worked things out; and if you would like to hear some of the inspiration for *In a Mist*, play *Land of the Loon*. He loved Eastwood Lane and Cyril Scott. I don't remember ever sitting down to listen to popular records; generally we listened to symphonies that we liked. A few of the things that most of the boys didn't know was that Bix got to the point where he could read pretty well.

He had a love life that very few people ever heard of. This girl still cherishes the things she hears about Bix, and she has a wonderful reason to do so. If she ever wants her story to be told, I feel sure she will let me tell it.

I seem to be wandering from the point a bit. We folded the band and went to Detroit to join Goldkette; and to say that the band was a "killer" would be putting it mildly. Don Murray was everything Russ Morgan said he was, and a little more. He would bring a basket of beer and sandwiches to rehearsal, and he and Quicksell drove me "nuts." As I was conducting the band, I would ask the boys to make a cut on some arrangement, and Murray would take me at my word and actually cut that part out with a pair of scissors—his parts all looked like an old lace curtain. And if you wanted to put something back that was previously cut out, Murray would yell, "Oh, no you don't! Look at my part; you cut that out once." Now what would you do in a case like that? I roomed with Murray for a while, until I couldn't stand the ladders and red lanterns he and Quicksell would bring home.

RUSS MORGAN

There are just no two ways about it—the old Jean Goldkette band was the greatest band ever brought together! No band of today can compare with it. Why, when we played in the old Roseland in New York, we would give out with such tunes as *Tiger Rag* and *Riverboat Shuffle* on Saturday night and then play concerts in church the next Sunday morning!

I'll never forget our closing night in the Roseland. There were musicians from out of fifty-two different orchestras in the audience. After the last number was played, the people refused to leave the floor and the management had to call the cops in order to get the band off the bandstand.

When we arranged our music, we always gave Bix a newspaper to read for his part. He couldn't read music anyway and he would go off and smoke during rehearsal. And then, after we had played off the score, he would return to his chair, doodle a little, and then fill out his part with some of the most beautiful notes you ever heard. I can't recall ever hearing any clinkers or bad notes. Bix, you might say, was the cellophane wrapper around our basket of fruit.

Everybody loved Bix. The guy didn't have an enemy in the world. But he was *out of this world* most of the time. I remember one time three of us went out to play golf early in the morning and we came across Bix asleep under a tree. The night before he had decided to play some twilight golf and had lost all his golf balls. So he just laid down and went to sleep. We woke him up and he finished the course with us.

FRANK TRUMBAUER

When Bix and I played the Graystone Ballroom, and Whiteman was in the balcony, I was leading the band. Backstage, after a set, Bix said to me, "That is our next move. I hear the big boy is getting his kicks, at least so the boys tell me."

One of the things most people have forgotten was the next band we were in. Adrian Rollini set up a band of All-Stars for a cafe—I believe the name was New Yorker. Frank Fay was the main attraction; Patsy Kelly was a stooge; and Franklin was the piano player. Well, we all know where Fay is today; also Patsy Kelly; and Franklin. Anyone who has ever been around the Paramount lot can tell you who he is. Needless to say, most of Fay's stuff was too fast for the public, even when we played the Strand Theatre in New York. This band contained Joe Venuti, Eddie Lang, Morehouse, Rollini (leader), Frank Signorelli, Murray, Bix, and myself and others.

Bix and I joined the Goldkette band on the same day. Also the All-Stars and the Whiteman band on the same day. When we joined "Pops" Whiteman at Indianapolis he said, "Boys, I hope you will be happy. I pay more than any other leader because I want the best, and I have to keep the best happy. Go get a red coat and sit in the next show."

Bix went to the brass section with no idea of what was going on, and I sat in front with the saxes; and I was just as groggy as he was. A great many stars of the times were in that band: Bing Crosby, Jack Fulton, the Dorsey brothers, Challis, Grofe, and Strickfadden —you people should know the roster of the band at that time— 1927.

Whiteman, during the show out in front—rightfully proud— pointed to Bix; the spotlight hit him. "Take the next one," yelled Pops. Bix looked over to where he thought I should be and smiled and cut one that cooled all the boys. I took the next one, and we didn't get fired, at least.

152

PEE WEE RUSSELL

I first met Bix I'd say in the latter part of 1926. That was in the Arcadia Ballroom in St. Louis. Frankie Trumbauer had the band there and he had brought Bix down from Detroit where both had been working with Jean Goldkette. This was a summer job and we worked the season at the Arcadia. After we finished the season we went to Hudson Lake. You see, this was a Goldkette unit. We had the book and Jean was at the office from where he sent bands out. I had heard Bix on records before—those Gennett records with Tommy Dorsey and Paul Mertz and the other guys—and I had heard him in Chicago. There used to be a band at the Rendezvous that Charlie Straight had. Those were the speakeasy days and Bix used to come late and play with that band. It would sometimes go to seven or eight in the morning. But I had never worked with Bix until St. Louis.

Sonny Lee, who later played with Jimmy Dorsey, was playing trombone with this band at the Arcadia, and Sonny used to live at my home. I came home one afternoon and there was Bix with Sonny in the living room playing Bix records. It gave me a kick—a big thrill to have Bix in my home. Among musicians, even at that time, Bix had a reputation. Very few of us understood what he was doing; even in Chicago only a limited number did. In fact, it was the guys like Krupa, Goodman, Sullivan, Freeman, Dave Tough, and Tesch, naturally, that really appreciated him. The other musicians, like in St. Louis, understood what he was doing on a much smaller scale. And as for the management, he wasn't even featured with the band.

The thing about Bix's music is that he drove a band. He more or less made you play whether you wanted to or not. If you had any talent at all he made you play better. It had to do for one thing with the way he played lead. It had to do with his whole feeling for ensemble playing. He got a very large tone with a cornet. Records never quite reproduced his sound. Some come fairly close but the majority don't.

Then there were the men he usually recorded with. He had a hard time with some of those records. I don't mean that the men he recorded with weren't musicians. I mean he wasn't in bad company, but they didn't belong in a jazz band and Bix had been raised in jazz. So it was all due to them that a majority of the records didn't quite catch what Bix could do. But Bix's disposition wasn't one to complain. He wasn't able to say, I don't like this guy, let's give him the gate and get so and so. He was never a guy to complain about the company he was in. Like I say, they were good musicians and they could make it with Goldkette where they were supposed to do certain things. But they weren't for jazz.

Without a doubt, music was all Bix lived for. I remember we used to have a Sunday afternoon thing at the Arcadia Ballroom. Ordinarily the band would complain about the extra work, but Bix would really look forward to it. He said he liked to see the kids dance on Sunday afternoon. He liked to watch them do things like the Charleston, et cetera. He said he liked it because the kids had such a fine sense of rhythm. And, in their way, the kids knew what Bix was doing. They knew he was doing something different because he made them want to dance.

We used to have little head arrangements, written by some of the men in the band. They were good musicians in the band. We had a bass player, for example, from the St. Louis Symphony for a while. We would do little things once in a while so drastic or rather so musically advanced that when we had a damn nice thing going the manager would come up and say, "What in God's name are you doing?" I remember on *I Ain't Got Nobody* we had an arrangement with five-part harmony for the three saxes and the two brass. And the writing went down chromatically on a whole-tone scale basis. It was unheard of in those days. "For God's sake!" the manager would yell out—and naturally we couldn't explain it to him. That sort of music became more or less of a novelty with the people though. And they'd say at times, "Play those awful things!" Bix was instrumental in things like that. Most of the writing at that time was done by Bud Hassler. He was a tenor player.

As for Bix's compositions, this is the background of *In a Mist*. Tommy Satterfield, who was working with the Skouras brothers at that time, I don't know if anybody knows this story—Tommy had an office and did all the scoring for the large pit bands. Being an arranger, he took a liking to Bix and what he was doing and he took down *In a Mist* for him. You see, Bix played it for him on the piano. It was the first time that the song had ever gotten written down. I think Ferdie Grofe helped Bix with *Candlelights* later and some of the others.

Bix had a miraculous ear. As for classical music, Bix liked little things like some of those compositions of MacDowell and Debussy —very light things. Delius, for example. Then he made a big jump from that sort of thing to Stravinsky and stuff like that. There'd be certain things he would hear in some modern classical music, like whole tones, and he'd say, why not do it in a jazz band? What's the difference? Music doesn't have to be the sort of thing that's put in brackets? Then later it got to be like a fad and everybody did it, but they wouldn't know what the devil it was all about.

We would often order a score of a new classical work, study it, and then request it from the St. Louis Symphony. And we'd get ourselves a box for those concerts when they did a program we all liked. It would be Bix, Hassler, and I. We'd haunt them to play scores that we wanted to hear. Stuff like the *Firebird Suite*.

Rudolf Ganz was conducting at that time. We got to know him. We had the connection through Trumbauer's bass player. There was a soloist clarinet in the St. Louis Symphony, Tony Sarlie. I used to try to get him to teach me, and I studied with him a little. I wish I had studied more.

Anyway, we'd get those requests in. We weren't exactly like jitterbugs. It was on a different scale. I guess you could call us a different type of jitterbug. At least we were trying to learn something. And we wanted to hear these scores played well. You see, we knew what was supposed to happen because we had taken the scores with us and followed the work with them. Later on, Don Murray, Bix, and I used to go to concerts in New York. Murray was a very, very clever arranger. He and Bill Challis.

PAUL WHITEMAN

Bix Beiderbecke, bless his soul, was crazy about the modern composers—Schoenberg, Stravinsky, and Ravel—but he had no time for the classics. One evening I took him to the opera. It happened to be SIEGFRIED. When he heard the bird calls in the third act, with those intervals that are modern today, when he began to realize the leitmotifs of the opera were dressed, undressed, disguised, broken down, and built again in every conceivable fashion, he decided that old man Wagner wasn't so corny after all and that swing musicians didn't know such a helluva lot.

PEE WEE RUSSELL

I think Paul Whiteman will bear me out on this story. Anyway, we were all living in the Forty-forth Street Hotel in New York and there was a concert at Carnegie Hall. I forget what the program was. Whiteman had a box for it, and on that night his band was doing the Chesterfield Hour. Whiteman invited Bix and Murray, and Bix invited me and, at the last minute, Whiteman said he couldn't make it. So the three of us were quite despondent and we ordered some more whiskey. Whiteman called back and said, "Bix, I called the place and told them it was okay for you to use the box." So we stopped in to celebrate our new thing and we drank some more whiskey. We were feeling pretty good. We were dressed for the part and enjoying it immensely.

When we were in the box, I remember Don Murray was sitting right on the edge of his chair. There were lorgnettes all around us. We smelled awful bad, but we looked good. So Murray was sitting on the edge of his chair—remember we had all been celebrating—the chair slipped and Murray fell off. Bix and I were gentlemen enough to not notice anything. We were on our best behavior. Murray quietly got up and sat down again on the edge of his chair. At intermission, Don apologized profusely. After intermission, in the middle of the next movement, Murray became excited—the chair slipped again—and he fell off. Bix and I didn't say a word. Neither did Murray. We pulled apart the curtain that led into the box and we left. None of us saying a word to each other. We went into a bar and stood there drinking. You see, we were ashamed and were conscious of the other people at the concert. It was no fault of Murray either. But at that bar at first we still didn't say a word—we didn't want it to be any more embarrassing for him than it already was. Finally, Murray started berating himself so we told him not to.

JIMMY McPARTLAND

Bix didn't talk much, and there was certainly no conversation when a record was on. After it was over, we'd talk about how the chords resolved and, in Stravinsky or Holst, how different and interesting the harmony was.

He did like to talk about Stravinsky, Holst, Eastwood Lane, Debussy. I remember, about 1929 in New York, he took me to a Stravinsky concert at Carnegie Hall given by the New York Philharmonic. We used to talk about writing a jazz symphony. The plan was to give the soloists a terrific background with a good beat and then let them take off. Nothing ever came of the idea, but, as you know, he was very interested in writing. I wish he'd put down on paper more of what I know was in his head.

At sessions he'd often show me sections of what he'd written— things that later became *In a Mist, Flashes,* et cetera. He'd play a section and ask what I thought of it and then would play it another way to see if it could sound better.

In his own cornet playing, Bix could read well enough but was never a quick sight reader. He'd practice a part over by himself and then play it skillfully with the large band. Actually, he could create better than those guys could write.

As for why he never switched to trumpet, he used to say that the trumpet had a "pee-wee" tone. One thing about his jazz records is that I think it's remarkable he sounded as good as he did, carrying all that dead weight he had for accompaniment.

Bix contributed a lot to jazz. I think he helped bring it polish. He made it more musical. His technique was excellent, his intonation was great. So was his harmonic sense and his application of it on the cornet and piano. He was the first man in jazz I heard use the whole tone or augmented scale. I think almost any jazz musician— besides all the brass men—have one way or another been influenced by Bix.

One thing we talked about a lot was the freedom of jazz. People used to ask Bix to play a chorus just as he had recorded it.

He couldn't do it. "It's impossible," he told me once. "I don't feel the same way twice. That's one of the things I like about jazz, kid, I don't know what's going to happen next. Do you?"

LOUIS ARMSTRONG

And the first time I heard Bix, I said these words to myself: there's a man as serious about his music as I am . . . Bix did not let anything at all detract his mind from that cornet and his heart was with it all the time.

I shall never forget those nights in Chicago, when Bix was with the great Mr. P.W. and I was playing for Joe Glaser at the Sunset at Thirty-fifth and Calumet Streets. That's when Earl Fatha Hines, Tubby Hall, and Darnell Howard was in the band. It was Carroll Dickerson's band. That's when the Sunset was really jumping.

Bix came through with Mr. P. and they opened up at the Chicago Theatre. I shall never forget that incident because I caught the first show that morning . . . hmm ᵢ . . . I had to stay up all night to do it.

But Bix was in that band and this was the first time I witnessed him in such a large hellfired band as Mr. Whiteman's . . . I had been diggin' him in small combos and stuff. Now my man's gonna blow some of these big time arrangements, I thought . . . and sure enough he did . . . as soon as I bought my ticket, I made a beeline to my seat because the band was already on, and they were way down into their program, when the next number that came up, after the one they were playing when I came in, was a beautiful tune called *From Monday On* . . . My, my, what an arrangement that was.

They swung it all the way . . . and all of a sudden Bix stood up and took a solo . . . and I'm tellin' you, those pretty notes went all through me . . . then Mr. Whiteman went into the Overture by the name of *1812* . . . and he had those trumpets way up into the air, justa' blowing like mad, but good . . . and my man Bix was reading those dots and blowing beautifully . . . and just before the ending of the overture, they started to shooting cannons, ringing bells, sirens were howling like mad, and in fact everything was happening in that overture.

But you could still hear Bix . . . the reason why I said through all those different effects that were going on at the ending you could still hear Bix . . . well, you take a man with a pure tone like Bix's and no matter how loud the other fellows may be blowing, that pure cornet or trumpet tone will cut through it all . . . all due respect to the men.

After the show, I went directly around backstage to see Bix, and say hello to a few of the other musicians I knew personally. After a long chat and when they went on the stage for their next show, I cut out and went straight to a music store and bought *From Monday On* . . . and put it with the rest of my collectors' items of his.

The recordings from *Singing the Blues* on down to *In a Mist* . . . they all collectors' items. . . .

When Bix would finish up at the Chicago Theatre at night, he would haul it out to the Sunset where I was playing and stay right there with us until the last show was over and the customers would go home.

Then we would lock the doors. Now you talking about jam sessions. . . . huh. . . . those were the things . . . with everyone feeling each other's note or chord, et cetera . . . and blend with each other instead of trying to cut each other . . . nay, nay, we did not even think of such a mess . . . we tried to see how good we could make music sound which was an inspiration within itself.

After a while we would sort of rest up and Bix would get on the piano and play some of the sweetest things . . . real touching . . . that's when he was getting ready to record his immortal *In a Mist* . ... . the tune is still fresh today, as it was then . . . you couldn't find a musician nowheres in the whole world that doesn't still love Bix's *In a Mist*.

ARMAND HUG

I first met Bix in the fall of 1928. He had already left Frank Trumbauer and Jean Goldkette and had joined Paul Whiteman's orchestra on a tour of the United States. When the Whiteman orchestra came to New Orleans, Monk Hazel, Eddie Miller, and I went backstage to chat with Bix during the intermission. I can remember Whiteman passing while we were talking with Bix and Monk said, "Listen, Paul, if you don't let Bix play more horn we're going to tear this place down." Whiteman smiled and very obligingly replied, "Don't worry, I'll let him take over when we go back on." During the rest of the program we heard wonderful jazz.

At that time, Bix's piano composition *In a Mist* had not yet been published and I had been trying to learn it from the records. I'd been having trouble with it and I asked Bix to show me how it went. Bix sat down next to me at the piano and began playing the parts with which I'd been having trouble. I shall remember that piano lesson as long as I live.

Another tribute to his genius came one evening when Bix sat in with King Oliver's Band at the Plantation Club. Lynn Harrell, of Dallas, Texas, who was present that evening says that tears rolled down Oliver's face and Oliver said that Bix was the greatest he had ever heard. Louis Armstrong, who was playing second trumpet with Oliver at the time, was also high in his praises of the boy from Davenport.

JIMMY McPARTLAND

Sometime before I began to travel with Ben Pollack, Bix had already joined Paul Whiteman. They were on a tour and were heading for Chicago. I got a call at eight one morning from Bix. He'd left his tuxedo at the cleaners in the last town, and he asked if he could borrow mine. Then and always he could have anything I had.

All during the date at the theater, a troupe of us gathered between shows and at night at the Three Deuces and jammed. Bing Crosby would play the cymbals or the drums if there were no drummer. Bix always preferred to play piano at a session, and this time he asked me to play his new Bach cornet, the best horn he'd ever had.

I fell in love with it, and Bix asked, "Would you like to have a horn like this?" He took me over to the Dixie Music House after the next show, put down one hundred dollars and said, "That's all the money I have with me. But I guess you can scrape up the other fifty. You can give it back to me sometime."

I'll never forget that week. We played almost all the time he wasn't on stage. I never did see the tux again. Do you think I cared? I still have that horn, by the way. Bix warmed it up at the theater for a few shows, then I used it for some time. Now my four-year-old grandson, Dougie Kassel, has it.

People have asked me often what Bix was like as a person. Well, he was very reticent. His main interest in life was music, period. It seemed as if he just existed outside of that.

I think one of the reasons he drank so much was that he was a perfectionist and wanted to do more with music than any man possibly could. The frustration that resulted was a big factor, I think.

PEE WEE RUSSELL

As I said, Bix was not one to complain about the company he was in. He was a very gentle man. He had a very, very good sense of humor. For him there was nothing better than a good laugh. He was a perfectionist for himself in music though I don't say he became despondent if he ever missed a note, but he'd swear like anybody does when he missed one.

MEZZ MEZZROW

Late in '27 sometime, Bix suddenly fell into town. He was playing at the Chicago Theatre with Paul Whiteman's orchestra, and, soon as we got the news, Eddie Condon and I shot over to knock him some skin. He came backstage with Bing Crosby (Bing was singing in Whiteman's trio, The Rhythm Boys, with Harry Barris and Al Rinker). The first thing he said when he dug us was, "Come on, let's go get a drink." Down through the Loop he led us, along State Street, until just off of Lake Street we met up with a blackened-up old store that looked like it had been condemned before the Chicago fire. A peephole slid open, an eye appeared in the hole and gunned Bix; then the door swung open like a switch-blade. I guess the mug of that bottle baby was known to every peephole attendant in the Western Hemisphere.

JIMMY McPARTLAND

My last period of association with Bix was in New York. The Pollack band hadn't been working for almost two months. Eight of us, including the Goodman brothers, were in one hotel room, and we were really scuffling for food. Then at a cocktail party on Park Avenue I ran into Bix who'd just come back into town with the Whiteman band. I told him that this was pretty ironic. Here I could get all the drinks I wanted for free but didn't have enough money for a sandwich.

Bix took me into a corner and pulled out two hundred dollars. I told him ten was enough but he said, "Don't worry about it, kid. You'll be making money soon. Then when you see your way clear, you can pay it back." I did, in about eight months, after I'd been working for some time in the pit for Sons of Guns.

In the last months of his life, I'd see Bix quite often at a little speakeasy on Fifty-third Street called Plunkett's. Most of the musicians hung out there. I'd see him, too, backstage whenever Whiteman played town. We'd jam in the dressing room with Bing always on the cymbals or a snare drum.

At Plunkett's we'd sit and talk. Bix was ill, looked bad, all swollen up. He drank, didn't eat, stayed up late, got very depressed. Whiteman had sent him home to Davenport for a while, but it didn't seem to help.

I remember one night he had a very bad cold, and he was broke besides. I told him to go home and stay there until he got over the cold and lent him some money. "Thanks, kid," he said, "I'll be all right. I've got a job at Princeton in a couple of days." That was the last I saw of Bix. Naturally, I cried when he died. I loved him both as a person and as a musician.

PEE WEE RUSSELL

As for what caused Bix to destroy himself, well, in that era, naturally where he started, around Indiana, there was that thing with the hip bottle and the gin—the 'twenties and all that stuff. Later, when he had acquired a name, he could get a bottle of whiskey any time of day or night. Now Bix enjoyed a drink but he was human too. Everybody likes privacy. Privacy enough to sleep and eat. But it was impossible for him to get any. There were always people in his room. They would knock on the door even at six A.M., and it was impossible for him because of the kind of person he was to insult anybody, to say get out of here.

I remember how, at one hotel, he used to leave word that he wasn't in. So some fellows would check into the hotel, take a room on the floor below Bix's room; then they'd come up and rap and pound on the door and you'd have to answer. He even had a piano in the room, and, when he had a spare moment, he'd try to get a composition started, but with all those people always hanging around he didn't have a chance. In a sense, Bix was killed by his friends. But I think the term is being used loosely. Because they weren't his friends. They were the kind of people who liked to be able to say, "Last night I was up at Bix's and oh, was he drunk. Gee, you should have seen his room!" You know that type of people. They wanted to say they were there. I don't think I have to say any more about that type of people. And Bix couldn't say no. He couldn't say no to anybody.

I remember one Victor date we did. Bix was working in the Whiteman band at the time. He had hired me for the date but rather than hurt anybody's feelings he also hired Jimmy Dorsey and Benny Goodman and Tommy Dorsey and everybody.

Every time somebody would walk into the door at Plunkett's, the bar we hung out at, Bix would say, "Gee, what am I going to do?" So he'd go up to the guy and hire him for the date. He didn't want to hurt anybody's feelings. So he went way over his budget and we had to scrape cab fare to get back from the date.

Bix came from a good home life. He had the best. His people were very well-to-do. Anything more I could tell you about Bix is all history anyway and has been written about.

HOAGY CARMICHAEL

Bix was sick. Whiteman had sent him home and he had come back again to New York, but he hadn't rejoined Whiteman's band and that had hurt him. He was drinking pretty hard, and staying to himself in his hotel room for days at a time. His only recreations were moving pictures such as WINGS and HELL'S

ANGELS. He was crazy about flying; occasionally he would visit the city morgue.

Jazz was dying and the man who was its epitome was dying, too. He worked occasionally on his piano compositions. *Flashes, Candlelights, In the Dark.* Whiteman's arranger, Bill Challis, came at times to get them on paper. Thanks to Bill, these beautiful things were preserved. The darkness was closing in on Bix and he didn't seem to care.

I went by Bix's room one day. I met a maid in the hall. "What's the matter with that fellow, anyway?" she asked. "Who is he? He hasn't been out of his room for three days."

Tell the maid. Who is he?

I looked at the maid's blank face. "Just a guy," I said. I went on to his room.

"Hi, Hoagy." Bix was lying on the bed. He looked bad, there was something missing, as if part of him were already "in the dark."

"Hi, Bix." I sat down. I was uneasy. "How's it goin', fellow?"

Bix smiled wanly. "What are *you* doing?"

"Been listening to the publisher's theme song: '*It's Not Commercial.*' "

Bix looked away and then I heard his voice. "Don't worry, boy. You're . . . ah, hell. . . ."

"Get out your horn. Let's doodle a little."

He shook his head. "Ran into a girl the other day," Bix said, "she's going to fix me up in a flat out in Sunnyside."

"Swell. Get out of this dump and you'll feel better. You might eat something."

He looked at me and the veil went from his eyes for a moment. "How's for bringing her over some night?"

"Sure, any time," I said.

And Bix brought the girl and came to my apartment one night. We didn't have a drink, we didn't talk music, and it soon became apparent that this girl had no idea who Bix was. And then the terrible thought struck me—I didn't know either.

164

PART III

"Travelin' Light"

11

*. . . to Harlem, which really jumped—on through
the 'twenties to the depression years. Armstrong came
to town, and everybody knew the great pianists like
James P. Johnson and Willie "The Lion" Smith, and
bands like Charlie Johnson's, Cecil Scott's, Sam
Wooding's, and the Cotton Pickers. King Oliver and
Jelly Roll had had their day, and among those coming up were Chick Webb, at the Savoy, and Billie
Holiday, singing those depression blues.*

MEZZ MEZZROW

Just on Seventh Avenue alone, going north from 131st Street,
the line-up was: a barbershop, a drugstore, the Performers and
Entertainers Club and under it the dicty Connie's Inn, then the
Lafayette Theatre, then a candy store, the Hoofers' Club down
in the basement, and finally, Big John's famous ginmill. Around
on 132nd Street were Tabb's Restaurant, and next to it the
Rhythm Club, where you could call any hour of the day and
night and hire a musician. And back on 131st Street, soon as you
turned into it, you found a fine rib joint called the Barbecue, the
entrance to a gang of upstairs halls where top bands like Armstrong's and Count Basie's and Jimmy Lunceford's and Cab Calloway's and Erskine Hawkins' used to rehearse, and a speakeasy
and night club called the Bandbox. Most important of all, there

was an areaway running all around the corner building there, a wide alley with entrances from both Seventh Avenue and 131st Street. This alley led to the Lafayette's backstage entrance and also to a special bar in the rear of the Bandbox, and here it was that most of our social life was spent. Louis Armstrong was heading the Connie's Inn show (it was HOT CHOCOLATES, written by Fats Waller and Andy Razaf and staged by Leonard Harper, and it was doubling at the Hudson Theater down on Forty-sixth Street) and all the cats from the show would come out in the alley and mingle with the other great performers of Harlem who were appearing at the Lafayette, and they would be joined by visitors from all over, including a lot of white musicians.

DUKE ELLINGTON

There wasn't near enough work for everybody that could blow horns, and what musicians didn't have steady jobs would spend their days standing out on the street gabbing, always arguing about the respective merits of everybody else. The Rhythm Club was the great hangout and sure enough if you landed a gig and wanted to hire some guys to work it with you, you'd walk down that way and find enough good guys to work another three jobs.

And at nights everybody used to carry their horns round with them and wherever there was a piano you'd find hornblowers sitting in and jamming. There'd be maybe a piano player, and a drummer, and about six different cornet players; everybody trying to outblow everybody else. And whoever owned the place would stand drinks all night long. It was O.K. by him, he got free music that way.

It was still too early for the fellows to get real big-time about money, and all the musicians who weren't working steady played gigs round town and didn't bother about reputation. A lot of the guys liked to play so much that, in spite of being on a regular job, they'd still hire out to work matinees, or breakfast dances. The ginmills were wide open at that time, and there weren't restrictive regulations about closing hours. Nobody went to bed at nights, and round three and four in the mornings you'd find everyone making the rounds bringing their horns with them.

The earliest bands I can remember (about 1923) were those of Fess Williams, Wilbur Sweatman, Jack Hatton the trumpet-player, and the famous trumpeter, Johnny Dunn. Mamie Smith had a wonderful band working at the Garden of Joy, which was built on top of a rock which is now 140th and Seventh Avenue. Bubber Miley was playing trumpet; Sidney Bechet, soprano; Earl Frazier, piano; and Cecil McCoy, clarinet. There were many colorful hot spots scattered about Harlem, and no curfew to dampen the spirits or curtail early morning activities. Small's Paradise was always jammed and there was a band at Conners where Bubber Miley sometimes worked. Count Basie was playing piano in a band at Leroy's and Harry Smith was playing trumpet with him.

Tricky Sam was working at The Bucket of Blood, while the Green Cat was another popular spot. There weren't many organized bands around New York but there were any number of fine musicians working in and out of the dance schools and cabarets. There were a dozen great piano players who entertained nightly at parlor socials. The king was James P. Johnson. At that time Fats Waller was just a big kid beginning to find his way around. Then there was Basie, and Earl Frazier, and Seminole, who was part Indian, and whose left hand was something to listen to. And there was Willie Smith, "The Lion."

WILLIE "THE LION" SMITH
Jimmie (James P. Johnson) gave me the title because of my spunk and enterprise. "The Lion" named him "The Brute." Later we gave Fats Waller the name "Filthy." The three of us, "The Lion," "The Brute," and "Filthy," plus a guy called "Lippy," used to run all over town playing piano.

DUKE ELLINGTON
Small's was the place to go, the one spot where everybody'd drop in. And a lot of musicians from downtown too. Jack Teagarden used to bring along his horn, and Benny and Harry Goodman, Ray Bauduc, and a gang of others. Then on Sundays, Small used to hire a guest band, the best he could get, and there'd be a regu-

lar jamboree. Matinees on Sunday were something too. Elmer Snowden did the hiring for a while, and all kinds of musicians worked that job, Johnny Hodges, and guys from Chick's band, and a lot of others. There was always plenty of whiskey around those places, and the music would jump and everything else besides.

LOUIS ARMSTRONG

My manager and agent sent for me to come to New York alone, to join that big show which was in rehearsal at that time called GREAT DAY. Instead of my going alone, I took the whole Carroll Dickerson band with me. We were so attached, we just wouldn't part from each other. I borrowed twenty dollars apiece for every man in the band and myself. We had about four old dilapidated cars among us. We just piled in them and went on to New York. On our way we went sightseeing, stopping in a lot of towns where they had been listening to us over the radio from the Savoy in Chicago. They treated us royally. Our money was counterfeit.

We arrived in Buffalo, New York, and went forty miles out of the way to dig Niagara Falls. Half of the cars didn't reach the "Apple" (New York). They burned out before they reached halfway there. Of course, my agent bawled me out, but I told him, "Just the same, my boys are here in New York, so find something for us to do." He did. We opened at Connie's Inn and stayed there six months. All the musicians came up and gave me a very beautiful wrist watch. Every musician from downtown was there that night. What a memory of those fine days.

ZUTTY SINGLETON

When Louis was fixin' to make his next trip to New York (the first one on his own) Lil Armstrong loaned everybody in the band twenty dollars and off we went—without a job set or anything. I'll never forget that trip across the country in Louis' Hupmobile. I did most of the driving 'cause Louis spent most of the time sleeping in the back seat. And every big town we'd come to, we'd hear Louis' records being played on loudspeakers and stuff. Louis was surprised—he didn't know he was so popular. If we'd known that, we could have had an agent line us up one-nighters all the way to New York.

We got to New York on Friday and by Sunday we'd lined up a job for that afternoon. Duke Ellington was playing the Audubon Theatre in the Bronx, but he couldn't make the first show because he had something else to do. So our band played it.

The pit band looked pretty surprised when the curtain went up and there we were on stage. But then Louis played the *St. Louis Blues* and I saw something I'll never forget as long as I live. When he finished, even the band in the pit stood up and applauded for him. It was a wonderful, wonderful reception.

We played the Savoy after that, then Connie's Inn. Louis got an offer then to play downtown and decided to break up the band. I wanted to go with him, but he told me he was breakin' up the band. "Pops," he said, "you got a steady job, you better stay here."

CECIL SCOTT

My band went into the Capitol Palace early 1926. This was a highly thought of cabaret on Lenox between 139th and 140th, an immense hall. The Capitol was a strong rival of the famous Cotton Club. But the Cotton Club closed at three or four in the morning, while we played till dawn and even past sometimes to seven A.M.

At the Capitol Palace there were no restrictions on the hours we might play. The patrons had to purchase a bottle of sparkling water at about a dollar a bottle plus a bucket of ice. Everyone carried their own liquor in a hip flask for these were the days of prohibition and bathtub gin.

When the other clubs closed, one by one their band members and patrons would drift into our spot, and musicians from such places as the Cotton Club, Club Alabam, Roseland, Paradise Inn, used to vie for the chance to sit in with us. We usually had a waiting line holding their horns against one far wall waiting turns. Fellows like Johnny Hodges, members of Fletch Henderson's gang, Fats Waller, Earl Hines, and fellows from Charlie Johnson's band, Luis Russell's band—all these and many others. They were eager to blow since on their regular job they were restricted from righteous playing because they would have to play stock arrangements for floor shows. "Cutting contests" developed. Sidney de Paris and Rex Stewart kept trying to top one another night after night on tunes such as *Tiger Rag, Nobody's Sweetheart,* or *China Boy.* Most mornings we would jam from four on to six or seven. We might be dead tired physically but hopped up eager to play more because we were fired with the surge of the beat.

Often we would pile out of the club about dawn, shouting and too excited to go to bed. There was an iron fence which divided Lenox Avenue at 135th Street and we would line up along it; it became a regular musicians' hangout. We would cluster as thick as thieves discussing music and gossiping about fellow players until maybe noon. Then home for an afternoon's sleep and that evening we'd begin the same routine. Music was our entire world. Early morning jamming eased the tiredness of the hard work of the evening previous.

LLOYD SCOTT

While at the Savoy we were at the peak. On one evening there in 1928 we won an extraordinary battle of music against eight bands, including those of Fletcher Henderson and Charlie Johnson, at what they termed a "South Sea Island Ball." Another contest was called the "Arabian Nights Ball"; that was in the following year, also at the Savoy. We were placed second to Ellington. These battles were fiercely contested affairs for much prestige was at stake. Bands would have extensive preparation ahead of time for the largest of these battles and would fire their best in the way of arrangements at one another. One particularly brutal one was a victory over three bands—Fess Williams, Cab Calloway, and Fletcher Henderson. Our winning was clear cut but only after an all-night struggle which ended at seven o'clock Sunday morning.

172

GENE SEDRIC

In 1925 I played with Sam Wooding's band at the Club Alabam on Broadway. It was one of the hottest clubs in New York at the time. Among the musicians that were in it were Garvin Bushell and Tommy Ladnier. He had come from Chicago. Louis Armstrong had recommended him to the band because we were going to Europe and we wanted a good hot man. Before that, he had taken Louis' place with King Oliver when Louis had come to New York to join Fletcher Henderson. Sam Wooding's band also had Herb Fleming, Jerry Blake (alto), and Doc Cheatham.

I rate Tommy Ladnier among the great musicians. He played the greatest blues you'd ever want to hear.

Tommy had a wonderful sense of humor but he got into a little matrimonial trouble and started drinking heavy. He used to try to solve world problems, get juiced, and just let himself go.

MUGGSY SPANIER

I first met Tommy (Ladnier) in 1921, when I was playing in back rooms along North Clark Street in Chicago. Tommy was playing in some hole-in-the-wall out on Thirty-ninth and State. Whenever I wasn't working a night I was always out listening to Tommy, and, on his nights off, I generally managed to get him to come to whatever joint I was playing at. I was in seventh heaven when he sat down to play beside me!

If you're not familiar with his work, get hold of Noble Sissle's old Brunswick records like *Basement Blues* (Tommy's chorus is right after Sidney Bechet's) or the Rosetta Crawford records on Decca, or those old New Orleans Feetwarmers sides.

Take it from me, when old Gabe blows that horn one of these days, he'll probably use the fingering that Tommy Ladnier taught him.

JOE TURNER

I arrived in New York City, which is a three hours' train ride from Baltimore, with only a dollar twenty-five in my pocket and a suitcase made of cardboard. (I had told my mother I had a job in New York, which explained my reason for not taking more money with me. But in reality I had no job; I was just trying to make my luck in the Big City.)

I asked the first person I met where I could find the colored people in town. I was told to take the L-train to 130th Street in Harlem. There I asked where the musicians were hangin' out. They told me that it was a place called the Comedy Club.

Going there, I had a drink, set my bag down, and noticed that anyone who wished could go to the piano and play. Realizing that none of the pianists who had performed before me had done anything special, I walked over to the piano and started to play. After a warm-up number, I went into the *Harlem Strut*, and then I went to the climax with *The Carolina Shout*.

When I had finished, people swarmed around me and wanted to know where I came from. After I told them, someone in the crowd reminded me that the composer of the last two numbers I had played was in the room—James P. Johnson! Of course, you can imagine how I felt! I must have impressed him, however, since he left his table, came up to the piano, and played the same two numbers as nobody in the world could!

After it was over, someone asked me if I wanted a job, and, of course, I said, "Yes!" Then I asked, "When do I start?" To which he replied, "Right now, just come with me."

I went with him to Baron Wilkins Club (most famous piano club in Harlem, all the best pianists having played there at one time or another) where I met for the first time, and played with, Hilton Jefferson, the great alto man.

When the boss told me he could pay me only thirty a week, I almost fainted, because until then I had never made more than twelve dollars a week.

I worked there successfully a few months, then I joined the red-hot band of trumpeter June Clark, who was a carbon copy of Louis Armstrong. June and Jimmy Harrison were known as the greatest brass team of that (wonderful) period. "Jazz" Carson (a fine drummer) completed our quartet.

During these first few months in New York, I visited Clarence Williams' office once, where I met what I considered a truly great pianist, Eddie "Blind" Steele, who played a very full piano.

This was also the time when we had the world's most exciting piano contests, night after night, with the following pianists regularly present—James P. Johnson, Willie "The Lion" Smith, Thomas "Fats" Waller, and Joe Turner. Very rarely did other pianists dare to play. Of course, there were times when Stephen "The Beetle" Henderson was getting into the contest, and he demanded the greatest respect for his perfect left hand. And there would be two others who would try their luck occasionally in the contests—"Corky" Williams and, especially, Willie Gant. . . .

After my first few months in New York, I had a tour out West as accompanist to Adelaide Hall, or rather, as one of a piano-duo accompaniment, for I went with my good friend, the late Alex Hill. However, before long we had trouble with Alex, and so Francis Carter, also a good pianist, joined us.

Benny Carter told me that when I reached Toledo I shouldn't play any piano because there was a blind boy there, named Art Tatum, and I would not be able to touch him. When the Adelaide Hall troupe finally got to Toledo, I asked where Tatum could be found, and I was given the address of a buffet flat where he appeared every night at two o'clock sharp, after his work.

After finishing at the theater at midnight, I went there and waited for Art to come. In the meantime I played some good stuff on the piano there, and two girls sitting near the piano started an argument over my playing in comparison with Art's. One girl said, "He'll wash Art away," while the other was insisting, "Just wait until Art gets here and you'll see how he will cut this boy."

Art Tatum arrived at two o'clock sharp. I got up from the piano and greeted him. He asked me if I was the Joe Turner who had made a reputation with a fine arrangement of *Liza*. I said it was me and begged him to play piano for me. After he had refused to play before hearing me (and, of course, with Art I lost the argument), I played first *Dinah* for warmin' up and then my *Liza*.

When I had finished, Art Tatum said, "Pretty good." I was offended because everywhere else I played *Liza* it was considered sensational, and there was Art Tatum saying "Pretty good." After that Art sat down and played *Three Little Words*. Three thousand words would have been an understatement! I had never heard so much piano in my life.

We became the greatest of friends after that. Art came to my home the next morning and, even before I left my bed, I heard him in the parlor play my arrangement of *Liza*, note for note, after hearing it only once the night before.

I want to mention some more pianists who really gave me solid kicks in my life—Lucky Roberts; Fats Waller, who was the best friend I ever had; Willie "The Lion" Smith, the most unpredictable pianist of all times, because if Tatum played, if Fats played, if James P. played, if anyone in Harlem played, we could pretty well guess what their feature number would be. But, when "The Lion" roared, you never knew what was coming.

WILLIE "THE LION" SMITH

I wanted to become a rabbi. I got as far as becoming a cantor. Because of my devotion to Judaism, I was called "The Lion of Judea," later abbreviated to "The Lion."

ETHEL WATERS

I was learning a lot in Harlem about music and the men up there who played it best. All the licks you hear, now as then, originated with musicians like James P. Johnson. And I mean *all* of the hot licks that ever came out of Fats Waller and the rest of the hot piano boys. They are just faithful followers and protégés of that great man, Jimmy Johnson.

Men like him, Willie "The Lion" Smith, and Charlie Johnson could make you sing until your tonsils fell out. Because you wanted to sing. They stirred you into joy and wild ecstasy. They could make you cry. And you'd do anything and work until you dropped for such musicians.

WILLIE "THE LION" SMITH

During the first war, I was one of the few to volunteer to go to the front and fire a French seventy-five—and of those who did, few returned. I stayed at the front for fifty-one days without relief. I was known from that time on as Sergeant William H. Smith, "The Lion."

CHARLIE GAINES

In 1920 I went to work at a wild spot called the Garden of Joy up at 140th and Seventh Avenue in Harlem. That club was way up on a high hill which was really a mountain of rock. Coleman Hawkins played tenor there, and we had a fast pianist named Ginger Young. That was about the time Sam Wooding had one of the first organized bands in Harlem. Fats Waller played organ at movie houses, and Don Redman had just come to New York with Billy Paige's outfit. It was then I first began to record with Clarence Williams.

I don't recall my first record or many of the titles of others that followed. Guess this was because one recorded with Williams on a routine, mass-production basis. He never engaged a man for specific dates. He had a stable of musicians on a weekly payroll. You might be called for several dates every day or maybe none for a week, but you received a standard sum of about eighty-five dollars each week. Williams had only one day to pay, and if you were out of town it accrued on the next week's salary. We liked that arrangement, but it created a lack of interest in the work you recorded as to recalling outstanding details. But that is how Clarence did business. He lived up on 137th Street in Harlem. He had an office elsewhere but did most of the operating of it out of the top of his hat and his black memobook.

I know we recorded for every label possible, it seemed. Sometimes as a band playing instrumentally and also back of scores of blues singers. On most sides I was on, clarinet was played by Bob Elliott, Charlie Irvis was trombone, and a West Virginia boy played washboard—can't recall his name—but Clarence seldom played piano. I know we recorded with Bessie Smith at one point. I had worked with her in Atlantic City with Taylor's band prior to that.

FRANK WALKER

I'll never forget one of the first electrical recording sessions we ever had at Columbia, back in 1926, I believe. It was quite a procedure. We built an enormous tent in the studio on the theory that the conical shape would keep the sound in. There was only one light hanging from the ceiling from a long cord, and inside of the tent was Bessie Smith, Fletcher Henderson at a piano, Don Redman, and myself. Anyway, there were four or five people and a piano in that thing. Then the wire broke. Down came the sides of that tent and, I'm telling you, it was the wildest scramble you ever saw.

To go back a little before that, I can remember when Columbia began to get interested in going into the rhythm and blues field (we called them "race" records, then). I'd hear about some singer or band, or perhaps see somebody good on one of my trips through the South or Midwest and then we'd either send for them or else record them in their own towns. Clarence Williams worked for me then.

In those days, we would carry our equipment with us and set up in almost any place we could find. In New Orleans I remember sessions on the second floor of some shaky old building. Why, the musicians would stomp their feet as they played and the walls and floor would be shaking and the microphones would rock. So we'd take out the cardboard pads from the record boxes and spread them on the floor. When that didn't work, we'd have the musicians take off their shoes. Now, there would always be some that didn't have stockings, and so there they would be a band playing the wildest kind of natural jazz in their bare and stockinged feet.

I've always said that when musicians began to wear shoes, it was no longer the original jazz.

New Orleans was what I like to call "The University of Jazz." Oh, lots of musicians and bands came from places like Kansas City and Chicago, but there was something—a certain combination of hot weather, dumps, and dives and people—that only New Orleans could provide.

There was one time I was driving out in the country and stopped at a place, a shed-like affair with a place to park your car, called the Halfway House. I dropped in for a cold drink or something to eat. The band that played there had five musicians, and I don't believe that any one of them could read a note of music. Well, I sat there and listened and listened and listened. They didn't seem to know much of anything, but finally I asked them to play a favorite of mine, a waltz called *Let Me Call You Sweetheart*. They knew that one all right. They knew it just well enough to tear it apart. A few weeks later I recorded that band playing *Let Me Call You Sweetheart*, and, believe me, it wasn't in three-quarter time either! This was the band that became the nucleus of the New Orleans Rhythm Kings.

I prefer to think that there are two kinds of jazz—"natural jazz" and "musical jazz." The natural kind is what came out of New Orleans and folk music. "Musical jazz" is what happened to it when the trained musicians got hold of it. I had my share of recording both kinds—from Louis Armstrong's first record, Bessie and Clara Smith, Fletcher Henderson, Benny Goodman, Bing Crosby, Glenn Miller—right up to George Shearing.

CLARENCE WILLIAMS

Ever since Frank Walker hired me to work for him, I'd guess that I've been on or else made about five thousand records. There was one time I figured I was losin' money being under contract to Okeh, and so I recorded under lots of different names, the Blue Five, Lazy Levee Loungers, the Blue Four, Washboard Footwarmers, Jazz Kings, and many others. And they were for companies like Grey Gull, QRS, Pathe, Edison, Columbia, Gennett, Paramount, and all those other labels they had then.

ED ALLEN

When we recorded with Clarence Williams, he would pick most of the tunes, those that the record company didn't pick. Of course, he picked a lot of his own numbers, but we would use anybody else's tunes, too. The companies liked to feature mostly blues at that time—blues from all over the country. They weren't so much on popular numbers as they are today. We made records for several people, and sometimes the boys would record under different names for different companies. At one time Clarence made records for every company in New York; on one record it would be "Clarence Williams Washboard Beaters," and on another simply "The Barrelhouse Five."

A bunch of records we made, we used Willie "The Lion"

Smith or James P. Johnson on piano and Clarence would sing and be the director. These records, before the time that radio became really popular, they sold very well; mostly they used to send them down South. Nowadays, with the jukeboxes so popular, it's very tough on musicians—you make one record and they play it forever and you don't get anything out of it. Right now, there are a couple of dance halls on Broadway that are using jukeboxes and, of course, that means less jobs.

MARY LOU WILLIAMS

I was glad of the chance to meet Clarence Williams and Jelly Roll Morton. I had admired Williams' compositions for some time, and I found him a kindly man who seemed to like me and who was reassuring about the things I played him. I have never seen Clarence again, though he lives in New York to this day.

Mr. Jelly Lord was a more frightening proposition. He was considered a big deal then, and he had me scared. When the guys dragged me into his office downtown, we were surprised to see him playing duets with an ofay piccolo player.

At a convenient break, they introduced me and told Jelly they would like for him to hear me. Indicating that I should park my hips on the stool, Jelly gave over the piano and I got started on my favorite Morton piece, *The Pearls*. Almost immediately I was stopped and reprimanded, told the right way to phrase it. I played it the way Jelly told me, and when I had it to his satisfaction, I slipped in one of my own tunes. This made no difference. I was soon stopped and told: "Now that passage should be phrased like this."

Jelly Roll had a mouthful of diamonds and spoke with a stammer when he got excited. He was what we call a "big mouth," and the sound of his voice had me shaking in my boots. Any minute I was expecting to get off the floor because I had played his *Pearls* wrong.

That's how they trained you in those days (half those chorus girls had black eyes!), and Morton had the reputation of being a demanding taskmaster.

Musicians—they really have it easy now!

JELLY ROLL MORTON

Not until 1926 did they get a faint idea of real jazz, when I decided to live in New York. In spite of the fact that there were a few great dispensers, as Sidney Bechet, clarinet, William Brand, bass, New York's idea of jazz was taken from the dictionary's definition—loud, blary, noise, discordant tones, et cetera, which really doesn't spell jazz music. Music is music. Regardless of type, it is supposed to be soothing, not unbearable—which was a specialty with most of them. It is great to have ability from extreme to extreme, but it is terrible to have this kind of ability without the correct knowledge of how to use it. Very often you could hear the New York (supposed-to-be) *jazz* bands, have twelve-fifteen men; they would blaze away with all the volume they had. Sometimes customers would have to hold their ears to protect their eardrums from a forced collision with their brains. Later, in the same tune, without notification, you could hear only drums and trumpet. Piano and guitar would be going but not heard. The others would be holding their instruments leisurely, talking, smoking reefers, chatting scandals, et cetera.

Musicians of all nationalities watched the way I played; then soon I could hear my material everywhere I trod, but in an incorrect way, using figures behind a conglomeration of variations sometimes discordant, instead of hot-swing melodies.

OMER SIMEON

Those people at Victor treated Jelly like he was somebody special, which he was, being the best in the country at the time in his style, and they paid us boys a good deal over scale to work with him. See, Jelly Roll was mighty particular about his music and if the musicians couldn't play real New Orleans, he'd get somebody else.

I'll tell you how he was in rehearsing a band. He was exact with us. Very jolly, very full of life all the time, but serious. We used to spend maybe three hours rehearsing four sides and in that time he'd give us the effects he wanted, like the background behind a solo—he would run that over on the piano with one finger and the guys would get together and harmonize it.

The solos—they were ad lib. We played according to how we felt. Of course, Jelly had his ideas and sometimes we'd listen to them, and sometimes together with our own, we'd make something better. For me, I'd do whatever he wanted. In other words I just cooperated with him, where a lot of the fellows wouldn't. It was my first big break.

I always called him the Dizzy Dean of music, he was so belligerent and braggadocio. He was a real fanatic over the music. He wanted real New Orleans style and he wanted it played just so. So the boys figured him for a radical. Different arguments came up. And, by him being one of the pioneers of jazz, he'd come right back at them when they disagreed with him. Well, they felt they was as big as he was—those that had been in music any length of time—and so, naturally, he had a hard time keeping the same personnel.

It was really a show when Jelly got in an argument. We used to all be standing around the Famous Corner at 131st and Seventh and Jelly would be telling what a great composer he was. So Chick Webb would kid him about his "old-fashioned" music just to get Jelly started. I'll never forget Jelly's favorite expression, "I'm the master," he'd say. "I'm the master." And he would tell all the big musicians, "Listen, fellow, anything you play on your horn, you're playing *Jelly Roll*."

Lots of those boys would get hot at that. But, one thing I always noticed about Jelly, he would back up everything he *said* by what he could *do*.

JELLY ROLL MORTON

I have been robbed of three million dollars all told. Everyone today is playing my stuff and I don't even get credit. Kansas City style, Chicago style, New Orleans style—hell, they're all Jelly Roll style. I am a busy man now and have to spend all my time dealing with attorneys, but I am not too busy to get around and hear jazz that I myself introduced twenty-five years ago, before most of the kids was even born. All this jazz I hear today is my own stuff, and, if I had been paid rightfully for my work, I would now have three million dollars more than I have now.

LOUIS METCALF

Jelly resented the agencies beatin' bands out of money and wouldn't give in. And because he wouldn't give in, he was pushed aside. In those days if you had a song you wanted played or recorded, Mills or somebody else would buy it for fifty dollars. After that it could make a million, but the fifty was the last you ever heard of it.

I was with Jelly for about six months and Luis Russell and Paul Barbarin were in the band with me. Jelly was really advanced; in fact, he was talkin' way over our heads most of the time. Every once in a while these days, I begin to understand the message he was trying to get over. He kept talkin' about playin' the melody. But in those days playin' jazz was the only thing in the world for me besides eatin' and sleepin' and I didn't understand what Jelly was drivin' at.

You just gotta respect men like Jelly, King Oliver, Henderson, and those other pioneers. They were proving something and had a rough time. Jazz was known then as "jig" music, and those men had to fight all the way. There were a few white musicians too— men like Bix Beiderbecke and Benny Goodman, the Dorsey boys and Jack Teagarden. They didn't care nothin' about color, or that jazz had a bad stamp to it. Why, Bix would come uptown and blow with us, eat with us, sleep with us. He was one of us.

Those guys shouldn't be forgotten, 'cause if they hadn't scuffled, jazz wouldn't be known now. It hurts me to see guys, fine musicians, walkin' the streets or workin' as porters or in men's rooms. And these young kids—I overheard one of them listenin' to Red Allen a little while ago and sayin', "Man, why doesn't that cat give up?" Seems as though they want us to die out.

It shouldn't be.

BUSTER BAILEY

There was a time when King Oliver began to slip. Joe was suffering from pyorrhea and he got to the place where he couldn't get over G. Couldn't even hit C or B-flat. After Louis left him, he'd hire guys who'd actually do most of the playing.

I used to shoot a lot of pool with Joe. I won most of the time and I was no hell at it. He was a great eater, Joe, and he liked a lot of sweet things. He was a great snorer, too. He'd alarm the whole neighborhood.

JOE OLIVER

Pops, breaks come to cats in this racket only once in a while and I guess I must have been asleep when mine came. I've made lots of dough in this game but I didn't know how to take care of it. I have been under the best management in the country but didn't know how to stay under it.

I have helped to make some of the best names in the music game, but I am too much of a man to ask those that I have helped to help me. Some of the guys that I have helped are responsible for my downfall in a way. I am the guy who took a pop bottle and a rubber plunger and made the first mute ever used in a horn, but I didn't know how to get the patent for it and some educated cat came along and made a fortune off of my ideas. I have written a lot of numbers that someone else got the credit and the money for. I couldn't help it because I didn't know what to do.

I am in terrible shape now. I am getting old and my health is failing. Doctors advised me a long time ago to give up and quit but I can't. I don't have any money and I can't do anything else, so here I am.

I have been under management of both colored and white bookers in the last few years and I haven't had one yet to deal fair with me. I had one booker who collected deposits on all the dates I played for him and skipped out. I had another who bought a bus for my band and had me sign papers that put all the fellows' instruments under mortgage. I gave him money to make the payments and he kept it for personal use. The company took the bus and the instruments, but I pleaded with the manager to let me keep the instruments and told him how I had been gypped, and he opened up his heart and gave back the instruments. After this we made jobs for a week in a coal truck, as we didn't have enough money to rent cars or bus. Then my band broke up, and I had contracts for some very nice jobs so I was lucky enough to get Maurice Morrison and his band to fill the dates for me until I got another band together. Things changed a little for me after this. I got a new and better band and a bus and headed south for Florida, where I became the victim of another crooked booker and my band broke up by degrees. I played my last job under him with four men, including myself. I then went to Georgia and organized another band, the band I have now, and if you don't do something to help me I will lose them.

LETTERS FROM JOE OLIVER TO HIS SISTER

Savannah, Georgia
November, 1937

Dear Sister:

I'm still out of work. Since the road house close I haven't hit a note. But I've got a lot to thank God for. Because I eat and sleep. Look like every time one door close the Good Lord open another. I've got to do my own cooking, as my landlady and daughter both work out. I am doing pretty fair. But I much rather work and earn my own money. Soon as the weather can fit my clothes I know I can do better in New York.

Joe

Dear Sister:

I received your letter which found me well and getting along pretty nice. I looked up another job. With little money. If hours was money I'd be drawing more money than Babe Ruth at his best. We are still having nice weather here. The Lord is sure good to me here without an overcoat. I have to see by lamp here. *Smile.*

Sincerely yours, Brother

Sunday evening

Dear Sister:

Well I hope you don't feel like I am lying down on you. I put in such long hours until I don't feel anything like looking at a bottle of ink or picking up my pen and you know I'm one who love to write. But I am

185

going to see to you hearing from me often. I will get some cards when I go to town and will be able to drop you a card from the place. I am feeling pretty good, but just can't get rid of this cough. Don't like that sticking on me so long. I just can't get rid of it. I've tried most everything. My heart don't bother me just a little at times. But my breath is still short, and I'm not at all fat. . . .

I would like to live long as I can, but nothing like making all arrangements in time. Don't think I will ever raise enough money to buy a ticket to New York.

I am not the one to give up quick. If I was I don't know where I would be today. I always feel like I've got a chance. I still feel I'm going to snap out of the rut I've been in for several years. What makes me feel optimistic at times. Look like every time one door close on me another door open . . . Look how many teeth I had taken out and replaced. I got teeth waiting for me at the dentist now. I've started a little dime bank saving. Got $1.60 in it and won't touch it. I am going to try and save myself a ticket to New York.

Joe

Dear Sister:

I open the pool rooms at 9 A.M. and close at 12 midnite. If the money was only ¼ as much as the hours I'd be all set. But at that I can thank God for what I am getting. Which I do night after night. I know you will be glad when the winter say goodbye.

Now Vick before I go further with my letter I'm going to tell you something but don't be alarmed. I've got high blood pressure. Was taking treatment but had to discontinue. My blood was 85 above normal. Now my blood has started again and I am unable to take treatments because it cost $3.00 per treatment and I don't make enough money to continue my treatments. Now it begins to work on my heart. I am weak in my limbs at times and my breath but I can not asking you for money or anything. A stitch in time save nine. Should anything happen to me will you want my body? Let me know because I won't last forever and the longer I go the worst I'll get unless I take treatments.

It's not like New York or Chicago here. You've got to go through a lot of red tape to get any kind of treatment from the city here. I may never see New York again in life. . . .

Don't think I'm afraid because I wrote what I did. I am trying to live near to the Lord than ever before. So I feel like the Good Lord will take care of me. Good night, dear. . . .

Joe

Editor's note: *Joe Oliver died on April 10, 1938.*

LOUIS ARMSTRONG

He would have been *big*, because there wasn't nobody doing nothing except Joe Oliver in those days. Bunk hadn't even been heard of; he was down there in the cotton fields wrestling with those bales, and forgot all about trumpet. They tried to get Joe to come to New York when he got hot, but he wouldn't come. And all the time the cats were coming out from New York with those big shows and picking up on what he was playing. Joe Oliver was *the* man in Chicago. But he came to New York too late. When he got there, everybody was playing him. Even I had been here long before him. And it was all his own fault, too, because he had Chicago sewed up. The agents and everybody coming from New York had wanted to bring him in someplace, *any* night club, with his band. But Joe wouldn't leave. "I'm doing all right here, man," he'd tell them. He had good jobs with good tips. So time ran out on him. He looked around, and when he came to New York—too late.

From then on he began to get what I guess you could call a broken heart. When you wind up playing with little old musicians down in some place like Tampa, Florida, with cats that didn't even know him . . . And if you lay off for two days, the band breaks up. And the landlady commenced to hold his trunks. I saw him at that time; it was in Savannah, when I was on some one-nighters, and as far as I'm concerned that's what killed him—a broken heart. That's what killed Joe Oliver.

I was with him until they buried him; I was at his funeral. Most of the musicians turned out. The people who really knew him didn't forget him. It would have been nice if they'd had a parade for him, but instead they took him into the chapel across from the Lafayette—that big rehearsal hall in Harlem. I didn't like the sermon the preacher gave. Just because the Guild buried him was no reason for rubbing it in. They said he made money, and he had money, and didn't keep it. The Guild isn't supposed to say that; that's what we donate our services for when they give benefits. A lot of us didn't like that sermony, and even after all these years I still don't like to think about it.

He was a great man. I'll always remember him. But I don't care to remember him in Savannah, or the funeral. I'd rather think about a time like 1928, when I played two nights with Luis Russell's band at the Savoy, as a guest. Joe Oliver was there each night, with a new set of clothes, and that Panama hat like he usually wore. And he looked pleasant and happy. He was standing right in front of that trumpet. That was a thrill. I had run errands for his wife; he had brought me up to Chicago. And he stood there listening, with the tears coming right out of his eyes. It knocked me out.

DUKE ELLINGTON

Then, after a while, there was a lot of talk about McKinney's Cotton Pickers up in Detroit. They were another bunch that made a gang of musical history, and their records had everybody talking about them.

GENE KRUPA

There was a band which had few equals in those years, McKinney's Cotton Pickers. Came my first lesson in showmanship, for which Cuba Austin was responsible. Question any musician who knew that wonderful organization and be assured that Cuba played no little part in the success of the outfit from the standpoints of commercialism and musicianship. Years later, when asked by people about the antics of jitterbugs and so-called ickies, I always tempered my replies, remembering that one night in Chicago when I stood open-mouthed, completely awed and fascinated, and cheered more lustily, grew far more excited than any of the most obnoxious ickies that ever got in the hair or became a general nuisance to a performing band. No indeed, I'll never forget the Cotton Pickers, or just say I'll be a long time remembering Cuba Austin.

CUBA AUSTIN

When I was sixteen, I started working at a hotel called Kate's Mountain Club over at White Sulphur Springs, West Virginia. I was hopping bells and made extra money as a tap dancer in the floor show.

In 1924, the Prince of Wales made a whirlwind tour of the United States, and in September he came to Charleston for a rest. We entertainers beat it there from all over trying to get a chance to play before royalty. Why, the town filled overnight with singers, dancers, and such trying to catch his eye. One act that came was a little ragged jazz band called the Synco Jazz Band.

A fellow named William McKinney got that band together back in Springfield, Ohio. He was a drummer and was about twenty-six years old. First, he had drums and piano—that was Todd Rhodes; then, let's see—he added Milton Senior on sax and Dave Wilbourn on banjo and for vocals. After a bit, he brought in Claude Jones, a trombone player, and Wesley Stewart, sax and hot fiddle. Also he had June Cole, bass tuba. McKinney called them the Synco Septette—meaning six men and himself for seven. Later he changed it to Synco Jazz Band after he got more men.

We had made a hit with the Prince. I did my tap dancing and the band backed me. One night he sat in with us on drums and was pretty fair. Some photographs were made of that and our booker said they would help our reputation a lot. He also said the name of Synco Jazz Band lacked appeal, so we decided on McKinney's Cotton Pickers.

We were a pretty scrubby bunch. Most of the boys should have been in school still, and all of them were still wearing knickers.

That summer we were booked for a season at Manitou Beach, Michigan, and we added George (Fathead) Thomas on alto; John Nesbitt, a Norfolk musician, on trumpet; and Wesley Stewart switched from fiddle to tenor. We then had three saxes, one trumpet, one trombone, piano, banjo, and drums. It was at Manitou Beach that the band started coming on. Nesbitt was making the arrangements and teaching us all how to read.

It was here that the term "woodshedding" originated. When one of the gang wanted to rehearse his part, he would go off into the woods and practice until he made it. If anyone would biff a few too many, Nesbitt would send him off to the woods for a private rehearsal. Sometimes, more than half of the band would be woodshedding.

On Sunday, we would give our afternoon concert and we would play the easy parts of *Poet and Peasant Overture,* Victor Herbert songs, and similar numbers. From Manitou Beach, we went to Arcadia Ballroom in Detroit. Detroit was a wide-open town in those days and the great Jean Goldkette and the Orange Blossoms band were also in Detroit.

We played a season at the Arcadia and moved to the Graystone. Our personnel when we entered the Graystone was: Don Redman, Prince Robinson, James Dudley, Joyce Thomas, saxes; Langston Curl, Joe Smith, John Nesbitt, trumpets; Cuffee Davidson, trombone; Rhodes, Weldon, myself, and Bob Escudero made up the rhythm section. Redman and Nesbitt were making the arrangements and the band really jumped.

All the boys around Detroit at that time loved to jam and it wasn't a surprising sight to see Bix Beiderbecke, Don Murray, Hank Biagini, Joe Venuti, and others all on our bandstand jamming.

Goldkette used to have sort of a music school in a locker room at the Graystone, and he and Don Redman would take turns at the blackboard, explaining arrangements and teaching us to read better.

While we were at the Graystone, we would make trips to Chicago for our first recordings. Among our first waxings were *Four or Five Times* and *Milenberg Joys*.

The boys were wild with excitement about recording, and on the train to Chicago for (our first) date there was a lot of drinking, laughing, talking, and everybody was in great spirits. We just kept walking and cutting up the length of the train through the entire night—most of us didn't even go to bed or get any sleep.

Next morning (July 11th, 1928), we showed up at Victor in very boisterous spirits and we trooped into the studio shouting and rarin' to go. We made *Four or Five Times, Put It There, Crying and Sighing,* and *Milenberg Joys*. We had a lot of trouble with the engineers. In those days everybody took off their shoes and had a pillow under his feet so the thud from beating the rhythm didn't ruin things. Well, on *Milenberg Joys* the band was beating a fast rhythm and then, bit by bit, the pillows kept sliding away. We ruined several takes that way.

Now the worst of all was Prince Robinson. Don (Redman) hit on the idea of lashing Prince's ankles and knees together with rope to hold him steady. We started another time and things went smoothly 'til Prince started a solo; then he began to bob up and down with his feet tied together, and finally gave up in the middle of it—looked up at Don and said, "Aw, Don, I can't play tied up like this." But finally we got by with a good one.

The next day we made some more—*Stop Kidding, Nobody's Sweetheart, Some Sweet Day,* and *Shim-Me-Sha-Wobble*. We made *Cherry,* too, but we were sorry Guy Lombardo beat us to record the same tune—only he called it *Little Coquette*. After that we called it *Little Croquette,* just for a joke.

There isn't anything that can ruin a band quicker than a booker who keeps jumping it all over the country for one-nighters. You play nine to three, then hop in a bus and ride. You pull into the next stop maybe around sunset the next day. No time to get a rest in a bed or even to clean up and get the grime off of you. You get a hot meal someplace and then it's back on the stand. That goes on night after night. On the trip back from the West the Cotton Pickers were grumbling and talking under their breath in an undeclared war with Pat Moore. Soon they began to break into little groups within the band, talking and lying about each other. Things just seemed to get worse all the time.

You've seen boys on the stand making out they were laughing and talking with each other during the numbers—that's all in the game. You never know when you see them up there that any of those men might be in pain. No, I'm not fooling—he might be sick or tired—he might be worried about his family or a lot of other things, but he has to smile and make the crowd think he is happy.

That's the way with us. We had to pretend on the stand but instead we were sick inside with hate for Moore and his booking us all over at whistle stops. Every time we complained, Moore would say, "do it or else." The boys knew what "do it" meant and I guess we decided to find out what "or else" was like for a change.

When the boys quit the stand one night they just solemnly voted to stop for good. Then Don said that he would form a new band and asked how many would come with him and how many would stay with McKinney. Some of the boys said "yes" or "no" that night but most of them waited until after we had ridden back to Detroit in the bus, which was the next morning. The main ones who went with Don were Quentin Jackson, Claude Jones, Langston Curl, and Edward Inge. The rest said they would stick with McKinney and so they formed a new band.

DUKE ELLINGTON

McKinney was having a little trouble with John Nesbitt, the trumpet player, who was something of a 'lushy. Finally Mac told him things'd start happening if he didn't quit coming to work high.

So Nesbitt says O.K. For a couple of nights he comes to work sober, nobody sees a bottle anywhere around him. But, when intermission comes on, and the guys haven't been off the stand, Nesbitt climbs down so high he's weaving. Nobody can figure out what goes on. Nobody's seen him take a drink, but he's high all right.

So it turns out he's got a bottle in the inside pocket of his coat, and he's got him two straws! He's leaning down and dragging on these straws every time the brass lays out. No wonder he's high. Being truthful about it, he had something there. Quite a few guys have worked the same gag since.

Around 1931 McKinney's band was still doing fine, but on the way back from the Cotton Club in California, it seems McKinney and Don agreed to disagree. So Don made arrangements to get his own band together. Several of the Cotton Pickers went with him. Prince Robinson, Inge, Curl, Buddy Lee, and Quentin Jackson. Don started off by taking a few of the guys, and then the Cotton Pickers broke up, and he got a couple more.

Before McKinney's finally broke up, they sent for Rex Stewart, Cheatham, and Benny Carter from New York, but luck was against them, and those days wrote finis to a great history-making band. Don's line-up in the fall of '31 read like this: saxes—Don, Rupert Cole, Inge, Bob Carroll; trumpets—Curl, Buddy Lee, Shirley Clay; trombones—there were several switches here among Claude Jones, Freddy Robinson, Gene Simon, Big Green, Quentin Jackson, and Benny Morton. The rhythm was Manzie Johnson, drums, Tylcott Reeves, guitar, and Escudero, bass. Later on Sid de Paris took Buddy Lee's chair, and Clarence Holliday replaced Reeves.

Don went into Connie's Inn, where the band did very well, staying about a year and a half. Later on they made a successful road tour working as a theater unit with the Mills Brothers. Around the same time they were featured on a commercial air program, together with the Mills Brothers, for Chipso soap flakes.

A while earlier, Chick Webb had blown in from Baltimore, and John Trueheart with him. After a while they landed a job up at the Savoy Ballroom, shortly following its opening. They only had eight pieces and couldn't read a note of music, but that was a band. There was Elmer Williams on tenor, and Johnny Hodges was with Chick then. Bobby Stark was playing trumpet, and Slats Long, trombone. Trueheart, of course, was playing guitar, Leon England, bass, and Chick at the drums.

When they opened up at the "track," they were just a band without any particular leader, so the guys decided they might as well use Chick's name, though at that time Webb wasn't thinking anything about getting along on his own, his mind was all on the drums, no getting away from that. They worked up a gang of arrangements, even though they didn't use any music; in those days, anything good just got memorized.

Webb was always battle-mad, and those eight guys used to take on every band that came up to play there. And most times they did the cutting, regardless of the fact that half the time the other bands were twice the size. But the unforgettable and lovable Webb ate up any kind of fight, and everybody in the band played like mad at all times. They figured out a bunch of original numbers, and it was generally too bad for the guy on the opposite stand.

MARY LOU WILLIAMS

The Savoy was a place of tremendous enthusiasm, a home of fantastic dancing. And Webb was acknowledged King of the Savoy. Any visiting band could depend on catching hell from little Chick, for he was a crazy drummer and shrewd to boot.

The way I made it out, Chick would wait until the opposition had blown its hottest numbers and then—during a so-so set—would unexpectedly bring his band fresh to the stand and wham into a fine arrangement, like Benny Carter's *Liza*, that was hard to beat. Few visiting bands could stand up to this.

DUKE ELLINGTON

Most of all the great horn-blowers worked for Chick Webb some time or other, but Chick was always dogged by bad luck, and never managed to work steady for long. But every time he'd get a job, he always could hire first-rate musicians. Then the band would have a lay-off, and some of the guys would have to take work somewhere else. Johnny Hodges came over to me in 1928; Toby, Rudy Jackson, and Carney were our saxes at the time.

By 1934, Chick had one of the best bands he'd ever had. He was working steadily at last at the Savoy, after having taken it on the chin for a good long time. Webb never was a quitter—and in the end he got the success he was after. In '34, the line-up of his band was, trumpets—Mario, Bobby Stark, and Taft Jordan; saxes—Pete Clark, Wayman Carver, Elmer Williams, and Edgar Sampson; trombones—Sandy Williams and for a while, Claude Jones; Trueheart, guitar; Kirby, bass; and Joe Steele, piano.

The band made some fine records during those years, and Chick got properly started, making a reputation for himself. Maybe that was the best band he ever had, certainly the best organized one. He didn't discover Ella Fitzgerald until a year or so later. Claude Jones tells a story about his big heart. When he was leaving to join Cab, he owed Chick sixty dollars. Chick wouldn't take his money, telling him to wait till after he got set, afterwards he couldn't get over his surprise when Claude came round to let him have it.

GENE KRUPA
The Dunbar Palace in New York's Harlem—appearing in person the most luminous of all drum stars, the master, the little giant of the big noise, Chick Webb! For those who have never heard the Chick, I feel no small amount of compassion. Of course, records are made like *Liza*, for instance, but somehow, this genius never could get himself on wax. Chick gassed me, but good, on one occasion at the Savoy, in a battle with Benny's band, and I repeat now what I said then, I was never cut by a better man.

MARY LOU WILLIAMS
One night, scuffling around Harlem, I fell in the Savoy. After dancing a couple of rounds, I heard a voice that sent chills up and down my spine (which I never thought could happen). I almost ran to the stand to find out who belonged to the voice, and saw a pleasant-looking, brown-skinned girl standing modestly and singing the greatest. I was told her name was Ella Fitzgerald and that

195

Chick Webb had unearthed her from one of the Apollo's amateur hours.

Later, I learned that Ella never once forgot Chick for giving her the break when others turned their backs—others who wanted her when success came.

DANNY BARKER

Success didn't come to many when I came up from New Orleans to New York in 1930. I played at Harry White's Nest Club and I played a few engagements with Fess Williams (they called him "Professor"). He had a fabulous band called the Royal Flush. I played with Billy Fowler and with Luis Russell for a while. Then I went back into the Nest Club with Dave Nelson and doubled in the Mae West show. This was in 1933. THE CONSTANT SINNER. That was the first chance I had to get a taste of a little loot in the depression. I worked with Cliff Jackson at the Lenox Club and with James P. Johnson at Small's.

But, for the most part it was the depression and the depression for musicians in New York—man, it was a bitch! I was working, I remember, in the Lenox Club, and there was a ten-piece band, eight chorus girls, four waiters, two bartenders, two managers, a doorman, a porter, and a "whiskey man." The whiskey man was the cat who used to hide the whiskey downstairs so when somebody wanted to drink he'd go down and come up with it mysteriously.

On weekdays they had but one or two parties a night. On week ends it was a little better. The hours were like from ten in the evening to five in the morning. Well, whatever they picked up in the register in the course of the night, at the end of the night they would pull a table into the middle of the floor and spill out the receipts of the night on the table and give everybody an equal share. Some mornings we'd make seventy-five cents, other mornings we'd get twenty-five. Everybody cooperated because there was nowhere else to go and, in fact, nobody had nothin'.

Also during the depression there were a few jobs for musicians in dance schools. We'd go to work at eight P.M. and play until three A.M.—continuously—without stopping. These were taxi

196

dance halls. There were thirty to forty dime-a-dance girls. We played on a commercial kick—all the current pop tunes. We only played a chorus or a chorus and a half to make the dances shorter. You'd keep your bottle, if you could afford one, on the stand with you and you'd bring your lunch and each of us would take turns taking a break while still on stand to eat or drink while the drums kept playing. The only time they had a real full band were on the introductions and ending of the tunes.

Most of the time the bands in the taxi dance halls had six or seven pieces. A few of the schools had twelve to fifteen. Benjie Madison and Billy Cato had wonderful bands in taxi dance halls, so jazz guys worked there and everywhere. Ward Pinkett worked at a dancing school on 125th Street.

I worked at the Stroller's Club with Chu Berry and Roy Eldridge. But a gangster shot up the joint, so we were unemployed. There was cabaret entertainment there while we were there and one show had Lizzie Miles, Clara Smith, Tracy Smith, Neka Shaw (she was a beautiful chick—a singer). In fact, there were about fifteen singers who went on continuously, but I doubt if anyone was getting much loot. The band was Paul Barbarin's—my uncle. This was about 1935. Chu Berry had gotten his stamp with Benny Carter. When you made Benny Carter's band in those days the stamp was on you. Then you could go with Chick Webb or Fletcher Henderson or any of the other bands. Every time Benny got a band together all the cats would want to know who was in his band because if you could make Benny Carter's band, that was it. It was like major- and minor-league baseball.

CECIL SCOTT

In 1931, we left the Savoy and signed with another hall—The Renaissance, opposite Horace Henderson. Later we went back to the Savoy. This was the end of the trail for several reasons. The main one being that the early 'thirties were difficult, for money was scarce. With repeal of Prohibition folks no longer had to come to speakeasies to buy liquor sold by racketeers. Harlem's hot music suddenly cooled off because the patrons could buy a bottle and drink at home far cheaper.

COLEMAN HAWKINS

You know what used to happen during the depression? We used to play a lot of jobs and didn't get paid. Everybody belonged to the union and everything, but it seemed like there wasn't anything we could do about it when that happened. I was still with Fletcher then and we used to do quite a few nights for which we didn't see any money.

BILLIE HOLIDAY

I used to run errands for a madam on the corner. I wouldn't run errands for anybody, still won't carry a case across the street today, but I ran around for this woman because she'd let me listen to all Bessie's records—and Pops Armstrong's records of *West End Blues.*

I loved that *West End Blues* and always wondered why Pops didn't sing any words to it. I reckoned he must have been feeling awful bad. When I got to New York, I went to hear him at the Lafayette Theatre. He didn't play my blues and I went backstage to tell him about it.

I guess I was nine years old then. Been listening to Pops and Bessie ever since that time. Of course, my mother considered that type of music sinful; she'd whip me in a minute if she caught me listening to it. Those days, we were supposed to listen to hymns, or something like that.

This is the truth. Mother and I were starving. It was cold. Father had left us and remarried when I was ten. Mother was a housemaid and couldn't find work. I tried scrubbing floors, too, but I just couldn't do it.

We lived on 145th Street near Seventh Avenue. One day we were so hungry we could barely breathe. I started out the door. It was cold as all-hell and I walked from 145th to 133rd, down Seventh Avenue, going in every joint trying to find work. Finally, I got so desperate I stopped in the Log Cabin Club run by Jerry Preston. I told him I wanted a drink. I didn't have a dime. But I ordered gin (it was my first drink—I didn't know gin from wine) and gulped it down. I asked Preston for a job, told him I was a dancer. He said to dance. I tried it. He said I stunk. I told him I could sing. He said sing. Over in the corner was an old guy playing the piano. He struck *Travlin'* and I sang. The customers stopped drinking. They turned around and watched. The pianist, Dick Wilson, swung into *Body and Soul*. Jeez, you should have seen those people—all of them started crying. Preston came over, shook his head and said, "Kid, you win." That's how I got my start.

First thing I did was get a sandwich. I gulped it down. Believe me, the crowd gave me eighteen dollars in tips. I ran out the door. Bought a whole chicken. Ran up Seventh Avenue to my home. Mother and I ate that night—and we have been eating pretty well since.

CARMEN McRAE

As for Billie Holiday, I don't know what to say about her. As far as I'm concerned, she is her worst enemy. She's a queer woman. She has temperament. I guess she was born with it—I mean I don't think it's because she's a star. She's been very unhappy for a long time. I don't know about now. I think all her troubles have stemmed from her unhappiness.

I'll say this about her—she sings the way she is. That's really Lady when you listen to her on a record. Whether it's a jump tune or a ballad, whatever you get out of a record of hers is really Lady. Singing is the only place she can express herself the way she'd like to be all the time. Only way she's happy is through a song. I don't think she expresses herself as she would want to when you meet her in person. The only time she's at ease and at rest with herself is when she sings. I mean by that when she can sing, not when she's under the influence of liquor or whatever she's on.

Lady is a very unpredictable woman. Some nights people will listen to her sing and feel sorry for her, thinking she's through. Then the next night she sings her ass off, pardon my expression.

She used to be my idol. She could do no wrong. I remember when she was happy—that was a long time ago. Then she could reason with herself better than she can now and she wasn't using anything. She has the greatest constitution in the world, that girl. Her mother fed her well and loved her so. Maybe that's what helped to carry her before. Maybe after she lost her mother, she kind of goofed.

Sadie, her mother, was the only relative, I believe, she had. After her mother died, she had no living relative in the world. I knew her mother very well and loved her. I remember coming back from her mother's funeral, Billie was telling Joe Guy, her husband then, she was telling him over and over again, "Joe I don't have anybody in the world now except you." She needed someone to say that to. She felt completely alone.

BOBBY TUCKER

I played for Lady Day for about two and a half years and I guess you'd call it quite an experience. I was with her until the time she got busted and sent away to Lexington—and man—I'll always remember the concert at Carnegie when she got out. It was one of the greatest thrills of my life.

One thing about Lady, she was the easiest singer I ever played for. You know, with most singers you have to guide 'em and carry 'em along—they're either layin' back or else runnin' away from you. But not Billie Holiday. Man, it was a thrill to play for her. She had the greatest conception of a beat I ever heard. It just didn't matter what kind of a song she was singin'. She could sing the fastest tune in the world or else something that was like a dirge, but you could take a metronome and she'd be right there. Hell! With Lady you could relax while you were playin' for her. You could damn near forget the tune.

Man, but gettin' her to work was another thing. Lady was in terrible shape then. When a person's hooked, nothin' in the world is more important than dope. The worst part of it is that she's one of the nicest people I ever met, and, most important, she really fought that stuff. But, well, she had a terrible childhood and had a lot of real bad breaks—and she made some herself. Let's say, she made mistakes. There's one thing about Lady you won't believe. She had the *most* terrible inferiority complex. She actually doesn't believe she can sing—that might have had somethin' to do with her troubles. Another thing—money didn' mean a thing to her

—or big names or prestige and things like that. And she stood by her friends.

Isn't it a shame?

BILLIE HOLIDAY

I don't think I'm singing. I feel like I am playing a horn. I try to improvise like Les Young, like Louis Armstrong, or someone else I admire. What comes out is what I feel. I hate straight singing. I have to change a tune to my own way of doing it. That's all I know.

12

. . . and there were Fletcher Henderson and the great musicians who worked for him—Louis Armstrong, Coleman Hawkins, Joe Smith, Jimmy Harrison, and the rest.

DUKE ELLINGTON
Musicians mostly remember that band, during those years, as the greatest dance band anyone ever heard. They played some formidable music, and, personally, the musicians themselves were a great gang.

JO JONES
Fletcher Henderson had a wonderful dance band because he was a competent musician. Before Henderson jazz musicians just picked up horns and played. Henderson put class to jazz music because his musicians were hired on their ability to play music. His bands largely led to jazz as we have it now.

FLETCHER HENDERSON
It was back in 1922, down in New Orleans, when I heard this young man playing the trumpet in a little dance hall. I was accompanist for Ethel Waters, who was the headline attraction at the Lyric Theatre, and I decided that the youthful trumpeter would be great in our act. I asked him his name and found he was Louis Armstrong.

Louis told me that he would have to speak to his drummer, because he couldn't possibly leave without him. The next day Louis was backstage at the theater to tell me he'd have to be excused, much as he would love to go with us, because the drummer wouldn't leave New Orleans. Some years later I heard that he was playing with King Oliver at the old Dreamland Cafe in Chicago. Knowing the way that horn sounded, I had to try to get him for my band that was scheduled to open at the Roseland Ballroom. Truthfully, I didn't expect him to accept the offer, and I was very surprised when he came to New York and joined us.

The band at first was inclined to be a bit reserved toward the new arrival and there seemed to be a little tension in the air. At rehearsal he was perplexed by the trumpet part I gave him to a new arrangement of a medley of beautiful Irish waltzes. Now, those parts were well marked with all the dynamics of the music, and at one point the orchestration was indicated as *fff* with a diminuendo down to *pp*.

The band followed these notations and was playing very softly, while Louis still played his part at full volume. I stopped the band and said, "Louis, you are not following the arrangement."

Louis objected, saying, "I'm reading everything on this sheet." I said, "But, Louis, how about that *pp?*" and Louis broke us all up by replying, "Oh, I thought that meant 'pound plenty.'" There was no tension after that.

There were a lot of serious musicians in that wonderful orchestra of mine, and they were a little too stiff at first for Louis' taste. Finally, a fight developed between the trombonist and the bass player, and they had their coats off and were really going after each other before I quieted them, and this eased everything for Louis. For the first time he said, "Oh, I'm gonna like this band."

LOUIS ARMSTRONG

Along about the latter part of 1923, I received a telegram to go to New York to join the great Fletcher Henderson's orchestra. That's how I felt about "Smack" Henderson, years before I had seen him in person, from recordings he made for years by himself, with Ethel Waters and Revela Hughes. He had the first big colored band that hit the road and tore it up. When I explained to the King that it was my one big chance to see New York, where people there really *do things*, he dug me. I knew he would, and he released me so I could knock it.

When I arrived in New York I had to go straight to rehearsal. And don't you know that when I got into that rehearsal, I felt so funny. I walked up to old "Smack" and said, "Er, wa, I'm that boy you sent for to blow the trumpet in your band." And "Smack," all sharp as a Norwegian with that hard-hitting steel-gray suit he had on, said, "Oh, yes, we're waiting for you. Your part's up there" (meaning the bandstand). I said, "Yassuh," and went on up there with my eyes closed. When I opened them I looked square into the faces of Coleman Hawkins, Don Redman, Kaiser Marshall, Long Green, Escudero, Scotty, Elmer "Muffle Jaws" Chambers, and Charles Dixon.

They all casually looked out of the corner of their eyes. You know how they do when a new man joins a band, they want to be real friendly right off the bat. But they'd rather hear you play first. I said to myself these boys look like a bunch of nice fellows, but they seem a little stuckup. That was the opinion I had of them right off the reel. I guess they had theirs about me, too. Where I had come from I wasn't used to playing in bands where there were a lot of parts for everybody to read. Shucks, all one man in the band had to do was to go to some show and hear a good number. He keeps it in his head until he reaches us. He hums it a couple of times, and from then on we had a new number to throw on the bands that were advertising in the wagons on the corner the following Sunday. That's how we stayed so famous down in New Orleans. We had a new number for the customers every week. Now I was in New York getting ready to join the biggest band in New York at the time. We played the first number down. The name of the tune was *By the Waters of Minnetonka*. I had the third trumpet part, which was so pretty.

Still nobody said anything. Finally, one of the boys said something to Long Boy Charlie Green, the great trombone man. Oh yea, it was Escudero, the tuba great. Escudero was a devilish sort of fellow, and it seemed he got a great bang out of teasing Green. I didn't know all this. Anyway, Escudero leaned over and played Green's trombone part, note for note, on his tuba. Ump! You never heard such language in all your life. I commenced to relax —you know—feeling at home. The boys didn't really hear me *tear out* until one night we all were mugging on *Tiger Rag*, and believe me, it was on.

BUSTER BAILEY
Louis made the same impact in New York that he had made in Chicago when he first came there. He always made the greatest impression on musicians when they heard him.

DUKE ELLINGTON
So when Smack's band hit town and Louis was with them, the guys had never heard anything just like it. There weren't the words coined for describing that kick. And Louis was no exception, he carried his horn round just like everybody else, and sat in and played anywhere he happened to drop in. Everyone on the street was talking about the guy.

LOUIS METCALF
To my mind, the controversy about the two different styles of playing, Eastern and Western, came to a head when Louis Armstrong joined Fletcher Henderson, taking Joe Smith's chair. It was a real jazz feud with all the musicians taking sides. Louis represented the Western style of jazz, while Joe Smith was the Eastern. It was the most terrific thing I ever heard—that midnight show at the Apollo Theatre when Henderson showed off Louis. I don't remember if anybody knew about it in advance, but Joe Smith was sitting in the pit with the house band, and, believe me, when he opened the show, it tore the house down. He did five or six encores and probably played better than he ever did before in his life. I guess he did it just to prove that he was still *the* Joe Smith.

Well, I believe that they took out part of the show so Henderson could go right on—to bring it to a head, so to speak. To find out who was who.

The first number they played was *Copenhagen*. And Louis' solo was *so* good. But different, and the audience didn't know about how much to applaud. The next number was even better and the people began to dig and were sayin', "Here's another great trumpet player." After the third piece, they really made their minds up. They were sayin', "Now here's another *King!*" And the house was his.

It was a real thrill for me, because Louis comin' out of New Orleans and me from St. Louis were both of the same style, and he was backin' up everything I had been tryin' to tell—only *he* made them understand.

REX STEWART
Then Louis Armstrong hit town! I went mad with the rest of the town. I tried to walk like him, talk like him, eat like him, sleep like him. I even bought a pair of big policeman shoes like he used to wear and stood outside his apartment waiting for him to come out so I could look at him. Finally, I got to shake hands and talk with him.

LOUIS ARMSTRONG
Our engagement at the Roseland was great. Our road tour was the same. I stayed with "Smack" Henderson until way up until 1926. Lil, my wife at the time, had the band at the Dreamland Cabaret in Chicago, and suggested that I come home because it was easier for us to starve together than be apart so long. Then I was a little homesick too. So, I cut out from those fine boys who treated me just swell. We all are just as glad to see each other right now as we were in those days.

BUSTER BAILEY
Louis had been afraid to come to New York. He liked Chicago. It was the same with me. The first week we were both in New York we both said, let's go back to Chicago. There were more

bands there—more everything—more money. Chicago was far ahead of New York at that time. I stayed with Fletcher from around 1924 to 1929. Louis stayed for only a year. He came back to Chicago in 1925. It was not only that he was homesick, but Lil was there and Louis had a chance to buy a home. So he joined Erskine Tate.

REX STEWART

About 1925 it was customary every Monday morning for the artists and musicians from the Club Alabam, Plantation, Cotton Club, Small's Paradise, et cetera, to gather in one club to enjoy themselves dancing and drinking. All the big-shot musicians would sit and sip and then if the urge struck them, they would grab a horn and how they would blow to that wonder audience.

One particular night in my memory the Gala was held at 129th and Lenox. When a tall, distinguished man, closely followed by a short, heavy-set, widely smiling young man were escorted to a ringside table, the air was electric with whispers. That's Fletcher Henderson and Louis Armstrong! I looked, gulped, and almost swallowed my mouthpiece. Louis Armstrong! Then panic struck and I told Elmer Snowden, who had the band, that I was sick and had to go home. He just grinned and said, "You'll stay right here and blow that horn." Boy, but I was scared.

I didn't think I would ever see my idol from a distance much less sit in the same room and blow while he was watching me, so I replied, "No, I'm sick and I've gotta go." But when I started to get up, Elmer cuffed me, so I sat down and started to try. The guys in the band kept encouraging me and I took chorus after chorus. I guess the whole deal stimulated something unusual because after the number Louis came over and asked my name and congratulated me while I almost passed out. The Great Man had actually spoken to me!

In the fall of 1925, while playing with Pop Snowden at the Nest Club in Harlem, the phone rang. The call boy said, "It's for you, Rex," and here is a conversation I'll never forget. "Hello," says I. "Hello," answers a voice, "this is Louie." "Louie who?" "Louie Armstrong. Do you want a good job?" "Sure," says Rex, thinking the rumors I had heard about Louis getting a band of his own were true and he wanted me to work with him. "Fine," said Louie, "you take my place with Fletcher in two weeks." "No, no," I shouted. "I can't do that. I thought you wanted me to work in your band." To which Louis replied, "I'm only going to have a small band in Chicago." "I'm sorry, Louie, but I just haven't the nerve to sit in your chair."

But the King just laughed and said, "We'll be up to see you tonight." Well, it took six months and Snowden had to fire me before I'd take the job, and even then I couldn't stand the pressure, so after nine months I took off my uniform, hung my horn in my locker, caught a train to Washington and they saw me two months later. I didn't intend to be a character, but I just couldn't take it.

BUSTER BAILEY
When I came into New York I was asking Louis one night about the different guys in the Fletcher Henderson band. He told me about Big Charlie Green and about a tenor saxophone player—Hawkins—he said that guy really swings. That was the first time I had heard the word used that way, and I didn't dig what he meant. Louis tried to explain it. He said, "Man, he swings! He swings out of this world!" I caught on to what he meant, because after I got to work that night I heard Hawkins. So I knew what he meant. How would I define it now? Swing. A guy that's . . . I still have to use the word swing. I mean a guy who's got a beat—a certain accent—a certain attack. Part of it is that you are playing along with the beat.

COLEMAN HAWKINS
I joined Fletcher Henderson in 1925. I was just a kid. I had been studying since I was six. I began on piano and used to play cello and started in on my tenor when I was nine. I was aware of jazz right from the start as a kid. I used to sit up and practice all day —all day long. Then when I was through with my lessons I would play jazz all the rest of the day. I became aware of jazz through records and I also used to go to all the classical concerts.

208

We used to buy season tickets (that was in Topeka, Kansas) and see everything at the auditorium. When I was a kid, I saw the early jazz musicians like Louis Armstrong and Earl Hines the first time I was in Chicago. I was going to school there and I was able to play in school bands. I was about fourteen.

We had a little orchestra that played school dances—this was both in Chicago and Topeka. I used to go down to the South Side to hear the jazz musicians. I was as big then as I am now. When I was twelve I had a mustache and everything and started using my father's razor at ten even though there was just fuzz.

Louis and Earl impressed me a good deal, also Jimmie Noone. When I was a kid, that was the best music you could listen to. Benny Goodman, as I remember, used to hear Jimmie Noone a lot too. You can't miss that in his playing. And then there was Buster Bailey. I used to think he was a very good technician and everything.

At the time I joined Henderson I didn't take music seriously. I was about seventeen. I started out when I was very young reading music so I had no trouble with Henderson's book. Some people say there was no jazz tenor before me. All I know is I just had a way of playing and I didn't think in terms of any other instrument but the tenor. I honestly couldn't characterize my style in words. It seems like whatever comes to me naturally is what I play. That's the way it's always been. It's influenced by a lot of things I hear unconsciously and I find myself playing a lot of things I have developed out of something. But I never made any particular study of how and why I play as I do—it just comes out naturally. As for my full tone, I always did play with a kind of stiff reed. When I started I also used to play very loud because I was trying to play those solos over those seven or eight other horns all the time. I used to work on those reeds all night to make them sound, and, doing that, having to play loud, developed the fullness of the sound. Now I don't blow so loud any more but the sound is still full.

Joe Smith used to have a very pretty tone. He had some kind of a way of his own with a plunger in his bell. He was a very sensitive player. Joe may have played quiet but he wasn't a quiet man. He used to have a very good time and did a lot of running and everything. He was a real nice fellow.

FLETCHER HENDERSON

I remember when Joe came to New York in 1923, starting with Mamie Smith's Jazz Hounds. He finally learned to read—but not according to Hoyle. He used his own system by remembering if a note was so far from another note, then it had to be *that* note it was supposed to be. Lines and spaces meant nothing to him, and he did very well with this curious method.

Soon, he was almost as well known as Hawk in Mamie's band, and that same year he joined my outfit at the Roseland Ballroom. Several months previously we had worked together with Ethel Waters on Black Swan records in a combo called the Black Swan Troubadours, and toured the country. Joe was the most soulful trumpeter I ever knew, and when he used a felt hat for a mute, it was difficult for me to tell if *he* was playing or if it was one of the saxophonists. His beautiful tone was the best ever executed with a plunger.

TINY PARHAM

He put so much oomph into his horn that I've seen a drunken noisy cabaret crowd get quiet as a mouse when Joe started off on a sweet sentimental tune. Once a drunken fellow, crowding up close to listen, bumped the bell of his horn, hitting Joe's mouth a hard lick. This would have made the average musician mad as hell. Joe just smiled and said, "Pops, be careful. You don't know what you're doing to me." Joe was like that. He played the cleanest, purest trumpet of all time. His tone had soul and packed so much emotion that it could easily have been mistaken for a woman singing.

PARKER BERRY

I remember Joe came to Cincinnati in 1920. His first job was with an outfit named Brownie's Band. Joe, who carried his horn with him at all times, would bash at numerous functions and house-rent stomps along Carlisle and John Streets in Cincinnati's black bottom, in the same neighborhood where Mamie Smith was born. Other nights he could be found down on the levee at the Silver Moon Saloon, at Deadman's Corner where a man was killed at least once a week, and where the Box Back Boys (pimps) used knife blades to keep their whining guitars talking all night long.

KAISER MARSHALL

I first met Joe Smith around at the Amsterdam Musical Association, which is a musicians' club. In 1919, we played gigs together and later started working together at a dancing school on Forty-eighth Street near Broadway. We did not stay there so long, as gigs were much better than a steady job in those days.

Well, later we went to work at the Club Alabam at 44th Street and Broadway for Fletcher Henderson. But Joe liked to roam about. So he left on his own will to go with a show called Chocolate Dandies, where he played with the pit band and did his trumpet specialty on the stage, with his plunger. I have never seen anyone get the tone and sweetness out of a trumpet with the plunger like Joe could. He could play hot, sweet, and also swing.

Well, Joe got tired of the show and rejoined Fletcher's band again when we started at the Roseland Ballroom at Fifty-first Street and Broadway.

Of course, by that time he had made many records with the Smiths, which is our late Bessie Smith, Clara Smith, and Mamie Smith. Bessie always wanted Joe and Big Green for her record dates. Joe also made some fine records for Ethel Waters, such as *I'm Coming, Virginia*, in which he used the plunger and played sweet behind Ethel's voice. That was one of his masterpieces, not to say about all the ones he made with the Smiths, especially Bessie, and the many ones with Fletcher.

Well, Joe left again to go shuffle along, but he came back. He could always find a seat in Fletcher's band, or else Fletcher would make room for Joe.

Well, later Joe left again to go with Don Redman, who at that time had left Fletcher and was directing McKinney's Cotton Pickers out in Detroit, and later on I was sent for to play with Don and Joe. Well, this brings it to a little tragic part, because during that time George Thomas, who was known as Fat Head and could sing, play, and scat out of this world, was killed in my automobile, in which Joe was driving from Springfield, Massachusetts, to Bridgeport, Connecticut. I happened not to be in the car. I was in New York with McKinney on business and would meet the band passing through New York to Philadelphia, which was our next date. Although McKinney had a big Greyhound bus for the band, Don and I always traveled in our cars, and Joe and Fat Head always rode with me. Well, that accident caused me to leave the band in Pittsburgh, as I had to come back to New York and see about my car and get my name straightened out, as Joe had my driving license, and my name was in the papers instead of Joe's. Well, after many months, everything was O.K.

Then, I started my band and Joe started playing with me, also Chu Berry. Well, we were in Boston, so Joe had roaming fever come on him again, and he left me in Boston to go back to Don and McKinney's Cotton Pickers. I really think that it was that accident that put Joe where he spent his last few years, as Joe and Fat Head loved each other.

His favorite dish was a great big juicy steak, with onions, and he would keep a pocketful of garlic, and you could tell every time Joe had his steaks, as the smell of garlic would certainly tell you, and, of course, he had to have his small bottle of corn whiskey.

I made a special trip to Charleston, West Virginia, to attend Fat Head's funeral, as the band was booked up and had to carry on. Well, anyhow, we certainly do miss one swell person who could really play trumpet and make everybody like it, and that person is our dear, beloved Joe Smith.

Then there was Jimmy Harrison. I first met Jimmy at Small's Fifth Avenue Club, in 1923, where he was playing with June Clark's five-piece band. I used to visit the Club at least three or four times a week to hear Jimmy and June (who plays trumpet, or at that time, cornet), many nights staying until they finished. It would be nine or ten in the morning sometimes.

Jimmy played riffs and often played his trombone very high, so that sometimes you would think two cornets were playing instead of one. Well, from there Jimmy went to Bamboo Inn on Seventh Avenue, between 139th and 140 Streets. I had the pleasure of opening up Bamboo Inn, as Fletcher was the attraction there for three nights, playing from two until three, because we finished at the Roseland Ballroom, where we were playing, at one o'clock.

Well, Jimmy had a one-year contract with Charlie (Johnson). So, at that time Fletcher wanted him and had to buy his contract in order to get him. Well, Jimmy came in our own band. At that time we had Don Redman, Buster Bailey, and Coleman Hawkins, reed section; Big Green and Jimmy, trombone; Cootie Williams, Bobby Stark, and Red Stewart, trumpets; Dixon, guitar; Fletcher, piano; and Escudero, bass. Jimmy really did his share in the band. He did his preaching act, his Bert Williams act, his comedy, and plenty of playing. And to think his father who was a preacher wanted Jimmy to be one. So, I can see where Jimmy learned his preaching act. When he used to put on his frock tail coat, high hat, and wear his glasses, we played a slow blues behind him, while he did his preaching. He used to bring the house down.

Well, from Fletcher, Jimmy went back to Charlie Johnson, then back to Fletcher, and to Chick Webb, where he spent his last days.

Jimmy and I had an apartment together, and many a morning, we would sit up with Hawkins playing pinochle, which was his favorite game. Jimmy did not drink much, sometimes a little wine, and smoked very little, but, my, how he could eat! He liked plenty of ice cream and cake, and baked spareribs and candied sweet potatoes.

He was crazy about Louis Armstrong, and some of the same things that Louis made on his cornet or trumpet, Jimmy could play the second part of it, in fact, like I said, before you could think, two trumpets were playing. He liked Jack Teagarden, who used to come to our house often, sometimes staying all night, and we would have a slight jam session between Hawkins, who lived only a few doors from us. So Jack would play the piano, Jimmy trombone, Hawkins tenor, and myself on my rubber-pad I kept at home. Then Hawkins would play piano, Jack and Jimmy trombone. My, what fun we had! Of course, we brought home, in my car, twelve bottles of beer, some wine, whiskey, ice cream, cake, barbecue ribs, and some chittlins, to make our morning complete.

Jimmy was well liked by everybody and had a swell disposition —always the same way, never a bad word for no one. He also liked Dicky Wells, who, I think, plays on Jimmy's style at the present time, and who also is a great and wonderful trombonist.

Well, to come to the sad and touching part, Jimmy died at Wiley Private Sanitarium, as we all have to go when the Master calls. Jimmy had ulcers of the stomach. I believe it came from eating too much sweets and his baked spareribs, but, my, what a man and perfect gentleman he was.

Well, if you can get some of the records Jimmy made, do so, as they are the last words. So, long live the King, Jimmy Harrison, the one and only.

BUSTER BAILEY

Fletcher had all the blues singers served up for all the companies so far as accompaniment went. We did accompaniment for all the blues singers. All the Smith girls—Bessie, Mamie, Clara. None of them were related, you know. There were different names like Clarence Williams' Blue Five, Perry Bradford's Jazz Hounds, et cetera. Louis, when he was with the band, and I and Big Green were on almost all the dates because we had the beat. Later Joe Smith did a lot of them. He was pretty in the middle register—he didn't go above high C. Then there was Tommy Ladnier. Did you ever hear any of his records? There's a guy who had a natural swing. Listen to the way he plays on those records. The way he takes a melody and swings it. That's what I mean by swing.

DUKE ELLINGTON

In those days, between 1926 and 1930–31, there was a lot of interchanging of the better-known musicians going on amongst three or four particular bands.

By 1926, there'd been a lot of changes in Smack's band. They were doing terrific at the Roseland at that time. Joe Smith was with them, his brother Russell, playing first, and Bobby Stark on trumpets. Benny Morton joined the band, replacing Big Green, and afterwards Green left and Jimmy Harrison came back. Big Green and Jimmy switched a couple of times. The saxophones were Hawk, Don Redman, and Buster, and the rhythm was still Escudero, Dixon, and Kaiser. And then came June Coles and later Kirby, taking Escudero's place.

The only trumpet player that stayed on through all those years was Bobby Stark. For a while there was Bobby, Rex Stewart, and Cootie Williams. Both of the latter have been working with our band now for several years. Cootie came over to us in 1929 and Russell Smith went back to Fletcher. Cootie had been playing open horn all that time, and when the guys heard about the change he was making, he got kidded a lot. The one and only Bubber Miley had died and we were hiring Cootie to take his place. Everybody told him he'd have to use a plunger and growl all night long. How was he going to make out, they wanted to know. But he didn't pay them any mind. He caught onto a lot from Tricky Sam, and before you knew it everyone was saying nobody could work with a plunger like Cootie.

REX STEWART

About that time Fletcher inaugurated one-night stands. Every April we would pile into our assorted Packards, Buicks, and Caddies and hit the coal fields of Pennsylvania until September; and each year we went further afield. In 1930 we opened at the Graystone Ballroom in Detroit. Charley Horvath and Charley Stanton were in charge and they said there were only two great dance bands in the country, Jean Goldkette's Victor band and us. Well, we scoffed and took it very lightly. After all, men like Buster Bailey, Don Redman, Hawk, Big Green, Russell Smith had been everywhere, and if this was such a hell of a band, they would have known about it. As I recall it, we closed the Graystone on a Sunday night and had a few days off until Friday to open at Roseland in New York. Most of the guys came right back to Harlem, but Redman went to West Virginia to see his people and didn't make it to New York.

Opening night and no sign of Don, but Smack had a boy from Harlem, Benny Carter, to sit in until Don returned. We thought it strange when Brecker informed Fletcher we were to open because we always were the featured band and played last. We had no idea of who was to be our relief. We finished our set and went outside for some air, but I was wondering who the other band was, how did it sound, and could I learn plenty with a capital "P." It was that Victor band with all those never to be forgotten names, but my special kick was Bix, whose work I have always admired.

JOHN HAMMOND

In 1932, I conducted my first recording session at the old Columbia studios at 55 Fifth Avenue, with Fletcher's band. Columbia was then in bankruptcy and had virtually no recording budget, but pressure from English Columbia for "hot" jazz made them agree to my proposal for four Henderson sides for the grand total of three hundred dollars (scale was twenty dollars a session a man in those days). Needless to say, I received no pay for supervision, but my excitement was tremendous, for this was the greatest band of the era.

The session was scheduled for ten A.M., and everyone had been warned that promptness was essential. At eleven thirty there were exactly five men in the studio, and my realization came that this was a band with little or no morale. It was not until twelve forty P.M. that John Kirby finally arrived with his bass and the date actually started.

Miraculously, three of Henderson's greatest sides were cut in the space of forty-five minutes: *Honeysuckle Rose, New King Porter Stomp,* and *Underneath the Harlem Moon.*

An even worse experience took place in the theater with which I was connected the same year. Henderson's band was booked for the opening week, and it was soon discovered that the men were incapable of making time. There were something like sixty violations of the show schedule during the week's twenty-eight shows. But the music was nothing less than sublime, particularly since Red Allen was sitting in for Bobby Stark and the brass section had an added boost.

DUKE ELLINGTON

Smack's band was beginning to find the going a little tough around '32 and '33. Work was scarce, but the band was so fine, and the guys so attached to it, that nobody had the heart to quit. It was exceptional the way everybody stuck, hoping for a break. Almost each individual musician had money coming to him, and yet nothing ever happened. Finally, when they couldn't hang out any longer, the whole band got together, and everybody turned in their notice at the same time. That was the break-up of the Fletcher Henderson band. Maybe it was an appropriate finale for one of the greatest dance bands anybody ever heard.

That was in 1934 and the men in the band were: Pops Smith, Red Allen, and Mouse Randolph, Claude Jones, and Keg Johnson, Benny Webster (Hawk had already left for Europe), Procope, and Jeff, Walter Johnson, Lucie, Kirby, and Horace. Things had been so bad with Smack, the boys were working one-nighters for fifty dollars a week. And yet some of them, like Claude Jones, who had four hundred dollars coming to him, were refusing offers from Calloway and others, to stick till the end.

Incidentally, that was probably one of the party-ingest bands that ever was. They used to travel on the road in cars, instead of buses. As soon as they'd arrive at their destination they'd start in having a ball. When they got through at night, they'd pick up where they left off. They'd wait till the last possible moment before leaving for the next town, and they'd have to hold a steady seventy on the road to arrive on schedule (which half of them never did). There's a story about one of the boys when they were playing at the Roseland. He had a bottle of gin in his locker, and one night the rest of the band dipped into it lightly. When he showed up it was all gone, and he was hot. He went out and got another bottle—plus a bottle of colorless castor oil! He mixed them up, putting the bottle back, and telling the guys to help themselves. Most everybody did. There was murder on the stand that night!

BILLY TERNENT

I got to know Henderson in the 1935–36 period, when I was the arranger for Jack Hylton. We were appearing in Chicago, and I met F.H. through Benny Goodman, for whom Smack made so many arrangements. Benny, at this time, was playing at the Congress in Chicago (with Gene Krupa on drums and Jess Stacy, piano).

Every night, after I finished at the Gold Coast Room of the famous Drake Hotel, I used to call for Goodman, and we all proceeded to the Grand Terrace ballroom, where Henderson was appearing with his band.

For me, the first hearing of Smack's band was a thrill I shall remember as long as I live. The *jump* that this band had was simply amazing.

In the band was Roy Eldridge—to me the guy who could squeeze anything out of a trumpet—and I have never heard anyone reach so high in my life. Then there was Buster Bailey on clarinet—who Benny thought was the last word—and a tenor player, Chu Berry.

Yes, I agree that Coleman Hawkins was and is great, but Chu played choruses that really would "make the angels sing."

Anyhow, after the excitement was over, I met all the gang, and a couple of nights later I had a drink and a serious chat with Smack in his little flat, only a few yards from the Grand Terrace room.

Believe you me, I thought he was a sick man *then*—or perhaps I should say a man always full of depression.

LEORA HENDERSON

It's so long ago, it's like a dream. I first met Fletcher when we were playing a dance on a Hudson River boat. It was a gig. (We called jobs like that gigs then.) I was playing trumpet and he played piano. At that time, during the day, he had a job downtown at the Black Swan record company as a sort of recording director and band leader. Fletcher was on all of the Ethel Waters' records for Black Swan. He was her accompanist.

Before I met Fletcher, I could only play classics or else only what I saw on paper, and Fletcher said, "You better learn to jazz or you won't make no money." Then we heard somebody playing *Lady Be Good* on the radio and it had just the *prettiest* trumpet chorus! And that's how I think Fletcher started writing. He went right to the piano and wrote out that chorus for me. From then on, he did that for me many times. Later on, when Louis Armstrong came to the band, I used to sit and watch him, and Louis taught me how to make riffs. Oh, after that, I played a regular hot trumpet and got all the work I wanted.

Fletcher had a band at the Club Alabam for about a year, and in 1924, I think, went into the Roseland Ballroom. The band played there on and off for seventeen years, most of that time as the regular house band. Of course, they would go out on tour for a few months each year, and, do you know, in all that time he never had a contract!

It was considered an honor to get in that band. It had the hardest book in the business, and many a musician just couldn't play those arrangements. Why, there were times when there was an empty chair on the bandstand. Jimmy Harrison couldn't make it. Fletcher turned him away and he went out and studied before Fletcher would take him back. The same thing happened to Rex Stewart. They rehearsed 'most every night, and while there were drinkin' men in the band, I don't remember when any of them was ever drunk on the job. And, at that time, I don't think that there was any of that reefer smokin'. At least, if there was, I didn't know anything about it.

My! Some of those rehearsals were a pleasure to watch. They would have some real battles. "Cuttin' contests," you know. I would set off in a dark corner and watch while Charlie Green (we called him Big Green) would be playing something wonderful and then Jimmy Harrison would say, "Huh, you think *you* done somethin'," and then he'd try to cut him. It was that way with the whole band. I'm telling you, it was just thrilling!

And that would get them all prepared for the Battles of Jazz with

219

the bands that were playing at Roseland—the Dorsey Brothers, Casa Loma, Vincent Lopez, Jean Goldkette, and there was one band that they called The Buffalodians that had a little kid playing piano. He was the boy who wrote *Stormy Weather*. His name was Arlen . . . Harold Arlen.

But nobody could beat our band, not with people like Don Redman and Louis, Bobby Stark, Joe Smith, Coleman Hawkins, Buster Bailey, Benny Carter, John Kirby, Big Green, and all the rest of the fine musicians that Fletcher had in those years.

Just before one of those band battles were about to start Fletcher would say to the men. "Come on—let's take charge!" And they would *play!* But, you know, those other bands didn't mind at all. They'd be listenin' and getting ideas and inspiration.

On his tours, Fletcher would see or hear of some musician who would qualify for the band and then later on he'd send for him. And Fletcher wasn't like some other band leaders. The men liked to work for him. He'd exploit their names and bring them out so people would know them. And he had an easy disposition and a nice way about him. In fact, I never, in all the time I knew him, knew him to get real mad about anything.

Many of the musicians would come up to the house then. The only time any of them ever sat in with the band was during the last set, and afterwards they'd come home with us. Bix Beiderbecke would come all the time, and Joe Venuti and Eddie Lang and many more. Musicians seemed much nicer then. You didn't mind having them in your home. But mercy! I don't know about today. I wouldn't have all that reefer smokin' in my house!

For a while, a rage came along for blues singers—everything was blues, and Fletcher did a lot of work for blues singers. There was Bessie Smith and Clara Smith (she used to rehearse right here in this house) and many others whose names I don't recall. Sometimes Fletcher would work under different names because he was under contract, but it was so long ago, I guess it don't matter if I mention it now.

Around that time Paul Whiteman was called "The King of Jazz" and so people began calling Fletcher "The Colored King of Jazz." Whiteman would be playin' all those novelties and semi-classical numbers and Fletcher would turn right around and swing them. I recall that Don Redman even did an arrangement of *Rhapsody in Blue*, but later on they stopped the band from playin' it.

After the band would finish playin' at Roseland about one A.M., they'd sometimes play for dances in Harlem, till about three thirty in the morning. There'd be a band on before Fletcher got there, but when he and the men arrived, everything would stop. Folks would get out of the way, and then Fletcher would start off with *Sugar Foot Stomp* and the crowd would go wild.

And there were no singers then like there are now. We didn't need 'em. Oh, Louis would carry on with a lot of foolishness— jump up and down and shout like a down-South preacher. And Jimmy Harrison was all fun and comedy too. He'd act like Bert Williams and sing *Somebody Loves Me* just like Williams—and things like that.

Joe Smith was wonderful too. He drank heavy and got real sick and passed later on. But, you know, I didn't know about any drinkin' or carryin' on in the band. The boys would keep that from me—and me being Fletcher's wife, there were *lots of things* I didn't know.

But about Joe Smith. (I used to call him "Toots.") I knew Joe before he could even play trumpet. He was always botherin' me to use my horn. But I used to get real mad. I didn't want anybody blowin' on my trumpet. I used to worry him about going out and finding himself a job . . . maybe learning to play drums or something.

Then he went away for about two years, and one day I found a note under my door. It said, "Back in town" and it was signed "Toots." At that time I was playin' in the pit of the Lafayette Theatre and he came down to see me.

He came in sly-like and said, "I learned to play clarinet." And he picked up a clarinet and started to play.

"That's not so good, Toots," I told him, and started to tell him again about settlin' down and gettin' a job. But when the time came to do the show, he came into the pit with me. I didn't know it, but he had hidden a trumpet there, and when some blues singer (I just can't remember her name) began to sing, Joe played. And the people started to howl. I'm telling you, I couldn't play another note that night!

He came to the theater every day after that and I helped to make him read and he really could play anything. That is, except that Spanish music. But finally he conquered that too. Joe had such a big soft beautiful tone. Bessie Smith was just crazy about his playing and he was on lots of her records later on.

There was one other musician I'd like to mention. He was *so* good. That's Hilton Jefferson. I don't know why people don't appreciate him—one of the finest saxophone players I ever heard. His record of *Who Can I Turn To* with Cab Calloway is so beautiful.

Believe me Fletcher was never the same after he had that automobile accident down in Kentucky. He was going to Louisville to see my mother in that big open Packard he had, ridin' with Big Green, Coleman Hawkins, Bobby Stark, and Joe Smith. Some woman wouldn't pull over and the car went off the road and fell fourteen feet and turned right over. Fletcher was the only one who got hurt. He had an awful hit in his head and his left shoulder bone was pushed over to his collar bone. You know, it was the left side that got paralyzed later on. That was the only accident he ever had, and after that—why, he just changed.

Everything would seem comical to him and he never achieved to go higher than he was. He never had much business qualities anyhow, but after that accident, he had even less. And worst of all, he would get careless. He had a wonderful ear and if a bell would strike somewhere in the street, Fletcher would tell you what note it was. But one day I went to a rehearsal and the boys were blowin' and I said, "Fletcher, can't you tell, one of them horns is out of tune." But he didn't seem to care much. It was the men in the band that kept up the morale then.

Then the managers of Roseland lost confidence in him too. The band was broken up and one day John Hammond came over and asked Fletcher to do some arranging for Benny Goodman. I'm telling you that nobody could have done more than John and Benny. Benny did everything he could to build up Fletcher's name and would tell people that his band was nothin' compared to Fletcher's on those arrangements. Later on Fletcher worked with Benny's band and when he got sick and John arranged that special broadcast, Benny got some of his old men together and made that record so we could get the money.

The last job that Fletcher had before the stroke was in that Jazz Train show that played in that place on Broadway, Bop City. He worked so hard on that. He was really trying to make a comeback—workin' days and nights on arrangements and rehearsals. But all of it was for nothing.

The day Fletcher died he had one of his biggest audiences out here on the street what with the ambulances and the oxygen tanks. Louis Armstrong sent the most beautiful floral piece I've ever seen—shaped like an organ, pipes and all. Louis and Joe Glaser came to the funeral—and, you know, the people from Roseland sent a man up here to see how I was gettin' on.

13

"Ellington plays the piano, but his real instrument is his band."

REX STEWART

Ah, those were the days—top and bottom, breakfast dances, and real jam sessions. Let's pause here and pay tribute to Willie "The Lion" Smith, Stephen "The Beetle" Henderson, James P. Johnson, and Willie "The Tiger" Gant. Those fellows were the inspiration of most of the guys who were on the New York scene, many of whom became greats in the swing world—Fats Waller, Benny Carter, Jimmy and Tommy Dorsey, Goodman, and, oh yes, there was a five-piece band from my home town, Washington, who, rumor said, existed on the earnings of its pool-hustling drummer, Sonny Greer, because they worked very little.

DUKE ELLINGTON

The memory of things gone is important to a jazz musician. I remember I once wrote a sixty-four-bar piece about a memory of when I was a little boy in bed and heard a man whistling on the street outside, his footsteps echoing away.

And take my *Harlem Air Shaft*. So much goes on in a Harlem air shaft. You get the full essence of Harlem in an air shaft. You hear fights, you smell dinner, you hear people making love. You hear intimate gossip floating down. You hear the radio. An air shaft is one great big loudspeaker. You see your neighbors' laundry. You hear the janitor's dogs. The man upstairs' aerial falls down and breaks your window. You smell coffee. A wonderful thing, that smell. An air shaft has got every contrast. One guy is cooking dried fish and rice and another guy's got a great big turkey. Guy-with-fish's wife is a terrific cooker but the guy's wife with the turkey is doing a sad job. You hear people praying, fighting, snoring. Jitterbugs are jumping up and down always over you, never below you. That's a funny thing about jitterbugs. They're always above you. I tried to put all that in *Harlem Air Shaft*. . . .

The music's mostly written down, because it saves time. It's written down if it's only a basis for a change. There's no set system. Most times I write it and arrange it. Sometimes I write it and the band and I collaborate on the arrangement. Sometimes Billy Strayhorn, my staff arranger, does the arrangement. When we're all working together, a guy may have an idea and he plays it on his horn. Another guy may add to it and make something out of it. Someone may play a riff and ask, "How do you like this?" The trumpets may try something together and say, "Listen to this." There may be a difference of opinion on what kind of mute to use. Someone may advocate extending a note or cutting it off. The sax section may want to put an additional smear on it. . . .

I got my first break when I was about seventeen, down in Washington, and Louis Thomas sent for me to play piano one night. Thomas was the leader of a society band whose only competition was Meyer Davis. I was to get a chance to play in his third band on the condition I would learn to play the *Siren Song* well enough to perform it that night.

I spent the whole day learning the tune. When I arrived on the job I found that the band was a legitimate one, they wouldn't play any "jumps." The musicians started talking to me about correct chords, and I knew that in a few minutes I'd be sunk. Then somebody requested the *Siren Song*, and in great relief I started plunking out the number. I'd often watched Lucky Roberts who had come down from New York to play the Howard Theatre. He had a flashy style, and a trick of throwing his hands away from the piano. It occurred to me then that I might try doing what he did.

Before I knew it the kids around the stand were screaming with delight and clapping for more.

In two minutes the flashy hands had earned me a reputation, and after that I was all set. I got a hunch about having my own band. I put an advertisement in the telephone book just as large as Louis Thomas' and Meyer Davis', and bigger than Doc Perry's. Whenever anybody wanted anything in Washington, they looked in the telephone directory. Especially so where bands were concerned. If somebody wanted to hire some music and didn't know what musicians they wanted, I figured they were just as likely as not to pick on the biggest advertiser in the book. My hunch worked out pretty well, and before long, I had about three bands working. It was the hands that turned the trick.

Things were swell for two or three years, and after a while I was averaging about a hundred fifty to two hundred a week. By around 1922 I had myself a pretty good band. The Miller brothers were with me. These were three low-down musicians who came from one of those "musical families" where everybody plays some instrument. There was Bill Miller, Brother, and Felix. Being all of twenty or so, they were sophisticates, and imbibed corn whiskey and gin heavily, either one serving as a chaser for the other. Otto Hardwicke, or "Toby" as we all call him, was just growing up at that time. I think he was sixteen.

He was playing bass fiddle with Carroll's Columbia Orchestra that year, and he was so small his father used to carry his bass to work for him. I, considering myself a veteran, decided I would break Toby in. He got himself a saxophone; in those days it was a C melody. I got him a job and later on I used to send him out on other jobs and pretty soon he got to be known as one of the best saxophone players in town. Artie Whetsol used to work with us sometimes too. Afterwards he joined my band and was for years one of its most indispensable members. Elmer Snowden played banjo in our band, and was considered to be very fly. Juan Tizol came to town that year too. He was with the band from Puerto Rico that Marie Lucas brought back to play in the pit at the Howard. We had to acknowledge that was a hell-fired band, all the musicians in it could switch instruments, and at that time, that was extraordinary.

Then someone sent for Sonny Greer from New York. We had heard about Sonny. He was supposed to be a very fly drummer, and anybody from New York had the edge on all of us. But maybe, we thought, he wasn't all that he was cracked up to be. We watched him work in the pit, and he used a lot of tricks. He was flashy, but our minds still weren't made up. We decided to give him the works and find out just what sort of a guy he was, maybe he hadn't done any more than just pass through New York. We stood on the street corner and waited for him. Everybody used to stand on street corners then and try to look big-time. Here comes Sonny. "Whatcha say?" we ask him. I take the lead in the conversation because I'm sure that I'm a killer with my new shepherd plaid suit, bought on time. Sonny comes back with a line of jive that lays us low. We decide he's O.K.

Later on Sonny quit the Howard Theatre to join me . . . Everybody in our band at that time was a juice-hound, juice meaning any kind of firewater. We all thought we were extra special, and liked to smoke big cigars, and look like Stuart Holmes in the movies. Toby had a weakness for ninety-dollar suits, and he ended up by buying himself a Pullman automobile. We called the car the "Dupadilly." You always had to push to start it, and it didn't have a crank-handle. It inevitably stalled on a hill. One day it stopped somewhere and we got out and left it and that was the end of the Dupadilly. Before that, though, Otto bought another car from Dear-Me. That was his name, we never did know the rest of it, everybody called him Dear-Me.

Claude Hopkins had a car, and I had a Chandler, and Toby and Felix and Bill used to race our two cars and the Dupadilly. After work we'd set out, going nowhere, and as fast as we could. We didn't bother about street crossings or anything else. I don't know why we never cracked up.

After work, musicians usually gathered at the Industrial Cafe, where they would hold a general gab fest and jam session. Every guy would try to tell a bigger lie than the last one, and that's where

Sonny showed us what he was made of. He always carried off all honors. Band contests were very popular in those days, and one that I remember was arranged between Elmer Snowden's eight-piece band with Artie and Toby, and our three pieces including Sonny, Sterling Conway on banjorine, and myself. Sonny and I decided we'd have to put our heads together for that, and we worked out a lot of tricks between drums and piano. They went over so well we walked away with the cup. The next contest was with Blind Johnny's band. Johnny played a whole lot of piano and he won that one. Whenever we had a contest to play we used to go all out for psychology. We'd tell the fellows in the other band they were going to get cut that night. They'd be so rattled they'd even get to calling out the wrong numbers.

For a long time I had been rehearsing a riff to make the piano sound like Jimmy Johnson. Everybody was trying to sound like the *Carolina Shout* that Jimmy had made on a player-piano roll. I got it down by slowing up the roll. I had it so close that when Jimmy came to town to play one night, they made me get up on the stage to cut him. I took him out that night for a tour of the Southwest district, and I stayed up till ten A.M. listening to him.

All at once it looked like the big break had arrived. Wilbur Sweatman sent down from New York for Sonny, and eventually that meant Toby and myself too. But when we got there we found out the work that wasn't so good. We just had some theaters to play and they were split-weeks. Sweatman performed every night with his three clarinets in his mouth at one time. But at night it was mellow.

We went out every evening regardless of whether we had money or not, and we met all the hip guys. I got a big thrill when I strolled into the Capitol Club at 140th and Lenox, down in the basement, and found "The Lion" working there. We went the rounds every night, looking for the piano players. We didn't have any gold, but then Sonny was good at that sort of thing. He would stride in, big as life, and tell the man . . . "Hello, Jack, I'm Sonny. I know So-and-So, and he told me to look you up. Meet my pals, Duke and Toby." Then the man would hear that Duke played a whole lot of piano. I'd sit down after "The Lion," and then Fats Waller would

228

sit down after me. Fats used to follow Jimmy Johnson around, and "The Lion" used to say of him, "Yeah, a yearling, he's coming along, I guess he'll do all right."

Jimmy Johnson used to get all the house-rent parties to play. There were so many of them that he turned a lot of them over to Lippy. Lippy had heard so much piano that he couldn't play any more. He only thought piano. Lippy gave a lot of piano players work, and then he'd remember me. One time, things were so bad that even Sonny took a job playing piano. Lippy knew every piano and player-piano in town. He used to walk around all night long with James P., "The Lion," Fats, and myself. I was one of the main hangers-on. Lippy would walk up to any man's house at any time of night. He'd ring the doorbell. Finally somebody would wake up and holler out the window about who was it making all the disturbance. Lippy would answer, "It's Lippy, and James P. is here with me." These magic words opened anybody's door, and we would sit and play all night long.

It wasn't long after that that I found the fifteen dollars in an envelope on the street. It bought me a new pair of shoes, and the fare back to Washington for the three of us. When I finished eating that first home-cooked breakfast, I made up my mind I'd stay put for a while and organize another band.

After I'd gone back home to Washington and stayed for a while, Fats Waller came through town with a burlesque show. Bushell was with the band too, and Clarence Robinson and Bert Adams were the featured dance team with the show. Sitting in my house, eating chickens by the pair, Fats told us they were all going to quit; that we'd better come on up to New York and get the job.

Then there was a wire from New York saying that Fats had decided not to leave, so Artie Whetsol, Sonny, Toby, and Snowden went up alone. Then they sent for me; everything had been fixed, the job was a cinch for me! On the way up, I travel in style, blowing all my money on the train. After all, I'm a big shot, I've got a job waiting for me in the big town. I have just enough left for cab-fare uptown. There they are, standing on the corner. "Whatdya know? how's things? and give us some gold," they say. They're busted!

The job was set back time and time again, and it got so that it looked very bad. We were living with some nice people and they told us we could stay on until we found some work. We kept right on auditioning, but nothing ever happened. There was no work. Then Bricktop came along, and she saved the day for us. I'd worked with Bricktop, the famed Bricktop of Montmartre, Paris, at the Oriental in Washington. Barron's was then a very popular spot, and she knew Barron well.

She got him to let his band go and hire us instead. We'd scuffled for five weeks, and here at last we were to go to work. That day we got hold of some money and blew it going out to Coney Island. We went to a fortune teller, and for fifty cents he told us we'd start to work on Monday. Though it had all been figured out beforehand, somehow we must have spent a nickel too much. Somebody was minus subway fare home.

Everybody seemed to like us at Barron's, and at that time there were no other organized bands in Harlem. We were only five, but we had arrangements on everything, and it was what we've now named conversation music, kind of soft and gutbucket. We were Toby, Whetsol, Sonny, Snowden and myself, and we let Snowden handle the business. I didn't have my mind on leadership, but then Snowden got a raise and we didn't know it till later, so we decided to make a change. They made me take his place.

There were lots of "Mr. Gunions" who came into Barron's. A "Mr. Gunion" is anybody with lots of money. We used to make thirty dollars a week, and the tips ran into twenty apiece per night. There were nine of us who had to split, the four entertainers and ourselves. We used to see fellows throwing twenty dollars in halves on the floor.

It was after Snowden left that we got Freddy Guy. It was funny the way it came about. We used to hang out a lot at a spot called the Orient. Earl Dancer ran the place, and Freddy had the band. But Earl owed Freddy so much money, that the latter was practically owner. Fats Waller was working for him there, and when we first walked in, Freddy big-timed us, asking Fats who we were. Fats spoke his little piece, and we were all relieved when Freddy okehed us. Later on we got to be good friends, and Freddy liked our band so much that when Snowden quit, he decided to come with us.

In September, 1923, we landed a job through Leonard Harper, at the Hollywood Cafe at Forty-ninth Street and Broadway. Harper had the revue there, and it was a hot show. Later on the name was changed to the Kentucky Club. We did well there, and our run lasted well into five years. During that time Sonny's drums got burned up three different times, because of the club's periodic fires. Station WHN was just opening up around then, and they started broadcasting us every night after two A.M.

All that air-time helped to build up our name. The Kentucky Club definitely became the place to go, and the biggies and musicians used to drop in every night. We had plenty of swell times all during those days. Many of the boys with the Wolverines used to come by, Bix Beiderbecke with them. Then we were friendly with the fellows from Paul Whiteman's band, and from the California Ramblers, and we used to often see Jimmy and Tommy Dorsey, Lopez, and a dozen others around who were coming up at that time.

After a while we decided to add another man, and we got Charlie Irvis on trombone. He used to play with a special cone-shaped brass mute. Then Whetsol left us, and went back to Howard University to finish studying medicine. Bubber Miley was still young then, but we had him join. Our band changed its character when Bubber came in. He used to growl all night long, playing gutbucket on his horn. That was when we decided to forget all about the sweet music.

Charlie Irvis could play lowdown on the trombone, and there was never anyone to sound like Bubber. Together he and I wrote out our theme, the *East St. Louis Toodle-Oo*. Bubber was very temperamental, and liked his likker, he used to get under the piano and go to sleep when he felt like it. In fact all our horn-blowers were lushies, and I used to have to go around and get them out of bed to see they got to work.

The band had been at the Kentucky Club about three and a half years when I first met Irving Mills. We were playing the *St. Louis Blues*, and he asked what it was. When I told him, he said

231

it sure sounded nothing like it. So maybe that gave him ideas. He talked to me about making records. Naturally, I agreed, and we got together four originals. They were for the Vocalion and Brunswick labels, and we made *East St. Louis* and *Birmingham Breakdown* for the first. On the second date I remember we waxed *Emigration Blues*.

I'd been doing a bit of writing during that previous year and had scored the show THE CHOCOLATE KIDDIES in 1924. Joe Trent was the lyric writer, and Robbins had the score. At that time Robbins was on Broadway, with only one small room. The show never did play New York. It went to Berlin to play the Winter Garden where it ran for two solid years.

In 1927 we left the Kentucky, and Irving Mills submitted us for the Cotton Club. Everybody was betting we wouldn't last a month. We had one friend by the name of "Mexico." He ran the hottest ginmill on 133rd Street and you were always seeing cats walking along the streets, tubas on their shoulders, making their way over to his "cutting contests." Mexico bet one hundred dollars and a hat that our band would make the grade. He did all right for himself because we were starting a five-year run. We used to hang out at his place, drinking up his booze. We called it "a ninety-nine per cent," one more degree either way would bust your top, we said.

That was during Prohibition and we used to stick around till morning watching Mexico make up the stuff. Tricky Sam was official taster. We opened up at the Cotton Club, December fourth, in 1927. Jimmy McHugh and Dorothy Fields had scored the show, and Jimmy had been instrumental in getting us the booking. Clarence Robinson and Johnny Vigal were the producers, and the big tunes were *Dancemania* and *Jazzmania*. Later on we played the same show in the Lafayette and Standard Theatres, and these originated the type of entertainment featured at the Apollo today.

We were broadcasting at five P.M. every day over WHN. Then we really got a break. Columbia sent Ted Husing down to see about putting the band on the air. He got everything settled, and went right to work announcing our programs. He did such a terrific job that our band soon became widely known. By that time, we had twelve men in the band. Bubber and Artie were the trumpets and later we added Metcalf. Johnny Hodges was still with Chick Webb, but we had Toby and Ruby Jackson, and we'd just hired Carney.

Carney was only a kid at the time, and we had to tell him everything. He wanted to know what the money was, and when we told him seventy-five dollars, he could hardly credit his ears. By then we were recording almost every day, and for all the labels. We used a dozen different names. We were signed with Victor, but we'd wax for other companies as the "Jungle Band," "Joe Turner and His Men," "Sonny Greer and His Memphis Men," and the "Harlem Footwarmers."

We started doubling at theaters and neighborhood houses, like the Audubon, the Bronx Crotona, the Broadway, and the Brooklyn. We'd been playing a three-day run at the Fifty-eighth Street Theatre when along comes a guy and says we open the Palace the following day. Situated at Forty-sixth Street and Broadway, the Palace was the big thing at that time, and we were naturally tickled. There was only one hitch. They told us it was necessary for me to emcee!

I didn't know the first thing about how to emcee and the thought of it had me half scared to death. Then there we were on the stage, and I opened my mouth and nothing came out. Finally, I moved down to the footlights, and things got a little better. The audience actually seemed to be listening. I guess we must have growled them almost out of their seats. They wouldn't let us off the stage, and the main act had a hard time coming on.

So that was our first year at the Club. Afterwards we made further changes in the band, and soon there was so much work that we were doubling all the time.

IRVING MILLS

The first time I heard Duke Ellington was at the Kentucky Club in New York, where he had come in with the five-piece band he had been appearing with in Washington, D.C. I had gone to the Kentucky Club that night with the late Sime Silverman of *Variety* who, like most newspapermen, liked to go out for an evening of relaxation after putting his paper "to bed" for another deadline. I think the number that caught my attention that night was *Black and Tan Fantasy*. When I learned that it was Duke's composition, I immediately recognized that I had encountered a great creative artist—and the first American composer to catch in his music the true jazz spirit.

Shortly after that, when I was producing a new show for the Cotton Club, I built as much of it as possible around Duke's band and his music. The budget, incidentally, did not provide for a band as large as Duke felt he needed—ten pieces. I paid the salaries of the additional musicians out of my share of the project. I did it gladly, because I had complete faith in Duke Ellington and firmly believed that together we were launching something more than just a dance orchestra.

LOUIS METCALF

In those days, they almost came to blows in Harlem—musicians, I mean, about the two different styles of playing. Why, when I joined Duke Ellington at the Cotton Club, about 1925, I guess, the men in the band were always fighting about which was the better style, Eastern or Western. 'Course, when I say Western, I mean everything that came out of New Orleans, Chicago, St. Louis, Kansas City and places like that. The Western style was more open . . . open horns and running chords and running changes. With Ellington, it was the new men like myself and Johnny Hodges and Bigard against guys like Bubber Miley and Tricky Sam Nanton. They were playing wah-wah music with plungers and things. Actually, our coming into the Ellington band made them change somewhat.

The Cotton Club was a class house and, considering that Duke was still organizing his band, the fact that we were makin' about seventy-five a week with him showed how much he was thought of. But, believe me, Duke had to fight every inch of the way to get what he wanted. Some of the guys used to tell him he was a fool to give in so much to management, but Duke knew what he wanted, and I guess to get what you want, you have to compromise.

234

NED E. WILLIAMS

I first heard the Ellington band in 1927, which was the year it made its debut at the famous Cotton Club in Harlem. That year I was the press agent for the celebrated song team of Van and Schenck and for the Silver Slipper, where Gus and Joe were appearing in the heart of Times Square.

Dan Healy was the producer of the floor show at the Slipper, and it was as his guest that I visited Harlem. We were driven there by an affable member of the Slipper mob, Johnny Irish, who had his girl friend with him, the dancing star of the Slipper show, Ruby Keeler, who a few months later became the bride of Al Jolson.

I can't say that I was too much impressed with the Ellington crew on that visit. It definitely didn't have the form and the polish that it acquired later, of course. I was bewildered by the elaborate floor revue at the Cotton Club, even then comparable with the top Broadway musicals, and fascinated by the dispatch and lack of commotion with which a belligerent drunken guest was subdued and evicted by the club attachés.

The next time I heard Ellington was three years later on the stage of the Oriental Theatre in Chicago. That occasion was memorable for the rendition of *Mood Indigo* by the original trombone, clarinet, trumpet combination, Tricky Sam Nanton, Barney Bigard, and Artie Whetsol. It never has sounded the same since.

Subsequently, I was to hear the fabulous Ellington band on countless occasions, in rehearsals, recording sessions, theaters, one-nighters, and in the Cotton Club during its heyday. There was the early era in which the Duke had just received general fame, when Paul Whiteman and his arranger, Ferde Grofe, visited the Cotton Club nightly for more than a week, finally admitted that they couldn't steal even two bars of the amazing music.

There was the unforgettable night when Ethel Waters stood in the spotlight, with the Ellington band pulsating behind her, and sang, for the first time in public, a song by Harold Arlen and Ted Koehler called *Stormy Weather*. I heard Ed Sullivan introduce Arlen on television the other night merely as the writer of *Over the Rainbow*! Oh, well.

Then there was that later night at the Cotton Club, when the entire brass section of the Ellington band arose and delivered such an intricate and unbelievably integrated chorus that the late Eddie Duchin, usually a poised and dignified musician, actually and literally rolled on the floor under his table in ecstasy.

Duke always has had a penchant for pinning nicknames on those most closely associated with him, usually nicknames that stick. Thus, Freddy Jenkins, the little trumpet player who held the uninhibited spot in the band later graced by Ray Nance, became Posey. Johnny Hodges, alto star now out on his own, still is called Rabbit by those closest to him.

The late Richard Jones, Duke's valet for years, jumped only to the call of Bowden, and Jack Boyd, erstwhile manager of the band, whose given name is Charles, for no explainable reason was always just Elmer to the Duke. It was Elmer in turn who dubbed Ellington as Dumpy, and I can't remember when I've called him anything else in direct communication.

It may be a signal honor, but Duke went into a big corporation routine for me, never addresses me nor refers to me except by my first two initials, N. E. Another leader, while playing trumpet for Ellington, won the name which he still uses professionally, Cootie Williams, and there are many other instances.

For favored feminine acquaintances, Duke lapses into the old southern custom of adding May to everything, Daisy May, Evie May, Willie May, no matter if the resemblance to your own given name is very slight. Even the antiquated revolver, toted around in the trunks by the troupe for years against possible holdups (no one knows who would use it) always has been designated Sweetie May.

An odd instance of the thirteen (Friday or not) superstition in the Ellington make-up comes to mind. It was the year that he was writing, with the collaboration of Henry Nemo and others, the entire score for a Cotton Club show. He had completed twelve songs, but he decided that unless he turned out thirteen, it wouldn't be lucky.

So, he composed a thirteenth song, which strangely enough was presented as a production number in that show, since the producer and the dance directors already were spinning on their heels with the wealth of Ellington material. But it was played regularly on the nightly broadcasts from the Cotton Club.

It was called *I Let A Song Go Out Of My Heart*.

Speaking of song titles reminds me of the amusing go-around we experienced with radio censorship about fifteen years ago, when we were celebrating Duke's tenth anniversary in music business (and his birthday) with a matinee party at the Cotton Club and a special broadcast to England through the facilities of BBC.

We had cleared the numbers for the broadcast in customary fashion when this worried girl assistant 'phoned from the station. They were in serious doubt, it seemed, about the propriety of two of the titles scheduled, *Hip Chick* and *Dinah's in a Jam*.

My efforts to assure her (and the censor board) that the *Hip* in the first title had nothing to do with hips, and that the jam version of *Dinah* was not even remotely connected with pregnancy were unavailing. Since both were instrumental numbers, we switched the titles to more innocuous ones and played them anyway.

I've often wondered since about the condition of the wigs of the busy radio censors if they ever learned the truth about the significance of such recorded titles as *The Skrontch*, *T. T. on Toast*, *Warm Valley*, and others.

BILLY STRAYHORN

In 1934, in Pittsburgh, I heard and saw the Ellington band perform for my first time. Nothing before or since has affected my life so much. In 1939, I became his protégé, enabling me to be closer and see more.

His first, last, and only formal instruction for me was embodied in one word: Observe. I did just that and came to know one of the most fascinating and original minds in American music.

Ellington plays the piano, but his real instrument is his band. Each member of his band is to him a distinctive tone color and set of emotions, which he mixes with others equally distinctive to produce a third thing, which I like to call the "Ellington Effect."

Sometimes this mixing happens on paper and frequently right

on the bandstand. I have often seen him exchange parts in the middle of a piece because the man and the part weren't the same character.

Ellington's concern is with the individual musician, and what happens when they put their musical characters together. Watching him on the bandstand, the listener might think that his movements are stock ones used by everyone in front of a band. However, the extremely observant may well detect the flick of the finger that may draw the sound he wants from a musician.

By letting his men play naturally and relaxed, Ellington is able to probe the intimate recesses of their minds and find things that not even the musicians thought were there.

Lately, personnel changes have prompted the comment that what I call the "Ellington Effect" has been replaced by something different. This, I believe, comes about from listening with the eyes instead of the ears. The same thing has happened every time there has been a change during my stay, and, even before my time, the advent into the band of the very people who have left brought forth the same remarks.

The same comment accompanied my arrival, but has long since simmered down to a whodunit game indulged in by the band (which always puzzles me, because I think my playing and writing style is totally different from Ellington's).

The Ellington Effect has touched many people, both listeners and performers, princes and paupers, the loved and the unloved, and will, as long as there is, and after there is—Ellington.

DUKE ELLINGTON

I like great big ole tears. That's why I liked Whetsol. When he played the funeral march in *Black and Tan Fantasy*, I used to see great, big ole tears running down people's faces . . . Bubber used to say, "If it ain't got swing, it ain't worth playin'; if it ain't got gutbucket, it ain't worth doin'."

14

Bessie Smith—"The Empress of the Blues."

FRANK WALKER

I don't think there could have been more than fifty people up North who had heard about Bessie Smith when I sent Clarence Williams down South to get her. Clarence did a lot of work for me then. He was very important in coaching and teaching and working on our artists. He could somehow manage to get the best out of them, and to this day hasn't received the credit he really deserves.

Clarence really wasn't much of a pianist though, he'll tell you that himself. When he was back home in New Orleans he played piano in one of those honky-tonks and could only play by ear— maybe knowing a half a dozen songs. Then some inebriate might come in and ask for a song he didn't know, and Clarence would say, "Come back tomorrow night." The next day he'd go down to the five-and-ten-cent store, to the sheet music counter, and pull out the song for the piano player to demonstrate. He would hear it once and know it. If that customer came back, Clarence would play the song and maybe pick up a dime tip. It was like some of our hillbilly artists say about songs, "I can write them down, but I can't note them."

Anyway, I told Clarence about the Smith girl and said, "This is what you've got to do. Go down there and find her and bring her back up here."

He found her, and I'm telling you that the girl he brought back looked like anything *but* a singer. She looked about seventeen—tall and fat and scared to death—just awful! But all of this you forgot when you heard her sing, because when Bessie sang the blues, she meant it. Blues were her life. She was blues from the time she got up in the morning until she went to bed at night. Oh, she had a sense of humor all right, and she could laugh too. But it didn't last long.

Her first record was *Down Hearted Blues* and it was a tremendous hit. And there was one line in that blues that did it. It was the first time it was used and it made that record a hit. It was "Got the world in a jug, got the stopper in my hand."

I don't know that there was anyone closer to Bessie than I was. She came to me for advice; I took care of her money and bookings (at one time she was probably the highest-paid Negro performer in vaudeville—next to Bert Williams, that is). She knew that we looked at her and treated her as a human being and not as a piece of property.

It was all a matter of feeling with her. It was inside. Not that there was any repression. It all came out in her singing. Almost all of the blues she sang told sort of a story, and they were written especially for her. I don't want to give you the idea that Bessie Smith was incapable of writing her own blues, not at all. She probably could have. She would get an idea, then we would discuss it. But once she started to sing, nobody told her what to do. Nobody interfered. That was one of the reasons she liked Fletcher Henderson so much. He was quiet and never butted in. He did what Bessie told him to.

I suppose that lots of people remember and think of Bessie as a rough-and-tumble sort of person. Still, that wasn't the only side of her. They didn't know about things like her buying a rooming house for her friends to live in, and hundreds of other little things which cost her barrels of money. Yes, Bessie had a heart as big as all outdoors, but she gave it all away.

Later on, when the blues began to spread out and became established, new people were coming along and Bessie began to lose heart. You might say she didn't have a hitching post to tie her horse to. She began to lose interest in life. She had no heart left and was singing differently.

There was bitterness in her, and, you know, the blues aren't bitter.

CLARENCE WILLIAMS

Here's something I don't think anybody knows about Bessie Smith, even Mr. Frank Walker. I had worked with Bessie on T.O.B.A. time, in vaudeville and colored theaters, and I thought she was terrific, and this was long before Mr. Walker's time at Columbia Records. Well, Bessie was about twenty then, and she was dancin' too, and sometimes played a man's part, wearin' a tuxedo.

I spent two or three hundred dollars for a dress for her to try out in for a new Broadway show, and while she was up here (the show just didn't happen), we cut an audition record for the people who were at Columbia. That record was *I Wish I Could Shimmy Like My Sister Kate*, which A. J. Piron wrote and I published. Anyway, they didn't like it, said it was coarse and loud, and they didn't want any part of it. Do you know something? They all got fired just a few weeks later because I wished them bad luck. I wished that God would punish them, and when they were fired, I knew that God had answered my prayer.

I sure wish I had a copy of that audition record now. I loaned it to Bessie once, and she never gave it back. I'll bet it's worth twenty-five thousand dollars now!

When Mr. Walker came into Columbia, he asked me to get that Bessie Smith I had been talkin' about. I said that those others had said that her voice was too rough.

"You just get her here," he told me.

MAY WRIGHT JOHNSON

In 1921, I was playing at the 81 Theatre on Decatur Street in Atlanta, and Bessie Smith was at the 91, just down the street. My husband, James P. Johnson, was leading the band at the 81, which was the bigger theater (you know it had to be big because it had sixteen boxes) and I was the principal, not just a chorine. I was workin' under the name of May Wright.

The 91 was a smaller and rougher theater. Bessie had her own show there, and it sure was funny. I still fall out with laughter when I think about it, even today. You won't believe this, but Bessie was the smallest woman in that show. And you know how big *she* was. Well, that opening number was the funniest thing I ever saw. The curtain went up, and the floodlights came on, and there was the entire chorus dressed in close-fitting bloomers, bent over with their backs to the audience. The orchestra struck up *Liberty Bell*, and there was that whole chorus shakin' every muscle in their bodies. I tell you I couldn't even keep a straight face when I was doin' my own show after that.

Years later, I was on the same bill with Bessie up North, and you know what I had the nerve to do? I sang the blues! It's just lucky I went on before she did. Yes, she was terrific, and there's been nobody since that could sing the blues like Bessie Smith.

She would come over to the house, but, mind you, she wasn't my friend. She was very rough.

ETHEL WATERS

Bessie Smith was booked into 91 Decatur Street while I was working there. Bessie was a heavy-set, dark woman and very nice looking. Along with Ma Rainey, she was undisputed tops as a blues singer.

Bessie's shouting brought worship wherever she worked. She was getting fifty to seventy-five dollars a week, big money for our kind of vaudeville. The money thrown to her brought this to a couple of hundred dollars a week. Bessie, like an opera singer, carried her own claque with her. These plants in the audience were paid to throw up coins and bills to get the appreciation money going without delay the moment she finished her first number.

Bessie was in a pretty good position to dictate to the managers. She had me put on my act for her and said I was a long goody. But she also told the men who ran No. 91 that she didn't want anyone else on the bill to sing the blues.

I agreed to this. I could depend a lot on my shaking, though I never shimmied vulgarly and only to express myself. And when

242

I went on I sang *I Want To Be Somebody's Baby Doll So I Can Get My Lovin' All The Time.*

But before I could finish this number the people out front started howling, "Blues! Blues! Come on, Stringbean, we want your blues!"

Before the second show the manager went to Bessie's dressing room and told her he was going to revoke the order forbidding me to sing any blues. He said he couldn't have another such rumpus. There was quite a stormy discussion about this, and you could hear Bessie yelling things about "these Northern bitches." Now nobody could have taken the place of Bessie Smith. People everywhere loved her shouting with all their hearts and were loyal to her. But they wanted me too.

When I closed my engagement in that theater Miss Bessie called me to her. "Come here, long goody," she said. "You ain't so bad. It's only that I never dreamed that anyone would be able to do this to me in my own territory and with my own people. And you know damn well that you can't sing worth a ——."

DANNY BARKER

Bessie Smith was a fabulous deal to watch. She was a pretty large woman and she could sing the blues. She had a church deal mixed up in it. She dominated a stage. You didn't turn your head when she went on. You just watched Bessie. You didn't read any newspapers in a night club when she went on. She just upset you. When you say Bessie—that was it. She was unconscious of her surroundings. She never paid anybody any mind. When you went to see Bessie and she came out, that was it. If you had any church background, like people who came from the South as I did, you would recognize a similarity between what she was doing and what those preachers and evangelists from there did, and how they moved people. The South had fabulous preachers and evangelists. Some would stand on corners and move the crowds from there. Bessie did the same thing on stage. She, in a sense, was like people like Billy Graham are today. Bessie was in a class with those people. She could bring about mass hypnotism. When she was performing, you could hear a pin drop.

ZUTTY SINGLETON

Now there was a woman! I mean Bessie Smith was ALL woman! I remember about 1923 or 1924, when I was playing with Robichaux's orchestra at the Lyric Theatre in New Orleans—that was her headquarters. I think she must have played there four or five times a year maybe. And man! She always did pack that house, every show, with big lines always waiting.

Her act was really something. She'd have a regular recording studio setup on the stage, with that big old horn they used to use and everything. Then she'd sing things like *Gulf Coast Blues* and *Baby Won't You Please Come Home* in that big wonderful voice of hers, and, believe me, she looked like a queen up there. She was a *big* woman with that beautiful bronze color and stern features. Stately, just like a queen. And nobody called her just "Bessie" either, 'least I didn't have the nerve to. She was always "Miss Bessie" to me.

Yeah, she was ALL woman—really the Queen of the Blues.

BUSTER BAILEY

Bessie Smith was a kind of roughish sort of woman. She was good-hearted and big-hearted, and she liked to juice, and she liked to sing her blues slow. She didn't want no fast stuff. She had a style of phrasing, what they used to call swing—she had a certain way she used to sing. I hear a lot of singers now trying to sing something like that. Like this record that came out a few years ago—*Why Don't You Do Right?*—they're trying to imitate her.

We didn't have any rehearsals for Bessie's records. She'd just go with us to the studio around Columbus Circle. None of us rehearsed the things we recorded with her. We'd just go to the studio; Fletcher would get the key. This, by the way, applied not only to Bessie but to almost all the blues singers. The singers might have something written out to remind them what the verse was but there was no music written on it. On a lot of the records by Bessie you'll see lyrics by Bessie Smith and music by George Brooks. That was Fletcher.

We recorded by the horn. You know the way they used to record in those days. We'd monkey around until we had a good balance and we'd make two or three takes but we never made more than two masters on a tune. We'd make only two sides in a session and at that time we got more money for that than we do now.

For Bessie, singing was just a living. She didn't consider it anything special. She was certainly recognized among blues singers—a shouter, they called her. They all respected her because she had a powerful pair of lungs. There were no microphones in those days. She could fill up Carnegie Hall, Madison Square Garden, or a cabaret. She could fill it up from her muscle and she could last all night. There was none of this whispering jive.

CARL VAN VECHTEN

Porter Grainger brought her to my apartment on West Fifty-fifth Street. Fania Marinoff and I were throwing a party. George Gershwin was there and Marguerite d'Alvarez and Constance Collier, possibly Adele Astaire. The drawing room was well filled with sophisticated listeners. Before she could sing, Bessie wanted a drink. She asked for a glass of straight gin, and with one gulp she downed a glass holding nearly a pint. Then, with a burning cigarette depending from one corner of her mouth, she got down to the blues, really down to 'em, with Porter at the piano. I am quite certain that anybody who was present that night will never forget it. This was no actress; no imitator of a woman's woes; there was no pretence. It was the real thing—a woman cutting her heart open with a knife until it was exposed for us all to see, so that we suffered as she suffered, exposed with a rhythmic ferocity, indeed, which could hardly be borne. In my own experience, this was Bessie Smith's greatest performance.

MEZZ MEZZROW

Bessie was a real woman, all woman, all the femaleness the world ever saw in one sweet package. She was tall and brown-skinned, with great big dimples creasing her creeks, dripping good looks—just this side of voluptuous, buxom and massive, but stately too, shapely as a hourglass, with a high-voltage magnet for a personality.

You ever hear what happened to that fine, full-of-life female woman? You know how she died? Well, she went on for years, being robbed by stinchy managers who would murder their own mothers for a deuce of blips, having to parade around in gaudy gowns full of dime-store junk and throw away her great art while the lushes and morons made cracks about her size and shape. She drank a lot, and there must have been plenty of nights when she got the blues she couldn't lose, but she went on singing, pouring out the richness and the beauty in her that never dried up. Then one day in 1937 she was in an automobile crash down in Mississippi, the Murder State, and her arm was almost tore out of its socket. They brought her to the hospital but it seemed like there wasn't any room for her just then—the people around there didn't care for the color of her skin. The car turned around and drove away, with Bessie's blood dripping on the floor mat. She was finally admitted to another hospital where the officials must have been color-blind, but by that time she had lost so much blood that they couldn't operate on her, and a little later she died. *See that lonesome road, Lawd, it got to end,* she used to sing. That was how the lonesome road ended up for the greatest folk singer this country ever heard—with Jim Crow directing the traffic.

BUSTER BAILEY

Alberta Hunter was another singer of the type I mean. She didn't need a mike. Bricktop was also in that gang. She was a good singer and she could dance. You had to sing and dance in those days. Bricktop was the one who later had a club of her own in Paris and now has one in Rome. Ma Rainey was good—you can't leave her out. But they all considered Bessie the best, like they put Louis on top. Bessie was the Louis Armstrong of the blues singers. She had more original ideas for blues and things than the others did.

ALBERTA HUNTER

The blues? Why the blues are a part of me. To me, the blues are—well, almost religious. They're like a chant. The blues are like spirituals, almost sacred. When we sing blues, we're singin' out our hearts, we're singin' out our feelings. Maybe we're hurt and just can't answer back, then we sing or maybe even hum the blues. Yes, to us, the blues are sacred. When I sing:

"I walk the floor, wring my hands and cry.
"Yes, I walk the floor, wring my hands and cry. . . ."

what I'm doing is letting my soul out.

Blues are a part of me, and when I knew nothing about music, or even about such a thing as music being written down, I was singing blues and picking them out on the piano with one finger. I was less than eleven years old when I started writing *Down Hearted Blues*, just before I ran away from home. Later on, I recorded it for Paramount Records and it was a tremendous hit. That was before Frank Walker sent for Bessie Smith. Bessie made it after it had been recorded on almost all the labels and even on piano rolls. We thought that it was exhausted, but it was Bessie's first record and it sold 780,000 copies!

No, they don't have blues singers now like they had then, except maybe Dinah Washington. There was Sara Martin, Ida Cox, Chippie Hill, Victoria Spivey, Trixie Smith, and Clara Smith and Mamie Smith, who made it possible for all of us with her recording of *Crazy Blues*, the *first* blues record.

But Bessie Smith was the greatest of them all. There never was one like her and there'll never be one like her again. Even though she was raucous and loud, she had a sort of a tear—no, not a tear, but there was a *misery* in what she did. It was as though there was something she had to get out, something she just had to bring to the fore. Nobody, least of all today, could ever match Bessie Smith.

As for musicians who could play the blues? Well, the ones that didn't know music could play the best blues. I know that I don't want no musicians who know all about music playin' for me.

But then there was Lil Armstrong—she played a mighty blues. And don't ever forget Lovie Austin. She wrote and played a *mess* of blues. Lovie worked at the Monogram Theatre in Chicago where all the T.O.B.A. shows played. Lovie wrote *Graveyard Blues* for Bessie Smith and made hundreds of those early records.

247

It was Lovie who helped me copyright my blues. I was just a child and didn't know a thing about those things. She copyrighted them under her name but had me down as the writer. But you know something? I never collected a quarter on any blues I ever wrote!

MARY LOU WILLIAMS

And there was usually something worth hearing in town those days, even if Pittsburgh was not one of the jazz centers. One Saturday night I went to a theater on Frankstown Avenue where all the Negro shows were booked. But I hardly noticed any part of this show, for my attention was focused on a lady pianist who worked there.

She sat cross-legged at the piano, a cigarette in her mouth, writing music with her right hand while accompanying the show with her swinging left! Impressed, I told myself, "Mary, you'll do that one day." (And I did, traveling with Andy Kirk's band in the 'thirties on one-nighters.)

The lady turned out to be Lovie Austin, who was working with the pit band and making all the orchestrations. It so happened that she was behind time, and hurriedly arranging a number for one of the acts further down the bill.

Another week, the fabulous Ma Rainey came into a little theater on Wiley Avenue. Some of the older kids and I slipped downtown to hear the woman who had made blues history.

Ma was loaded with real diamonds—in her ears, around her neck, in a tiara on her head. Both hands were full of rocks, too; her hair was wild and she had gold teeth. What a sight! To me, as a kid, the whole thing looked and sounded weird.

When the engagement ended, and Ma had quit the scene, rumor had it that the jewelry was bought hot and that Ma was picked up and made to disgorge—losing all the loot she had paid for the stuff.

SAM PRICE

. . . and then there was Trixie Smith. Her record of *Freight Train Blues* is one of the greatest blues records ever made. Trixie had depth, real warmth, and appeal. What was she like? She was just another woman called Smith—but she could sing like hell!

Another great blues singer was Blind Lemon Jefferson, and when I was a record salesman for R. T. Ashford's store in Dallas, I was the first to recommend him for records. You know, I don't trust those stories about this one and that leading Blind Lemon Jefferson through the streets of Dallas. Seems to me he didn't need any leadin'. He had a really uncanny sense of direction. He'd walk around those Dallas streets singin' the blues—a chunky little fellow wearing a big black hat. Everybody knew him.

There was one thing he could do. He had a bottle of whiskey home and he could tell by just holdin' that bottle and shaking it how much was in it. If he'd come home and shake that bottle and find less in it than when he'd left, his wife would get a beating.

T-BONE WALKER

The blues? Man, I didn't start playing the blues ever. That was in me before I was born and I've been playing and living the blues ever since. That's the way you've gotta play them. You've got to live the blues, and with us that's natural—it's born in us to live the blues.

I think that the first thing I can remember was my mother singing the blues as she would sit alone in the evenings in our place in Dallas, Texas, where I was born. I can't remember the words to those blues, but she could sing you blues right now like you never heard before. I used to listen to her singing there at night, and I knew then that the blues was in me, too. Everyone down there sang the blues. In fact, they still do. Go any place where there's a group of Negroes, and you'll hear them singing blues you never heard of—wonderful blues.

After I heard my mother play the blues and sing them, then I started in. I didn't know the words because there weren't any set words. I made them up as I went along. That's the way we do, you know. Right today I can make up blues faster than I can sing them. I could sing the blues for you a whole day and never repeat a verse. Anyhow, when I first started singing, I used to take an old Prince Albert tobacco can that I had and strum it kind of like a guitar. There wasn't much tone, you know, but the bluesy beat was there and a kind of melancholy note, too, that I liked when I sang the blues.

You know, there's only one blues, though. That's the regular twelve-bar pattern and then you interpret over that. Just write new words or improvise different and you've got a new blues. Now, you take a piece like *St. Louis Blues*. That's a pretty tune and it has kind of a bluesy tone, but that's not the blues. You can't dress up the blues. The only blues is the kind that I sing and the kind that Jimmy Rushing sings and Basie plays. I'm not saying that *St. Louis Blues* isn't fine music, you understand. But it just isn't blues. Now, *Blues in the Night* is a lot better blues than St. Louis. That's because the first part of *Blues in the Night* is really blues on the right pattern. Of course, when they get to the bridge of the tune, it isn't blues any more. It's pretty but it isn't blues. It's even more spiritual than it is bluesy, with that whistle cry in it. Blues is all by itself.

Blues is all in the way that you feel it. One person can feel it and another can't. Count Basie's band can play wonderful blues because he and all the band feel the blues. Duke Ellington, with all his fine musicians, can't play good band blues. Some of his men can, but the band can't. The way it is with bands is the same with singers. Louis Jordan, for instance, plays good blues and he sings them like they were originally sung, too. Take his *Outskirts of Town*, that's really fine old blues. But then you listen to Dan Grissom sing *Outskirts* and that isn't blues, with the same melody and everything. It takes a bluesy feeling and the old twelve bars. Grissom sings sweet but the blues aren't sweet. You've gotta feel the blues to make them right.

Of course, the blues comes a lot from the church, too. The first time I ever heard a boogie-woogie piano was the first time I went to church. That was the Holy Ghost Church in Dallas, Texas. That boogie-woogie was a kind of blues, I guess. Then the preacher used to preach in a bluesy tone sometimes. You even got the congregation yelling "Amen" all the time when his preaching would stir them up—his preaching and his bluesy tone. Lots of people think I'm going to be a preacher when I quit this business because of the way I sing the blues. They say it sounds like a sermon.

The first blues that I heard, the ones my mother used to sing, were always homey things or things that were troubling her. She might sing about the dinner burning or anything like that. I guess that obscenity was built up with commercial playing of the blues. Usually I don't think it's bad because a good blues singer is so sincere in the things that he sings that he has a feeling and a meaning beyond the dirty words of his song. Some people just go to hear that kind of stuff, but anyone who understands blues goes beyond that to the real blues that's there. And people are beginning to really understand blues now, the whites are getting it and I'm glad. They're missing something without the blues.

JELLY ROLL MORTON

Please do not misunderstand me. I do not claim any of the creation of the blues, although I have written many of them even before Mr. Handy had any blues published. I had heard them when I was knee-high to a duck. For instance, when I first started going to school, at different times I would visit some of my relatives per permission, in the Garden district. I used to hear a few of the following blues players, who could play nothing else—Buddie Canter, Josky Adams, Game Kid, Frank Richards, Sam Henry, and many more too numerous to mention—what we call "ragmen" in New Orleans. They can take a ten-cent Xmas horn, take the wooden mouthpiece off, having only the metal for mouthpiece, and play more *blues* with that instrument than any trumpeter I had ever met through the country imitating the New Orleans trumpeters. Of course, Handy played mostly violin when I first arrived in Memphis. Violinists weren't known to play anything illegitimate even in New Orleans.

Tony Jackson used to play the blues in 1905, entitled *Michigan Water Tastes Like Sherry Wine*. He never sang anything on the stage but blues, such as *Elgin Movements In My Hips, with Twenty Years' Guarantee*. Blues just wasn't considered music—there were hundreds, maybe thousands, who could play blues and not another single tune.

W. C. HANDY

The blues is a thing deeper than what you'd call a mood today. Like the spirituals, it began with the Negro, it involves our history, where we came from, and what we experienced.

The blues came from the man farthest down. The blues came from nothingness, from want, from desire. And when a man sang or played the blues, a small part of the want was satisfied from the music.

The blues go back to slavery, to longing. My father, who was a preacher, used to cry every time he heard someone sing *I'll See You On Judgment Day*. When I asked him why, he said, "That's the song they sang when your uncle was sold into slavery in Arkansas. He wouldn't let his masters beat him, so they got rid of him the way they would a mule."

Then in the First World War, all Americans got a taste of what we had had for years—people being torn from their families and sent to faraway places, sometimes against their wishes. And blues and jazz began to have more meaning for more people. Then the depression was a new experience for many. But we had been hungry for years and had known hunger and hurt.

So the blues helped to fill the longing in the hearts of all kinds of people. They took it to their hearts and felt the same thing we felt. Now when you hear a white person sing the blues, he can put as much into it as a Negro. The blues and jazz have become a part of all American music and will be developed farther and farther on into infinity.

Like I said, we look for truth in music as in everything else. It won't always take shape as we think it will. There will always be some surprises. But so long as it's good, it doesn't matter whether it's Negro or white. What we want in music is something to build on.

15

. . . and spreading his special brand of musical joy—
Fats Waller.

JAMES P. JOHNSON
Some little people has music in them, but Fats, he was *all* music, and you know how big he was.

MAY WRIGHT JOHNSON
Right after James P. heard Fats Waller playing the pipe organ, he came home and told me, "I know I can teach that boy." Well, from then on it was one big headache for me. Fats was seventeen, and we lived on 140th Street, and Fats would bang on our piano till all hours of the night—sometimes to two, three, four o'clock in the morning. I would say to him, "Now go on home—or haven't you got a home?"

But he'd come every day and my husband would teach. Of course, you know the organ doesn't give you a left hand and that's what James P. had to teach him.

Then finally Fats got his first job—it was at Leroy's Cabaret on 135th Street and Fifth Avenue, and I was working there then. Fats was afraid to perform and so I taught him to play for me. That's how he started.

COUNT BASIE
The first time I saw Fats Waller, I had dropped into the old Lincoln Theatre in Harlem and heard a young fellow beating it out

on the organ. From that time on, I was a daily customer, hanging onto his every note, sitting behind him all the time, fascinated by the ease with which his hands pounded the keys and manipulated the pedals. He got used to seeing me, as though I were a part of the show. One day, he asked me whether I played the organ. "No," I said, "but I'd give my right arm to learn."

The next day he invited me to sit in the pit and start working the pedals. I sat on the floor, watching his feet, and using my hands to imitate them. Then I sat beside him and he taught me.

MARY LOU WILLIAMS

I stayed in New York, eyes and ears open to all the attractions Harlem had to offer. Like most other pianists, I revered the amazing Fats Waller, who had lately made a splash wailing on organ at the Lincoln. (When he quit New York, his admirers wouldn't let anyone follow him on organ, and those frantic kids were likely to throw most anything if you tried.)

Naturally, it was a great day for me when some musicians took me across to Connie's Inn on Seventh Avenue to meet Fats, working on a new show. The way Waller worked was anything but slavery.

The OAO (one and only) sat overflowing the piano stool, a jug of whiskey within easy reach. Leonard Harper, the producer, said, "Have you anything written for this number, Fats?" And Fats would reply, "Yeah, go on ahead with the dance, man." Then he composed his number while the girls were dancing. He must have composed the whole show, with lyrics, while I was sitting there—ears working overtime.

Meanwhile, he bubbled over with so many stories and funny remarks that those girls could hardly hoof it for laughing. The girls, thirty-five to forty-dollar-a-week chorus beauties, were loaded with enough ice around their shapely ankles to sink a battleship, for these were generous days in New York.

After the rehearsal, one of the boys—knowing my memory—bet Fats I could repeat all the tunes he had just written, a bet Fats snapped up at paying odds.

Falling apart with nerves at having to play before this big

254

name, I was prodded to the piano but managed to concentrate and play nearly everything I had heard Fats play. He was knocked out, picking me up and throwing me in the air and roaring like a crazy man.

MEZZ MEZZROW

I'll never forget when I first met Fats personally and began to associate with him in the fall of '28 and the spring of '29. He invited me to come to his rehearsals and to his home while he was writing the music for Connie's HOT CHOCOLATES.

He and the celebrated Andy Razaf were then working together. Andy, of course, writing the lyrics, and what a team they made! I'll never forget when they were writing *Black and Blue, Ain't Misbehavin', That Rhythm Man,* and *Sweet Savannah Sue.* Fats, his coat off, collar opened, sitting at the piano at Connie's Inn, which was in a cave, with the inevitable bottle of gin (and, of course, this was bathtub gin, for they were Prohibition days) on the cover of the piano. He went over the numbers time after time, and finally finding some new embellishments for the particular number he was playing at the time, his face would light up with such an expression that it was transmitted to everybody in the room. He was so magnetic, with such a robust personality, that you could never be sad in his presence. Andy Razaf would be sitting on the side, changing the lyrics here and there. Suddenly, he'd come to Fats' piano, and with a pleasant voice, full of enthusiasm, he'd sing his new version to us. I'll never forget my impression of the two the very first time I heard them together. I asked Fats why they didn't take a part in the show as a team and Andy chimed in and said, "Yes, Mezz, I've been telling him the same thing for a long time." But Fats answered, "Mezz, you know, I am a musician and not an actor."

Can you imagine hearing Louis Armstrong playing the trumpet with Fats Waller at the piano, getting the flavor of the numbers together? The late Leonard Harper (one of the greatest Negro producers that ever lived) calling his chorus to the floor, and giving them the routine. Comedians repeating their parts on the side. All the gaiety, laughter, and enthusiasm.

Yet, what stood out most was Louis and Fats. To see these two geniuses at work, two of the most magnetic personalities in the world, to me, is something I'll treasure for the rest of my life. Louis would play the tunes at first in the lower register, with a tone as broad as Fats himself. These low, thick, round notes that come out of Louis's horn on the lower register, I have never heard come out of another trumpet in all my life—and I've heard many a trumpet in my days. Fats was always kidding with Louis, and I remember when they started one time to rehearse *Ain't Misbehavin'*. Fats sat down at the piano and began to sing it to Louis, and what an accompaniment he gave to it as he sang! Pure unadulterated blues. If you don't think that's possible—try a piano and sing it.

LOUIS ARMSTRONG

I've seen Fats Waller enter a place, and all the people in the joint (I mean the place) would rave and you could see a gladness in their faces . . . honest . . . and Fats wouldn't be in the place a hot minute before he would tell them a fine joke and have everybody holding his side from laughter . . . Haw haw haw haw, he kills me.

Why I could tell you a joke that Fats told me and you would all just roar with laughter. But I'd better not, maybe. In other words, it's not commercial enough for this particular occasion. Fats used to use some bigger words than that, and I mean bigger.

He and I used to play in the Symphony Orchestra in Chicago in 1925. It was at the Vendome Theatre, a motion picture house. That was in the days of the silent films. The orchestra was directed by that fine leader, Erskine Tate . . . We used to play for the films, and during the intermission, we would play a big Overture and a Red Hot Number afterwards. And folks, I'm telling you, we used to really romp.

TOMMY BROOKINS

One day I was going into Dave's Cafe at the corner of 50th Street and Garfield Boulevard in Chicago to get a drink and to say hello to my friends when Fats Waller recognized me.

"Hey, Tommy Boy!"

We drank together. Fats was always a happy guy and while he drank his glass of gin he said, "Tommy, when you leave the club come to the Hotel Trenier. We'll drink and we'll play, and we'll sing and have a ball." I answered, "At that time of morning?" (I ought to say that it was already between four and five.) "O.K. I'll be there," I told him.

After work, I went to Fats' hotel and knocked on his door, and while it was being opened I could hear the rough voice of Fats and then I saw him appear with a glass of gin in his hand.

"There's my man, Tommy. Come on in."

He took me by the hand and presented me to his guests. There were fifteen. Then to my great astonishment I saw that Fats had installed right in the middle of the room a Hammond organ, and as I showed my surprise Fats answered, "Lyon and Healy gave it to me." (That was a large musical instrument store in Chicago.)

"Sit down and put yourself at ease." And then, without waiting any longer, he began to play on the organ, and how he played!

Fats played all that you can imagine. I knew what a great organist he was from having heard him at the Regal Theatre, but I never heard him play as well as he did in his hotel room that night.

After three hours of concentrated music by Fats and although it was already nine in the morning, no one showed any sign of fatigue.

"Have another glass and I'll play you my favorite piece."

I knew Fats' entire repertoire, but when he began to play *Abide With Me* I fell back and tears came to my eyes.

Who would imagine that that was the favorite song of the great Fats?

CHARLIE GAINES

While at Connie's Inn at 132nd Street and Seventh Avenue in Harlem, Eddie Condon and Fats Waller came in one night. They had a date for Victor next morning (March 1st, 1929) and wanted me to play on it. They wanted to talk more about it so waited till I finished at four. By then, Fats, who had been drinking gin, was in wild shape. We never discussed arrangements or ideas and ended up making the sides cold next morning.

Fats arrived in high spirits, still without any ideas of what we would play. He just sat down and kicked off in E-flat and we used our own ideas. We had no rehearsals whatever. Didn't even have a name for the sides. Later they called them *Harlem Fuss* and *Minor Drag*, and they were under the name of Fats Waller and His Buddies. Besides Fats, Condon, and myself, we used Charlie Irvis, trombone; Arville Harris, clarinet and alto; but didn't have a drummer. Years later, Herman Autrey told me plenty of those pops for Victor were made the same way, without hardly any rehearsal at all.

LEORA HENDERSON

Fats Waller is the first and only man I ever bought whiskey for. I don't believe in whiskey and don't want my money to go that way. I had bought a brand-new piano and just *had* to have Fats Waller play on it. When I saw him I told him so. "Miss Lee," he said, "I just ain't got time to play for you now."

"Fats," I said, "to show you just how much I want you to play, I'll buy you a quart of whiskey."

Well, you should have heard him. He played for more than an hour and drank up that whole quart of whiskey.

Another time I was playing with a band of white girls at the Astor Hotel at some sort of a big party and they announced some singer and his Arabian accompanist. Well, I nearly died laughing 'cause who should this Arabian be but Fats—all dressed in one of them turbans and a long white robe, with his arms folded like a priest or somethin'. He walked out on stage by me and winked his eye. He said, "Uh" at me. "Uh-huh," I answered. Later on that night he took me home, but you should have seen those girls swarm all over him while he was playin' between sets at that party. It was really something to see.

SNUB MOSELY

I remember I was on a theater tour with Fats, and with us was Hank Duncan, who was Fats' protégé. Fats would let Hank play a while and then he would sneak up and say, "Watch out, boy, I'm gonna getcha."

And you want to know something? There were a few times when he didn't catch Hank!

Fats was one of the first to keep an organ in his apartment. At that time he was living up on Morningside Avenue. Well, sometimes he'd get home at five or six in the morning and start playin'. He'd have an inspired moment and maybe play a little loud, you know? Sure enough the super in the building started raising hell and so Fats had to go out and buy himself a house.

MAY WRIGHT JOHNSON

I sold Fats his house—just a few blocks from ours, and every once in a while he'd come in at four or five in the morning to go to bed here. He'd say, "The kids too noisy over at my house."

MAURICE WALLER

As for my piano playing, the thing I remember most emphatically from what my father used to show me is the importance of the left hand. I remember his emphasizing the use of tenths in the bass, for example. And he used to tell me that a piano man without a left hand is a very weak pianist.

He also told me never to let the body, the richness get out of the piano. A pianist should be rich with sound and cover a distance, too. I mean by that he should really play open chords—tenths, elevenths, et cetera. I play close stuff once in a while like Shearing, but mostly, I believe in playing very open.

There was a Sunday morning I especially remember. When my father got up that day, he went downstairs to the Hammond organ we had in the house, and then called me down—I was about thirteen—to listen to a new idea he had. He'd awakened with the tune on his mind. In about ten minutes flat, the tune was finished and it was *Jitterbug Waltz*.

He was a remarkable musician, my father. He had, however, a terrific personality that overlorded his true greatness at the piano. I remember back to when I was seven and eight. I used to sit listening to him play the piano at home until four in the morning sometimes. That's when he wasn't entertaining, just playing. From those evenings I know what he was trying to say. His ability and technique were overpowering even though he never had a chance to study the way he should have.

My father spent a lot of time composing things that have never been published. They're on the order of the *London Suite*—things like that. Some are finished; some are not. Half of them didn't have a name. They weren't commercial; they weren't the type of thing he was supposed to have done.

It was a matter of his getting at his inner self in them. Often I heard him play stuff that amazed me, and yet, most people will tell me first when they talk about him, "Yes, I used to like to hear him sing." They seem to go after that personality and his playing ability was hidden by it.

W. T. ED. KIRKEBY

My association with Fats Waller started in 1935. I had just been appointed Artists' Repertoire Manager of RCA-Victor for which Fats, of course, recorded. After a year, I left to join the band division of NBC, and it was at that time that I was asked to handle Fats' business affairs.

Our first venture together was a flop. It was when Fats tried fronting a big band on a southern tour. I tried looking around for new territory. Why not Europe? Fats' records had already made him famous there.

We asked twenty-five hundred a week for an eight-week tour—big money in those days. But we came to London on those terms and, as you know, opened at the Palladium in 1938.

The recent issue of Ted Heath's recordings of Fats' *London Suite* reminds me how this music was written. Fats had arranged to record some of his piano pieces for Jimmy Phillips, and Jimmy had fixed the studio around midday—pretty early for Fats.

I got him out of bed in good time, but he was feeling heavy after a late night. "Man," he said, "fetch me my liquid ham and eggs." This was the four fingers of straight whiskey that started Tom's day. Such an early date required a second helping. After that, Fats was ready to go.

But he'd had no breakfast. And though he played well, I could see it wasn't the day for his fastest fingering. "How about working on those pieces you wanted to write about London?" I suggested.

I gave him a rapid word picture of Piccadilly, Bond Street, Chelsea, Whitechapel, and so on. In three minutes he'd rounded off Piccadilly. And will you believe me when I tell you that those six pieces in the *Suite*—all original conceptions—were composed and recorded within the hour! Jimmy Phillips will bear me out on this.

What a musician! And Tom was a great guy, too. His heart was as big as the grand piano he played.

GENE SEDRIC

As for the record sessions, it seems like they would always give him a whole lot of junky tunes to play because it seemed as if only he could get something out of them. We were on the road a lot, and while we were on the road there was no chance to record so we'd need a hit when we did.

Well, Fats would get a good job and stay up all night with his co-writer, Andy Razaf, and they'd turn out a hit. They'd never miss.

In the recording studio, we had recorded so much that Fats was the most relaxed man I ever saw in a studio. And so he made everybody else feel relaxed. After a balance had been taken, we'd just need one take to make a side usually, unless it was a kind of difficult number.

W. T. ED. KIRKEBY

I had booked a date with Muzak to do some transcriptions with Fats and his Rhythm. As we had three shows daily at the Loew's State Theatre, we had to sandwich this recording session in between our stage work. The recording studio was just across the street from the stage entrance, so it was no job to get there. Fats and I had quite a hassle with the stagehands' union which was insisting on putting on an extra electrician at Fats' expense. One hundred bucks a week just to plug in a line for his Hammond organ. "Take yo hand outa ma pocket," Fats had screamed, and was glad to get away from the scene of the holdup.

261

Once in the studio we lost no time. The first show at the theater had keyed up the boys, and with a fine Steinway piano and an excellent "studio sound" Fats looked forward to having himself a ball. Everyone was keyed up and in the proper frame of mind for musical stimulation—and the panic was soon on. The boys played like there was no tomorrow. They knew all the tunes and the masters piled up at a truly amazing rate. With the next show ahead Fats had to keep a terrific pace, but with all the drive there was always that feeling of relaxation, of Fats having fun. He would chuckle and grin, raise his eyebrows in glee; and when Gene Sedric would come up for a solo Fats' booming voice would urge him to greater effort with, "Get on yo feet, Baby Bear, and earn yo salary." Or to Slick Jones who would be frantically chewing a wad of gum, "Gimme some skin, man gimme me some skin!" And as the pace became more torrid and the joint really began to rock, Fats would scream to Buggs Hamilton, "Ah send me, send me. . . . SEND ME. . . . YEAH!" And Buggsy's trumpet would soar to the clouds and do fine things under the spell of the Waller drive. Yes, it was happy music and it made for a joyous day not only for those who made the music, but for us in the control room who were lucky enough to be in on the session.

The date was over for Fats and his Rhythm with a grand total of twelve sides recorded. "On stage!" at the theater was only ten minutes away and the boys disappeared fast. Fats got away with "I'll see you later," for he was to return after the second show for a session of piano solos. And late that afternoon he did just that. Four more solo records seemed like play, and that powerful left hand was a one-man rhythm section. No one could doubt after that second record session, in addition to his three shows at the theater on the same day, that the tremendous drive and vitality that characterized Fats' work was really without equal anywhere.

Yes, Fats was a volcano all right, alone in his class. That alternating strength and delicacy in his playing, his tongue-in-cheek singing, and his ebullient songs like *Ain't Misbehavin'*, *Honeysuckle Rose*, and *Keeping Out Of Mischief* leave one with the feeling that he thought life was rather a good joke and not to be taken too seriously. "One never knows, do one?" said Fats slyly in the movie, STORMY WEATHER, and stole the show.

Fats' flair for witty remarks has been the birth of many of his song titles. His tongue-in-cheek jibes on his records, off stage and on stage, and even in his everyday conversation have caused many a smile, chuckle, and uproarious laugh from the lucky listener. Here's one instance of many that happened to me.

Los Angeles was the halfway mark in our coast-to-coast tour of playing one-nighters. We had to open a day earlier at the Paramount Theater than originally booked. Fats had counted on that day off for a rest, but good trouper that he was, the show had to go on, so he got through the rehearsal with Rochester (Jack Benny's sidekick) but had no time before curtain time to go over the act with Kitty Murray, the dusky comedienne with Rochester's act. So they went through a quick "talkover" rehearsal, and the show was on.

Well, Fats was doing the M.C. chore in the show, and time came for Kitty to come on stage. Fats introduced her and on she walked. Now Kitty was of no mean proportions. Just try to picture two hundred and twenty pounds of womanhood dressed like an Indian squaw. Red feather upright in her raven braided hair; and old black evening gown cut off unevenly above the knees and showing Kitty's ample arms, shoulders, and sturdy legs, and a pair of stage shoes miles too big. Kitty clomps across the stage to the umpty ump . . . umpty ump of the bass drum, stops on the cymbal crash, strikes a pose, and stares at Fats with her jaws furiously working on a cud of bubble gum. Fats, open-mouthed, with his right hand stroking his chin in amazement, turns to the audience with those raised eyebrows and that pixie look and cracks, "Look at all dat meat and no potatoes!"

The audience "fell in the aisles" and another song title was born.

Yes, Fats gave his all to people. It was obvious in Chicago at the Sherman Hotel where the Panther Room was packed with people night after night, week after week, as Fats and his Rhythm "gave out" to the dancers. Fats also entertained as a single on the floor, and with that famous derby hat cocked over his left ear, and his pixie smile as natural and warming as a child's—and with just the same hint of coyness he slayed the crowds to thunderous applause. *Ain't Misbehavin', Honeysuckle Rose, I've Got a Feeling I'm Falling, Black and Blue, I'm Gonna Sit Right Down and Write Myself a Letter, Your Feet's Too Big, Two Sleepy People, Handful of Keys.* On and on went the requests and Fats went right on obliging.

Intermissions would find Mother Waller's two hundred and eighty-five pounds of pride and joy backstage and steaming. Between signing autographs, he would mop the perspiration from his grinning face and prepare for his upcoming nightly radio broadcast. From hundreds in the Panther Room, Fats' audience on the air literally jumped to millions, for it was these airshows that were the talk of the town. For Fats, always having fun, reveled in his wisecracks and tongue-in-cheek remarks. He would "Wonder what the poor people were doing. I'd like to be doing it wid 'em." A little later he'd cajole the damsel in the lyric of the song he was singing, or completely change the lyrics of *Shortnin' Bread*. Fats' changes and alterations were always humorous—most of them slipped out on the spur of the moment—but often they were more than a bit on the suggestive side, just enough to make them typically Fats' own. This went on *ad infinitum* until the manager of the Sherman went nuts thinking the FCC was about ready to take the hotel off the air. Consequently I was on the carpet every other day with demands that I gag Fats. But Fats wouldn't be gagged and just went on "livin' the life I love!"

GENE SEDRIC

Fats Waller was sometimes very unhappy about his music. You see, he was appreciated for his showmanship ability and for that amount of piano that he played on records, but very few of Waller's record fans knew how much more he could play than what he usually did on records. He didn't try to prove anything by his singing. It was a matter of fun with him. But I deeply believe that, in his later years, his novelty singing and his showmanship in general overshadowed his playing. He was one of the great showmen and he was so good at it that people paid less attention to him as a musician.

264

Yet, he wanted to do great things on organ and piano—which he could do. There were many times when we played engagements during which he felt like himself and wanted to play great. But when he played as musically as he could, many people in the audience would think that he was lying down and they'd yell, "Come on, Fats!!" He'd take a swig of gin or something and say resignedly, "Aw right, here it is."

One of Fats Waller's greatest performances publicly occurred at his last concert at Carnegie Hall. It was around 1943, I think. The first part was wonderful. He played organ and piano straight and the audience reaction was wonderful. As for the last half, everybody got kind of half-high and it ended up in a clambake.

Fats was really a truly great artist. Only his very personal friends knew how much he could play. He could play all styles from modern on down. What is generally called the Waller style is more or less the style he became known by commercially. He had a much wider range than most people realize.

Fats was a very generous man. He always had a good word for everybody. And you never heard him knocking another pianist. He had a thorough knowledge of the classics and had a large library of classical music. He especially loved Bach.

Fats was often broke. He once sold a song to Irving Berlin for twenty-five dollars. And he sold other songs to publishers for as little as that when he needed money.

I remember when we were playing the Yacht Club. All the publishers used to go there. They liked Fats and they'd all want his songs. I remember one night when he played *If I Had You*. He started crying. It turned out he was thinking about his earlier days and about all the hits he had given away. Jack Robbins, the music publisher, once told me that, if Fats had completed all the songs he'd gotten advances on, Robbins would be a millionaire again.

That time when he was feeling so sad about all the hits he had given away was before his last comeback which started in 1937. He'd been playing, you know, since the age of seventeen. He made piano rolls when he was very young and he was one of the leading sellers on Q.R.S. He kept broke because he was always busy balling and having a good time and he just didn't care.

Shortly after he came out of the alimony jail—that must have been around 1935 and I guess he spent not quite a year there—he did very well. He went to Cincinnati and played on station WLW where he had a very successful midnight program. This business of the alimony jail happened before I joined him. As I remember, I think Paul Whiteman got him out of there.

Like I said, Fats liked to ball. He'd go three or four days without sleep and then go to bed for forty-eight hours. Yet he was very religious, very religious. He was a Bible student. I believe that had he lived his ambition was to have a big traveling religious show.

I worked with Fats from 1938 to 1943 and I'd been on records with him ever since 1936. It was the greatest to work with him. He kept everybody connected with him happy all the time and he was very seldom angry about anything that happened inside the band.

FATS WALLER

When I look back at the ground I've covered from way back in 1919 when I wrote my first professional song, *Squeeze Me*, I guess I've been more used to being written about than being on the writing end. Give me a piano to beat up and that's me; but as to this writing business, *I'm like a bear from the fair, I ain't nowhere.*

But there are a couple of things I'd like to say, and one is: that I'm very glad to see that jazz has finally come back to his pappy, Melody. Now that the jitterbugs are cooling off, and the shag is no more, we're beginning to give the old masters a rest and concocting some melodies of our own.

It is my contention, and always has been, that the thing that makes a tune click is the melody, and give the public four bars of that to dig their teeth into, and you have a killer-diller. And if you doubt this statement just take a look at the weekly Hit Parade.

Now I'm not a cat to preach without practicing what I preach, and, in all the long line of hits I have had the fortune to write, there has always been a melodic line. Regardless of how sweet that line, how fast or slow, the good old left hand can always swing it out.

266

And it's melody that gives variety to the ear. That's what makes popular music endure. The fad of boogie-woogie piano playing is burning itself out. Why? Because it's too monotonous—it all sounds the same.

Ashton Stevens, music critic of the *Chicago American* wrote: "The organ is the favorite instrument of Fats' heart; and the piano only of his stomach." Well, I really love the organ. I can get so much more color from it than the piano that it really sends me. I have one at home, and a great many of my compositions originated there. Included is *We Need A Little Love, That's All.* Ed. Kirkeby collaborated with me on this, and I remember we stayed up until eleven o'clock the *next* morning finishing it up. That's the way songs are born. I will never forget how on a tour through the English provinces we were playing the Empire Theatre, in Sheffield. After theater is our usual time for relaxation, and following dinner I roamed restlessly through the beautiful park there. At dawn the birds awakened, and out of their lively chirpings one short strain stood out. I went back to the hotel, and by ten o'clock that morning, with the aid of some delicious Amontillado Sherry, we had finished *Honey Hush.* You see, it's fifty per cent inspiration and fifty per cent perspiration.

Another thrill of my life was making the records in my organ album. I'll never forget sitting down at the console of that magnificent organ in the H.M.V. studio on the outskirts of London. It reminded me of that Wurlitzer Grand I played at the Lincoln Theatre in Harlem when I was a kid sixteen years old. I had myself a ball that afternoon, and the records really came easy.

Next to a grand organ there's nothing finer than a magnificent symphony orchestra. I get my kicks out of that kind of music as well as spontaneous jazz. Both kinds for different moods are solid senders, and each type has its place in this everyday world of ours.

W. T. ED. KIRKEBY

Fats was only thirty-nine when he died. He had plenty to live for. He was at the peak of his fame. His first solo venture as composer of a full-length score for the Broadway musical, HOT CHOCOLATES, produced in 1929, was a big success, and producer Richard Kollmar was negotiating with him to write another musical that would be staged with an all-Negro cast. Fats was a family man, had a wonderful home, and a six-thousand-dollar Lincoln.

I'll never forget that tragic morning of December 15th, 1943.

The Santa Fe Chief was crossing the Kansas plain. It was as cold as an icebox. I eased open the door of our berth. "You okay, Tom?" I said. Fats said he was fine. But I knew how tired he was. He'd already been sleeping the best part of two days.

Soon, though, everything would be dandy. We were en route to Fats' home at St. Albans, New York, for a well-earned vacation. From now on we'd take it easy for a while. A few good dates, then maybe that picture with Abbott and Costello. Fats' records were selling well. He could afford to relax.

That night I turned in late. Tom was sleeping peacefully. But I woke up in the early hours to find him shivering and gasping for breath. I rang for the porter and ran up the corridor to get help. But it was five A.M. and few people were around.

The train had pulled into Union Station, K.C., where a doctor was on hand (he had been summoned for another passenger who had been taken ill). I told him Fats was very sick and hurried him to our car.

The doctor took one look. "This man is dead," he said.

LOUIS ARMSTRONG

Fats is gone now . . . but to me, he's still here with us. His very good spirit will keep him with us for ages. Right now, every time someone mentions Fats Waller's name, why you can see the grins on all the faces, as if to say, "Yea, yea, yea, yea, Fats is a solid sender, ain't he?"

16

New York's "second line"—the men who played with Whiteman and Goldkette, Red Nichols and Ben Pollack.

JOE SULLIVAN

It was a lot like the old days in Chicago. Most of the Chicago gang had gone to New York around 1928 and plenty more musicians were streaming into Manhattan to get their kicks and grab their share of the fantastically high salaries which were being paid at the time.

New York seemed to be stricken with the same fever regarding jazz that Chicago had experienced five or six years before. It was great while it lasted.

ARTIE SHAW

I became a part of the circle of young jazz musicians who were then drifting around New York. There was Artie Bernstein, the bass player, with whom I roomed. Artie was at that time going to Columbia University and preparing to become a lawyer; but, although he finally graduated and passed his bar exams, he never did go into law but kept right on playing bass fiddle instead. The last time I ran into him he was working in one of the large Hollywood studio orchestras. There was Jack Teagarden, the phenomenal young trombonist who had just blown into town from the wild and wooly Southwest, and through whose completely new style the entire concept of what a jazz trombone could sound like was being changed; Jack's younger brother, Charlie, who played trumpet and sounded like a lazier, higher-pitched version of Jack himself; Joe Sullivan, Gene Krupa, Eddie Condon, Bud Freeman, Benny Goodman, Red Mackenzie, Davey Tough, Max Kaminsky, George Wettling, Jess Stacy, Wingy Manone, the whole "Chicago crowd," who had also come to New York at about the same time and were hanging on to try their luck at getting set somewhere in the Big Apple. There was Bix Beiderbecke, recently out of Paul Whiteman's large dance orchestra, where he had never belonged in the first place—now on the downgrade. There was Jimmy Dorsey, a saxophone player with an astounding technical equipment, who had already established himself in the higher echelons of the radio and recording fields but who still came around now and then for one of our periodic "sessions"; Tommy Dorsey, Jimmy's brother, who was already beginning to make a name for himself as a "high-note artist" on the trombone; Bunny Berigan—also dead now, after an unsuccessful and frustrating battle with life and that Old Demon Rum—but at that time a young lad fresh out of Madison, Wisconsin, flat broke like most of the rest of us, also trying to find himself any little job so he could earn some kind of living with his trumpet, any old kind of job just so he could pick up a few bucks to keep going, pay for a hotel room, feed himself, and buy a drink now and then.

There was Dick McDonough, the guitar player, who is also dead, for much the same reasons as Bix and Bunny. Another guitar player, who had developed an entirely different style of jazz guitar from Dick's, but in its own way a whole new approach to the guitar as a jazz instrument, was a blond, long-nosed, good-natured guy named Carl Kress. There was a crazy drunk of a trombonist named George Troop (now dead too), also a "high-note artist" but, unlike Tommy Dorsey, unable to stay sober long enough at any one time to keep any job he might start on; there was a very young, bright-eyed, intense young kid named Joey Bushkin who played piano and hung out with the Chicago crowd, who is today beginning to make a name for himself around New York. There were any number of others, almost without exception hard-drinking, fast-living, wild-eyed young guys living out their crazy, boozey, frantic lives, and without one single exception, every last one of them was chockful of energy, facility, and enormous musical talent in a world that had not yet come to the point where it was interested in what they had to offer musically, aside from whatever commercial use the budding radio industry was occasionally able to make of their skills.

RAY BAUDUC

I got to New York before a lot of the Chicago boys turned up. I had been working with the Dorsey Brothers' Wild Canaries, their first band, in the Midwest and in Pennsylvania, and the going was rough. Sometimes we didn't make enough to cover the feed bill and we'd all end up at Tommy's house with Mom Dorsey taking care of all of us.

Even then the boys were always fighting and I would be in the middle. Tommy and Jimmy would argue over anything. (Do you know that later on they actually broke up their big band over an argument over what tempo the band would use on a number—*Night and Day*, I think it was—something like that.)

Anyway, Jimmy got tired of scuffling and called Joe Venuti, who was in Atlantic City, for a job. Joe needed a drummer too, so Jimmy asked him, "How about Ray?" and I was in.

After a while we ended up in New York playing in a cellar called The Playground on Fifty-first Street between Broadway and Seventh—where the Basin Street is now. It was Tommy Guinan's place, Texas Guinan's brother, and some of the guys in the band were Joe Venuti, Chummy McGregor, Red Nichols, myself, and Eddie Lang.

LONNIE JOHNSON

I well remember Eddie Lang. He was the nicest man I ever worked with. Eddie and I got together many a time in the old Okeh record studios in New York, and we even made many sides together with just two guitars. I valued those records more than anything in the world. But one night not long ago someone stole them from my house.

Eddie was a fine man. He never argued. He didn't tell me what to do. He would ask me. Then, if everything was okay, we'd sit down and get to jiving. I've never seen a cat like him since. He could play guitar better than anyone I know. And I've seen plenty in my day.

At the time I knew Mr. Lang, I was working for the Columbia record people in New York. That's all I did—just make sides. But the sides I made with Eddie Lang were my greatest experience.

FRANK TRUMBAUER

His musical mentality could be termed a natural one, as he carried the entire Paul Whiteman library, as far as his parts were concerned, on the back of a small business card in his coat breast pocket. There would be some intricate modulation to play, and rarely in radio rehearsals would he have time to actually set these things, so Whiteman would say, "You take the modulation, Eddie." During the program that night, just before the modulation, the excitement of the entire band could be felt because it hadn't been rehearsed and the boys were wondering if Eddie remembered. All Eddie had was a few marks on that little card— marks that meant nothing to anyone but Eddie himself.

Came the modulation—and the master played it from another world. Everyone breathed a sigh of relief and from that day on, when Eddie would say "I got it," everyone realized he knew what he was talking about.

Evidence of this genius can be heard on all of our early Okeh recordings, as Eddie did practically all of them. Too many, in fact, for me to recall here in detail. Those of you who are acquainted with the recordings will recall many a masterful lick that would do credit to present-day records. Inseparable with Joe Venuti, the early recordings stand to prove that these two great artists presented guitar and violin masterpieces that will live forever as the ultimate for such a combination.

JOE VENUTI

Eddie (Lang) and I started to play together when we were in grammar school. You know, Eddie and I went all through grammar school and high school together. We used to play a lot of mazurkas and polkas. Just for fun we started to play them in four-four. I guess we just liked the rhythm of the guitar. Then we started to slip in some improvised passages. I'd slip something in. Eddie would pick it up with a variation. Then I'd come back with a variation. We'd just sit there and knock each other out.

Eddie and I were kids together in the same neighborhood in Philadelphia. We were together all through school except for a couple of years I put in at the University of Pennsylvania. Everybody in my family played music—string instruments mainly: violin, cello, mandolin. It was just taken for granted.

Formal training? I think a cousin started to teach me when I was about four. Solfeggio, of course. That's the Italian system under which you don't bother much about any special instrument until you know all the fundamentals of music. It's the only way to learn music right. Later, when I started to study fiddle seriously, I had several good teachers. I even put in six years in a conservatory.

Did I plan to be a concert violinist? Sure, every fiddle player does. But even when I was in the conservatory, I used to play jazz in between times for the professors. They loved it.

Eddie and I played our first real job together at a place in Atlantic City in 1921 with Bert Estlow, a piano player. The band also contained a drummer and a saxophone player. When we had time off we used to go to hear and sit in with the Scranton Sirens (Jimmy and Tommy Dorsey, Russ Morgan, et al.). And they, and other musicians, used to come to hear us.

But we never played any jazz on the job with Estlow. We would go into the men's room and play for them there. You could say the first real jazz concerts were played in the men's room of a joint in Atlantic City. Rube Bloom, who recorded with us later, first heard us there. So did Red Nichols, who was always scouting around looking for musical talent.

RED NICHOLS

I made my first phonograph record with the Syncopating Five, or as we might have called it, the "Syncopating Five Plus Two." I'll let discographers struggle with the subject of my records, but

I'll mention this one because I doubt if even the professional collectors know about it.

The titles were *Toot, Toot, Tootsie, Goodbye* and *Chicago*— and WE EACH PAID THE COMPANY TWENTY-FIVE DOLLARS FOR THE PRIVILEGE OF MAKING THE REC-ORDS! We each got twenty-five copies for "promotional pur-poses." I don't know what became of mine. I didn't even save one for myself. Maybe someone can turn one up somewhere.

It was about this time that I first heard and met Bix. The Wol-verines, briefly under the leadership of Vic Berton, followed us at a Midwest resort. We had already heard plenty about them, mainly via the musicians' grapevine, so of course we stuck around to hear them.

Bix made a tremendous impression on me, and I'd be the last one to deny that his playing influenced mine. But I did not con-sciously imitate him. I had already evolved the "style" identified with me in later years, and the same was true of Bix. We both de-rived our inspiration from many of the same sources. Only a per-son who is musically ignorant finds any marked similarity be-tween my work and that of Bix.

Early in 1923 we went into the Ambassador in Atlantic City, following Paul Whiteman, but we had to change our name there to the Royal Palms Orchestra. Joe Venuti and Eddie Lang were working at the Knickerbocker Hotel there, playing with the dinner-concert orchestra.

I also believe I first heard the first Memphis Five in person in At-lantic City at that time. During that period the Memphis Five contained such musicians as Phil Napoleon, trumpet; Frank Signo-relli, piano; and—most important to me—Miff Mole, who exer-cised a great influence not only on the development of jazz in gen-eral but especially on me.

I was doing very well with the Royal Palms Orchestra, but I got my first opportunity to organize and head a band of my own at the Pelham Heath Inn in New York.

It was comprised of Freddy Morrow, alto; Dudley Fosdick; mellophone; Gerald Finney, piano; Joe Ziegler, drums; Joe Venuti, and myself. I tried, but wasn't able, to get Eddie Lang. The Pelham

Heath band was the first in which I began to get the sound and feeling we later brought to a high point in the Five Pennies recording units.

Because of the influence the bands and musicians working around New York at that time exerted on jazz trends, I'll mention a few—Duke Ellington, Ben Selvin, Sam Lanin, the Memphis Five, and the California Ramblers—a name used later by many recording groups but at that time under the leadership of Arthur Hand.

Louis Armstrong was with Fletcher Henderson at the Roseland. Louis and I used to play for each other in the musicians' room downstairs. We were happy to exchange ideas. He was very interested in the false-fingering ideas I was working out and I showed him how it was done. The jazz musicians of that day were a kind of fraternity—all working together to promote and advance the music and each other. It's quite different now.

We quit the Pelham Heath job because the management wouldn't go for our forty-five-minute intermissions, and I went to work with Sam Lanin. Sam aided me in forming my first recording groups, which accounts for the appearance, on records, of "Sam Lanin's Redheads."

The history of the various Five Pennies recording groups is too long to tell, and much of it is well known. The name itself was supplied by Vic Berton. The numerous names under which jazz units recorded during that period were usually just last-minute thoughts at the completion of a session (we sometimes did as many as ten and twelve a week), often designed to preserve the anonymity of the musicians, who frequently had conflicting contractual commitments.

Small wonder jazz collectors are still trying to unravel and identify the personnel of some of those bands. At the time we weren't thinking much about it. We were all making lots of money playing with successful commercial dance orchestras. When we got together for a recording session, the principal aim was to turn out something that met the approval of your fellow-musicians right there in the studio.

The rest of my story can be telescoped. The important period for me was the five years between around 1925 to 1930 that was marked by a virtual partnership, musical and personal, between Miff Mole and myself. That story can only be told in the discographies and by our records.

On those records it was my good fortune to be associated with such musicians, to name a few, as Benny Goodman, Jimmy Dorsey, Artie Schutt, Vic Berton, Adrian Rollini, Eddie Lang, Miff Mole, and many, many others.

MIFF MOLE

Vic Berton, Arthur Schutt, Bix Beiderbecke, Jimmy Dorsey, and I decided that we were going to make the greatest records ever made. We took along two quarts of gin and went up to the Gennett studios. Well, we drank for an hour and a half, played about half an hour, and were then told, not too politely, to leave. We hadn't cut any records, but we didn't mind. We climbed to the top of a Fifth Avenue bus and played there, all the way home.

I quit WOR and went up to NBC. Stayed there ten years—a steady job. I played mostly classical music, and at that time I studied harmony with Vivasky. The only time I studied trombone was during my first job. Bought a euphonium, though and almost learned to play it. It has a lovely tone. Tommy Dorsey, who was living nearby, borrowed it and I've never seen it since.

Tommy was living in Merrick, Long Island, and I was living in Rockville Center, so that I could drive him out to Merrick. We were usually loaded at that point and would stop off at my house for a few drinks, then have some more at Tommy's house. Then he'd insist on driving me home, and so on. We missed more record dates that way.

RED NICHOLS

To wind up my own story, I'll go back to when I joined Paul Whiteman, in 1927. Miff was expected to join the band also, but when he declined (at that time) I quit because I was unhappy without Miff. Furthermore, Paul, flush with his success at that time, was not devoting his full attention to the band. Many times he didn't show up on a job. On such occasions Henry Busse would front the band. I would have to take over Henry's book and sit there while Henry played his muted solos.

276

Since that time I have hated the thought of a mute in a trumpet or cornet and have never used one since, except when called for on commercial radio or studio engagements.

When I quit Whiteman, my chair was taken by Bix Beiderbecke. To me that is still the greatest honor I have ever received.

With the coming of the early 'thirties, interest in the small-band intimate type of jazz played by the Five Pennies seemed to wane. I think it would have come back sooner had it not been for the extraordinary success of Benny Goodman with his big-band, swing-style type of jazz that dominated the music scene up to and through the war years.

JOE VENUTI

When the Dorsey brothers went to Detroit to join Jean Goldkette, who was building one of the great bands of that day—or any day —they persuaded Eddie and me to join Goldkette. When we got to Detroit, we dropped in at the Pelham Heath to see Nichols. Red waylaid us and we played with his band there for a time before joining Goldkette.

We stayed with Goldkette until his band broke up in New York and most of us joined Whiteman in 1927. Everyone knows that story of the days when Whiteman was assembling a band made up of almost all of the great jazz musicians of the day.

Don't ever make fun of Paul Whiteman. He did great things for American music. He took pride in having the finest musicians in the world as sidemen, and he paid the highest salaries ever paid—five hundred and six hundred a week, and even more for those who also were arrangers.

JIMMY McPARTLAND

But there were a few big bands, aside from Whiteman's that had *more* room for jazz.

BUD FREEMAN

It must have been 1927 or '28 when I was with Ben Pollack. We went into the Little Club—Gil Rodin, myself, and Benny Goodman on saxes; Glenn Miller on trombone (Jack Teagarden came later); Al Harris on trumpet (he's on the Coast now doing studio work); Jimmy McPartland played jazz cornet; Benny's brother, Harry, was on bass; Vic Briedis, piano (he later became Ruth Etting's accompanist and then committed suicide); Dick Morgan on guitar (he's the guy who invented "icky" language); and Ben Pollack, of course, on drums.

We were only there a couple of months and were continually getting in trouble with the boss. We were just an independent bunch of individuals and were always fluffing the boss off and getting just as fed up with him as he was with us. It was a pretty swank place and he couldn't see our sitting with the customers or anything like that.

In a way, those were the happiest days of our lives, only we didn't know it then, and maybe we don't even know it now.

JIMMY McPARTLAND

Ben Pollack—now there was a drummer, one of the finest that ever lived! He used to be with the New Orleans Rhythm Kings, and he produced as good a beat as I've heard. When he got behind you, he'd really make you go—yes, he'd send you.

And he had a marvellous band. That band really swung. We didn't play all jazz, naturally—we had to play popular tunes of the day for the customers. But everything we did was musical. The intonation was fine, the band had tonal quality. It was a ten-piece outfit, and it played nice, danceable music.

In New York, we all moved into nice places to live and spent our money fast. Bud Freeman and I put up at the Mayflower Hotel; then suddenly Pollack quit, over an argument about the show. So we were out of a job.

It was a tough layoff; no work, nothing saved up, of course. But there were always the cocktail parties. This was 1928, before the stock market crashed, and there was plenty of money floating around—though we didn't have any of it for the time being.

A lot of people gave a lot of parties, and often we would be invited. You could get all you wanted to drink but nothing to eat. Just the same, it was better than nothing at all.

We couldn't pay the rent, though, so after a couple of weeks we moved into the Whitby Apartments, where Gil Rodin, Dick Morgan, Benny Goodman, and Glenn Miller had a suite. We all moved into that, practically the whole band, with the exception of Pollack, sleeping on chairs, couches, the floor, anywhere.

The number of that apartment was 1411. And that is how that title came up, *Room 1411*, by Benny Goodman's Boys. We had been out of work about five weeks when Benny came home and said, "I've got a recording date with Brunswick. We can get some money, buy some food, eat!"

We made that date—Goodman, Miller, myself and two or three more, playing different kinds of numbers like *Blue* and *Jungle Blues*, and this one we named *Room 1411*. After the session was just about over, we started kidding around and playing corny.

Out comes the recording manager from his booth, and he says, "That's it! That's what we want, just what you're playing there!" We were playing as corny as possible. As a matter of fact, Tommy Dorsey had come up and was standing listening to us, and he picked up a trombone and started playing, kidding around, too.

The manager said, "You gotta do that." That is what he wanted. So we sort of used the *St. Louis* chord progressions and blew all this cod Dixie, and we called the number *Shirt Tail Stomp*. It sold more than any of the others; or I should say that it sold the rest of the sides because it was corny. It shows the taste of people; still the same, I guess, the world over.

This was not the first time I recorded under Goodman's name. After we made those Victor records with Pollack that I mentioned, Benny got a date with Brunswick for a small band. There were just the Goodmans, Miller, Briedis, Morgan, myself, and drummer Bob Conselman, and I think we made only two titles— *Jazz Holiday* and *Wolverine Blues*.

A week or two later we went to work again, with short engagements in Atlantic City, Syracuse, and so forth. Back in New York, I was having a couple of drinks with Bud Freeman and Pee Wee Russell one evening in a little speakeasy on 51st Street, when Pee Wee began talking about a trombone player, the greatest thing he had heard in this life.

We said we would have to hear the guy, and Pee Wee said, right, he'd just pop over and get him. Two drinks later, Pee Wee was back with the guy, who was wearing a horrible-looking cap and overcoat and carrying a trombone in a case under his arm.

Pee Wee introduced us. He was Jack Teagarden, from Texas, and looked it. "Fine," we said. "We've been hearing a lot about you, would sure like to hear you play."

The guy says "All right," gets his horn out, puts it together, blows a couple of warm-up notes and starts to play *Diane*. No accompaniment, just neat; he played it solo, and I'm telling you he knocked us out. He really blew it. And when he'd done with that he started on the blues, still by himself.

We had to agree with Pee Wee, we'd never heard anyone play trombone like that. We were flabbergasted. They were going to a jam session later, up on Forty-eighth Street where Jack lived, so we went back and told Gil Rodin and a couple of the others how wonderful Teagarden was.

The other guys scoffed, but Rodin didn't. He came with us on the session that night, and when he heard Jack he reported back to Pollack and the whole band, and next night they all came up to hear the new trombonist.

Glenn Miller was among them, and he was gracious enough to bow to a real jazz player like that. It was the greatest he had ever heard, too. Until then, Miff Mole had been Glenn's idol, the person he'd patterned himself on. Teagarden was earmarked for the Ben Pollack band.

JACK TEAGARDEN

I was playing with Ben Pollack, but cut a lot of records independently under various labels, many with Red Nichols. Glenn Miller did the arrangements for Nichols, and we had Benny Goodman on clarinet, Gene Krupa on drums, Glenn and I on trombones, and my brother Charlie with Red and Manny Klein on trumpets.

I was home in New York the evening before the *Basin Street Blues* record date when Glenn called me from his apartment in Jackson Heights. "Jack," he said, "I've been running over *Basin Street* again and I think we could do a better job if we could put together some lyrics and you could sing it. Want to come over and see what we can do? My wife will fix us some supper."

After we had worked out a first draft of verse and chorus, Glenn sat on the piano bench and I leaned over his shoulder. We each had a pencil, and as he played, we'd each cross out words and phrases here and there, putting in new ones. We finally finished the job sometime early in the morning.

Next day, we cut the record. It's been the most popular I've ever done! The lyrics were later included with the sheet music, but it never carried our names.

KAISER MARSHALL

In 1928 Louis Armstrong got some of us together for a record date—Jack Teagarden on trombone, Happy Cauldwell on sax, Joe Sullivan on piano, Eddie Lang on guitar, and myself on drums. We had been working the night before and the record date was for eight in the morning, so we didn't bother about going to bed; I rode the boys around in my car in the early morning hours and we had breakfast about six so we could get to the studio at eight. We took a gallon jug of whiskey with us.

After we recorded the number the studio man came around with his list to write down the usual information, composer, name of tune, and so on. He asked Louis what the tune was called, and Louis said, "I don't know!" Then he looked around and saw the empty jug sitting in the middle of the floor and said, "Man, we sure knocked that jug—you can call it *Knockin' a Jug*." And that's the name that went on the record.

TONY PARENTI

When I came to New York in 1928, I was shackin' with my old friend, Ray Bauduc, a New Orleansian too. Ray was with Ben Pollack at the Park Central Hotel at the time and also doubling in the show HELLO DADDY. The Pollack band was definitely one of the greatest white bands of all time—for that kind of music, I mean. It was big-band jazz with a firm beat, plenty of room for solos and some fine arrangements by Glenn Miller. I played with the band many times, sitting in for Benny Goodman when he was playin' a fraternity dance or a society gig or something of that sort.

Those jobs, incidentally, accounted for us makin' a lot of money in those days. Society band leaders like Meyer Davis and Joe Moss always wanted to have at least one good jazzman in their bands, somebody like Tommy or Jimmy Dorsey, Benny, Teagarden, McPartland, and so on. They wouldn't play jazz at those high social functions of course, but they did want a man with them who could play a couple of solo choruses on the up-tempo of things.

Other jobs to be had then were in radio because, you know, big name bands weren't popular yet. I played with Freddie Rich at the studios and Artie Shaw was playing sax; Bunny Berigan, trumpet; Jerry Colonna, trombone—lots of good jazzmen worked radio.

The big hangout for musicians in those days was Plunkett's on Fifty-third Street between Seventh and Eighth Avenues—where the old "el" used to be. Man, I drank a lotta whiskey in Plunkett's. So did all of us, in fact. We hung out there because Jimmy Plunkett was such a great guy—he'd lend us money till payday, cash checks, and do the musicians all kinds of favors.

RAY BAUDUC

We made a lot of records with the Pollack band at the time we were playing the Park Central. Gil Rodin sold the band to Irving Mills on the idea of making records, and for a while we made records for just about every company you could name. That was about 1929, I think, and some of the names we used were the Toe Ticklers, Mills' Musical Clowns, the Mills Hottentots, and so many more I couldn't possibly remember them. It was funny the way we would switch our arrangements just a little this way and that for those record dates.

Speaking of records, just a few years before that, when I first came to New York, I was on what I think were the first Memphis Five date. It was for Pathe, and Miff Mole was on trombone; Phil Napoleon on trumpet; Jimmy Dorsey, clarinet; Frank Signorelli, piano; and I played cymbal and wood blocks (that's all we used on record dates then). The tunes were *The Chant, One Sweet Letter From You, Go, Joe, Go,* and *Missouri Squabble.*

BEN POLLACK

We had some good runs, like the Southmoor Hotel in Chicago, in 1926, later the Little Club in New York—and that long run, a year, at the Park Central, part of the time doubling as featured band with a stage show, HELLO DADDY.

With recordings and other outside work those kids were making themselves two hundred and fifty to three hundred a week—in 1929! But as soon as we were out of a job they were broke and hocking everything they owned. Me—it seems I was always paying out more to sidemen than I was taking in. On one job I lost two hundred and fifty a week.

As I recall it now, everywhere the band played it was the talk of the town—with musicians—but I was generally going in the hole because I wanted to have a great band. But for all of us it was pretty much the same—weeks of starvation between jobs, followed by periods of high living and prosperity when we were working.

17

From Kansas City, a musician's town, came stories of fabulous jam sessions, good times, and the swinging band of Count Basie.

SAM PRICE
Jam sessions in Kansas City? I remember once at the Subway Club, on Eighteenth Street, I came by a session at about ten o'clock and then went home to clean up and change my clothes. I came back a little after one o'clock and they were still playing the same song.

JO JONES
Some places in Kansas City never closed. You could be sleeping one morning at six A.M., and a traveling band would come into town for a few hours, and they would wake you up to make a couple of hours' session with them until eight in the morning. You never knew what time in the morning someone would knock on the door and say they were jamming down the street.

MARY LOU WILLIAMS
In those years around 1930, Kaycee was really jumping—so many great bands having sprung up there or moved in from over the river. I should explain that Kansas City, Missouri, wasn't too prejudiced for a Midwestern town. It was a ballin' town, and it

attracted musicians from all over the South and Southwest, and especially from Kansas. Kansas City, Kansas, was right across the viaduct, just about five or six miles distant. But on the Kansas side they were much snootier. A lot of their musicians were from good families who frowned on jazz, so the musicians and kids would come across to Kaycee to blast. In Kaycee, nothing mattered.

I've known musicians so enthused about playing that they would walk all the way from the Kansas side to attend a jam session. Even bass players, caught without streetcar fare, would hump their bass on their back and come running. That was how music stood in Kansas City.

JO JONES
Before I came to Kansas City, I had heard practically everything that had happened in jazz since 1923, so I had something to base my comparison on. I had heard the McKinney Cotton Pickers and I had heard Fletcher Henderson. I had gone up and down the country in carnivals, and playing the Chautauqua Circuit. I had done singing and dancing and dramatic skits. I had played YMCAs and church festivals and athletic clubs, and I had studied music for about twelve years—trumpet, sax, and piano. (It's a funny thing, I could always play drums and everything I played on other instruments was drumming.)

So I knew the entertainment business and I knew something about music. But Kansas City had always been a phobia for me. I mean by that that I had a phobia about going there. I felt I wasn't qualified to compete with what was happening there and, yet, when I got there, I couldn't leave.

One of the reasons I was afraid about going there was that I'd been in a shell—I'd been isolated in Omaha for three or three and a half years.

After I got into Kansas City, I remember walking into the Sunset, and there was Pete Johnson and a drummer named Merrill and an alto player named Walter Knight. This was about 1933. I have never heard anybody play a sax like he did in my life. I can hear a little of it in Charlie Parker today. They only had three pieces in that group. But since that club had sessions so late and the other clubs closed early, they would soon have an augmented bandstand.

There were jam sessions I used to watch there and other places in Kansas City, even before I got with the Basie band, that were unlike any other jam sessions I have heard since. It has to do with what I will try to explain to you about head arrangements in the Basie band and how we didn't have to rehearse back in Kansas City. It was just there and we played it.

Now it was a very strange thing at these jam sessions in Kansas City. Nobody ever got in nobody's way. Nobody ever had to point a finger and say: "You take it now. You take the next chorus." Any place in Kansas City where there was a session the guys would just get up on the bandstand, and spiritually they knew when to come in. They could tell when a guy had played his three or four choruses and was ready for someone else to take over. Like when there were either two tenors and two trumpet players on the stand no one had to point to you and tell you to follow the trombone player. They just felt which one was coming next.

I remember sessions with guys like Dick Wilson and Ben Webster, and sometimes Pha Terrell would come right out of the audience and sing right in the middle of a number, and he knew exactly where to start. I haven't heard a jam session like that since I came to New York.

Around that time in Kansas City you could hear, at other sessions, "Pres" Young, Ben Webster, Herschel Evans, Dick Wilson, Lips Page, Irving Randolph (they called him "Mouse," and he later went with Calloway), Walter Page, and various other musicians. As for the lesser guys, they didn't attempt to play with the major leaguers. They would sort of work their way up from various clubs before they would get on the bandstand at a place like the Sunset. It's not like the present-day guys who try to run up on the grandstand and play with Charlie Parker and think they've accomplished something just sitting in. Some of these present-day guys don't realize that they don't have the background and accomplishment to sit in with a man like Bird yet. I don't mean it's a question of age—it's a question of experience.

As for me, I had a very good background of experience but

somewhere along the way there were influences that were going to destroy that background. If it hadn't been for the help I myself had had from other people I don't know what would have happened to me. I especially want to mention Alec Nabors, Wilson Driver, and Professor James H. Wilson.

But back in Kansas City even the so-called lesser guys—too many to mention—including some whose names I don't even know, always played with that feeling I've found nowhere else in jazz. These are men who were in the same age bracket of the ones back in New Orleans and Chicago. They had that feeling but were never written about—like Tommy Douglas and Walter Knight.

I went into Kansas City to join Tommy Douglas. He was and still is one of the most proficient sax players alive today. Several jazz musicians came up around him, and I think Parker brushed with him somewhere along the line. Like Benny Carter or Don Redman were regarded in the East, Douglas was in Kansas City. I remember he played clarinet and sax and played a little of both. And Knight had such a great big, open tone on alto. Another aspect of his playing that made it so good was the way he used to bend his changes.

MARY LOU WILLIAMS

So I found Kansas City to be a heavenly city—music everywhere in the Negro section of town, and fifty or more cabarets rocking on Twelfth and Eighteenth Streets.

Kirk's band was drawing them into the handsome Pla-mor Ballroom when my husband, John Williams, had me return to him in Kaycee. This was my first visit to Missouri's jazz metropolis, a city that was to have a big influence on my career.

With my sisters, Lucille and Louise, who knew every speakeasy in town, I began to make the rounds from Hell's Kitchen on Fifth Avenue to a club on Eighteenth where I met Sam Price. Sammy was playing an unusual type of blues piano, which I thought could hardly be improved on. I had the luck to hear him again when we were both in New York during 1934.

One night, we ran into a place where Ben Pollack had a combo, which included Jack Teagarden and, I think, Benny Goodman. The girls introduced me to the Texas trombonist, and right away we felt like friends.

After work, he and a couple of musicians asked us to go out, and we visited most of the speaks downtown. One I remember particularly, because it was decorated to resemble the inside of a penitentiary, with bars on the windows and waiters in striped uniforms like down-South convicts. In these weird surroundings, I played for the boys and Jack got up and sang some blues. I thought he was more than wonderful. While they stayed in Kaycee, Jack and some of Pollack's men came round every night, and I was very happy to see them.

Now, at this time, which was still Prohibition, Kansas City was under Tom Pendergast's control. Most of the night spots were run by politicians and hoodlums, and the town was wide open for drinking, gambling, and pretty much every form of vice. Naturally, work was plentiful for musicians, though some of the employers were tough people.

For instance, when Andy Kirk moved from the Pla-mor, the orchestra went to work for a nationally feared gangster. He was real bad; people used to run when you just mentioned his name. At that time, Andy was playing tuba, and the band was conducted by our singer, Billy Massey. Billy was a man not easily scared, and one day at the new job he ran off his mouth to the boss. The hood concluded he was crazy (which was not far wrong), and told all the band to pack and leave—but fast. The rest of the guys were too nice, he said, for him to think about killing Billy.

I heard that Count Basie later worked for the same dracula, and also had a slight misunderstanding. As a result, Basie had to work two weeks without pay.

At the head of the bands was Bennie Moten's, led by pianist Bennie and featuring his brother, Buster, on accordion. Then there was George E. Lee, whose sister, Julia, played piano in George's band and took care of the vocals.

From Oklahoma came Walter Page, with a terrific combo named the Blue Devils. Page, known as "Big One," was one of the very first to use the string bass as well as tuba, and he also doubled on bass saxophone.

JO JONES
The greatest band I ever heard in my life was Walter Page's Blue Devils band. Musically, Page was the father of Basie, Rushing, Buster Smith (Buster was an alto player that used to be called Prof, and he was Charlie Parker's musical father). And Page was a musical father to me too because without him I wouldn't have known how to play drums. For two years Page told me how to phrase, he taught me how to turn on what the kids now call "dropping bombs."

Now bombs are just pure accents. The accents in drum playing are going to be here for years to come just as they've been for millions of years before now. Aside from that, Page also told me a few of the moral responsibilities that go into making up a musician's, an artist's, life.

MARY LOU WILLIAMS
I loved to see Jo teaming with Walter Page, the bassist. Page showed Jo what to do and when to do it, and it was really something to dig those two great musicians. I have caught Basie's orchestra at times when there was no one on the stage except Page and the horns and, believe me, "Big One" swung that band on his bass without much effort.

JO JONES
You would hear music twenty-four hours a day in Kansas City. Practically all the little places had piano and a set of drums. I had a little group in one of them with Lester Young and George Hunt on trombone (he later took the solo on the Basie record of *One O'Clock Jump*) and Ed Durham on guitar. Any drummer who wanted to could sit in because I could play piano.

The place was run by "The Chief." His name was Ellis Burton. He was a father to a lot of the musicians. Anybody in music or anybody in the entertainment profession could always go to him and get a favor or food. Maybe he couldn't get money but he could get food and favors. The first thing any performer would do when he came to Kansas City would be to look up The Chief. Basie was his favorite son.

I had left Basie's band for a while, and I was in St. Louis at one point in 1936. I left to make some money and to get a set of drums. When I got back to Kansas City I was flushed. I had five dollars. First thing I wanted to do was to find The Chief. I ran into Joe Keyes, one of the most wonderful musicians I have known in my life. He was a trumpet player. He was also a guy who taught me how to think. Well, Joe told me The Chief was dead. Then we ran into Basie. Basie literally broke the door in when they wouldn't let anybody in to see The Chief. I never said anything then to Basie or since about it but you can see what The Chief's death meant to us.

The Chief, by the way, played a very important part in keeping the nucleus of the Basie band together. He gave us a lot of encouragement. And, at that time, just before he died, there were some people who were interested in backing him in a night club operation. After all those years of scuffle he had been through during the depression, when it looked like somebody was going to let him have about thirty thousand dollars to open a club of his own, he was looking forward so much to seeing Basie and to telling him, "Get the band together. I've got a place for you guys to play and you've got nothing to worry about any more." I expect all that excitement proved a little too much for him.

Like that Ellis Burton was the daddy of us, so was Piney Brown the big brother. He was very much in the family. I don't think anybody's ever been to Kansas City who hasn't received the hospitality of Piney Brown. He's the one Joe Turner sings about on the record of the *Piney Brown Blues*. He came up after The Chief. He took up that slack. No performer, small or large, ever came into town but what Piney Brown was willing to help him. He loved professional people. But it had to be up to you. You had to be yourself. He didn't like any phonies. A phony could hardly get served in a bar in Kansas City—a real guy could. Like a guy could come up to Piney Brown's bar and say, "I only have thirty-five cents." Piney would serve him what he wanted, take the thirty-five cents and let it go at that.

Piney Brown ran the Sunset where I first ran into Joe Turner. I remember we used to play behind Joe there. There was a place close by (across the street in fact) called the Lone Star. Joe Turner would start to sing the blues at the Sunset, and then he'd go across the street and sing the blues at the Lone Star, and we were still playing all this time. Joe would socialize there for a while and stop in the front and have breakfast and then he'd come back in to the Sunset, go up to the microphone, and sing some more blues and we'd have been playing all the time. Often we'd play for an hour and a half straight like that.

At that time it wasn't unusual for one number to go on about an hour or an hour and a half. Nobody got tired. They didn't tell me at that time that they used to change drummers so I just sat there and played the whole time for pure joy. And I never realized that an hour and a half had gone by. In later years, that was to help me build up a lot of stamina. So now you can see some of the reasons why it was hard to leave Kansas City.

MARY LOU WILLIAMS

A wild Twelfth Street spot we fell in regularly was the Sunset, owned by Piney Brown, who loved jazz and was very liberal with musicians. Pianist Pete Johnson worked there with bass and drums, sometimes with Baby Lovett, a New Orleans drummer who became one of Kansas City's best.

Now the Sunset had a bartender named Joe Turner, and while Joe was serving drinks he would suddenly pick up a cue for a blues and sing it right where he stood, with Pete playing piano for him. I don't think I'll ever forget the thrill of listening to big Joe Turner shouting and sending everybody, night after night, while mixing drinks.

Pete Johnson was great on boogie, but he was by no means solely a boogie player. It was only when someone like Ben Webster, the Kaycee-born tenor man, yelled, "Roll for me—come on, roll 'em, Pete, make 'em jump," that he would play boogie for us.

In the summer, Kirk's band worked only from nine to twelve

at night, and afterwards we would drive by the Sunset—John Williams and me and the five or six that rode with us. Pete might be playing something like *Sweet Georgia Brown* or *Indiana* when we got there. I'd go home to bathe and change, and when I got back, ten-to-one Pete would still be jamming the same tune, and maybe some of the guys wailing along with him.

Of course, we didn't have any closing hours in these spots. We could play all morning and half through the day if we wished to, and in fact we often did. The music was so good that I seldom got to bed before midday.

It was just such a late morning session that once had Coleman Hawkins hung up. Fletcher Henderson came to town with Hawkins on tenor, and after the dance the band cruised round until they fell into the Cherry Blossom where Count Basie worked.

The date must have been early 1934, because Prohibition had been lifted and whiskey was freely on sale. The Cherry Blossom was a new night club, richly decorated in Japanese style, even to the beautiful little brown-skinned waitress.

The word went round that Hawkins was in the Cherry Blossom, and within about half an hour there were Lester Young, Ben Webster, Herschel Evans, Herman Walder, and one or two unknown tenors piling in the club to blow.

Bean didn't know the Kaycee tenor men were so terrific, and he couldn't get himself together though he played all morning. I happened to be nodding that night, and around four A.M., I awoke to hear someone pecking on my screen.

I opened the window on Ben Webster. He was saying, "Get up, pussycat, we're jammin' and all the pianists are tired out now. Hawkins has got his shirt off and is still blowing. You got to come down."

Sure enough, when we got there, Hawkins was in his singlet, taking turns with the Kaycee men. It seems he had run into something he didn't expect.

Lester's style was light, and, as I said, it took him maybe five choruses to warm up. But then he would really blow; then you couldn't handle him on a cutting session.

That was how Hawkins got hung up. The Henderson band was playing in St. Louis that evening, and Bean knew he ought to be on the way. But he kept trying to blow something to beat Ben and Herschel and Lester. When at last he gave up, he got straight in his car and drove to St. Louis. I heard he'd just bought a new Cadillac and that he burnt it out trying to make the job on time. Yes, Hawkins was king until he met those crazy Kansas City tenor men.

JO JONES

That was the first night Hawkins was really challenged. But when I say "challenged" I mean it was a respectful challenge. You see, nobody in those days would walk in and set up with Hawkins, except maybe in New York where Chu Berry was just coming up. But most of the time at sessions guys would just be trying to show Hawkins how they had improved since he had last heard them. Those sessions were held for the joy of playing. They weren't cutting sessions or contests. This was all part of our feeling about music in Kansas City.

Now those were pretty tough times and yet the guys did take the time to study, and when they had found something new they would bring it up to the session and they would pass it around to the other musicians, no matter what instrument they played. So they would try that particular riff or that particular conception at a session and perfect it. The idea of the jam session then wasn't who could play better than somebody else—it was a matter of contributing something and of experimentation. Jam sessions were our fun, our outlet.

MARY LOU WILLIAMS

Yes, Kaycee was a place to be enjoyed, even if you were without funds. People would make you a loan without you asking for it, would look at you and tell if you were hungry and put things right.

There was the best food to be had—the finest barbecue, crawdads, and other seafood. There were the races, and swimming, and the beautiful Swope Park and zoo to amuse you. There were

293

jam sessions all the time, and big dances such as the union dance given every year by our local.

As many as ten or twelve bands participated in this event, and you were sure to hear at least eight original styles there, as well as one or two outfits trying to imitate Duke.

For private entertainment we had our hot corn club every Monday, at which the musicians and wives would drink and play bridge, "tonk," or "hearts."

At these meetings, the boys drank corn whiskey and home brew—in fact, most anything with a high alcohol content—and they got laughs out of giving me rough liquor so strong it would almost blow the top of one's head off.

One of the regulars was Herman Walder, brilliant tenor player with Moten and brother of saxophonist Woodie Walder. Herman asked me if I'd like a cool drink one night, and not knowing the taste of corn, I gulped down a large glassful. The next thing I remember was people putting cold towels on my head. Being stubborn, I thought, "If they can take it, so can I." So each Monday I tried to drink, with much the same result.

JO JONES
We lost a wonderful piano player in Kansas City this way. We lost him because he tried to drink a pint of whiskey all at one gulp. Usually before drinking a lot, guys would eat a lot of chili because it had a lot of grease to line the stomach. Well, under those conditions, you see, this guy had drunk a pint of whiskey at one gulp. But this time he was doing it just on a bet and he'd had no preliminary conditioning and so we lost a wonderful piano player.

MARY LOU WILLIAMS
Speaking of piano players, at one place, we ran into Art Tatum. Art had a radio program, also a job in a dicty private club, but preferred wailing after hours.

It was this place every night then. Whenever I wasn't listening to Tatum, I was playing—Art inspired me so much. Chords he was throwing in then, the boppers are using now. And his mind was the quickest.

Art usually drank a bottle of beer while the other pianists took over, and didn't miss a thing. For instance, there was a run that Buck Washington showed me. (Buck, of the Buck and Bubbles team, played a lotta piano, especially when out jamming. Everything he did was unusual.)

Now Art heard me play this run, which consisted of F, E-flat, D-flat, C; (octave up) C, B-flat, A-flat, G; and so on all the way to the top of the keyboard. When he sat down, he played it right off. Other pianists had heard and tried, but taken time to pick it up.

In Kaycee, we had a kind of counterpart of Tatum, an ear man called Sleepy, who played almost as much as Art, and in the hard keys—A natural, B natural, E natural.

Another unsung piano player was Lincoln, known as a three-chord man. His harmonies were the worst, yet he was terrific with the beat. Martha Raye, then eighteen, stopped in Kansas City on her way to California and got hung up listening to Lincoln's nasty beat. She stayed close on to two weeks, and was down at the clubs digging the music and singing like mad, night after night. Martha hated to leave and nearly missed doing her picture. That was how Kaycee would get you, for there were always places open and music to hear.

Besides the players I've mentioned, and Bennie Moten, Count Basie, Pete Johnson, Sam Price, and Clyde Hart, there were three girl pianists, apart from myself. One was Julia Lee, who took little part in the sessions; another I recollect only as Oceola; the third was known as Countess Margaret. Countess was a friend of Lester Young, and when I was sick for a time, Kirk sent for her to take my place for a month.

The tour got her, I fear, for she died of tuberculosis before she had done very much, though I hear she was quite good.

JO JONES

So the city was full of musicians and I know no place was the hotbed of music that Kansas City was in the four years I spent there, and don't forget I missed 1930, 1931, and 1932. Men who used to come through Kansas City would go back to their various localities afterwards and improve on what they had there. The Kansas City influence first spread within a radius from Texas to Oklahoma and into Missouri. Men based in Kansas City would do one-nighters through all those territories. By being thrown into constant contact with each other, the musicians in the whole area were able to grow. And there were some very good bands based in those territories. Like Alphonso Trent in Dallas. Lips Page came out of Dallas too.

Hot Lips Page was the life of many a Kaycee jam session. After a soloist had blown nine or ten choruses Lips would start a riff in the background which the other horns picked up. Not many arrangers could improve on Lips when it came to backing up a soloist.

ORAN "HOT LIPS" PAGE

I was born and raised in Dallas, Texas. When I was a boy, my mother wanted me to be a doctor, and I went to college with that idea in mind, but I never finished. I was much more interested in music. I had always liked music. My mother gave me my first lessons. She had been a school teacher, teaching general subjects, but she also taught music on the side, taking private pupils at home.

My father died in 1916, when I was still in short pants. He had been in the moving business. After his death, to help out at home, I took to running errands and doing odd jobs around the neighborhood. I began to take music seriously when I discovered I could make more money blowing a trumpet than shining shoes. Originally, I wanted to play clarinet, but changed to trumpet because it stuck out in a brass band like a sore thumb. My first regular chance to play came when I joined what we used to call a kids' band. They were run by a man named Lux Alexander. Lux played in one of the big city bands. He was a bass drummer. However, he could play all the different instruments, and he used to form kids' bands to play for weddings, parties, picnics, parades, fire sales, and lodge meetings. Sometimes he used as many as thirty-five or forty kids in a band.

By the time I was fifteen, I was too old for kids' bands. That was the age limit, so the next summer I began to play for carnivals and minstrel shows touring through that section of the country. In those days, before big bands really came into their own, colored shows were very popular everywhere, and an organization named T.O.B.A. used to book shows all over the South. One summer, we went as far East as Atlanta, Georgia, where we played a theater date with Bessie Smith. At that time, Atlanta was considered quite a center. It was the town everyone wanted to play. Another time, we were booked for tent shows with Ma Rainey. She took an interest in my playing, and did what she could to encourage me, with the result that I got a chance to play with her when she worked at the Lincoln Theatre in New York City.

Following the early experiences that I have been telling about, the carnivals, minstrel shows, and stage shows for name singers, I had a chance in 1928 to join my older half-brother, Walter, the bass player. He had a band called "Walter Page's Blue Devils." King Oliver, of course, was the chief influence on the Blue Devils, then Jelly Roll Morton, and then Duke Ellington, in that order. We played all around the Southwest, and when we hit Kansas City in 1930, Bennie Moten came to hear us.

Bennie was a businessman first and last. He had a lot of connections out there, and he was a very good friend of Pendergast, the political boss. Through contacts of this kind, he was able to control all the good jobs and choice locations in and around Kansas City. In his day, you might say that he was stronger than MCA. However, he was also a very good musician. A real old-timer, he was an excellent ragtime pianist and he could play along with the best of them. Bennie liked our music, he liked the way we played, and he made us a proposition. If we would provide the music, he would provide the jobs, and that is how the Blue Devils became the nucleus for the best band Moten ever had.

Of course, we didn't need Bennie as a pianist. We already had Basie. I had sent for Basie some time before when a previous man had left us, and he had fitted in O.K. At the time, Basie hadn't been out West long. Originally, he had come from Jersey, and was still more or less unknown. Consequently, Moten only played when he felt like it and was good and ready. Often, he'd just stand up alongside the piano and smile. At other times, he'd go off and join some influential people in the audience. All that was good business.

Except for occasional changes in personnel, we all stuck together right up until Moten's death in 1934. During those years, we played all through that section. We also toured the East, playing New York City, Detroit, Cincinnati, and a number of big towns. And there's one thing I want to say about that band. I don't think that any other band of that period ever brought out the two-beat as definitely as Moten's.

JO JONES

Bennie Moten's band played a two-beat rhythm such as one-and-three. Walter Page's band played a two-and-four. It wasn't that they would stop to accent that beat, it was sort of like a bouncing ball, and when those rhythms met in the Basie band there was an even flow—one, two, three, four—like a bouncing ball.

COUNT BASIE

I'd traveled west from New York with a touring vaudeville show. I was just a kinda honky-tonk piano player with the show and we had more than our share of troubles. We didn't have any "names" in the cast and we didn't do much business. So, about the time we reached Kansas City, the unit was in pretty bad shape and then came the inevitable folding. When we folded, I was broke and didn't have any way to get out of town.

I knew I couldn't do any good by sitting around feeling sorry for myself or wishing I'd never left my home in Red Bank, New Jersey. I started making the rounds to see if there might be a spot in town for a piano player, and surprisingly fast found that spot playing the accompaniment to silent films at a local movie theater called the Eblon. I must say I got a lot of good experience in that job, because I was playing for all sorts of pictures, anything from a western melodrama to a crime thriller or one of those passion plays.

Well, I held that job at the Eblon for the better part of a year. Then, in 1928, I got a job with a band known as the "Blue Devils." The leader of this band was a guy named Walter Page, who played a mighty wicked string bass, and still does. Yes, he's the same Walter Page who later made with the rhythm in my band.

The Blue Devils did quite a bit of traveling between Kansas City and Oklahoma City, and in 1929 we picked up a blues singer in Oklahoma City. That was Jimmy Rushing, who for my money has never had an equal when it comes to the blues.

Back in the early 'thirties there was a band in Kansas City that more or less ruled the local jazz scene. It was that of the late Bennie Moten. Few people outside of Kansas City ever knew much about this band for the reason that way back then there were no such means of nation-wide exploitation as radio, records, and juke-boxes and local or territorial bands had to be seen to be heard. Well, the Blue Devils broke up and several of us, including Page and Rushing, joined Bennie. I played "third piano" in that band. Bennie, of course, was the big man at the keys, and his brother Bus played piano-accordion.

There were some great musicians in that Moten band. Five of those musicians have played with me right up to the present. In addition to Walter Page and Jimmy Rushing, they are Ed Lewis, my first trumpet player of long standing; Jack Washington, baritone sax; and Jo Jones at the drums. We also had such men as Eddie Durham, who played trombone and did a great deal of the arranging, and Hot Lips Page, who took care of a lot of jazz on trumpet.

I guess we played just about every jazz spot in Kansas City. The ones that are foremost in my mind are the Reno Club, the Tower and Main Street Theaters, the Fairland Park and Pla-mor Ballrooms, and the Frog Hop Ballroom in St. Joseph, not far from Kansas City.

I've heard a lot of conflicting stories as to how I came to go out as a bandleader in my own right. First, I will say that I did not take over the Bennie Moten band when Bennie died. In 1935 the band was booked for the Rainbow Ballroom in Denver, one of the leading dance spots in the West. Bennie, however, stayed in Kansas City for a tonsillectomy. In the meantime, the band went on to open in Denver. Just as we were getting under way on opening night, Bus Moten received a telephone call from Kansas City that

Bennie had died on the operating table. This news, of course, was a tremendous blow to every man in the band. We all thought a great deal of Bennie and our association went much deeper than that of musicians for their leader. We did our best to carry on and go through our opening night at the Rainbow. But without a leader, the band just didn't seem to mean very much any more. Bus Moten took over for the next six months or so and then we broke up.

The next move I made was to organize a small band of my own, in which several of my fellow members in the Moten band joined me. Then, in 1935, I enlarged this band at the Reno Club in Kansas City and this eventually became my present organization. Rushing, Page, Jo, Durham, Ed Lewis, and Jack Washington were among those who joined me.

I don't mind saying that it was a mad scuffle with that band. In fact, we were in and out of the Reno Club for about a year before things even started to look up. That's where Benny Goodman and John Hammond entered the picture. On one trip to Kansas City, John caught the band at the Club. He was just a youngster then, but just as much of a jazz enthusiast as he is now. John liked the band and went around talking about us to a lot of people, including B.G.

We were broadcasting over a local Kansas City station from the Reno Club, and John told Benny to listen in on one of the broadcasts. Benny did and he was interested enough to make a special trip to Kansas City to hear the band in person. I might add that Benny's own band was playing in Chicago at the time and, as he later told me, the only way he could pick up the station on which we were broadcasting was by going out into the middle of a vacant lot with a portable radio.

When Benny came to the Reno Club in the spring of 1936 to hear the band, none of us was aware that he was digging us. Benny went back to Chicago and phoned his own booker, Willard Alexander of Music Corporation of America, in New York. In the meantime, John mentioned us to Willard. Then Willard made a trip to Kansas City himself and signed the band with MCA.

Contrary to several conflicting stories, I got the name "Count" right in Kansas City in 1936 while at the Reno Club. I was known as Bill Basie at that time. One night, while we were broadcasting, the announcer called me to the microphone for those usual few words of introduction. He commented that Bill Basie was a rather ordinary name, and further that there were a couple of well-known bandleaders named Earl Hines and Duke Ellington. Then he said, "Bill, I think I'll call you Count Basie from now on. Is that all right with you?" I thought he was kidding, shrugged my shoulders and replied, "Okay." Well, that was the last time I was ever introduced as Bill Basie. From then on it was Count Basie, and I never did lose that nickname. It's funny the way those things will stick. I always get a big kick when an announcer or interviewer will ask, "Count, tell us how you got that royal title, willya?" That's usually the first question, and by now I can reel off the answer to that one without catching my breath.

Another popular question is the origin of our theme, *One O'clock Jump*. I'll answer that one right here because it too has a very strong connection with Kansas City. It also came out of one of our radio broadcasts. Back in those days, when you went on the air, you didn't have to clear songs and titles in advance as you do now. In other words, the band would just go on the air and play "heads" and anything that came to mind. One night we had about five minutes to go on a broadcast and the announcer asked me for the title of the closing tune. Well, it just had no title so it was up to someone to pick one out in a hurry. I glanced up at the clock. It was almost one o'clock. "Just call it the *One O'clock Jump*," I told the announcer. After that we used it for our theme and it's unquestionably the record most closely associated with the band.

In all the time he was with the band, Jimmy Rushing has been what I might call my right arm. There were times in the early days of the band that I'd have given it all up but for Jimmy's urging to stick with it.

JO JONES
We worked with Basie at a place called the Cherry Blossom. They used to have a piano they would roll on the floor, and Jimmy Rushing would go around serenading the people.

MARY LOU WILLIAMS

I remember the lovable Jimmy Rushing, "Mr. Five by Five," from when he was singing with Bennie Moten and later with Basie. Unlike the run of blues shouters, Jimmy could read music, and he could be heard ten blocks away without a microphone (they used megaphones then, anyway).

Jimmy was big brother to me and some of the other band wives. I remember him playing piano and singing wonderful ballads to us; other times he would keep us laughing with his risqué stories, getting a kick out of seeing us blush.

Basie drew Jimmy and several other of Moten's men into his outfit and built the band that blew up a storm at Kaycee's Reno Club.

While the Count was getting this group together, he sent out for Jo Jones on drums.

JO JONES

The second Basie band I was with started in 1936 as a small combo and it went up from seven to nine to ten to fourteen, and that's when we went to New York. Now, in that band the nucleus of that Kansas City spirit and feeling I was trying to describe was still there. When we first came to New York we tried to experiment. We tried to play some of the so-called modern arrangements of that era. Basie was of the opinion that the things we had been playing were old hat. So after a week of experimenting we found out that there was nothing old hat about what we had been doing. You know, we didn't have any idea at all that we would record *One O'clock Jump* and that it would be our first big record. We had twenty-five or thirty tunes we could have played—tunes we felt better in. In fact, we didn't want to record *One O'clock Jump* at all. I remember in the recording studio when it was decided we record that one, we wanted to go back to Kansas City. People should have had the privilege of hearing those other twenty-five pieces we had. They were all head arrangements. I'm afraid they're lost, though, because they were never written down.

BUCK CLAYTON

I was with Basie from 1936 until I went into the army in 1943. It was different at the beginning. When we first started out, we didn't have good arrangers writing just for the band. We used heads we made up on the job for the first four years or so, and then we began to get arrangements, too.

We all had a lot to learn. When the Basie band first came to New York, we didn't even sound in tune all the time. We had to learn ensemble technique. We had to learn how to choose good instruments. Some of us had come in with patched-up horns, instruments tied together with rubber and such things. And we had to learn how to record properly.

JO JONES

The Basie band had the feel of a small band. The arrangements were almost all "heads," and no matter how many men we had at any one time, there was all the freedom and flexibility of a small unit. This was not true of the other large bands contemporary with Basie, as good as they were in many respects.

We'd come into the studio, decide what we wanted to play, look at the "head," and bang! One take, or at the most two or three, and the record was made. Some of the best sides, like the small band classics, *Dickie's Dream* and *Lester Leaps In*, weren't even planned. We were fooling around between takes and they decided to cut them.

COUNT BASIE

Some of you know that our band featured a "heavy" brass section. I guess the word "heavy" is okay in this instance, because our brass included four trumpets and three trombones. The saxes, four of them, were also phrasing the way I wanted them to phrase, and their intonation—which gave us a little trouble back in the days when the band was organized—apparently was up to the par we set. Of course, we were a little rough when we made a change as a result of Herschel Evans' death, but George (Buddy) Tate caught on in a hurry and fit right in.

I am sure that the rhythm section was right. It's the one section that gave us no trouble at any time. And when I speak of the rhythm, I mean, bass, drums, and guitar. You can count me out.

Years ago when I was using nine pieces in a little club called "the Reno" in Kansas City, we had worked together a long while. We got so we coordinated every move, every solo, perfectly. That was how Walter Bales, John Schilling, Don Davis, and a few other Kansas City cats found us playing; that's how we got to broadcast every night. It was nine pieces that saw Basie get his biggest break with Benny Goodman, John Hammond, and Willard Alexander, as a result of that radio wire and the raves of the men I just mentioned.

Now—and this is the point I want understood most, if you don't mind—I wanted my fifteen-piece band to work together just like those nine pieces did. I wanted fifteen men to think and play the same way. I wanted those four trumpets and three trombones to bite with real guts. BUT I wanted that bite to be just as tasty and subtle as if it were the three brass I used to use. In fact, the only reason I enlarged the brass was to get a richer harmonic structure. I said that the minute the brass got out of hand and blared and screeched instead of making every note *mean something,* there'd be some changes made.

I, of course, wanted to play real jazz. When we played pop tunes, and naturally we had to, I wanted those pops to kick! Not loud and fast, understand, but smoothly and with a definite punch. As for vocals, Jimmy Rushing and Helen Humes were handling them the way we felt they could best be handled. Earl Warren, who played lead alto, also sang occasionally. That's all the comment I have on our purposes, style, and our vocalists.

My piano? Well, I don't want to "run it in the ground," as they say. I love to play, but this idea of one man taking one chorus after another is not wise, in my opinion. Therefore, I fed dancers my own piano in short doses, and when I came in for a solo, I did it unexpectedly, using a strong rhythm background behind me. That way, we figured, the Count's piano wasn't going to become monotonous.

304

FREDDIE GREENE

. . . and Basie's piano certainly contributes to making the rhythm smooth. He contributes the missing things. I feel very comfortable working with him because he always seems to know the right thing to play for rhythm. Count is also just about the best piano player I know for pushing a band and for comping soloists. I mean the way he makes different preparations for each soloist and the way, at the end of one of *his* solos, he prepares an entrance for the next man. He leaves the way open.

COUNT BASIE

We got a lot of questions about personnel in that 1939 band. It included Earl Warren, alto; Lester Young, tenor; Jack Washington, alto and baritone; and George (Buddy) Tate, tenor; Ed Lewis, Wilbur (Buck) Clayton, Shad Collins, and Harry Edison, trumpets, in that order; Benny Morton, Dickie Wells, and Dan (Slamfoot) Minor, trombones, in that order; and Jo Jones, drums; Walter Page, bass; Freddie Greene, guitar; and Basie, piano. That was it. Of that number, Lewis, Clayton, Washington, Young, Jones, Page, Minor, and Jimmy Rushing all had been with me since the old Reno Club days in Kansas City. They are a great bunch, and any success we had is due entirely to the grand spirit among us.

I'd like it known that the band worked hard—rehearsals three hours long were held three times a week, on the average—and that we got our kicks from playing.

DON LAMOND

Jo Jones reminds me of the wind. He has more class than any drummer I've ever heard and has been an influence on me ever since I first heard him with Basie. Man, he could drive that band! With Jo there's none of that damn raucous tom-tom beating or riveting-machine stuff. Jo makes sense.

JO JONES

Did the Count Basie band rehearse? I personally don't know how to explain that—how to explain how those things happened. I never understood quite fully how those head arrangements came out. All I knew was that I was just there, and we started playing, and they weren't rehearsed. They just happened.

It's like my drumming—the way I use cymbals and the hand-drum solo I've been doing for twenty-three years. It all happened almost unconsciously, through the bare necessities I had to work with at the time I was learning drums—in carnivals.

When I was traveling with a carnival I didn't travel with much. I used to walk into a grocery store and get a wooden box and whittle it down until I had some sticks. I had a sock cymbal and a top cymbal and I used a coat hanger as a cymbal holder. I rarely had a snare drum. When we used to get into town I would ask some of the people in the carnival to scout around and find a bass drum for me. With this limited amount and kind of equipment I had to do something. So I'd run around stage during the course of the act—I'd had quite a lot of background in singing and dancing.

At that time, when musicians were advertised for they had to do more than just play. You might have to be a dancer or a straight man. Now the carnival I was with had a three-piano act—I was about eighteen or nineteen at the time—and when one of the pianists quit, I had to double in that act too.

Many jazzmen came up from or through the carnivals. There were good musicians too in the Ringling Brothers band. P. G. Lowery was the band leader and a lot of good musicians would join his band to make the season. In the carnivals you had some great drummers. There was Snag Jones, for example, out of Chicago. The carnival drummers were flashy but they also could play. Then a lot of men came up through the minstrel shows like the Riverboat Minstrels, and a lot also came up through traveling rodeo shows like The One-O-One Ranch.

Men who came up through a background like that were guys like Edgar Battle, a wonderful trumpet player, and R. C. Hicks, a trumpet player who later played with Basie for a spell.

GENE SEDRIC
I used to play shows on the Columbia burlesque wheel and other carnival shows. A lot of jazz guys used to do that. It was forty-two

weeks' steady work with a Pullman berth and all the trunks you could carry. In those days, that was big time and you did get a chance to play a few things.

LESTER YOUNG

My father, William H. Young, was a carnival musician. He could play all the instruments, although he liked the trumpet best. He taught voice, too, and kept up traveling with carnival minstrel shows and teaching music until he died, in the 'forties.

I was born in New Orleans, August 27th, 1909. My mother, Lizetta Grey, lives in Los Angeles now. I stayed in New Orleans until I was ten, when my sister Irma, brother Lee, and I went to live with my father. He took us to Minneapolis, where we went to school. During the carnival season, we all traveled with the minstrel show, through Kansas, Nebraska, South Dakota, all through there.

I played drums from the time I was ten to about thirteen. Quit them because I got tired of packing them up. I'd take a look at the girls after the show, and before I'd get the drums packed, they'd all be gone.

For a good five or six years after that I played the alto, and then the baritone when I joined Art Bronson's band.

Ran away from my father when I was about eighteen. We were in Salina, Kansas, and he had a string of dates down through Texas and the South. I told him how it would be down there, and that we could have some fine jobs back through Nebraska, Kansas, and Iowa, but he didn't have eyes for that. He was set to go.

That was when I joined Art Bronson and his Bostonians. Played with him two or three or four years. He lives in Denver now, and all the men in the band've got families, like to stay close to home— all except me. Anyway, I was playing the baritone and it was weighing me down.

I'm real lazy, you know. So when the tenor man left, I took over his instrument. But we stuck to Nebraska and North Dakota. Only time I went through the South was with Basie, and it was different then.

I worked at the Nest Club in Minneapolis when I first heard

Basie's band. Band at the Nest wasn't anyone's, really; they gave it to different people every week.

Used to hear the Basie band all the time on the radio and figured they needed a tenor player. They were at the Reno Club in Kansas City. It was crazy, the whole band was gone, but just this tenor player. I figured it was about time, so I sent Basie a telegram.

He had heard me before. We used to go back and forth between Minneapolis and Kansas City. When I joined the band he had three brass, three reeds, and three rhythm. I'd sit up all night and wait to go to work.

But Basie was like school. I used to fall asleep in school, because I had my lesson, and there was nothing else to do. The teacher would be teaching those who hadn't studied at home, but I had, so I'd go to sleep. Then the teacher would go home and tell my mother. So I put that down.

In Basie's band there always would be someone who didn't know his part. Seems to me that if a musician can't read, he should say so, and then you help him. Or you give him his part before. But Basie wouldn't. I used to talk to him about it, but he had no eyes for it. You had to sit there and play it over and over and over again. Just sit in that chair.

I joined Fletcher Henderson in Detroit in 1934. Basie was in Little Rock then, and Henderson offered me more money. Basie said I could go.

Was with Henderson only about six months. The band wasn't working very much. Was with Andy Kirk for six months about that time, too. Kirk was wonderful to work for. Then back to Basie until 1944 and the army.

JO JONES

I have known Lester Young about twenty-three years. He's been playing the same horn all along. He's been Lester and nothing else. He hasn't changed. What people don't realize is the environment he has to be around in order to play the kind of horn he's capable of. Sometimes when a good musician has inferior men with him it's like Stan Musial playing sand-lot baseball with a bunch of kids around Central Park.

MARY LOU WILLIAMS

I remember Lester Young from when he was blowing cool sounds at the Subway on Eighteenth Street back in Kansas City. This was a small place with only one entrance, really a firetrap, yet groovy. The first time I heard Lester I was astonished. It took him several choruses to get started—then, brother, what a horn. Then, too, there was Herschel Evans.

JO JONES

Herschel Evans was a natural. He had a sound on the tenor that perhaps you will never hear on a horn again. As for the so-called friction between him and Lester, there was no real friction. What there was was almost like an incident you would say could exist between two brothers. No matter what, there was always a mutual feeling there. Even in Lester's playing today, somewhere he'll always play two to four measures of Herschel because they were so close in what they felt about music. I was always a sort of go-between between them. I roomed with Herschel, and I had a liking for Pres and I was always trying to get them together in a cafe or in a restaurant booth. It was some childish thing that had started it—I never knew exactly what. It may have started in part that night Coleman Hawkins came to Kansas City with Fletcher Henderson and Herschel, Lester, and Ben Webster played for him.

That night, Herschel played all over the horn—played it the way it was supposed to be played because Hawk was his idol. You couldn't say anything bad about Hawkins to Herschel. Some of that friction between Herschel and Pres may have had something to do with that night and with Hawkins. Lester, you know, has always been an unlimited soloist, and he was still playing at the session when everybody else was finished.

And then, too, there was something about tone. Hawkins had a full tone and Herschel's was full, too. But Lester's tone was different. It was lighter. Some people would tell Lester that he didn't have a good tone, that he should change his tone. And that would cause friction. These people never think in terms of the physical features of an individual and how each one has different physical characteristics and that these make him play the way he does play.

BILLIE HOLIDAY

I was with Basie's band for a time, and Lester used to live at home with my mother and me. I named him the "President," and he named me "Lady" and my mother "Duchess." We were the Royal Family of Harlem.

Pres and Herschel Evans were forever thinking up ways of cutting the other one. You'd find them in the band room hacking away at reeds, trying out all kinds of new ones, anything to get ahead of the other one. Once Herschel asked Lester, "Why don't you play alto, man? You got an alto *tone*." Lester tapped his head, "There's things going on up there, man," he told Herschel. "Some of you guys are all belly."

Normally, I don't go in for those saxophone battles, but those cats really hated each other, and it kept them both blowing all the time. Of course, Herschel had the big beautiful tone; Lester had less tone, but a whole lot of ideas.

Yes, he was President and I was Vice-President. I used to be crazy about his tenor playing, wouldn't make a record unless he was on it. He played music I like, didn't try to drown the singer. Teddy Wilson was the same, and trumpet player Buck Clayton.

LESTER YOUNG

The trouble with most musicians today is that they are copycats. Of course you have to start out playing like someone else. You have a model, or a teacher, and you learn all that he can show you. But then you start playing for yourself. Show them that you're an individual. And I can count those who are doing that today on the fingers of one hand.

LEE KONITZ

Then there was the sound of Lester on the old Basie records—real beautiful tenor saxophone sound, pure sound. That's it. For alto too. Pure sound. How many people he's influenced, how many lives! Because he is definitely the basis of everything that's happened. And his rhythmic approach—complex in its simplicity. How can you analyze it? Shall we tag some words on it? Call it "polyrhythmic"?

JO JONES

There are too many musicians out of New Orleans still hanging on Louis Armstrong's coattails—musicians who can't play. But in Kansas City all those guys, even the ones who were playing twenty years ago, were, and still are, individualists.

In Kansas City, in that time, some of the younger kids would gather across the street from the clubs where jazz was being played in order to listen. They were individualists too, and they were kids who were eager to learn—Gene Ramey, Charlie Parker, and other guys. A lot of the kids, for example, that played and were to play with Jay McShann's band. In fact, some of those kids had a little band of their own then in Kansas City, a little Basie band and they intended to take over and make something new.

MARY LOU WILLIAMS

Two other pianists I met in Kaycee during the mid-thirties were Tadd Dameron and Thelonius Monk. I was to get to know both of them well in New York in later years.

Tadd, who came from Cleveland, was just starting out playing and writing for a band from Kansas. Though very young, he had ideas even then that were 'way ahead of his time.

Thelonius, still in his 'teens, came into town with either an evangelist or a medicine show—I forget which. While Monk was in Kaycee, he jammed every night, really used to blow on piano, employing a lot more technique than he does today. Monk plays the way he does now because he got fed up. I *know* how Monk can play.

He felt that musicians should play something new and started doing it. Most of us admire him for this. He was one of the original modernists, all right, playing pretty much the same harmonies then that he's playing now. Only in those days we called it "zombie music," and reserved it mostly for musicians after hours.

Why "zombie music"? Because the screwy chords reminded us of music from FRANKENSTEIN or any horror film. I was one of the first with these frozen sounds, and after a night's jamming, would sit and play weird harmonies (just chord progressions) with Dick Wilson, a very advanced tenor player.

JO JONES

The men from Kansas City, as things began to kind of peter out and Andy Kirk and Dick Wilson and Count Basie left, began to migrate to Chicago and to California, and they carried that Kansas City feeling with them.

What I mean is that I was in New Orleans and I was in Chicago but I never heard music that had the kind of feeling in jazz I most admire until I went into Kansas City in November, 1933. Some musicians retain that feeling for a short period of time and some, like the ones from Kansas City, still retain it. Men like Ben Webster and Lester still have it and Count Basie does. It's hard to describe it exactly. For example, I don't know why the feeling at jam sessions is different in New York from the way it was in Kansas City. But it is. Now, New York is the greatest city on earth. It affords everything contained in Kansas City, Chicago, Cleveland, Detroit, or anywhere, but we had in Kansas City an unselfishness you don't find here. We didn't have time for selfishness. We were more concerned with our fellow man and with music.

DON LAMOND

You know, it's a funny thing, but of all the places the Woody Herman band went, Kansas City was the best so far as kicks and finding musicians to join with were concerned. And remember I'm talking about a time as late as 1947 and '48. That town just has a different atmosphere.

18

*The Swing Era—big bands, big money, jitterbugs,
one-night stands, commercialism, and the breakdown
of some racial barriers.*

BENNY GOODMAN

When the band started, we didn't have any special ambition or goal, and we didn't know what it was exactly that made the band sound the way it did. But it was work, and detail—and arrangements. Why, do you know, when a new arrangement would come in, it would be an occasion. We couldn't wait to get started on it, and we'd work for three or four hours on it right away. And *know* if it wasn't ready. We'd play it for a few nights before letting it go over the air, for instance. When a new arrangement by "Smack" or Jimmy Mundy would come in, we'd work on it, and if we liked it, you'd be sure to hear some of the guys say, "C'mon, let's play it again."

When we started the band, the only purpose we had was to play music, and Gene Krupa, Teddy, Hampton, Jess, Hymie, and the rest, they had a purpose. It was their life, it was important to them.

A lot of guys today, they don't know what they want, do they? Maybe I don't either. But something happens when you find out that what you're doing is no longer music—that it's become entertainment. It's a subtle thing and affects what you're playing. Your whole attitude changes.

As far as I'm concerned, the most important or the most exciting thing that ever happened with the band was when we opened at the Palomar in Los Angeles. (When was it—1935?) We had just laid a big egg in Denver and were pretty low. And we figured that the further West we went, the worse it would get. Before we hit L.A. we played a few one-nighters, one in San Francisco that wasn't too bad. When we opened at the Palomar we had a "what've we got to lose" attitude and decided to let loose and shoot the works with our best things like *Sugar Foot Stomp*, *Sometimes I'm Happy*, and the others. Actually though, we were almost scared to play.

From the moment I kicked them off, the boys dug in with some of the best playing I'd heard since we left New York. I don't know what it was, but the crowd went wild, and then—boom!

That was the real beginning.

DICK CLARK

We were all sort of scared and worried until that night at the Palomar, and never really got going until that night. Then it happened, and it's great to feel that I was there and had a part in it. Though now I'm glad to be settled down, in radio and recording work, I can thank Benny for that too.

GENE KRUPA

Had Benny thrown in the towel before his first great triumphs at the Palomar in Los Angeles and the Congress in Chicago, there's little doubt but what many of us who have enjoyed success, prominence, and considerable financial reward since the late 1930's would have ever attained these heights.

Benny built himself a band playing musicians' music, but didn't shoot over the heads of the public. It took the people time, but once they grasped the Goodman musical sermon, they easily understood, accepted, and followed. Being a part of this band was the fulfillment of a dream for any young musician. It allowed us to play the way we honestly wanted to play, with good pay and before huge, appreciative audiences. In the days before the Goodman era, we played that way, too, but in smaller bands with no similar success, or in sessions held in empty halls with no one to appreciate our efforts but the fellows playing the other instruments.

For all that Benny did for music, for jazz, for musicians, and for me, I, for one, doff my cap in a salute of sincere appreciation.

BENNY GOODMAN

By the time we finished our job in THE BIG BROADCAST OF 1937, which was made in the summer of *1936*, we had a pretty good idea that the public for real jazz was a big one, and growing all the time. Even when we opened at the Pennsylvania, some of the people around the hotel were skeptical, saying the band was too loud. After the band was set in the room and the crowds started to come and keep on coming, we didn't hear much more comment on the band being loud. But I don't think that any of us realized how strong a hold it had on the youngsters until a certain day early in March, 1937.

We had undertaken to double at the Paramount Theater in New York in addition to playing our job at the Pennsylvania, with no expectation that we would do more than fair business. After all, our only previous theater bookings had been something less than sensational. So when we arrived at the theater for an early morning rehearsal before the first show and found a couple of hundred kids lined up in front of the box office at about seven A.M., we couldn't help feeling that every one of our most loyal supporters in the five boroughs was already on hand.

However, this wasn't a patch on what happened even before we got on stage. All through the showing of the picture, the folks backstage said there were noises and whistling coming through from the house as Claudette Colbert did her stuff in MAID OF SALEM. The theater was completely full an hour before we were supposed to go on, and when we finally came up on the rising platform, the noise sounded like Times Square on New Year's Eve. That reception topped anything we had known up to that time, and because we felt it was spontaneous and genuine, we got a tremendous kick out of it.

However, we didn't know half the story until we got off the stage and were back in our dressing rooms. It seems that my manager, Willard Alexander, was sitting in the mezzanine with Bob Weitman, the manager of the Paramount. They got the same thrill out of this enthusiasm that we did, up to the point where a couple of youngsters got up and started to shag in the aisles. Then a few more started to climb over the rail towards the orchestra, and Bob jumped up and rushed out, yelling, "Somebody's going to get hurt there any minute. There'll be a panic."

He ran down the steps to the back of the orchestra, and as soon as the ushers saw him, they snapped to attention and started saluting.

"The hell with that," he shouted. "Get down there and stop those kids from killing themselves!"

As he went from aisle to aisle to get the ushers organized, he had to go through this same routine of being saluted by each one before he could get things under control.

By three o'clock in the afternoon, eleven thousand, five hundred people had paid their way into the theater, and the total for the first day's attendance was twenty-one thousand. Another thing about that first day which caused talk around the theater was this: The total for the day's sale at the candy counter was nine hundred dollars—which is some kind of a record, too.

It was during this engagement that we found out what this particular sort of success means. We played five shows a day at the Paramount, beginning around ten thirty in the morning, and in between the two evening shows, we did our usual stint at the Pennsylvania, going back there after the last show (about ten thirty) to finish up the dance session, until two A.M. Then, of course, there was the radio commercial once a week, with the special rehearsals that go with it. There was also the problem of moving the stuff up to the studio, which in our case was the CBS Radio Theatre at Broadway and Fifty-third Street. Just how we managed to stand up under that grind, I don't know—except that once you get into that groove, you just keep on going.

Right after this we got the first taste of what comes with being a really successful band. I didn't have any more love for one-nighters than I had before, but that summer we filled a schedule of bookings that lasted almost two months, and we never played the same town twice. As a matter of fact, we finished up with a string of thirty consecutive dates on as many nights, in the middle of a broiling Midwest July.

Traveling with a band on tour is the next thing I can think of to moving a circus. There's the music to be taken care of, the instruments to be checked, the trunks and other baggage to keep in line, all of which was in the care of a general handyman, porter, and looker-outer. In our organization he was an efficient fellow by the name of Peewee Monte, who had made a career out of nursing bands. Later it was Popsie Randolph.

But there also had to be someone on hand to manage the actual work of making hotel arrangements for the men, taking care of the transportation, ironing out the difficulties that come with the promoters in the various halls and pavilions that we played, acting as contact man for the press, and generally doing all the things that I couldn't possibly do myself.

On a typical one-nighter around the New York territory, we traveled in a Greyhound bus that stayed with us throughout the entire tour. Generally it rolled up to the place late in the afternoon, and if we hadn't been there before, we had to find out about the P.A. (the public address system) and hook up the one we carried along, if the permanent installation wasn't any good. Then the stands had to be set up and the music laid out—and in most places, some kind of a rope or a guard rail put around the stand so that we could work without stepping on the fingers of the kids that hung around the band.

By this time, Hymie Schertzer's nose for corn-beef had led him, without fail, to the best place in town for his favorite food, and a few of the boys went along with him. The rest of us picked out some likely looking place for the kind of food we wanted, and got through with the meal just in time to change our clothes and get on the bandstand. The crowd started coming in, the requests started piling up, and another job was under way.

We played right through until about one o'clock, with the trio and quartet coming out for a session around midnight. What happened after that depended on the distance to the next booking. If the jump was a fairly short one, say two hundred miles or so, we spent the night at a hotel in the same town, and made the trip the following day. If it was closer to three hundred or anything up to four hundred, we piled into the bus when the job was finished, and made the jump at night, when we could make better time, and allow for any incidents that might come up on the trip. That brought us into the next town around nine or ten o'clock in the morning—and after eight hours bumping around in a bus, trying to catch a few winks of sleep, the only thing you wanted to do was crawl into bed at the hotel, and get some sleep before it was time to go to work again. There are more towns in America that I have only seen after dark than I would care to think about.

It was while we were out on the Coast that we engaged Martha Tilton. After Helen Ward left us, we had been trying out various girl singers, some of them well-known, others that weren't. But none of them could sing with the band like Helen did, and it wasn't until we heard Martha that we found what we were looking for. Martha was a hard worker and improved consistently when she was with us, and really had a personality that everybody liked.

Of course, when Teddy Wilson joined us and later, Lionel Hampton, there was talk about the problems of presenting a band with a mixed group like the trio and the quartet. However, I found few places where the crowds were not wonderfully responsive to Lionel and Teddy. Most of the people who listened to us appreciated what swell musicians these boys are, and recognized that what they did was something that was just unique, that nobody played piano or vibes just the way they did.

About the only unpleasantness that we ever had in this connection happened in this same summer of 1937. It was after we finished HOLLYWOOD HOTEL and were working our way back East by way of the Southern route, stopping off for a couple of weeks to play a big fair in the Southwest. We opened to a fine crowd, and through the first day or two everything was swell.

But we noticed about the second day, that a couple of city police on duty around the place didn't like the attention that Lionel and Teddy were getting. They didn't say anything, but every time one of the kids came up and asked either of them for an autograph (naturally calling them "Mr. Hampton" or "Mr. Wilson") they'd act nasty, because it seems that isn't done in their circles.

On the third night, after we had finished a session with the quartet, one of the guests thought he'd express his appreciation by sending some champagne back to Lionel. As he got to the stage door, one of these officers stopped him and said, "Where you goin' with that?"

The waiter answered, "It's for Mr. Hampton."

"The hell with that stuff," this guy yelled, and flung out his arm, knocking the tray, glasses, ice, and champagne out of the waiter's hand.

Well, we were up against it. We didn't want to complain because the fellow might have gotten some of his boy friends together and really made trouble for us—and at the same time, we couldn't stand for any jive like this.

Luckily, one of the boys was friendly with a local police official (who happened to be a jazz fan) and he went to him confidentially that night and told him what was happening. He came right back with Leonard, walked up to this officer (who knew well enough who he was, because he had made a name for himself all over the Southwest by capturing Bonny Parker and Pretty-boy Floyd), grabbed him by the shoulder, and said, "Get the hell off these grounds and stay off. And if any of your pals have an idea to start trouble here, I'll see to it that you're kicked off the force."

Jumping around the way we did, playing for every kind of audience in the most varied places, we got a reaction that represented a pretty good cross-section of opinion. I know that for a lot of people that came to hear us, the quartet was a special kick—and when we played, nobody cared much what colors or races were represented just so long as we played good music. That's the way it should be.

I know, for example, that our 1938 concert in Carnegie Hall would have lost a lot if we didn't have the cooperation of fellows like Johnny Hodges, who is by far the greatest man on alto sax that I ever heard, or Harry Carney, who is just about the same on baritone, or Cootie Williams, whose trumpet playing is like nobody else's. Then in the jam session, we had such other great colored players as Lester Young, who is one of my favorite musicians, that swell guitar player, Freddie Greene, Count Basie on piano, and Buck Clayton to play his own particular kind of trumpet, with Walter Page doing wonderful things on bass.

Actually that jam session was a real thrill—not the way it worked out in the concert, unfortunately, because it is always a difficult thing to know how such a setup will turn out on any particular occasion—but when the boys first came together, just to try things out, a few days before. There was Count, with his hat on the back of his head, picking notes at the piano; Johnny Hodges (in a sweater, I think); bashful Harry Carney, hiding behind his baritone; and all the rest, sitting down with Gene, Harry James, and Vernon Brown (who plays fine hot trombone) from my band. I went down in the Hall to get an idea of how it sounded, but before they had done more than five or six choruses on *Honeysuckle Rose*, the thing was jumping so much that I had to rush up and get in on it. We probably would have kept on playing all night if there hadn't been jobs waiting for us.

That night at Carnegie was a great experience, because it represented something—a group of musicians going on that stage and playing tunes by Gershwin and Berlin and Kern in arrangements by Fletcher and Edgar Sampson, getting up and playing the choruses the way they wanted to, each of them just being himself—and holding the attention of all those people for two hours and a half.

One thing I found out is that there wasn't much difference in the people you played for, East or West. They wanted to hear the same tunes when they were new, or the same standbys they'd heard on the air, or the things we'd made records of. *Sing Sing Sing* (which we started doing back at the Palomar on our second trip there in 1936) was still a big thing, and no one-nighter was complete without it . . . they wanted *Big John Special, One O'clock Jump, King Porter, Blue Skies*, or the quartet doing *I Got Rhythm*, and, of course, *Don't Be That Way*.

Pretty soon, people and places became pretty much a blur.

You start thinking (if you ever get a chance to)—was it in Cincinnati that Bud Freeman played those three terrific choruses on the *Yam*, each one better than the last? Was it in Scranton that Lionel sat in on *Sing Sing Sing* and gave that tough old setup the work-out of its life, or was it in Buffalo? Was it in Detroit that we first started doing these descending trumpet runs in the last chorus of *One O'clock Jump* (so that everybody started referring to it as *Two O'clock Jump*) or was it in Philadelphia?

JOHNNY GUARNIERI
I'm probably the best guy to tell about those swing days because I'm probably the only one who was ever sober. When I joined Benny Goodman, it was like a fulfillment of a beautiful dream for me. It was what I had lived and worked for, and, because I was a sober individual and wasn't involved in rivalries, drinking, narcotics, money problems, and such, like some of the other musicians, I enjoyed every minute of it. It was all very vital and absorbing, including the traveling. In fact, I can say that I've had more fun than anybody in this business.

When I first joined Benny, he called me "Fletcher" for three months before he could remember my name. And then he told me I was the worst piano player he'd had since Frankie Froeba. He didn't like my so-called "imitating" other pianists. I'll tell you, though, both Lionel Hampton and Charlie Christian would tell me, "Don't let Benny scare you, you're a *piano player*, Johnny—and you *swing*." As a matter of fact, Lionel and Charlie were the only two guys in the band who would talk to me when I joined. All the other guys were "big shots" and I wasn't.

BENNY GOODMAN
I suppose I do have a hard time remembering names. There wasn't much of that trouble with the first bands I had though—all *those* guys were characters, weren't they? Bunny Berigan, Harry James, Jess Stacy, Harry Goodman, and the rest. But, later on, I suppose it might take me two months to learn a new man's name. You might say that a guy had to prove himself—or *make* a name for himself before I'd know who he was.

POPSIE RANDOLPH

Benny wanted what he wanted, that's all. If a guy worked for him, he had to do the job right. Sure, he was changeable all right, like the weather—a little fickle you might say. But man, he was a perfectionist. A guy would come into the band one day and two days later Benny'd say he was no good—and out he'd go.

But he was real good to the boys, and me, too. I was his band-boy from 1941 to 1947, only in 1945 he made me road manager when he re-formed the last band.

When a guy got in trouble or something, Benny'd take an interest and help out with emergency money. He'd always lend the guys money and things like that. Sure, some of the guys didn't appreciate it—said he was buttin' in, but I don't know of another leader in the business who took as much interest in the men as Benny—except Woody, maybe.

I remember once he sent me over to Mark Cross to buy the guys wallets for Christmas, and he put a fifty-dollar bill in each. And on Christmas day, I was feelin' kinda low 'cause I didn't get one. Benny and I were in Philly and we were ridin' back to the hotel on the trolley car when he says to me, "You got my wallet, Pops?" I had a couple of blank checks with me and he wrote me a check for five hundred dollars. He told me, "Now, that's better'n a wallet, isn't it?"

One thing he didn't tolerate and that was drinking—or for that matter, any of the vices. Benny didn't go for that playboy style.

The guys that Benny liked a lot and talked about were Jess Stacy, Mel Powell, Teddy Wilson, Harry James, Ziggy Elman, Manny Klein, Vernon Brown, in fact, all the guys from his early bands. They're his idols for playin'. He also respected people like Basie, Teagarden, Artie Shaw, Tommy Dorsey, for their playin' too.

He thought a lot of Gene Krupa too. I wasn't with Benny when Gene was with him originally, but right after he got out of jail for that dope thing, he came up to the Paramount where we were playin' and was in the dressing room wearing dark glasses. Benny says to me, "Popsie, we're gonna have Gene in the band." We went on a tour of army camps after that. In the band were Teddy Wilson and Red Norvo. There were lots of kicks.

JOHNNY GUARNIERI

I guess I could have been a big name with Benny if I played up to him, but after a while I left him to join Artie Shaw, went back to Benny and then back to Shaw again. It was with Artie Shaw that I played harpischord on those Gramercy Five records. All Artie ever wanted was for you to tell him how good he was, or more, how much better he was then Benny. He lived to cut Benny and Benny lived to cut him. But they were both great musicians. Each was great in his own style.

ARTIE SHAW

By the time we got to New York and the Lincoln Hotel, our opening night there was like a madhouse. From then on I couldn't think straight. My life wasn't my own. *Life* magazine, autograph hunters, everything all at once, plus all kinds of disagreeable pressures being put on me.

The bigger our success, the more dissatisfaction there seemed to be in the band. Billie Holiday, who had gotten along fine with Helen Forrest, began to resent her. Georgie Auld came in for a hundred and twenty-five dollars while the rest of the band, getting scale, objected. Buddy Rich joined us and the older guys didn't like it when he got so much applause. Instead of a bunch of guys that were happy to be struggling toward a common objective, we became a bunch of cliques, and I became gradually estranged from the men.

When we went into the Strand Theatre, it was even worse. People jumping up on the stage, cops, riots—things that were almost impossible to live through. I was making more money than I had ever thought existed, and I guess I got carried away by it.

BUD FREEMAN

The big bands *needed* individualists—they *needed* stars. Certainly, leaders might have had trouble with some of us, but we believed what we were doing, we grew up with jazz, felt strongly about

323

our music and each of us developed in his own way, becoming both distinct individuals and *soloists*. We weren't just another sideman!

Back in the 'twenties, it was almost unheard of for a musician to sit in, let alone work with just any band. We had to like the music the band was playing. Nowadays, in order to make a living, a musician may have to do anything to keep working.

Take Benny Goodman. He needed stars, didn't he? After all, although he's a great performer, he isn't creative and I don't think he would have been as important without all of those wonderful individual musicians.

Of all the big bands I played with, I suppose I enjoyed being with Tommy Dorsey most. Tommy allowed me more freedom, more opportunity to play. And the same went for Dave Tough. I think he was happier with Dorsey than anywhere else too.

As for Bunny Berigan, who was also with Tommy in those days, well, Bunny was a true musician, but he just hated the music business. Bunny loved music, he loved people, but you have to be tough to get along in the band business. When he had his own band, he didn't want to do what he had to do.

RAY CONNIFF

Yeah, it was quite an experience working with the Berigan band. It was a tight little band, just like a family of bad little boys, with Bunny the worst of all. We were all friends. In fact, Bunny wouldn't hire anybody he didn't like. And all of us would take turns rooming with him. Oh, it was a mad ball. You should've seen those hotel rooms! Ribs, booze, and women all over the place.

Bunny didn't take much interest in arrangements and business and things like that. In fact, he wasn't much of a leader type. But as a musician, we all idolized him. Even when he was drunk, he'd blow good. And when he was sober—man! Whenever we'd play the Savoy up in Harlem, if we'd walk along the streets or go into a rib joint they would say, "Hey Pops, them's Bunny's boys." They loved him up there. He had that beat.

324

FERDINAND ARBELO

When you talk about bands that could swing, don't forget the Lunceford band! I was with them for three or four years, and I'm telling you that that was one swinging band! There were times when we played in some places and even the walls would shake.

Willie Smith was playin' on alto; Trummy Young, lead trombone; Sy Oliver as trumpet (and arrangin'); and Jimmy Crawford on drums. As for Jimmie Lunceford, he was out of Memphis and a wonderful musician who knew every corner of music. He knew what the people liked.

GENE SEDRIC

One-nighters were very rough. Many times there were halls with no windows and inside there were thousands of people shouting and fighting. And it was very rough when you had to go over mountains to make another town and you'd skid on ice. Man, there were some long hauls between states.

Many times we'd get into town, check into a hotel, and we'd actually hear them planning how they were going to start the fights and shootings where we were going to play that night.

There were some of those towns that had special prices just for the bands that came through, that were touring. When they knew we were coming, the prices would be higher by twice as much. Many times we'd get in earlier though, before they had a chance to change the signs.

EDMOND HALL

This incident will give you some idea of how terrible things were touring in the South. . . . This happened in 1934 or 1935 in Little Rock, Arkansas. I was in the Claude Hopkins band. We had been touring the country for about four months. On this Saturday night we were supposed to have the night off, but the booking agent had put us in a place ten miles out of town. The next night we were supposed to play a dance in Little Rock itself and we played on this Saturday night until about twelve fifteen.

We stopped because of the "blue law." But the man who ran the place said, "We don't close until three," and pulled out a gun and made us play until three. Some of the guys had gotten away, so not all of us were stuck there. The way some of us had gotten away was that the Casa Loma band had taken our place at Roseland and also had our radio wire and the guys who didn't have to take time to pack up their instruments had gone out to the cars to hear how the Casa Loma band was making out. Well, the ones that escaped called our road manager and told him what was happening. He called the sheriff and the sheriff said, "The best way is the easiest way. Tell them to keep on playing."

The furthest South we played with Claude Hopkins was Birmingham, Alabama. When we played there they had a rope right down the middle of the floor. There was white on one side and colored on the other.

That Claude Hopkins band had a big drawing power. It drew as well as any band on the road at that time. There were crowds wherever we used to go. One of the big factors in its success was Orlando Robeson. He was a romantic ballad singer. He sang *Trees* and songs like that.

MILT HINTON

The one-night scene in the South was just simply terrible. I had a better deal with Cab Calloway because we always traveled first class. Cab would always retain a Pullman. We'd pull into one of those Southern towns and we slept in. But we had meals in holes and things. Cab had it easier because of his great popularity, so when you traveled with his band you were as comfortable as a member of a Negro band could be in the South. But it was still pretty bad. At dance halls people would insult us.

I remember Longview, Texas. They had recently struck oil there. Before that they were all poor people, accustomed to nothing. Drought, strikes, and all and the oil had been seeping through the land, and they had been selling the land cheap because the oil had been making the cattle sick. But when they found out it was oil many of them became rich overnight. They had no education so they went berserk with the money. They had big riotous parties and hired large bands. At those dances the prejudice was terrible. Some of them would say, "I'd pay a three hundred dollar fine just to hit one of those boys." Invariably they would begin to fight. The promoter would say, "Come on downstairs," and he'd put us in a room to keep the people from getting at us. The dance would always end up in a fight. When they didn't see us they'd fight amongst themselves. I can tell you I was scared. Like when we were at a roadhouse. There was no way for us to get out. Cab eventually stopped going through the South because he had enough work without it.

I remember the dances at Fort Lauderdale, Florida. There were some Northern people there on vacation and some Northern musicians whom we used to know when we played at the Cotton Club. Both the people who used to know us from the Cotton Club where we were famous and those Northern white musicians would talk to us between sets. But the Southern people would resent it. Sometimes it would be so bad at intermission we couldn't get off the stand for a drink of water unless we had a police escort. I remember it. There were two police in front and two behind, and we had to walk through the dance hall that way just to get a drink of water. And you know they would poke at us through the police! So you can see we didn't feel like playing much. And Cab was less likely to knock himself out entertaining people like that. After intermission we always had a tough time because the drinking had started and the insults got worse.

Then there was Greenfield, Mississippi. One of the valets in the band was a young kid who had just gotten back from overseas where he'd been decorated. This was the late 'forties. And among the other things he would do was to sell programs at intermission. There was a police officer who asked him a question, and Paul answered "Yes" without putting "Sir" on it. This was a real musclebound cop. He swung at Paul but Paul with all his military training and G.I. know-how just kept ducking away from him. So this cop couldn't hit him. The cop pulled his gun on Paul and dared him to duck. The crowd was screaming. The dance hall parted, and just Paul and the cop were standing and everybody fell to the floor. This officer became ashamed of himself. The band had stopped playing; the girl singer, Mary Louise Jones, screamed; and that's what alerted the audience to fall to the floor so the cop became aware of everybody looking on and became ashamed of himself and said, "Go on with the dance." Our road manager then was Hugh Wright. He had formerly been a lieutenant colonel in the Army. He was about fifty-five or sixty, straight military bearing, pretty manly. He went over to the officer to try to straighten it out. The guy said to keep out of it and get out of town.

Eventually, Cab had to go back down South again when the band business was real bad. The guys in the other bands who had to go through the South had the same and similar experiences. We discussed them amongst each other sometimes. The same towns, the same officers. I'm telling you, some of those people came and paid their money just to heckle the Negro bands, like some people like to tease an animal, and we had no recourse. Did you know that in Miami, Florida, where we used to play after nine o'clock at night, Negroes had to be off the streets unless they had a note saying something like: "This boy works for me"? There were white musicians we knew from New York playing there. They had come to the dance and said, "Let's have a session afterwards." We could have gone to the Negro section for a session, but elsewhere it would be impossible because if the police saw them they would be in trouble too.

'We never had trouble with Southern musicians—they didn't fraternize with us much but they would come to listen and to learn. They enjoyed talking music with us and they weren't insulting. Most of them, however, didn't choose our company after the dances, but a few did. Of course, the white Northern guys were there just for the session, and they were the same guys we used to hang out with on Fifty-second Street.

ROY ELDRIDGE

One thing you can be sure of, as long as I'm in America, I'll never in my life work with a white band again! It goes all the way back to when I joined Gene Krupa's band. Until that time no colored musician had worked with a white band except as a separate attraction, like Teddy and Lionel with Benny Goodman.

That was how I worked with Gene at first; I wasn't treated as a full member of the band. But very soon I started sharing Shorty Sherock's book, and when he left the band, I took over. It killed me to be accepted as a regular member of the band. But I knew I'd have to be awful cool; I knew all eyes were on me to see if I'd make time or do anything wrong.

All the guys in the band were nice, and Gene was especially wonderful. That was at the Pennsylvania Hotel. Then we headed West for some one-nighters, winding up in California. That was when the trouble began.

We arrived in one town and the rest of the band checks in. I can't get into their hotel, so I keep my bags and start riding around looking for another place, where someone's supposed to have made a reservation for me. I get there and move all my bags in. Naturally, since we're going to be out on the Coast several months, I have a heavy load, at least a dozen pieces of baggage.

Then the clerk, when he sees that I'm the Mr. Eldridge the reservation was made for, suddenly discovers that one of their regular tenants just arrived and took the last available room. I lug that baggage back into the street and start looking around again.

By the time that kind of thing has happened night after night, it begins to work on my mind; I can't think right, can't play right. When we finally got to the Palladium in Hollywood, I had to watch who I could sit at the tables with. If they were movie stars who wanted me to come over, that was all right; if they were just the jitterbugs, no dice. And all the time the bouncer with his eye on me, just watching for a chance.

On top of that, I had to live way out in Los Angeles, while the rest of the guys stayed in Hollywood. It was a lonely life; I'd never been that far away from home before, and I didn't know anybody. I got to brooding.

Then it happened. One night the tension got so bad I flipped. I could feel it right up to my neck while I was playing *Rockin' Chair;* I started trembling, ran off the stand, and threw up. They carried me to the doctor's. I had a hundred-and-five fever; my nerves were shot.

When I went back a few nights later I heard that people were asking for their money back because they couldn't hear *Let Me Off Uptown*. This time they let me sit at the bar.

Later on, when I was with Artie Shaw, I went to a place where we were supposed to play a dance and they wouldn't even let me in the place. "This is a white dance," they said, and there was my name right outside, Roy "Little Jazz" Eldridge, and I told them who I was.

When I finally did get in, I played that first set, trying to keep from crying. By the time I got through the set, the tears were rolling down my cheeks. I don't know how I made it. I went up to a dressing room and stood in a corner crying and saying to myself why the hell did I come out here again when I knew what would happen. Artie came in and he was real great. He made the guy apologize that wouldn't let me in, and got him fired.

Man, when you're on the stage, you're great, but as soon as you come off, you're nothing. It's not worth the glory, not worth the money, not worth anything. Never again!

LENA HORNE

The statement by Roy Eldridge that he will never again work with a white band made me very unhappy. I love Roy. He is a great musician and one of my best friends. I don't want him, or anyone else, to feel as bitter as he evidently did when he made that statement.

I hope others will not be influenced by his decision, if he really meant what he said, because we can't lick a problem by running away from it.

We've all had to face very difficult situations. Many times when I was singing with Charlie Barnet I wanted to quit for the same reasons Roy mentions. I might have, too, had it not been for the wonderful support I always got in every way from Charlie and the boys in the band. And I'll never forget that it was Charlie who took a chance to give me my first real break.

Thanks to pioneers like Charlie, Benny Goodman, Gene Krupa,

Tommy Dorsey, Red Norvo, and others not so well known, all of whom knew they were letting themselves in for some real headaches, too, the greatest strides have been made in breaking down age-old prejudices.

If we all took Roy's attitude, we would be letting those fellows down. I'm sure Roy will snap out of it when he thinks this over.

JO JONES

Twenty and twenty-five years ago conditions were involved with far more ignorant attitudes, social conditions that is. You can just imagine how many fine musicians the world lost because of these ignorant attitudes and prejudices. In 1940, I remember when I played a date at Harvard telling the guys there that things were changing and were going to change in the South, and they didn't believe it. But then in 1948 I played in Florida with Lena Horne and I remember after the set another guy in the band and I stopped at the bar to have a drink and the guy, while we were being served our drink at the bar, said to me: "This is Florida?" And yet I remember when I couldn't cross the tracks in Florida.

I remember, years ago, a little white boy sitting in in a colored club, and the police caught him and whipped him. But things change.

BUSTER BAILEY

One thing I'm happy to see is the integration that's been happening among musicians. And I've been watching music a long time. I've been playing since I was eleven. Years ago, if it had been like this when I came up I would be able to play with some symphony orchestra. I would have had more of an incentive to study because there would have been more of a prospect of my making a living the way I wanted to. Sure, we played concerts and overtures and numbers like that in the theaters, but when I started you couldn't even think, if you were a Negro, of making symphony orchestras. So the highest I got was theaters. In later years, I would get a chance to do a few things, like I made some records for Victor with the New Friends of Music—a string

331

group. And they were good records. But as for making a career out of classical music, it was too late then. I have played with NBC and CBS symphony orchestras, and I could have made a career in symphony music like I said. We did have a mixed group going a few years ago, with Everett Lee conducting. It was called the Cosmopolitan Symphony, and we gave quite a few concerts at Town Hall. I guess you could say the only regret I have is that I didn't have a chance to make it in symphony music.

When I was starting up, they used to say the two races couldn't get along playing. They used to say stuff like they were afraid we'd go after their women. All that's been proved false, and everything else on that prejudice kick has been proved false.

PART IV

"*Undecided*"

19

*The experimenters—Thelonius Monk, Dizzy Gil-
lespie, Charlie Parker, Kenny Clarke, Mary Lou Williams, Charlie Christian—made their headquarters uptown, at a place called Minton's.*

CARMEN McRAE

Minton's was just a place for cats to jam. People didn't pay too much attention to what was going on, I mean those people there that weren't musicians. So when you went in you'd see cats half-stewed who weren't paying much mind to what was happening on stage. But the musicians were.

But then, there were always places in Harlem for sessions. Before Minton's became *the* place there used to be an after-hours spot right off St. Nicholas Avenue. Some of the greatest musicians of that time used to jam there—Lester Young, all the guys from Basie's band, Goodman, Shaw, and Art Tatum, who was a lover of after-hours spots. There used to be fabulous jam sessions there. It is true that Art, for one, definitely plays better after hours. I don't know exactly why. Maybe it's because of the atmosphere. A lot of people play and sing differently in different atmospheres. Certain people and certain clubs make you want to do things you couldn't do ordinarily. But as for Tatum he's so fabulous it's hard to tell what times he plays better than at other times.

MILT HINTON

On Sunday afternoons, in the early 'forties, some of the guys would get together at my house. Monk, Dizzy, John Collins, Ben Webster, and others. We'd have little sessions listening to records. We'd listen to a lot of Hawk's records. He was making some in Europe that we'd get. And we'd play things of our own. There'd often be a guitar, bass, two horns, and my wife would be in the kitchen cooking us something to eat. Then on Sunday nights we'd go to Lewisohn Stadium when the symphonic session was on. "We're going to church," we used to say.

Then, later that night, we'd go to the Savoy to hear Chick Webb. That was a band that really swung. Then, after the Savoy, we'd go to Puss Johnson's, an after-hours spot at 130th and St. Nicholas, I think. Everybody would come in there. All the guys from the bands downtown. I remember one particular session. Ben Webster and Pres were there and everybody knew about it.

Anyway, at this particular session, each had his individual rhythm section to play for him. A drummer and I played for Ben. Walter Page and Jo Jones played for Pres. The room was filled with smoke and loaded with musicians. Not only that night but many nights guys were so eager to play that bass players would actually line up behind the bass to take turns playing. I remember one guy brought his bass over to play one morning and, even though he had brought his own bass, he didn't play since nobody knew him.

This business of guys having their own rhythm sections behind them at the sessions happened pretty often. Like Hawk would often have his own rhythm section. I remember the night Hawk came back from Europe. All the fellows came to play for him. He was sitting at a front table. They wanted him to see how they had improved. And finally he got up to play. Hawk was most highly respected. He seemed to be the most creative man of the era. Everybody just thought he was the top man.

As for that session with Ben and Lester, there never could be a decision. The house was divided. Most of those there were musicians. There were very, very few outsiders except some real jazz fans. They used to sell lots of chicken and whiskey at those sessions. I don't know of any sessions like that now. This particular place was especially for Sunday nights, that was the off-night around New York at about that time. It would start about three in the morning and last to about nine or ten A.M. It was always bright daylight when we came out. It just blinded you.

This used to happen like from about 1939 to 1942 or '43. Charlie Parker was never there. Dizzy was everywhere at the time. He was a mischievous guy, and he was also trying so hard to accomplish what he eventually did. Diz at that time was practically ignored by the veteran musicians. Their accent was on good intonation and good tone—this he reached later. He was trying for harmonic evolution, and his tone was very thin and weak. He improved it later. But his ideas were sound, and they got sounder. It was the beginning of modern jazz.

DIZZY GILLESPIE

No one man or group of men started modern jazz, but one of the ways it happened was this: Some of us began to jam at Minton's in Harlem in the early 'forties. But there were always some cats showing up there who couldn't blow at all but would take six or seven choruses to prove it.

So on afternoons before a session, Thelonius Monk and I began to work out some complex variations on chords and the like, and we used them at night to scare away the no-talent guys.

After a while, we got more and more interested in what we were doing as music, and, as we began to explore more and more, our music evolved.

KENNY CLARKE

We often talked in the afternoon. That's how we came to write different chord progressions and the like. We did that to discourage the sitters-in at night we didn't want. Monk, Joe Guy, Dizzy, and I would work them out. We often did it on the job, too. Even during the course of the night at Minton's. We usually did what we pleased on stand. There was no particular time we had to get on or off stand. Teddy Hill, the manager of Minton's, turned the whole back room over to us. As for those sitters-in

337

that we didn't want, when we started playing these different changes we'd made up, they'd become discouraged after the first chorus and they'd slowly walk away and leave the professional musicians on stand.

MARY LOU WILLIAMS

Minton's Playhouse was not a large place, but it was nice and intimate. The bar was at the front, and the cabaret was in the back. The bandstand was situated at the rear of the back room, where the wall was covered with strange paintings depicting weird characters sitting on a brass bed, or jamming, or talking to chicks.

During the daytime, people played the jukebox and danced. I used to call in often and got many laughs. It is amazing how happy those characters were—living, dancing, and drinking. It seemed everybody was talking at the same time; the noise was terrific. Even the kids playing out on the sidewalk danced when they heard the records.

That's how we were then—one big family on West 118th Street. Minton's was a room next door to the Cecil Hotel, and it was run by Teddy Hill, the one-time band leader who did quite well in Europe and who now managed for Minton.

Henry Minton must have been a man about fifty, who at one time played saxophone and at another owned the famous Rhythm Club, where Louis, Fats, James P., Earl Hines, and other big names filled the sessions. He had also been a musician's union official at Local 802.

He believed in keeping the place up and was constantly re-decorating. And the food was good. Lindsay Steele had the kitchen at one time. He cooked wonderful meals and was a good mixer, who could sing awhile during intermission.

When Thelonius Monk first played at Minton's there were few musicians who could run changes with him. Charlie Christian, Kenny Clarke, Idrees Sulliman, and a couple more were the only ones who could play along with Monk then. Charlie and I used to go to the basement of the hotel where I lived and play and

338

write all night long. I still have the music of a song he started but never completed.

KENNY CLARKE

Things began at Minton's in terms of modern jazz in the latter part of 1940. Minton's was a rather drab place frequented by old men, old cronies of Mr. Minton. He had been the first Harlem delegate to Local 802. They had a little band in the back room which Happy Cauldwell had for a while. When Teddy Hill took over as manager in 1941 (he had disbanded in 1939) he asked me to bring in a band. Yes, even though he had fired me from his band several years before because I was beginning to play modern drums even then.

Anyway, when Teddy took over, Minton's changed its music policy. Teddy wanted to do something for the guys who had worked with him. He turned out to be a sort of benefactor since work was very scarce at that time. Teddy never tried to tell us how to play. We played just as we felt.

The first band, around the beginning of 1941, had Joe Guy, Monk, Nick Fenton, and myself. Teddy was the one who really hired Monk. It was a funny thing. He hired the musicians and then made the guy he thought the most responsible the leader. Monk and I wrote *Epistrophy* together, by the way. It was one of the first modern jazz originals.

People dug the music we were playing. They used to come from miles around—from Chicago, from everywhere to hear us play. Most of them were musicians, though there were others who weren't. People would make it a "must." Earl Hines and the guys in his band would drop by and play with us. Dizzy would be there and Roy Eldridge, Lips Page, and Georgie Auld.

TONY SCOTT

I remember always going to Minton's to play and listen even while I was at Juilliard. There was one night when Ben Webster, Don Byas, and Lester Young were there and the three of them blew together, each with a different style and each blowing.

339

KENNY CLARKE

There was a lot of sitting in. Charlie Christian was there a lot. He and Monk were hand in glove. If Charlie had lived, he would have been real modern.

Lester Young would come often too. It was a pleasure when Lester came in—a particular delight. Les never had much to say. Evidently he liked what was going on because he always came around. Jimmy Blanton, definitely the greatest bass player at the time for a rhythm section, used to come around too, another very reserved guy like Charlie Christian, except when it came to music.

We used to look forward to Charlie coming in. We used to wait for him to come in after finishing work with Benny Goodman. Charlie was so sold on what we were doing he bought an extra amplifier and left it at Minton's. In fact, I think it's still there. Charlie used to talk about the music at Minton's so much, Benny Goodman even used to come. He was all the rage at the time and we always got a great deal of pleasure when he came in. We used to just convert our style to coincide with his, so Benny played just the things he wanted to play. We did that for others too, and sometimes there were guest rhythm sections to conform to the style of particular soloists. Johnny Guarnieri was another who liked what we were doing then. And Mary Lou Williams, too.

MARY LOU WILLIAMS

Now, I want to tell you what I know about how and why bop got started. Thelonius Monk and some of the cleverest of the young musicians used to complain, "We'll never get credit for what we're doing." They had reason to say it.

In the music business, the going is tough for original talent. Everybody is being exploited through paid-for publicity, and most anybody can become a great name if he can afford enough of it. In the end, the public believes what it reads. So it is often difficult for the real talent to break through.

Anyway, Monk said, "We are going to get a big band started.

We're going to create something that they can't steal because they can't play it."

There were more than a dozen people interested in the idea, and the band began rehearsing in a basement somewhere. Monk was writing arrangements, and later Bud Powell and maybe Milt Jackson. Everyone contributed towards the arrangements, and some of them were real tough. Even those guys couldn't always get them right.

It was the usual story. The guys got hungry, so they had to go to work with different bands. Monk got himself a job at Minton's —the house that built bop—and after work the cats fell in to jam, and pretty soon you couldn't get in Minton's for musicians and instruments.

TEDDY HILL

Monk is definitely a character. He's the type of fellow who thinks an awful lot but doesn't have much to say. Yeah, I've known a lot of musicians who were characters, but none just like him.

He just doesn't seem to be present unless he's actually talking to you and then sometimes all of a sudden in the middle of a conversation his mind is somewhere else. He may still be talking to you, but he's thinking about something else.

When I had him here, the band used to come to work at ten. He'd come in at nine, but at ten you couldn't find him. Maybe an hour later you'd find him sitting off by himself in the kitchen somewhere writing and the band playing didn't make any difference to him. He'd say, "I didn't hear it."

I always used to be so disgusted with him, and yet you never knew such a likeable guy. Plenty of times I'd have been happy to hire the guy as piano player in my band but I couldn't depend on him. Everybody liked the guy. Dizzy and Kenny Clarke once said they'd assume responsibility for getting him there on time if I'd hire him, they liked him so much. Everybody wanted him but everybody was afraid of him. He was too undependable. He'd just rather mess around at home.

He doesn't run around with just any guy who falls all over

him. If a guy doesn't dig him, he doesn't waste any time with him.

He'll come in here any time and play for hours with only a dim light and the funny thing is he'll never play a complete tune. You never know what he's playing. Many times he's gone on so long I've had to come back and plead with him to quit playin' the piano so I could close up the place 'cause it was against the law to keep it open any longer.

Monk seemed more like the guy who manufactured the product rather than commercialized it. Dizzy had gotten all the exploitation because Dizzy branched out and got started. Monk stayed right in the same groove.

One reason for it, I guess, is that he was living at home with his own people. Maybe if the guy had to stand on his own two feet it might have been different. But knowing he had a place to eat and sleep, that might have had a lot to do with it. Dizzy had to be on time to keep the landlady from saying, "You don't live here any more." Monk never had that worry.

KENNY CLARKE
Monk had his own ideas about things, as far as harmonies were concerned. But Dizzy was more advanced than any of them. Diz, by the way, was the first one I heard play *How High the Moon* in any other tempo than what had been the usual slow tempo up to then. That was about 1941.

DIZZY GILLESPIE
I was with Cab then—when I first started hanging out with Thelonius Monk, and I don't think Cab could figure out at all what I was trying to blow out of my horn on his stand. It was just the new ideas Monk and I had worked out the night before.

MILT HINTON
Dizzy Gillespie came into the Calloway band in the early 'forties. The first impression he made was that he was very progressive— even more than Chu Berry. Chu and Dizzy didn't hit it off too well.

Dizzy and Chu had played together with Teddy Hill. Chu was

342

the star with Calloway and Dizzy wasn't, and Dizzy hadn't been playing up to par so Chu sort of looked down on him, a little. Another thing that led to Chu's lack of enthusiasm for him was the difference in their musical approaches. Dizzy was playing a new thing. But Chu's style was based on riff patterns and speed. Diz was working on a new harmonic structure.

Dizzy's music was much more exciting. It was the beginning of a new trend. Dizzy hadn't perfected it yet. There were things he attempted to do that he couldn't. He didn't wholly make everything he tried but he got to me, and I admired him for what he tried. Like he would try a long-range progression with a high note at the end and he missed it. Cab would get very angry. Some of the guys in the band would say, "Nice try kid, try it again." But most of them didn't think he had anything or would amount to anything.

I was a kind of laboratory for Diz in the Calloway band. It was easy to get a bass aside so I'd walk him on bass while he'd try different chords and progressions. At the College Club, for example, during intermissions we'd go up on the roof and practice. It was easy to bring a bass up on the roof.

DANNY BARKER

When Dizzy joined Cab Calloway's band he was always energetic and was always experimenting and he was a fine, likeable chap. This was around 1941. He had none of the jealousy or the envious traits that a lot of the big stars acquired.

Well, Dizzy and Milt Hinton, between those two-and-a-half hour shows at the Cotton Club (and they were very strenuous shows) would retire to the roof. Dizzy would blow his new ideas in progressions, and he and Hinton would experiment on different ideas and melodic patterns, and they would suggest that I come up and join them. But after that two-and-a-half hour show, sometimes I'd go up and sometimes I wouldn't. Because what they were doing called for a lot of mental concentration on harmonies. It was very interesting, but I couldn't see going up there and wasting energies on something not commercial.

Both Hinton and Dizzy were very studious and energetic and

they continued those "woodshed sessions." And sometimes those sessions continued into band time. Cab had some wonderful arrangements in his book. Sometimes after the show and just before intermission we'd play them for dancing. Dizzy would take his solos and Hinton would follow his patterns harmonically, would follow the changes that Dizzy was making. Often, what Dizzy was playing would be contrary to the arrangement. But Hinton would look at me and I'd bend the chord so it would fit in. It sounded interesting and beautiful to me, but it annoyed Cab and three or four of the guys in the band.

Dizzy was always jolly like a little bad boy who couldn't sit at attention. He was always running around and always experimenting. Cab would stop after a number sometimes, and if the arrangement had been changed, he would say: "Whoever is doing that, the so-and-so should stop it. And you," he would point to Dizzy, "I don't want you playing that Chinese music in my band."

Diz continued to work on these beautiful patterns, and I think that was the start of the new sounds. Next thing I heard of there was a character in town called Bird who had worked with Jay McShann and another called the Mad Monk, and they played at Monroe's. They would meet there in the mornings and play those sounds and experiment with harmonies. When I heard Bird for the first time I didn't pay it no mind because I had heard Benny Carter and Hilton Jefferson. They are still great today, and Hilton was then doing some of the same things. Ever heard Hilton run a progression right out of the key? It seems like as long as I have heard Hilton Jefferson he was always a cat who excited all the other sax players and had their respect. But to get back to Dizzy, he sure caused a lot of activity in Cab's band.

MILT HINTON

This is how Diz got fired from Cab's band. Dizzy was right for once. The whole thing started over a spitball. You see, Diz would help me with solos and things. This whole new chord structure idea was interesting to me, and I would walk the new chords behind his playing. We had a quartet called the Cab Jivers—Cozy

Cole, Chu Berry, Danny Barker, and myself—and we played a spot of our own in the show in theaters. We used to have a spot of our own on the air from the Cotton Club. So I would consult Dizzy about my solos that I'd take, and when we were playing this spot, I would look back to Dizzy in the trumpet section and get his approval. If he liked what I was doing he would nod his head. Or if he didn't, he would pinch his nose as if to say, "That stunk." That was if I goofed.

Well, we were playing the State Theatre in Hartford, Connecticut, and our quartet was playing a number. I had a solo in the spotlight. I looked back over my shoulder to see what Dizzy thought of it. It was evidently horrible. He had put his fingers to his nose with a gesture. At that exact moment, Jonah Jones had a spitball in his hand. He threw it in the air, and it landed in the spotlight right next to the bass and the paper just lay there in the spotlight. Cab was in the wings and saw it. Now, Diz was always clowning. And every once in a while he'd miss notes and Cab would bawl him out. Some of the guys in the band would too, for that matter, and Diz took it all good-naturedly.

Well, after the curtain came down on this particular show, Cab bawled the daylights out of Dizzy, and that was one time it wasn't Dizzy's fault. You see, Cab had seen that gesture when Dizzy put his fingers to his nose about my solo, and he didn't see Jonah Jones throw the spitball. So he thought Dizzy had done it. Dizzy resented being blamed for something that wasn't his fault, but he wouldn't tell on Jonah and Jonah had already gone out into the street. An argument ensued. Cab made a pass at Dizzy, and Dizzy came at him with a knife. I grabbed Diz's hand but he was stronger. Cab was nicked in the scuffle before they were separated.

Cab hadn't realized that he'd been cut until he was back in the dressing room and then he saw the blood. He walked out, came up to Dizzy and said, "This is it for you." Dizzy calmly closed his case, walked out of the theater, and went back to New York.

That theater date was on the end of our tour. After Hartford, we went back to New York and when we got there, there was Dizzy standing there to greet us. He greeted Cab, as well, with a big smile, and Cab couldn't resist saying "Hello" to him, and finally he grinned too. No, he didn't join the band again.

Later, Dizzy played with Earl Hines' band and became quite an influence on the younger musicians.

BENNY GREEN

In the summer of 1942, Earl Hines came through Chicago with Billy Eckstine and somebody recommended me to Budd Johnson, who was playing tenor and arranging for the band. He listened to me and asked me to join the band. I wasn't playing too much jazz at that time. Dizzy joined later in '42, and the band also had Bird and Shadow Wilson.

I used to listen to Diz a lot. He sat right behind me. Quite a few of the men in the band couldn't understand what he was doing, though they admired his control and execution. I didn't understand too much of it either, but I liked it.

Dizzy would take me to his house and show me on the piano the alternate chords and other things he was doing. It was like going to school. I remember starting to ad lib around an eight-bar thing he'd written up. It opened up a new era for me. Then I started practicing things he'd tell me, and before I knew it, I was ad libbing more and more.

TEDDY HILL

He was Dizzy like a fox. When I took my band to Europe— that was before he was with Cab Calloway—some of the guys threatened not to go if the frantic one went, too. But it developed that youthful Dizzy, with all his eccentricities and practical jokes, was the most stable man of the group. He had unusually clean habits and was able to save so much money that he encouraged the others to borrow from him so that he'd have an income in case things got rough back in the States.

CARMEN McRAE

I've known Dizzy for a long time, but I've known him much better in the past six or seven years. He's always been dizzy, but I don't mean the way the name would sound. He's got a lot of brains and good common sense. He's the kind of guy who has no inhibitions, but he's not a flip as far as business is concerned, and things like that.

I believe, personally, that his wife Lorraine has really been sort of a brace for him when he gets a little too carried away in certain things. She probably says, "Diz, cool it a little bit." She tends to be the more practical of the two. She stuck by him in the days when people used to say that progressive jazz was just a passing thing, and she's been with him a long time.

Yes, Dizzy has influenced a lot of young musicians, but, like everyone else in jazz, he was influenced too when he was young.

His man was Roy Eldridge, and Dizzy, at first, used to sound a little like Roy. I was surprised when I heard him change into what became his own style.

DIZZY GILLESPIE

When I was growing up, all I wanted to play was swing. Eldridge was my boy. All I ever did was try to play like him, but I never quite made it. I'd get all messed up 'cause I couldn't get it. So I tried something else. That has developed into what became known as bop.

KENNY CLARKE

At Minton's Roy and Dizzy used to get involved in cutting contests. Roy was the favorite at the time, I guess. People understood more what Roy was doing. As time went on though, musicians began to understand Dizzy and forgot about Roy completely, as far as Minton's was concerned.

Roy never stopped coming and he never changed his style. He would be the last person to admit he'd changed his style.

Roy had been important to me in my development in modern jazz, but in a different way. He encouraged me when I was working out my ideas on modern jazz drumming.

You see, the beginnings of modern jazz happened a long time ago as far as I'm concerned. I began to change my style about 1937. The bands I was with before and during that time included Edgar Hayes, Claude Hopkins, and Teddy Hill. It was with Teddy Hill when I really got the thing together that I wanted to play. I was trying to make the drums more musical instead of just a dead beat. As far as I was concerned, the usual way of playing drums had become quite monotonous. Around this time, I began to play things with the band, with the drums as a real participating instrument with its own voice. I'd never heard anyone else do it before.

Joe Garland, who played tenor, bass sax, and baritone with Edgar Hayes (he also worked with Louis Armstrong) used to write things for me. He'd write out a regular trumpet part for me to read. That's where I hit upon the idea of playing like that all the time. He'd just leave it to my own discretion to play the things out of the part that I thought the most effective. What I mean is, I played rhythm patterns, and they were superimposed over the regular beat.

Around 1940, I was playing with Roy Eldridge and it was chiefly through Roy that I began to play the top cymbal—superimposing rhythms with the left hand—and that helped me develop my ideas all the more. I'd seen most guys who'd played drums with Roy before just leaving their left hand idle, but I just had to find something to do with it. So I began to write out parts for myself which today they call coordinated independence in jazz percussion. All the drummers up to this time had been mostly copying Jo Jones and playing sock cymbal. Actually, I'd begun playing the top cymbal before I joined Roy, and the guys used to ride me for not playing the sock cymbal on the after-beat like Jo Jones.

I wanted to be original. I couldn't see copying anyone. With Roy I got everything I'd been trying to do together. This was just before Minton's. My style was just about set at this time. Roy liked it because it seemed to fit with the brass. Roy's reaction was different from Teddy Hill's. Hill had fired me. He said that I broke the tempo too much. In fact, he wasn't listening, because I was really keeping a beat going all the time. By my improvising with the left hand, I guess he got kind of confused.

Dizzy was with Teddy Hill too. He was getting his style together at the same time I was. It was the turning point of the whole business, because I could feel Dizzy changing his way—

he used to play like Roy—and he dug my way. Later, every drummer who worked with him, Dizzy taught to play like me. He really taught Max Roach and Art Blakey how to play their particular ways.

TEDDY HILL
Kenny Clarke kept playing those offbeats and little rhythmic tricks on the bass drums. I used to imitate him and I'd ask him, "What is that klook-mop stuff?" That's what it sounded like, and that's what we called the music they were playing. Later on we called it be-bop.

CARMEN McRAE
Kenny got called Klook. It really should sound like Kloog, because of something he used to do on drums, sort of a riff he played that sounded like klook-a-mop.

BILLY ECKSTINE
If you ever listen to Diz humming something, he hums the drum and bass part and everything because it all fits in with what he's doing. Like *Oop-Bop-Sh'Bam.* That's a drum thing. And *Salt Peanuts* was another. It was a drum lick; that's the reason Kenny Clarke's name is on it.

CARMEN McRAE
I've known Kenny Clarke a long time. When Kenny went into the Army, things were really popping. Especially for him. He had made a reputation at Minton's and he had his own group at Kelly's Stables. So they drafted Klook at a time when he was really on his way to presenting this new jazz to the people. He was kind of a bitter guy for a while when he came back and found how different things were. Other musicians felt it too. It took him a while to get adjusted.

KENNY CLARKE
Minton's lasted until and on through the war. I went into the Army in 1943, and Minton's was still going full blast when I left.

349

The music wasn't called bop at Minton's. In fact, we had no name for the music. We called ourselves modern. That bop label started during the war. I was in the Army then and I was surprised when I came out and found they'd given it a tag. That label did a lot of harm. It was due to a lot of die-hard musicians who couldn't play the music. They tried to kill modern jazz, but the music itself didn't cease to exist. I think it died commercially after the war because of the tag, but it kept on growing as music. I've seen a lot of die-hards who panned so-called bop so much, but you can hear the music in all the bands today.

MARY LOU WILLIAMS

So the boppers worked out a music that was hard to steal. I'll say this for the "leeches," though—they tried. I've seen them in Minton's, busily writing on their shirt cuffs or scribbling on the tablecloth. And even our own guys, I'm afraid, did not give Monk the credit he had coming. Why, they even stole his idea of the beret and bop glasses.

I happened to run into Thelonius standing next door to the 802 Union Building on Sixth Avenue, where I was going to pay my dues. He was looking at some heavy-framed sunglasses in a shop window and said he was going to have a pair made similar to a pair of ladies' glasses he had seen and liked.

He suggested a few improvements in the design, and I remember laughing at him. But he had them made in the Bronx, and several days later came to the house with his new glasses and, of course, a beret. He had been wearing a beret, with a small piano clip on it, for some years previous to this. Now he started wearing the glasses and beret, and the others copied him.

Yes, Thelonius Monk, Charlie Christian, Kenny Clarke, Art Blakey, and Idrees Sulliman were the first to play bop. Next were Parker, Gillespie, and Clyde Hart, now dead, who was sensational on piano. After them came J. J. Johnson, Bud Powell, Al Haig, Milt Jackson, Tadd Dameron, Leo Parker, Babs Gonzales, Max Roach, Kenny Dorham, and Oscar Pettiford.

Those men played the authentic bop, and anybody who heard the small combo that Dizzy kept together for so long in New

York should easily be able to distinguish the music from the imitation article.

Right from the start, musical reactionaries have said the worst about bop. But after seeing the Savoy Ballroom kids fit dances to this kind of music, I felt it was destined to become the new era of music, though not taking anything away from Dixieland or swing or any of the great stars of jazz.

I see no reason why there should be a battle in music. All of us aim to make our listeners happy.

ORAN "HOT LIPS" PAGE

The word bop was coined by none other than our old friend, Fats Waller. It came about when Fats was playing with a small group at Minton's. Late one night some of the younger generation of musicians would bring along their instruments in the hope of jamming with the band. Waller would signal for one of them to take a chorus. The musician would start in to play, then rest for eight or twelve bars in order to get in condition for one of his crazy bop runs. Fats would shout at them, "Stop that crazy boppin' and a-stoppin' and play that jive like the rest of us guys."

COUNT BASIE

I think all the guys like Bird and Dizzy contributed so much to making the steps of progress of modern music. It was the finest thing in the world that could happen because everything has to change. Those guys have wonderful minds. It must be wonderful to be pioneers like they are, and that's exactly what they are. And the funny thing is that it used to be that fifteen out of twenty people couldn't understand their music and didn't like it. Now if people don't hear it, they wonder what's wrong.

EARL HINES

As for bop, I certainly don't have to be convinced about the place it has taken in the jazz scene, because back in 1943, when I had men in my band like Dizzy and Benny Green and Charlie Parker (Charlie was playing tenor in those days), they were playing just the same style of music that they are playing now. They were very conscientious about it too. They used to carry exercise books with them and would go through the books in the dressing rooms when we played theaters.

Charlie had a photographic mind. When we would rehearse a new arrangement, he would run his part down once, and when we were ready to play it the second time, he knew the whole thing from memory. Naturally, I have respect for musicians of that caliber.

BILLY ECKSTINE

Progressive jazz or bop was a new version of old things, a theory of chords and so on. I said Bird was responsible for the actual playing of it and Dizzy put it down. And that's a point a whole lot of people miss up on. They say, "Bird was it!" or "Diz was it!"—but there were two distinct things.

The whole school would listen to what Bird would play; he was so spontaneous that things which ran out of his mind—which he didn't think were anything—were classics. But Dizzy would sit there, and whatever he played, he knew just what he was doing. It was a pattern, a thing that had been studied. He's got that mind of his that people often don't stop to figure on.

Now Diz is dizzy like a fox, you know. He's one of the smartest guys around. Musically, he knows what he is doing backwards and forwards. So what he hears—that you think maybe is going through—goes in and stays. Later, he'll go home and figure it all out just what it is. So the arranging, the chord progressions and things in progressive music, Dizzy is responsible for. You have to say that.

Monk, too, was a great creator with his songs and tunes. I knew Monk when he played ten times as much as he does now. I think he has got a little weird in his music today. But I tell you, Monk could play.

Let me tell you about Bird and how I first heard him play. It came about through my going to Chicago.

The vogue before the war was to have a breakfast dance on one day of the week. Every club in Chicago, at some time or another, would have a breakfast dance, with the show going on at six thirty in the morning.

One spot there, the 65 Club, had a breakfast dance one morning, and they had a little combo with King Kolax on trumpet; a kid named Goon Gardner, who could swing like mad, on alto; John Simmons on bass; and Kansas Fields, drums.

It was more or less a jam show, for after the show all the musicians would blow in there. We were standing around one morning when a guy comes up that looks like he just got off a freight car, the raggedest guy you'd want to see at this moment. And he asks Goon, "Say, man, can I come up and blow your horn?"

Now Goon was always a kind of lazy cat. Anybody that wanted to get on the stand and blow, just as long as Goon could go to the bar and talk with the chicks, it was all right with him. So he said, "Yes, man, go ahead."

And this cat gets up there, and I'm telling you he blew the bell off that thing! It was Charlie Parker, just come in from Kansas City on a freight train. I guess Bird was no more than about eighteen then, but playing like you never heard—wailing alto then. And that was before he joined Jay McShann.

He blew so much until he upset everybody in the joint, and Goon took him home, gave him some clothes to put on, and got him a few gigs. Bird didn't have a horn, naturally, so Goon lent him a clarinet to go and make gigs on.

According to what Goon told me, one day he looked for Bird, and Bird, the clarinet, and all was gone—back somewheres. After that, I didn't see Charlie for, I suppose, three years, not until he came up to New York with the McShann orchestra.

CARMEN McRAE

The nickname "Bird" comes from yardbird. He did a short stint in the army, and yardbird is what they call a recruit. What's Yard like—Rooh Boy! I've always known the good side of him, so all I could ever say is that he's the greatest progressive jazz man we have today, barring no one.

353

KENNY CLARKE

Bird came into New York during the war with Jay McShann. He was working at Monroe's, and the sessions were between Monroe's and Minton's. Monroe's usually didn't open until four in the morning, the time the rest of the clubs closed, and we'd go from Minton's to Monroe's, which had been open since 1935. Bird came into there about 1940 and George Treadwell, I think, had the band. They began to talk about Bird because he played like Pres on alto. People became concerned about what he was doing. We thought that was something phenomenal because Lester Young was the style setter, the pace setter at that time.

We went to listen to Bird at Monroe's for no other reason except that he sounded like Pres. That is, until we found out that he had something of his own to offer. Well, by continually listening to him, we discovered that he not only sounded like Pres, but also had something new. He used to play things we'd never heard before—rhythmically and harmonically. It aroused Dizzy's interest because he was working along the same lines, and Monk was of the same opinion as Dizzy.

Bird wasn't at all talkative. He had very little to say. He was very meek, very reserved. I don't think he was aware of the changes in jazz he was bringing about. Or at least he didn't talk about it much. Dizzy was more aware of what was happening and his own part in it.

CHARLIE PARKER

I remember one night before Monroe's I was jamming in a chili house on Seventh Avenue between 139th and 140th. It was December, 1939. Now I'd been getting bored with the stereotyped changes that were being used all the time at the time, and I kept thinking there's bound to be something else. I could hear it sometimes but I couldn't play it.

Well, that night, I was working over *Cherokee,* and, as I did, I found that by using the higher intervals of a chord as a melody line and backing them with appropriately related changes, I could play the thing I'd been hearing. I came alive.

As for my beginnings, I came up in Kansas City when the

354

joints were running full blast from nine P.M. to five A.M. Usual pay was a dollar and twenty-five cents a night, although somebody special, like Count Basie, could command a dollar-fifty. There were about fifteen bands in town, with Pete Johnson's crew at the Sunset Cafe one of the most popular. Harlan Leonard was in town then, along with George Lee's and Bus Moten's little bands. Lester Young, Herschel Evans, and Eddie Barefield were playing around. Top local pianists were Roselle Claxton, Mary Lou Williams, Edith Williams, and Basie.

I was crazy about Lester. He played so clean and beautiful. But I wasn't influenced by Lester. Our ideas ran on differently.

I remember the time I tried jamming for the first time when I was just starting to learn. It was at the High Hat at Twenty-second and Vine in Kansas City. I knew a little of *Lazy River* and *Honeysuckle Rose* and played what I could. It wasn't hard to hear the changes because the numbers were easy and the reed men set a riff only for the brass, never behind a reed man. No two horns jammed at the same time.

I was doing all right until I tried doing double tempo on *Body and Soul*. Everybody fell out laughing. I went home and cried and didn't play again for three months.

After I first came to New York, I played at Monroe's Uptown House. Nobody paid me much mind at first at Monroe's except Bobby Moore, one of Count Basie's trumpet players. He liked me. Everybody else was trying to get me to sound like Benny Carter.

There was no scale at Monroe's. Sometimes I got forty or fifty cents a night. If business was good, I might get up to six dollars.

BILLY ECKSTINE

There used to be a joint in New York, a late spot up on 138th, called Clarke Monroe's Uptown House, where the guys all jammed. I had learned trumpet—fool around with it, you know —and used to go out and jam at Monroe's. Bird used to go down there and blow every night while he was with McShann at the Savoy, and he just played gorgeous.

Now, by this time, I was with Earl Hines, who was starting out with his new band. Budd Johnson and myself got this band together for him, and it was all young guys—Scoops Carey, Franz Jackson, Shorty McConnell, little Benny Harris, and guys like that.

The war was on, and a lot of the guys had to leave to go in the Army. So we sold Earl the idea to go up and hear Charlie Parker. Now Budd Johnson had left the band and we needed a tenor player. Charlie was playing alto, of course, but Earl bought him a tenor, and turned Charlie over on tenor, and we got Bird in the band then.

We had about three weeks off to shape this band up, and we were rehearsing every day at Nola's Studios and going up to Minton's at night to jam. Bird couldn't get used to this tenor and used to say, "Man, this thing is too big." He couldn't *feel* it.

One night Ben Webster walks in Minton's and Charlie's up on the stand and he's wailing the tenor. Ben had never heard Bird, you know, and says, "What the hell is that up there? Man, is that cat crazy?" And he goes up and snatches the horn out of Bird's hands, saying, "That horn ain't s'posed to sound that fast."

But that night Ben walked all over town telling everyone, "Man, I heard a guy—I swear he's going to make everybody crazy on tenor." The fact is, Bird never felt tenor, never liked it. But he was playing like mad on the damn thing.

Now I'll tell you a funny thing about Bird when we were with Earl Hines. He used to miss as many shows as he would make. Half the time we couldn't find Bird; he'd be sitting up somewhere sleeping. So he often missed the first shows, and Earl used to fine him blind. You know, fine him every time he looked at him. Bird would miss the show, Earl would fine him.

We got on him, too, because we were more or less a clique. We told him, "When you don't show, man, it's a drag because the band don't sound right. You know, four reeds up there and everything written for five." We kind of shamed him.

So one time we were working the Paradise Theatre in Detroit, and Bird says, "I ain't gonna miss no more. I'm going to stay in the theater all night to make sure I'm here."

We answered, "Okay. That's your business. Just make the show, huh?"

356

Sure enough, we come to work the next morning, we get on the stand—no Bird. As usual. We think, So, he said he was going to make the show and he didn't make it.

This is the gospel truth. We played the whole show, the curtains closed, and we're coming off the band cart, when all of a sudden we hear a noise. We look under the stand, and here comes Bird out from underneath. He had been under there asleep through the entire show!

Another thing happened at the Paradise. You see, Bird often used to take his shoes off while he was up on the stand and put his feet on top of his shoes.

He wore those dark glasses all the time he was playing, and sometimes, while the acts were on, he would nod and go off to sleep. This particular time, the act was over and it was a band specialty now. So Bird was sitting there with his horn still in his mouth, doing the best of faking in the world for Earl's benefit.

Earl used to swear he was awake. He was the only man I knew who could sleep with his jaws poked out to look like he was playing, see? So this day he sat up there, sound asleep, and it came time for his solo.

Scoops Carey, who sat next to him in the reed section, nudged him and said, "Hey, Bird, wake up, you're on." And Bird ran right out to the mike in his stockinged feet; just jumped up and forgot his shoes and ran out front and started wailing.

Oh, we used to have some wonderful times in those bands. Like in the band I led myself after leaving Earl Hines.

That first band I had—that was a pretty fabulous bunch of guys. About nine of them came over from the Hines band. First I got Diz for MD (musical director), then tried to get most of the other guys that left Earl. But by that time the army had jumped in and taken Shadow Wilson. So, I didn't get Shad.

Bird, meanwhile, had been working with Andy Kirk and Noble Sissle, but by this time was back in Chicago. I called Bird from New York and asked if he wanted to come in with me. And Bird had all the eyes in the world to come in the band.

I went into Chicago to get Jerry Valentine, Gail Brockman, Tom Crump, and Shorty McConnell, and brought Bird back. We came back into New York to rehearse, and we were all buddies —like I told you before—we were the clique. We knew the style of the music we wished to play.

We wanted another alto player, and it was Bird's idea to send for a kid called Robert Williams—Junior Williams out of Kansas City, who had played alongside Parker with Jay McShann. So when we got him we needed a baritone player. Leo Parker (no relation to Bird) had been playing alto up to this moment, but I went downtown and signed for a baritone for Leo and put him on it.

So the reeds then were Bird, Junior, Leo, Tommy Crump, and Gene Ammons (who had been playing in Chicago, too, with Kolax). While we were in rehearsal the Army took Crump, and I got Lucky Thompson to make the first band.

Then, in the trumpet section we had Brockman on first, Dizzy, Buddy (who also used to play with McShann) and McConnell; and on trombones—Benny Green, Scotty (Howard Scott, out of Earl's band), and Jerry Valentine.

The rhythm was John Malachy, piano; and Tommy Potter, bass, who I'd taken from Trummy Young's little combo; and Connie Wainwright on guitar. Only three when I started. I had no drummer; I was waiting on Shad, and, as I say, the Army had grabbed him.

At that time Art Blakey was with Fletcher Henderson. Art's out of my home town and I've known him a long time. So I wired him to come in the band, and Art left Fletcher and joined me at the Club Plantation in St. Louis.

That is where we really whipped the band together—in St. Louis. We used to rehearse all day, every day, then work at night. Tadd Dameron had moved into Kaycee at that time and when we got there he used to work along with us, writing some things for the band like *Cool Breeze* and *Lady Bird*.

Of course, then, the whole style of progressive jazz was just a theory of chords, a new version of old things. As I've said before, Bird was responsible for the actual playing of it, more than anyone else. But for putting it down, Dizzy was responsible.

358

20

Downtown, Fifty-second Street was the proving ground for what became known as "bop." Young musicians and veterans were playing the new music on The Street.

TONY SCOTT

I used to hear Bird on Fifty-second Street in 1942. There was no such label as "bop" on The Street then. Each guy played a certain way. Coleman Hawkins, for example, had his own style. So, it seemed logical to him and to other musicians for the new-comers to have *their* own styles.

COLEMAN HAWKINS

They say what Monk and Dizzy and Bird were doing was so different. Well, whatever they were doing they did great, and whatever they did I liked, and I had no trouble sitting in with them. The reason is that I had studied music so long and completely—not just the horn—but composition, arranging, and all that.

TONY SCOTT

The first time The Street heard Bird, I think, was around 1942. There was a place that later turned out to be the Spotlite Club, next to the Famous Door. And Bird came in one night and sat in with Don Byas. He blew *Cherokee,* and everybody just flipped. That was probably about his first time on The Street.

When Bird and Diz hit The Street regularly a couple of years later, everybody was astounded and nobody could get near their way of playing music. Finally, Bird and Diz made records, and then guys could imitate it and go from there.

Everybody was experimenting around 1942, but nobody had set a style yet. Bird provided the push.

An odd thing about Bird's influence on The Street is that the style he was so influential in developing was played on all instruments but his own horn—the alto. The reason was that Bird was so supreme on the alto. I think I was one of the first to play alto like Bird, but I gave it up because he was so superior. So I continued to get influenced from listening to him in clubs, and I used that influence for the clarinet. Where else could a clarinet player go after Benny Goodman? That was why Bird was such a godsend to me, especially because I'd already been fooling around with altered chords from the time I was at Juilliard. And I liked what Bird did with his lines, and I liked the way he formed a chorus.

But let me tell you more about The Street.

Around 1942, Erroll Garner, Coleman Hawkins, Stuff Smith, and Don Byas, among others, were on The Street. Around 1938, four years before that, Kelly's Stables had been the strong point. Then, too, there was the Onyx Club, where the Spirits of Rhythm had had a long run.

About the time I began to be around, King Cole had recently played Kelly's Stables with his trio, and Billie Holiday was working there for seventy-five dollars a week. Coleman Hawkins, when he had first come back from Europe, also played Kelly's Stables and there was a young pianist there sometimes, who is now dead, Nat Jaffe. And about that time, the Hickory House had Joe Marsala and his wife, Adele Girard, the harpist.

BILLY TAYLOR
In 1943, I remember The Deuces, the Downbeat, the Onyx, the Famous Door, Kelly's Stables, and the Hickory House—Joe Mar-

sala was still there. The three big draws on The Street then were Art Tatum, Coleman Hawkins, and Billie Holiday. And things were flexible for musicians on The Street. Like Don Byas might have an engagement at the Three Deuces as a leader, and then he'd go next door to the Downbeat as a sideman with Coleman Hawkins.

The cutting sessions there were just fantastic. With all of the musicians regularly working on The Street and with all those sitting in, astonishing sessions were inevitable. There were nights with five trumpets on stand and five saxophones. And one night Leonard Feather had a session in the Three Deuces with four vibraphonists. The Three Deuces was a pretty narrow room, but every one of them on that Monday session had his own instrument set up, and each one was out to outplay the other.

TONY SCOTT

At that time, everybody used to sit in. Like Ben Webster and Roy Eldridge had a band at one club, and Erroll Garner would come in from across the street and sit in. It happened all the time.

I got out of the Army in 1945, and I used to work the off nights on The Street, maybe two nights, and the rest of the week I'd be down there jamming.

The feeling was so wonderful. Any time you came into a joint, they asked you to join them. If you walked in without your horn, they'd say, "What's your story?" Nowadays there's a different feeling. But then, they weren't bugged on sitting in. I remember Clark Terry came in in his navy uniform one night and knocked us all out. He had a tremendous talent then and now. The owners didn't care about people sitting in. They weren't looking for it, but they didn't care.

I used to go from one joint to another, every half hour, like from where Ben was playing to where Erroll was, to where Sid Catlett had the band. I'd make the complete rounds and I'd sit in at each club. I remember one night I'd finished a set blowing with Catlett and I walked over to the Three Deuces where Erroll Garner had his trio, with John Simmons and Harold West. Erroll didn't make the set and they asked me to play something (I was in uniform at this time). There was a guy juiced who said, "Hey buddy, didn't I just see you playing clarinet next door?" I said, "Yes," not to confuse him any more. "Thanks," he said.

BILLY TAYLOR

The club owners took advantage of the knowledge that a sideman could attract some business on his own if he were publicized.

But eventually sitting in got less and less frequent. For one thing, it got to the place where you had to protect your job. Jobs began to get scarce. Then a second factor is that, as modern jazz evolved, guys would rehearse groups and get things set musically. The patterns within a group got so involved that if you play horn now, you can't sit in unless you know the men and what they're doing in their writing and arranging. In time, everybody began to work on developing his own lines and everybody began to work on getting something different in group sounds, so it got harder and harder for just anyone to sit in.

In some respects, this constriction of sitting in hurts because it's so wonderful to be able to exchange ideas with other musicians. I remember Roy Eldridge and Chu Berry, for example, were famous for going into towns, sitting in on sessions, and cutting everyone in sight. But sitting in is always unpredictable. You never know what ideas other musicians that you don't know are developing. So there were always surprises. Even Roy and Chu were surprised a couple of times.

That sort of thing is good because it's stimulating. A man faced with the kind of challenge you get in a sitting-in session is not so prone to imitate. He's apt to concentrate on building better and more original solos. Because, if after the third chorus at a free session, a man is still imitating, the guys there who are playing original lines will make him sound pretty sad. So that was one of the very good things about The Street—the practice of sitting in all the time and the challenges that came out of it.

Coleman Hawkins was *the* saxophonist then, just as Pres is now. Each man playing an instrument had a certain standard, and for those who played tenor, it was Hawkins. You either had more or less tone than he did. Well, no one could have more, I guess, so I should say you had varying degrees of tone less than he did.

Coleman Hawkins was sympathetic to the newer musicians as The Street became more modern. And Clyde Hart, the pianist, was another transitional figure who was important. Clyde was one of the first of the traditional musicians to understand and command the harmonic background to satisfy modern musicians like Dizzy and to play modern jazz piano well. He had a lot to do with what early success Dizzy had with the public when he played with Dizzy's band. He helped people cross the bridge. Sid Catlett, the drummer, was another of the traditional musicians who made the transition.

Sid was a great soloist and a great showman. He was completely at home musically in whatever he was doing. I remember once on the Coast, when Buddy Rich, Dodo Marmarosa, and Buddy De Franco were all with Tommy Dorsey, they used to come into the clubs and cut everybody. Buddy was cutting all the drummers, but not Sid. It used to annoy Buddy so much. He'd play all over his head—play fantastically—and then Sid would gently get back on the stand, and play his simple, melodic lines—on drums —and he'd make his point.

It was Sid who steadied Dizzy on some of the first modern jazz records, like those on Guild. Max Roach at that time hadn't gotten his style together, and he was playing those far-out rhythm things. But Sid could play both with Dizzy and with the Dixieland musicians. He was the first guy I was aware of who was *the* complete drummer. He could play any style, and he could play equally well in a big band or in any kind of small band.

Sid was also the first drummer I'd heard who would play regular choruses—like thirty-two or sixty-four bars, et cetera—the way a piano or a horn might. He thought very musically. And if he had two blues choruses, he would take just twenty-four bars, and if you didn't come in on the twenty-fifth beat, he'd say, "What?" Another thing about Sid is that he had such a big heart. He was a wonderful person. And he was a really advanced drummer in his concern with a melodic approach to the drums. Even today, most drummers have the rhythmic approach with no attention to the melodic potentialities of percussion.

Jazz is a very personal way of playing music. Everyone has his own style if he's good. Like Nat Cole on The Street. Nat had that personal thing of his. Art Tatum could cut him up and down any way you go, but Nat had his own thing. I remember at a session he sat down after Art and without a rhythm section. Man, that's asking for it! Yet, Nat played his own way and played well. One thing about his style is that Nat was one of the greatest pianists for doing things with the blues. Nat had a trio on The Street in the early 'forties, and other trios began to follow.

The Stuff Smith Trio at the Onyx Club in 1944 was one of the greatest trios I ever heard. He had Jimmy Jones on piano; John Levy was on bass. Just three guys and no drums! It was one of the most rhythmic trios I ever heard. Their only records were made for Asch, but they didn't show what the trio could do. They had worked up some things for the session, but then Stuff goofed and played some other things instead, as he was likely to do.

TONY SCOTT

Then George Shearing came in and did a single at The Deuces. Nobody was listening to him at the time. I used to sit in with him and we used to kid around with little fugue-like things. While we were playing together, I used to change key at the end of a phrase to try to trick George, but he's a fantastic musician. I never considered him a great jazz musician, but he's got total recall, and once he hears something he has it.

Then there was Erroll Garner. He flipped me too, but in another way. He originally came from Pittsburgh, and, from what I hear, he's always played that way of his, back from when he was beginning in his home town.

MARY LOU WILLIAMS

In Pittsburgh, my home town, I was told about a great young pianist just coming up. When I asked my brother-in-law who this was, he said it could only be Erroll Garner, then going to West-inghouse High School with my niece.

I arranged to visit a friend's house to hear Erroll and was sur-prised to find such a little guy playing so much. And he did not even read music. The next few days were spent just listening to him. He was original then, sounding like no one in the world but Erroll Garner.

At one point, I tried teaching him to read by giving him first whole notes, then halves, then quarters. I soon found he didn't want to bother, so I skipped it but tried to guide him any way I could, as others had guided me. I realized he was born with more than most musicians could accomplish in a lifetime.

Some time later, I heard that Erroll Garner was opening at a place on Fifty-second Street. I could hardly wait to hear him again and got away between shows to catch his opening. He was playing more than ever before, yet seemed to have got on a Tatum kick, playing fast runs and all.

I reminded Erroll of his own original manner of playing which I had admired so much when he was working in Pittsburgh. Be-fore very long I was glad to hear him back on his own style.

In those times, Garner made a habit of going over to Inez Cava-naugh's apartment, an inspiring spot for musicians, where Erroll used to play and compose all day. She told me he once sat gazing at a subdued table lamp of hers, then composed something to fit the mood, which he titled, *Lamplight*. Often he gets ideas for his pieces from some object or scene that happens to catch his at-tention.

Some unpleasantness came up on the job at this time, so Erroll went out to California for two years or so. When he returned to New York, he was astonished by the reception he got. He had thought of the Three Deuces as just another job, he told me later, and was surprised to see it full of people like Robert Sylvester, Barry Ulanov, and Leonard Feather for his opening.

Garner had not realized the impact made by his best-seller, *Laura*, in the East. And to back this up, he had dozens of sides with small companies, all of which released his stuff at one time in an attempt to cash in while *Laura* was still hot.

So far as jazz pianists go, I guess Erroll has become the fastest seller on records in the world. And he surely deserves this success, for he is a fine and distinctive player.

Unknown to Erroll, I often won small bets on him. You see, many people have the idea that he lacks technique and cannot execute difficult passages. I have been able to prove them wrong.

Garner is modern, yet his style is different from bop. He has worked out a sound of his own, doing four beats in the left hand like a guitar. He often uses bass and drums but can play alone and still promote a terrific beat.

I like his playing for several reasons, primarily because it is original and has more feeling than almost any pianist I can think of. To me, he is the Billie Holiday of the piano. Some musicians put him down because he does not read music nor indulge in a lot of senseless modern progressions. But these are not the important things in jazz.

What would jazz piano have done for inspiration without Earl Hines, Teddy Wilson, Bud Powell, Monk, Tatum, Garner, and the older giants like Willie "The Lion" Smith, James P. Johnson, and Fats Waller? Without these individualists, many of today's pianists wouldn't be playing anything, for they lack the power of creative thinking. Garner has been an asset and inspiration to the jazz world.

ERROLL GARNER

I like to play certain tunes because of their melody. Why should I disguise that melody? Musicians today, lots of them, just aren't getting along with the people. They forget they are people themselves, they can't be artistic hermits. They're confused.

I got the idea of jazz from listening to records. My style? My own. Two people can't really play the same, so why kid? Maybe that's why nobody imitates me. Shearing, Oscar, Tristano—their style is theirs. To them it makes sense. I like William Kapell. Real great.

I know you can't be confused today. No matter who the artist is, he can't work for himself. Someday, somewhere, he'll want somebody else to see, hear, or read his work—to share it. I'm sharing mine.

BILLY TAYLOR

The Street became more and more modern. Dizzy had the first all-modern group there in 1943—the first pianoless group, by the way. The group had Dizzy, Bird, Don Byas, Max Roach, Oscar Pettiford. Bud Powell was supposed to make it on piano, but Bud was in Cootie Williams' band and was under age. Cootie was his guardian and wouldn't let him go. So the band opened without a piano.

I was working on The Street with Ben Webster at the time, and I used to go over between sets and sit in with Dizzy's band. I kept running back and forth like that until Alexander, the man who ran The Deuces where I had my regular job, got sick of it and fired me. George Wallington, by the way, finally got the regular piano job with Dizzy.

TONY SCOTT

Yes, more and more of the modern guys began to come onto The Street. Around 1947, J. J. Johnson had a group and Bud Powell had started. Al Haig had come in with Bird and Dizzy. That was in 1945. It was a fabulous thing—Bird and Diz both blowing together and blowing great. Dizzy finally got a big band together—with Kenny Clarke on drums—and that hit The Street toward the tail-end of The Street's importance in the jazz scene.

BILLY TAYLOR

The Street sort of folded gradually. The decline had begun around late 1946 and early 1947. Why? Well, with so large a number of hangers-on around, those hangers-on were finding a lucrative market for all the vices—drugs, et cetera—and were preying on the school kids and others who came down. They didn't care too much about traffic from the musicians themselves. Then, too, The Street was close enough to the East Side so that people from the East Side used to come down "slumming," and they were available too to those pushers and to the guys looking for a fast buck.

And the club owners didn't help much either, because of their own greed and the fact that they didn't police their clubs better. By their greed, I mean the small tables and the big cover charges didn't build up good will. And the owners got into booking wars. If Dizzy were working at the Onyx, The Deuces would have Roy Eldridge *and* Charlie Shavers. Or if Bird were at one club, another club would get all the other alto men available—like Pete Brown and fifteen others. That sort of thing was wonderful for listeners, but it didn't help music, having that kind of battle of attractions.

TONY SCOTT

The Street started to slow down after the war ended, after V-J Day. But while everybody was coming back, for another year anyway, things were pretty flush.

There was always a bad element, but it got worse and worse after the war and into the late 'forties. It was a hotbed, for example, for narcotics. Marijuana was the main thing then.

The bad element used to take especial advantage of out-of-towners and soldiers and sailors. The police started to make some arrests, and warnings were given, and things were made harder and harder on the club owners, and every once in a while something bad would happen.

There began a move away from The Street. The owner of the Downbeat Club, for one, felt there wasn't enough money on Fifty-second Street, so he opened the Clique on Broadway. It's now Birdland. Shearing and De Franco worked there. And there was the Ebony which had a line of girls, and Billie Holiday and Buster Harding worked there. And there was the Royal Roost on Broadway. And then there was Bop City.

Another place that was going in the late 'forties and kind of drawing attention away from The Street, was the Aquarium on Broadway, which featured all big bands—Basie, Hampton, Duke.

It seemed like the feeling just went out of the smaller clubs on Fifty-second Street. The war had ended and it was more profitable for the club owners to switch to all-girlie shows. And so The Street gradually became a place for strip joints. I remember Bud had left The Street to take a group into the Roost on Broadway with Miles Davis, who had come onto the scene. The last jazz club folded by about 1948. And The Street was no more.

368

But there were still places for informal sessions, as well as regular clubs for modern jazz. Minton's was going all the time The Street was going, even into the middle 'forties. When guys weren't working downtown, they'd go uptown to Minton's. And if they weren't working anywhere, but didn't feel like blowing just anywhere, they'd go uptown to Minton's.

And newcomers could still be heard at Minton's, often before they appeared on The Street—musicians like Fats Navarro, one of the great ones.

BILLY ECKSTINE

Dizzy Gillespie left my band in Washington, D.C., because he was going to organize his own bunch. He came and told me to go over to the Louisiana Club, where Andy Kirk was working, because there was a fellow with Kirk called Fats Navarro. "Take a listen to him, man," said Dizzy. "He's wonderful!"

So I went out to the club, and the only thing Fats had to blow (because Howard McGhee was the featured trumpet player) was behind a chorus number. But he was *wailing* behind this number, and I said to myself, "This is good enough; this'll fit."

So I got Fats to come by and talk it over, and about two weeks after that he took Dizzy's chair, and take it from me, he came *right* in. Fats came in the band, and great as Diz is—and I'll never say other than that he is one of the finest things that ever happened to a brass instrument—Fats played his book and you would hardly know that Diz had left the band. "Fat Girl" played Dizzy's solos, not note-for-note, but his ideas on Dizzy's parts and the feeling was the same and there was just as much swing.

Fats stayed with me, I imagine, about a year and a half. Then, when we went out as far as California, he decided he wanted to stay in New York and work his card out. So I got in touch with Miles Davis; he was out there working in a group with Bird, who also had left me by now.

I'd like to tell you about Miles. When I first heard him, he was working in St. Louis, which is Miles' home. He used to ask to sit in with the band. I'd let him so as not to hurt his feelings, because then Miles was awful. He sounded terrible; he couldn't play at all. But by the time we got to California, he had blossomed out. He'd been going to Juilliard, in New York, and playing with Bird, so he came in and took over the same book, the solo book which was originally Dizzy's. Miles stayed with me until I broke up, which was in 1947.

21

About a problem—narcotics.

JO JONES

What people don't realize is that there are not as many musicians as there are coal miners or steel workers, but when a musician gets into trouble, it's played up. This happens whenever a musician is caught in one of the so-called narcotics situations.

Now, some of the young musicians did get on dope. I wouldn't defend those who did get into trouble with narcotics, but I could try to explain how it comes about.

During the war, some of the kids were rushed in to replace guys with much more experience than they had, and so they were over their heads, like little boys given a man's job to perform. They didn't have an adequate amount of experience, and they hadn't had the chance to learn and to face the realities connected with playing music. They were young musicians who had just enough to get by on for a time but were building their careers without a foundation.

So, after the war, there were a whole lot of potential artists with no place to play. They didn't have the stick-to-it-iveness to band together, to exchange ideas, to work together. They weren't ready for that sort of thing.

There were guys of twenty-two and twenty-three who saw their salaries drop after the war and thought that was the end of the music business. They didn't realize they had a long life ahead of them. Then there were some that could play a little better, but, by being in contact with musicians of lesser talent, they began to get a closed-in feeling. Then there were those who could play in a big-band section but weren't qualified for playing in the small-band units that grew up after the war, and there was no place for them to perform. You see, there are some musicians who could play in big bands and can't play in small bands—and the other way around.

DON LAMOND

For an example of a guy who got on, there was Stan Getz. He was a featured tenor when he was sixteen years old! Hell, he never had a chance to grow up. And you know how it was during the war. There weren't any bands. There was nobody for these kids to dig except for a few guys who happened to be around, and some of those guys were on junk. And you know how kids are. Everything their idols did was right. So the kids did it too.

Stan was an impressionable kid like many of them. And he was a spoiled kid, coddled all of his life. The tragedy is that I can't think of anyone who has more talent. Stan is a natural musician. He has a fabulous ear, imagination, a retentive memory. What else do you need?

POPSIE RANDOLPH

Once in London, Ontario, we were playin' and Benny was up there with Liza Morrow, who was singin' with the band. Stan Getz was with us, and for a gag he wrote out a crazy sign on the back of some music and hung it up on the stand. We laughed, and Benny saw it and sorta laughed too. But later that night he said, "Popsie, get rid of him."

I thought Stan was keen then, but he was a cocky kid, just a cocky little boy. A wise guy. The other run-in Benny had with him that I know about was in San Diego. I don't know what it was all about, but Stan's mother and father were visiting him, and when Benny was ready to fire him Stan cried and his mother cried and so Benny gave him another chance. I don't think he was on junk or reefers or anything then. I think that came later on, in his hungry days in California. The wind-up was he got himself busted finally in Seattle in 1954 holdin' up a drugstore to get money to buy some stuff.

LETTER FROM STAN GETZ
TO EDITOR, *DOWN BEAT*

Dear Jack: April 21, 1954

I have many things to say, excluding excuses, regrets, and promises. Promises from me at this point mean nothing; starting when I am released is when my actions will count.

What happened in Seattle was inevitable. Me coming to the end of my rope. I shouldn't have been withdrawing myself from narcotics while working and traveling. With the aid of barbiturates, I thought I could do it. Seattle was the eighth day of the tour and I could stand no more. (Stan, you said no excuses.) Going into this drug store, I demanded some narcotics. I said I had a gun (didn't).

The lady behind the counter evidently didn't believe I had a gun so she told another customer. He, in turn, took a look at me and laughed, saying, "Lady, he's kidding you. He has no gun." I guess I didn't look the part. Having flopped at my first "caper" (one of the terms I've learned up here), I left the store and went to my hotel. When I was in my room I decided to call the store and apologize. In doing so, the call was traced and my incarceration followed. My "dope poisoning" was sixty grains of a long-acting barbiturate that I swallowed en route to jail. I'd had enough of me and my antics.

When I came out of the coma three days later, with a breathing tube inserted in my trachea, I realized that the doctors at Harbor Haven County Hospital had other ideas. God didn't want to kill me. This was his warning. Next time I'm sure he won't let me live. As I lay there alive, not wanting to live because of what I had done to my loved ones and all the people who had tried to help me, the nurse came in with a good many letters, telegrams, and 'phone messages—all saying the same thing. They told me not to despair, that they admired my music, that I should pray as they were praying for me, and, most important, that they forgave me.

I was never what you might call a religious person, beyond being Bar Mitzvahed (confirmed in the Jewish faith), but those people showed me that there is a God, not above us but here on earth in the warm hearts of people.

I realize what I have done has hurt jazz music in general. To say I'm sorry is not nearly enough. I can't blame what I've done on the pressures of creative music in this country. Tell this boy from Seattle that it's pure and simple degeneracy of the mind, a lack of morals, and personality shortcomings I have that he doesn't. Tell him that the really good musicians are too smart to mess with it, and don't need it, anyway.

I have much more to write, but we are allowed only three pages a day. Will try again tomorrow.

Stan

JOE NEWMAN

Fats Navarro was on too. He had everything a trumpet player needs—soul, a good lip, continuity, and a good sound (one of those big butter sounds). He had everything. A guy with as much as he had to work with couldn't have failed if he had remained level-headed and stayed off the stuff.

CARMEN McRAE

I met Fat Girl when he was with Billy Eckstine. He was a fat, lovable character, playing the most beautiful horn, forever practicing and forever striving. He and I used to sit up and discuss the way cats were using the stuff and he said he'd never do it.

Fats was a real sweet guy B.H.—before horse, is what I mean. He was jovial and always laughing; he was typical of his size.

374

He was really big before he got on the stuff. You should have seen him. They called him "Fat Girl" because he was sort of a cherub, big fat jaws and a big stomach, and he was so young, in his early twenties. He was still in his twenties when he died. I hear he was down to something like between one hundred and two and one hundred and ten pounds, and he used to weigh one hundred and seventy to seventy-five at least, and he wasn't tall, just fat, you know. He developed TB, which is how he died, and he wasted away to nothing.

MARY ANN McCALL

The habit is a false crutch. Don't get on the H. If you do, reach for a forty-five instead of a bindle. Blow your brains out—it's the best way out. You know, I was the "number one" girl vocalist in *Metronome, Down Beat,* and *Esquire* polls in 1950.

Look at me now. I had an eighteen-thousand-dollar home, and it's gone. I spent four to five hundred dollars a week for the stuff.

ANITA O'DAY

A business like ours can make us easy marks. Look at me. I was a kid still in my 'teens when I was singing around those Chicago spots. Then, next thing I knew I'm up there in front of a band, with a trumpet rocking the joint—remember things like *Let Me Off Uptown?*—and kids screaming. All that wartime excitement. Then the post-war slump, with its big letdown.

Well, I'm older now—thirty-three—and wiser. And I know I was lucky not to get in any deeper.

I've had a rough time. Out of the hospital after that operation, then feeling that things were coming my way again when I was out there on the Sunset Strip and hopeful of probation. Then, bang! I'm in the women's wing of the county jail. It was an education—in crime!

But they do the best they can, I guess—not enough money and facilities. So they have to keep us there—I was in the "tank," as they call it, for a month and a half—until they can transfer us to some other place where conditions are better.

375

There were girls in the county jail who were "kicking it off." I saw them suffer. Oh, they get medical attention. There just isn't much that can be done for the bad cases. Even the short time—it only seemed like a lifetime—I was there I saw some of these girls, young and old, go out and come back again within days. I said to myself, "Anita, when you go out of here this time, you're NOT COMING BACK!" And I meant it. Of course, we all do. But I think I can do it.

JO JONES

I have seen it before—this matter of musicians' losing the respect of the public and I have seen them regain it. It happened in the roaring 'twenties and then for a time in the 'thirties. By 1940 we were getting along all right. Then came the ten-year gap that disrupted everything for everyone.

We had practically a ten-year void that disrupted our whole civic mode of life. Up to 1940 or 1941 we had been elevating ourselves, and then things began to become very uncertain. The younger group of musicians had broken with what you could call the hand-me-downs that go along from one generation to another of musicians. Because of that disruption, due to the war and other things, they couldn't get to people who could give them those hand-me-downs.

Because of migrations, due to the war and war work and uncertainty in general, the younger musicians didn't always have the contact with the music and the musicians that had gone before. They were cramming themselves with academic and scientific music, but they became congested because they had no outlet. A musician has to absorb all kinds of sound and tone and other aspects of music, and, when you have no outlet for what you absorb, things can become very difficult.

As for what goes on inside of all those that got on—for whatever reason—and makes them turn to drugs, I don't think you can find a half-dozen competent psychiatrists who could delve into a musician's life and find out wholly why he started. But some of it was due to frustration. Being in the profession, I can understand the feeling of frustration.

376

I know how frustrating it is for me as long as I've been playing when I'm not able to play. I want to play twenty-six hours a day, even though I know I need sleep. I don't want to go near music when I can't play it. I sit there and the palms of my hands are perspiring. It's a real feeling of frustration. And when the young kids don't get a chance to play that's one of the things that happens.

And so, one of the things that got the kids into dope is to get something to bolster their courage. Also, there were some of them doubly demoralized because they had gotten so far into music before the realization set in that they weren't the musicians they thought they were in the beginning.

BUDDY De FRANCO

And it's time for young musicians to stop supporting dope pushers and to begin supporting good teachers. Let's not be hypocrites about this—whether you like it or not, there is a disgraceful number of addicts inside and out of the music business.

All these sick kids with weak minds and spines of jelly who must "get out of this cruel, terrible world" must come to their senses. They must learn to accept the responsibilities of being performers in public or else give music up.

GENE SEDRIC

I don't think all musicians are on junk by any means. Some are, but that's true of any profession. They overdo the blaming when they lay it all on music and musicians.

BILLY TAYLOR

It happens because so many musicians are immature in their approach to everything other than their music. Why? First, because to become a good musician, you have to spend so much time with your instrument. It doesn't necessarily follow, but it often happens that because so much time is spent on learning your instrument, you don't spend much time on the things that broaden you outside of music.

So many, for example, have grown up musically and then have

had to go back to catch up with the rest of their lives so far as maturity is concerned.

Don't forget that time involved in studying is huge for a musician. There must be no less than four hours of practice a day, plus the time for lessons, plus a couple of hours for other studies connected with music. So figure eight to ten hours of music a day, added to eating and sleeping, and there isn't much time for other things that would broaden a man. Also, a musician's hours aren't conducive to social relationships. A guy gets married, say, but he plays nights, so when will he meet his wife's friends? Or his own.

The prognosis for modern jazz musicians is a very individual thing. It's hard to generalize on something as personal as this is. But you can say that if a musician is lucky enough to be able to go to school and get a general background as well as a specifically musical foundation, he can mature.

One thing that would help is if the music magazines would minimize the hero worship that tends to cluster around the stars. Also, if the music magazines could spend time on young musicians—including teen-age musicians—in all sections of the country so these starting jazzmen can get some encouragement and moral support.

If an unknown youngster comes to New York, there's nothing for him to do. He has to get his work connections together, work out his union card, and sweat it out. If he's a strong person, he can withstand the temptation of falling into the habits of some of the men who have succumbed. He can hold himself back from conforming to the things he shouldn't conform to. But some youngsters can't.

There should be guidance for these young musicians from out of town and in town too, for that matter. And that guidance could come from the union as a regular AFM service. All of these young guys have to have some help growing up. Now, I know a youngster who right now is much more mature in his *playing* than many better-established musicians. But, emotionally, he's still young. But he isn't known, and unless he's lucky, he'll fall by the wayside, not because he lacks the musical talent to make it but because there are other things in his way. By not working, by just

378

being on the outside looking in, he can get discouraged enough to weaken.

CHARLIE PARKER

Any musician who says he is playing better either on tea, the needle, or when he is juiced, is a plain, straight liar. When I get too much to drink, I can't even finger well, let alone play decent ideas. And, in the days when I was on the stuff, I may have *thought* I was playing better, but listening to some of the records now, I know I wasn't. Some of these smart kids who think you have to be completely knocked out to be a good hornman are just plain crazy. It isn't true. I know, believe me.

Because the time came when I don't know what hit me—I was a victim of circumstances. High school kids don't know any better. That way, you can miss the most important years of your life, the years of possible creation.

I don't know how I made through those years. I became bitter, hard, cold. I was always on a panic—couldn't buy clothes or a good place to live. Finally, on the Coast, I didn't have any place to stay, until somebody put me up in a converted garage. The mental strain was getting worse all the time. What made it worst of all was that nobody understood our kind of music out on the Coast. I can't begin to tell you how I yearned for New York. Finally, I broke down.

TONY SCOTT

As for narcotics, I'll tell you this. The guys that are really taking jazz seriously, as part of their life, and that think there's a future in it—those like that that I know of—aren't fooling around with narcotics. I mean guys today that are doing the most for jazz, guys like Clifford Brown and John Lewis.

DANNY BARKER

People don't always seem to realize that musicians, too, are people who come from homes and families, and from fine families. The public thinks all the musician has to do is grab an instrument; that he doesn't have to go to school to learn to read and write like

379

everybody else; that he doesn't need competent teachers. They think he comes out uncouth, that he comes to work, plays his instrument, and gets whiskey and gets a chick each and every night, three hundred and sixty-five days a year. That seems to be the general conception of all the people. There are some non-musicians, of course, who know better.

More understanding is needed, and it's there that the press can be of great help. Blowing up stories of drug addiction is constructive in one way but demoralizes in another way. They shouldn't overemphasize the part that musicians play, because every day ordinary people in the community commit all sorts of crimes far worse than any musicians do. But when the members of the community land in court, everybody's there to help them. Like this boy that kicked a man's brains out, and yet all he got was ten to twenty years. It's a good thing he wasn't a musician.

MILT HINTON

When a man lives a decent life, takes care of his family, and is a contributing member of his community, that's not news. Such a man doesn't get into the headlines. But sometimes I think that sort of everyday achievement *should* be printed in the newspapers and magazines. Particularly when that man is a musician.

STAN KENTON

Working with a group of musicians over a period of time presents many problems that are emotional and psychological rather than simply musical.

There are some musicians who are immature emotionally, regardless of how wonderfully they may play. No matter how far developed their thoughts may be along musical lines, there still remains an emotional part of them that is less fully developed and can cause all kinds of disturbances.

Most of all, it seems to me, a musician needs affection. He has to be told when he plays well, applauded at the right time; he has to be shown that he is respected, and must get enough bows to satisfy his ego.

BUSTER BAILEY

Those people that make a big thing out of jazz musicians being mixed up with narcotics. They're wrong when they think that most musicians are dope fiends. You find more addicts outside of music than in it. Sure, there are a few of them that way but people are always quick to blame the musician first. They look on the musician as nothing. The very people who make a living out of musicians—agents, those damn valets, and salesmen—they're the first to low-rate you. They call you "suckers," and a musician is one for letting those people make a living off him, for letting them treat him like dirt. Then they want to sign you up and they draw ten to twenty per cent of whatever you get, and then you still have to go out and make your own gigs. Unless you're a Louis Armstrong or somebody like that.

I heard a guy last week make a lot of remarks putting a musician down. He makes his living out of musicians. It made me hot. I said to him, "Don't you guys ever do nothing but put down musicians?"

Like drinking, for example. Musicians are not the only people who drink. I know a hundred musicians who don't even drink or smoke. But they never say anything good about a musician. How many musicians do you ever see on the street, lying in the gutter? They take care of themselves.

JO JONES

The younger guys are beginning to realize their responsibilities and are beginning to learn from the experience in the past of those musicians who, shall we say, made mistakes.

MILT HINTON

Gene Krupa, Cozy Cole, and I are working on a plan. We hope to present it to the Board of Education in New York and to school boards in other communities. Under the plan, the three of us and other musicians would volunteer to play at the schools, to answer any questions about music the kids have, and to encourage the youngsters who are thinking about going into music.

We want to show the youngsters and their parents that most professional musicians take pride in their work, that the bad publicity in the papers only applies to the relatively few irresponsibles. We want to show that we have a deep-rooted interest in the future of our music. Professional musicians are not gypsies. We have a stake in the places we live and in the future generation of musicians.

22

New sounds from big bands—Stan Kenton, Woody Herman, and Dizzy Gillespie.

JO JONES
Within the next few years, I'm convinced we are going to hear the best jazz music we've ever had in America.

TONY SCOTT
I think a whole new spark for a healthy era in jazz again is the Basie band. Everybody's all excited about it, its beat, its spirit, and its fabulous ensemble work. Like when they closed after several weeks at Birdland a while ago, they got a standing ovation from a packed house at three o'clock in the morning. And many of the people in that audience were from inside music. That is one thing doesn't happen often.

Yes, a new era is beginning. I think for one thing that jazz groups are swinging more now, and more honest jazz is being recorded by the major as well as the smaller record companies. They're not trying so much any more for a "new sound" like Shearing's. And they're recording more originals now. People's ears are opening up, so you don't have to just hang a tune on the changes of a standard. People have gotten past the point where they have to *try* to hear something.

ERNIE WILKINS

Playing with and writing for Basie I can see that what I call the Kansas City blues are coming back. We notice it on the one-nighters. I was raised up around the blues. My mother had all the old blues records, Bessie Smith and all of them. The blues is basic to jazz but all blues isn't jazz. You have to give it a jazz feeling.

I try to write Basie style, happy, free-swinging style, and I look for something fresh, new figures, and avoid things that are trite. It's not hard to write for this band, though—the guys have such wonderful spirit.

TONY SCOTT

When it comes to bands, the big argument is still about Stan Kenton.

STAN KENTON

Jazz means my very life. Jazz can be arranged, can be out of tempo, can be written in any time, arranged in any fashion, use any type of solo or coloration. The prime thing is that it must have the communicative feeling of warmth from the individual musicians. People cannot believe that jazz can get away from a steady unchanging beat. Jazz is primarily a sound rather than an essential rhythm. Jazz should move you more quickly than symphonic music; it is, of course, a less subtle music. Everything in symphonic music is interpretation. The musician plays for the conductor, is indeed his puppet—the reverse is true in jazz. I guide the band—we create music for the musicians directly concerned—we don't merely score notes. This, to some extent like Ellington, is a strongly personalized conception of music. Don't misunderstand—the integrated composition is the thing, not the solo. And our music is not like, say, Hindemith's, because ours doesn't have that cold symphonic sound. We have developed in this country's jazz not only a specialized technique of using instruments, with respect to sectional blends, attacks and voicings, but also a completely different attitude toward the employment and sound of solo instruments. There is more freedom in jazz, more regard for individual emotion. Jazz is a new way of ex-

384

pressing emotion. I think the human race today may be going through things it never experienced before, types of nervous frustration and thwarted emotional development which traditional music is entirely incapable of not only satisfying, but representing. That's why I believe jazz is the new music that came along just in time.

Ours is progressive jazz.

NORMAN GRANZ

You know, I've been following the Kenton band for years, and the only things I ever liked were *Peanut Vendor, Lover, How High the Moon*, and things like that. It's a shame; this could have been a real swinging band, but it failed because Stan read a few books or something. He had some wonderful raw material, eager young musicians, and music; but as Stan is verbose, his band is the same way. If you have a musical idea to sell, you sell it on its own merits, you don't press-agent it with a lot of loud talk.

This band cheats; it uses gimmicks and advertising slogans. What did "progressive" mean, anyway? Goodman and Basie and Ellington never needed a slogan. I'd hate to hear Kenton mess with some of the swinging bands at the Savoy. Duke Ellington was the real pioneer in jazz concerts, and he can go into the Apollo or the Savoy and play the same music he plays at a one-nighter for dancing and at his concerts—things like *Cottontail* and *Ko-Ko* are good anywhere.

With Stan, it's twenty men for dancing one year, forty men for concerts the next. I guess next year he'll have to have eighty men, and the year after that one hundred sixty. If he has anything to say, he can say it just as well with sixteen men.

DAVE BRUBECK

People ask me why some of us are annoyed with the labels that have been pinned to our music. Call it contemporary. You can't really call today's jazz "progressive," because Jelly Roll Morton was doing the same thing thirty years ago . . . so why use the term?

Kenton? Well, there's an example of why not to use it. I don't think he or any of us are doing anything today that hasn't been done before by Stravinsky, Bartok, and the others. I'd like you to name me something that's completely fresh and progressive in jazz. Your best example would be Lennie Tristano . . . and Hindemith and Schoenberg are much farther out on the atonal limb than he, or any of us, and certainly they are exploiting the twelve-tone system and atonality.

What Kenton is doing is going more or less out in front of the rest of us with that tremendous personal drive of his, attracting a great amount of publicity. He's actually establishing an audience for Tristano, Gerry Mulligan, and myself, and other groups like ours, so I love him for it. Now I don't say I appreciate all the music he's done. His early stuff was wonderful, had the feel of jazz like I've never seen before.

COLEMAN HAWKINS

I'm told there are some listeners who think that jazz stopped with Johnny Dodds and there are others who think that jazz started with Stan Kenton. People who don't listen to what's in the middle are people I think with no sense of rhythm. Kenton's music to me seems to have no rhythm to speak of, but they tell me all his new records have changed completely and that he's gone on the rhythm side. Anyway, I think there's no question that in between let's say Dodds and Kenton we had the most swing in jazz we ever had actually in music. If music doesn't swing it may be a novelty but it isn't jazz.

LENNIE TRISTANO

Stan's writers generally don't write things that swing—and by that I don't mean they have to be in four-four. There's just no inherent pulsation. Stan is supposed to be a very sincere person, but I wonder if he's really with the music, enjoys it himself. Personally, even when I enjoy his things I still don't think they're jazz.

Primarily, Kenton's perspective is that of a composer throughout, and my feeling is that all the great jazz will come from improvising, not writing.

386

DAVE BRUBECK

Many jazz musicians today do not improvise. I have worked opposite a lot of the top ones, and night after night they play the same things. For me, if I didn't improvise every night, I'd quit. I've got to keep improvising.

TONY SCOTT

Good inspired improvisation can stand on its own two feet. It doesn't necessarily need elaborate arrangement or overarrangement or Stravinsky-like backgrounds to live for posterity. You can go back to records made fifteen and twenty years ago, and if the solo is good, it doesn't matter what the band sounds like to our ears now, because a first-rate jazz soloist is usually years ahead of his time. So, when people wonder in what direction jazz is going, I'd say it's only going in the direction the soloist wants it to go. We always have to depend on the soloist to point to new developments in jazz styles.

DAVE BRUBECK

You've got to classify what's going on in jazz: two things, either improvisation or composition. . . . That's why so many things done now fall short—for they are put out as composition while they don't have the form, the thematic material, or the development of any of the great contemporary composers.

But I would like to say one thing about Kenton. Who is offering to the young American composer anything near what Kenton is offering in terms of freedom to his arrangers? For that he deserves great credit.

STAN KENTON

There's *City of Glass*, compositions by Bob Graettinger, an extremely important figure in modern writing. It's an example of the kind of music jazz is going to become. Jazz for a long time was mixed up with pop music. Now, as it has always been in Europe, jazz is being differentiated from pop music as well as classical music. The modernists deserve the credit for proving that jazz doesn't have to be danced to.

As a matter of fact, I don't think jazz was meant to continue as dance music. People got the idea just because it was confused with pop music. Critics have written a lot of nonsense about whether a band swings or not. That's silly. Jazz is a matter of sound too. And jazz has to develop; it can't always remain just functional dance music.

And there's another fallacy—that jazz can only be played in small combos. What about Dizzy's big band, for one? It was a tragedy that band had to be broken up. The reason that jazz is blown mostly in small combos nowadays is purely economic, though Woody seems to be countering that trend.

WOODY HERMAN

My three Herds? Sometimes it feels like it should have been my eighty Herds!

But the three each could take a book in itself. To go back a bit, let's clear up who started this Herd thing, anyway. I'm always being asked how we got the name. George Simon was the one who put that label on us. And, oddly enough, the band he named wasn't the one that eventually got to be known as the Herman Herd and to the jazz fans as the First Herd.

It was the 1943-44 bunch with Cappy Lewis, Herbie Haymer, and Cliff Leemans. It was really the last edition of "The Band That Plays the Blues" and the group that immediately preceded the Bill Harris–Chubby Jackson–Flip Phillips band.

Each band that has been called the Herd—First, Second, or Third—has a particular place in my heart. It would be hard to say, really, that one is more important to me than another. I like them all for different things.

Of course, nothing ever will equal the kick of standing before those crowds and hearing the band roar with Pete Candoli on top through those great tunes. And very frankly, I'm proud of that band. There never will be a night again like the 1946 Carnegie Hall concert.

The band fulfilled itself that night. *Summer Sequence* was a great moment. And so was *Ebony Concerto*, that Stravinsky wrote for us. Funny thing, we played that the next night in Baltimore, and we were all the way down. But that night at Carnegie Hall!

It was marvelous, too, to work with Bill and Chubby and Flip, Ralph, Pete, and, of course, Sonny and Davey, too. That was an exciting group to be with. Ideas and whole new tunes sprang out of that group like sparks. Flip would blow something, Pete would grab it, and the first thing you knew we had a new number.

There was the "Wildroot Show" and the "Old Gold Show" and the "Esquire" broadcast and the weeks at the Paramount. It was a great band and a great, exciting, exhilarating experience to be associated with it. Right on down to the wire when we finally had to break up.

And let me clear up something right now. We were making money, please believe me—money like you don't make today. That was one of the highest salaried bands of all time.

Then there were the tremendous kicks out of the 1948 band, the Four Brothers band. We got off to a bad start. Those first sides for Columbia were all made in Hollywood in a studio where something was wrong with the board. All the things made there were muffled. They had to run them through an echo chamber to use them at all.

No one there will forget how the records sounded when they were played back. *The Goof and I, Four Brothers*, all of them were really only pretty pale imitations of what actually happened. But that was an exciting band, too. We didn't realize it when we started, but the band business was sliding down rapidly, and we were doomed.

The concert tour with Nat Cole was pure pleasure, and we made a lot of things with that band I'll always be proud of. We played a lot of jobs, too, where the band really wailed. It was really a wailing band, and it would be unfair not to admit I was proud of it.

Mary Ann was singing like no one ever, then. You know she really joined the band the first time back in 1939 and the first thing she recorded with us was a tune called *Big Wig in the Wigwam*. She was all of sixteen then. This was even before Barnet. But with the Four Brothers band, she won the *Down Beat* poll, and she deserved it.

It was a tremendous kick, too, for the band to win the poll that year after it had broken up. We simply couldn't go on with business conditions what they were.

As to the Third Herd, my current band. Well, when we thought the time was right, we started back in the band business again. Ralph wrote a book that kept the Four Brothers sound, and we've proved you can swing and still play commercial spots, like the Statler. We've kept a lot of numbers from the Four Brothers band and we've added a lot more.

In some ways, this band—although we went through a couple of hundred musicians to find the right ones and although the band right now has only a handful of guys from the group we started with—has been the biggest kick of all. To find these kids —several of them just past twenty—still coming along with enthusiasm and love for music is enough to keep you going yourself.

Then we went to work with this group just when everybody said the band business was through. And instead of being through, it's gotten better. The kids are dancing again, and it's wonderful to play for them.

23

The present—where paths cross—notably those of some of the younger jazzmen and some "serious" composers. The West Coast school develops, and the Dixieland revival takes shape.

DAVE BRUBECK

In New Orleans, of course, is where it all started. Kind of a combination of cultures, the fusion of which produced a uniquely American art form. There was the African influence, you know, the drive, the beat. Then, via French New Orleans, from Western Europe, came the harmonic sense, the tonal structure, the instruments employed.

Today, in addition to these primary influences, there are the newer influences of contemporary serious composers: Bartok, Stravinsky, Milhaud, and others.

KENNY CLARKE

When I was playing in Paris in 1949, Milhaud invited me to his home. It happened through Dick Collins, the trumpet player now with Woody Herman, who had been with Dave Brubeck before he went to Paris. Collins was a student of Milhaud. He had been telling Milhaud about me, and Milhaud asked him to invite me over. Milhaud began to take notes as we talked and while Dick and I played together. He used to ask us to stop just in the middle

of something, and he'd note it down. We'd talk and then begin
to play again. He'd ask things like, "What is swing?" I'd tell him
it was a feeling, more or less, and we'd illustrate it. He was interested in the cymbal beat, in what I did with my left hand. He
seemed to know quite a bit about jazz. We stayed there about
three hours. He was in his wheel chair, and he'd roll around the
room, very enthusiastic.

DAVE BRUBECK

It was Milhaud who encouraged me in my playing jazz. He felt
that playing jazz was an expression of American culture. He felt
a musician born in America should be influenced by jazz. At the
beginning of every composition class each semester at Mills, the
first thing Milhaud would ask was, "Are there any jazz musicians
here?"

PAUL DESMOND

I met Dave in 1944 when he was coming through San Francisco
on his way overseas as a rifleman. We had a quick session, started
playing the blues in B-flat, and the first chord played was G major.
Knowing absolutely nothing at the time about polytonality, I
thought he was stark, raving mad.

His appearance at the time supported this point of view admira-
bly. Wild-haired, ferocious-looking, with a pile-driver approach
to the piano, and the expression of a surly Sioux. It took much
patient explaining and several more listenings before I began to
understand what he was up to.

Since then, he's been the greatest, as far as I'm concerned. When
Dave is playing his best, it's a profoundly moving thing to experience, emotionally and intellectually. It's completely free, live
improvisation in which you can find all the qualities about music
I love—the vigor and force of simple jazz, the harmonic complexities of Bartok and Milhaud, the form (and much of the
dignity) of Bach, and, at times, the lyrical romanticism of Rach-
maninoff. You see, a lot of us in contemporary jazz look for these
qualities you find in certain classical musicians—but in an evolv-
ing jazz context.

392

WOODY HERMAN
Then there were the wonderful kicks of working with Stravinsky when he wrote *Ebony Concerto* for us. He was the most patient. He'd hum and sing the parts to us. A very great gentleman. It was a rather exceptional experience and a lot of kicks.

CHARLIE PARKER
I first began listening seven or eight years ago. First I heard Stravinsky's *Firebird Suite*. In the vernacular of the streets, I flipped. I guess Bartok has become my favorite. I dig all the moderns. And also the classical men—Bach, Beethoven, et cetera.

LEE KONITZ
I'm particularly fond of Bartok's string quartets. In fact they're some of the swinginest music I've heard, outside of Bach, in the classical form.

PAUL DESMOND
There are so many things we haven't done yet in jazz. We haven't, for one thing, taken complete advantage of polytonal and polyrhythmic possibilities in jazz.

DAVE BRUBECK
Yes, and there's also a twelve-tone potential in jazz, but the man who works in that direction isn't going to be me. Yet, if I did have command of the twelve-tone idiom, I'd probably use it. Offhand, I don't know anyone currently in jazz who has.

I had two lessons with Schoenberg. At the second one I brought him a.piece of music I'd written. He said, "That's very good. Now go home and don't write anything like that again until you know the reason each note is there. Do you know now?" he asked. I said, "Isn't it reason enough if it sounds good?" He said, "No, you have to know why." That was my last lesson with Schoenberg.

In any case, I'm getting more and more from jazz of what I had hoped to get out of formal composition. One of our tapes that hasn't been released yet has an *On the Alamo* that says as much for me in ten minutes of my best improvisation so far on record as any symphony I ever hoped to write when I didn't have as much command of the jazz idiom as I have now.

This past year especially has shown me there is as much possibility for me to say what I want to say through jazz as there is through composition. Before that I thought I *had* to compose to fully express myself. But listening to another of our recent tapes, for example, I heard four different takes on one tune. They all go six or seven minutes, and not an idea is repeated.

You see, for years I approached jazz, in one way, as a means of experimenting on the job, harmonically and otherwise. That way I thought I could build up a big backlog of ideas for when I start composing. I still do that, but I've now come to believe that any music that expresses emotion is the only music that's going to live. And jazz certainly does that.

In their intellectuality, most of the contemporary composers, including most of the twelve-tone system writers, are getting too far from the roots of our culture. And for American composers, our roots should be in jazz. So I hope that what I do eventually write has more of a jazz influence in it than any other influence. But I do not think there is any necessary dichotomy between jazz and what is called "serious music."

I think jazz can be as "serious" as any "serious music." If I could grow as much playing jazz every year as I've grown this past year, jazz would still keep all of my interest. Under those conditions, even if it were to work out that I didn't have time to compose, I wouldn't be frustrated at all. I don't see, however, how we can keep on growing as much as we have this year. But we might.

PAUL DESMOND

You know the real solution to this problem of playing jazz and composing? The real solution is always to travel with a tape recorder. That way you can keep what's good, you can keep what you need to go farther. And that way you could produce more music in a lifetime of playing jazz than in five hundred years of writing music.

ANDRE PREVIN

Fairly soon, I hope, the integration of classical music and jazz will hit some kind of a happy meeting ground, because more and more classical musicians are interested in jazz. I know that whenever I play with symphony orchestras it's kind of a pleasant shock to have the French bassoon player who still speaks with a strong accent come up and ask me where Bird is playing. It's a good sign.

More and more people are interested in jazz, like Copland and Bernstein and Sam Barber, and, of course, more and more arrangers seem to be much more well-schooled now than they used to be in the early days of bands. What I would love to see is to have somebody with the ambition, the time, and the inclination to write a piece for a symphony orchestra with jazz soloists; but I'm sure that a hundred people have said this before me.

Nobody's done it yet, I think, for a certain reason. Pete Rugulo and I were approached by someone in Los Angeles who wanted to have a kind of a *concerto grosso* kind of thing written for symphony orchestra and featuring one of the great bands mentioned, but I don't want to give it away, because it is a big secret project.

They asked Pete to write it, and they asked me to write it, and we both turned it down for kind of a selfish reason. Unless it were absolutely great, both sides would hate it. The jazz guys would say, "What's the symphony orchestra doing there?" and the symphony orchestra would say, "Well, what's the tenor sax soloist doing ad libbing in there?"

It's a big problem, but if somebody with real repute from both sides got together, like let's say Ralph Burns and Stravinsky, that could be a great thing.

JOHN GRAAS

A lot of this development is happening here on the West Coast. I don't mean that jazz is necessarily regional. There are men like Bill Russo in Chicago and John Lewis in New York who are also experimenting with extended form, as we are, along with emphasis on contrapuntal jazz.

But there is a different setting for jazz in and around Los Angeles. It goes back to when several of us were with Stan Kenton. It was about 1950 or so, and we were coming back from that second concert tour he had. There were Shorty Rogers, Shelly Manne, Art Pepper, Bud Shank, Bob Cooper, Milt Bernhart, Bob Graettinger, and myself, among others. I remember when we were riding back in the bus, we all decided we wanted to stay on the Coast, we wanted to live in California.

We knew it was going to be hard to find work. We even thought for a while of renting an old barn to use as a night club, but we hadn't realized that we'd need a liquor license and things like that. So things were rough at first. That was all Dixieland territory then. The club owners in Hollywood and Los Angeles wouldn't hear of anything but Dixieland.

Well, we had our cards in at the local so, in any case, we couldn't do any steady work for six months. I remember we'd meet after those occasional gigs—Latin jobs and stuff like that—and compare notes about how horrible it was and about the things we had to play to make it.

But then the Lighthouse in Hermosa Beach let Howard Rumsey start some modern jazz nights. Howard gave work to a nucleus of Shorty, Jimmy Giuffre, Shelly, Frank Patchen (and later Russ Freeman), with Milt Bernhart, Bob Cooper, Bud Shank, Art Pepper, et cetera, on week ends. I did my first blowing at the Lighthouse.

Then Shorty Rogers himself was a large influence in making modern jazz catch on. He began getting gigs and record dates and he'd give us—all the ones who had been together at the beginning —first crack at them, like when he did his album for Victor, the people at the record company had never heard of us, but Shorty insisted we be used.

Shorty brought a fairly complete knowledge of what was happening all over the country with him when he settled on the Coast. Then there was the effect of his own studies with Dr. Wesley La Violette which gave us a common language. Dr. La Violette has been a major influence on all of us. He's a composer and teacher and has a wonderful way of communicating the knowledge of form—especially counterpoint—to a musician, regardless of the musician's background. He himself has never written any jazz and I think he doesn't understand it much, but he's always encouraged us in our use of form in jazz. He's helped us absorb a lot of important theory, and he's given us confidence in the use of it. Besides Shorty, Jimmy Giuffre and Frank Patchen are among those of us who have studied with him, under the G.I. bill.

Several of us studied with Shorty too, including Shelly and a bunch of new men not of the Kenton group who became part of our group. Is there anyone on the Coast who *didn't* study with Shorty? He made us listen to Basie, Dizzy, Charlie Parker, Lester Young, et cetera. He said Parker knew every note Lester Young played. We listened in record store booths to everything. You don't have to buy the records at Music City, a big record shop out here.

Another factor on the Coast scene was Gerry Mulligan. Mulligan wandered in one day to a Kenton recording date, fresh from New York. This guy did something to the West Coast scene.

To me, Shorty and Gerry are fundamentally alike, but Mulligan's main contribution was to bring jazz dynamics down to the dynamic range of a string bass—and then to use counterpoint in a natural, unschooled way. Some have called it being a miniaturist but, anyway, it *was* the opposite of the sensationalism of a Pete Candoli or Maynard Ferguson. And I think we were all secretly happy at the success of Chet Baker, a guy who uses about one octave in a dynamic range of *ppp* to *mf*.

The West Coast restraint can be attributed then, I think, to Mulligan's influence. I would agree with some who say those of us who can use a wider range of emotion should do so and should not fall into the trap of being too confined in our range of expression. But I believe that the Mulligan influence served a great purpose in exposing lines and in requiring a softer type drummer like Larry Bunker and Chico Hamilton for some things.

As for the records we began to make, Shorty had formed his Giants within the Kenton band. And when he got a chance to record, he recorded us as the Giants for disc jockey Gene Norman who sold the sides to Capitol. Norman played the album to death on his, the *only*, night jazz program in town. You couldn't help but notice it. It had a great influence in a jazz-starved town. Then Pacific Jazz recorded Gerry and Chet, and the dam broke. Soon we all got a chance on records.

Now with the foundation that we've had and made out here on the Coast, I feel we individual musicians are branching out and are also being influenced by visiting musicians and by records from other places. I don't know if there is a West Coast school. Were these things happening in other places? Let's just say a lot of us had a *chance* on the West Coast. I might have left out some important contributors—Hamp Hawes, Curtis Counce, et cetera. And other facts that round out the story. But basically, this is the way I remember it.

One of the additional things happening now is that the movie producers have become very impressed with this West Coast jazz school. Shorty has already done a couple of movie scores and I just started writing the music for my first TV series. And there's a lot more to come for all of us.

Now after a few years, it's Dixieland that's sort of passe in the Hollywood–Los Angeles area. There are a number of clubs, all of them well patronized, that feature modern jazz. Like The Haig, The Tiffany, Zardi's, the California Club. And we have all kinds of record dates for big and small labels. Most of us have already been signed to exclusive recording contracts, as a matter of fact, by one or another label. Those that have been are kind of limited thereby, because several of the record company directors are reluctant to let a guy they've signed record for another company even as a sideman. It's a short-sighted policy, and it does jazz more harm than good, but anyway, you can see by all this recording activity how much in demand modern jazz has become out here as well as elsewhere in the country.

I remember as short a time as a year and a half ago, to give you another example of how modern jazz has grown out here, that the owner of Zardi's didn't know who Stan Getz was when Howard Rumsey suggested he book him in. Zardi's had just changed over from its Dixieland policy. Well, Stan, of course, packed the place, and the manager got real mad because he couldn't get him to stay there even longer.

And living conditions are different out here than in the rest of the country. For musicians life is freer, more relaxed. There's more space for one thing. We all have our own homes and the payments are less than the rent would be. So that's one thing. Nobody's going to take your home away. A musician here has some of the security people in other professions have, and that makes it easier to create. Like even if you are out of work for a while out here, you don't get panicked like in New York. And having space— yards and all that—means that you can practice your horn in peace. You really can't practice your horn well in a city apartment like New York.

It's different from New York out here too in that New York sort of scares you. At least, it does me. Things are so hard and fast there. New York may be more exciting, in a sense, but for a musician it leads, I think, to the fact that in New York the really outstanding talent is forced into more of a struggle for existence and has less opportunity to experiment.

Take the difference in the attitude of the club owners. Out here some of the jobs are about as close to permanent as a night club gig can get. Some guys have had jobs that have lasted for years. And many of them are good for months. You see, the owners of the clubs don't turn you out if business is bad like they do in the East. Maybe it's because the rent of most of the clubs here is lower so that the overhead isn't as high. Anyway, eventually a listening audience begins to develop and it becomes a steady one. The same thing would happen elsewhere if the club owners gave a band a chance to develop a following in a club.

Anyway, being able to work together for long periods of time has allowed a well-knit thing to develop here. We work out things over a period of time, we get to know how each other plays, and it becomes a kind of communal thing. Each of us creates separately but together too. And in the clubs, the audiences themselves seem to conceive our music as a kind of chamber music. Everybody is quiet, and if anybody does make any noise, he's put down quickly by the other people in the place.

A lot of us also have more financial security here what with film studio work, radio and TV and all the record sessions.

So I can tell you we live better and play better here.

BUSTER BAILEY
As for the future of jazz, it's hard to say. The longer I play the more I realize that I'm right back where I started. I'm playing the old jazz and making more money. It seems like more guys are learning or leaning towards Dixieland now because it's the only thing you can make steady money from or a steady job.

TURK MURPHY
As for us, we've found that Dixieland not only has a big audience on the West Coast, where our band started, but has a strong following every place we travel.

BOBBY HACKETT
It's certainly funny to hear those youngsters trying to play like old men.

TURK MURPHY
Well, the music we prefer to play is the music that best fits our own personalities and a man's work should be what makes him happy. Also, I don't want the work of people like Jelly Roll Morton, Richard M. Jones, and similar major creators to be forgotten, and I think our band is helping to perpetuate their work. Out of the two hundred and ninety tunes in our book, for example, thirty to thirty-five are by Jelly Roll.

It's true that Jelly Roll has left us records on which he can be heard himself, but there is a certain substance to a live performance that records cannot contain, and it would be kind of rough to expect Jelly Roll to sustain his work through live performances these days. And furthermore, it isn't that we copy him exactly. We use our own individual attempts to routine his compositions, and we play them as best we can within the bounds of our individual and collective musicianship.

We don't follow the "white school" of jazz at all. We go back quite far; we base our start on the music played in New Orleans during the Storyville period and in Chicago in the 'twenties by the New Orleans musicians who moved up North. Some of our tunes, by the way, date back even further—we use some material from the 1870's and '80's that suits our purpose.

Examples of the "white school" we *don't* like would be, let's say, the New Orleans Rhythm Kings or the Memphis Five. I don't care for the tunes they played or the way they played them most of the time. I hate to use the word shallow, but their music doesn't have the excitement of the jazz played by Morton and Oliver and Armstrong, and the playing of the "white school" of that period was too full of the popular clichés of that period. As a result, their music doesn't sound fresh now while the records of Jelly Roll and King Oliver still *do* sound fresh. Musicians like Oliver and Morton were playing more from their own mind than their white counterparts were; they weren't relying on the clichés of the period.

And Jelly Roll Morton is the man of that era I admire most of all—his musicianship and his writing ability and his taste, a taste that came from the fact that this was the music he knew best.

Let me point out further that playing in this idiom, as of 1954, requires a great deal of musicianship. I don't want to mention names, but some of the other bands who claim to be dedicated to this idiom narrow themselves by not learning theory and basic harmony. As a result, their conception is musically narrow. Almost everyone in my band, unlike some other bands in this style, has studied basic theory and harmony, and all of us have had years of seasoning with many different types of music.

WALLY ROSE

In my own playing of the Jelly Roll Morton compositions, I use a great deal of passing notes and other notes that were probably not used at that time. I feel I can contribute that to the music. Perhaps the one thing we can contribute to the music is that if there are any failings in the musical knowledge of that period, we can fill those gaps in now.

When I play ragtime, I don't copy either. Actually we have no way of knowing what the great ragtime players did. We have the sheet music but almost no records. So I interpret the ragtime music my own way. And let me tell you in answer to those who think playing ragtime is easy—look at the music and you'll see it needs a hell of a lot of technique to be played well.

I did make one LP of ragtime music on which the piano had been "prepared" with tacks in the hammers so that it would sound more "authentic." It wasn't my idea and I don't plan to do that again. I think, as a matter of fact, that the piano has been lost. At least I hope so.

DANNY BARKER

There is a so-called Dixieland revival going on. Well, you can't improve on an Oliver, Morton, or an Armstrong Hot Five even with the poor recording equipment of those days. And a lot of people who are picking up instruments and jumping on the jazz wagon are supposed to be playing jazz but that's not the kind of jazz that I've heard and the majority of the youngsters who are playing jazz in the so-called Dixieland revival seem to me to be taking third-rate records of the earlier periods and copying them, because they don't have the finesse, technique, soul, and feeling of a Louis or a Joe Oliver or a Noone or a Dodds.

DAVE BRUBECK

You ask about Dixieland today. I don't see any challenge in it for a young kid. Makes me sick to see a young kid playing Dixie . . . if that's all he can play. From an audience standpoint, it's even worse; there's so little challenge in it. Then you're limited to tonic, subdominant, dominant chords in practically all tunes.

One great thing about Dixie, though, is its use of counterpoint, which was lost in swing, where everything was arranged for unison, or the soloist playing against the rhythm section with no interplay between trombone, trumpet, and clarinet. You always have that in a Dixie group, and it's wonderful, a wonderful freedom.

Now, take a group like Lennie Tristano's, which added onto that same feeling, made it atonal, the chord progression more intriguing and challenging. But for a young kid to become a two-beat musician? Well, that's like a concert pianist studying Bach all his life, ignoring Bartok, Schoenberg, Hindemith, Stravinsky, Milhaud.

Why is it the Dixie audience is so much larger than that for contemporary jazz? Could this be one of the reasons: A lot of kids like to do what their fathers did, and their fathers listened to Dixie? You know, they get to school, join the same fraternity, they get all hung up in tradition and forget about, or are afraid to reach out for, something new. I know in Berkeley, California, the whole town used to be square . . . which is kind of like a disease in a town.

TURK MURPHY

Some of the revival music has been plagued with a phony romanticism. Like some romantic die-hards claim that the cornet has a magic sound and should be used instead of a trumpet in "traditional" jazz. Well, I remember once when Lu Watters was sick and tired of all this cornet versus trumpet nonsense. He went into another room and played a cornet and then a trumpet for some of these romantics. And none of them could tell one from the other.

BUSTER BAILEY

I have no special choice in the music I play. Jazz—legit—Dixieland—bop. I just like some of it to swing. If the beat is there, it's right for me.

Coda

CHARLIE PARKER

Music is your own experience, your thoughts, your wisdom. If you don't live it, it won't come out of your horn.

They teach you there's a boundary line to music. But, man, there's no boundary line to art.

MILT HINTON

What is jazz? What makes a great jazzman is experience. Unless you've had experience and lived, what could you have to say on your instrument except copy off records? A person has to have lived to play great jazz or else he'll be a copy. It's like the story of the young guy who was copying this fine modern jazzman. He copied him note for note, phrase for phrase. One night he went down to hear his idol at Birdland. And this copier was real high. Well, the man he had copied all this time wasn't up to par that night. So the copier went right up to him on the stand and said, "Man, you ain't you, *I'm* you!"

WOODY HERMAN

In every era we've had swing, boogie-woogie, et cetera, and each of these caused the same tumult that's going on now. Fortunately, it will all blow over, but the music will stay.

JO JONES

What is jazz? The closest thing I can get to saying what jazz is, is when you play what you feel. All jazz musicians express themselves through their instruments and they express the types of persons they are, the experiences they've had during the day, during the night before, during their lives. There is no way they can subterfuge their feelings. It is like some kind of guy will say with a great big smile, "Man, I dig you the most," and he'll start playing something that sounds entirely different. That's the same reaction an audience has sometimes. They may never have heard a man play before, and yet, when he brings his experiences onto the bandstand, he projects his feelings amongst the audience and he can either have them going out of the place smiling or in frowns. And that can prove disastrous after they get home. Because music, being such a medium as it is, can affect you all your life. Music is not only a God-given talent, it is a God-given privilege to play music. There shouldn't be any debauchery attached to it, and it should be presented in the exact spiritual vein originally intended. It is something within ourselves. That's why various musicians express themselves so individually with various instruments.

PEE WEE RUSSELL

What's jazz? It's kind of tough to get into words. You could use ten-syllable words and it wouldn't mean a thing. If I say something in the way of a definition I'd probably retract it a second later. I'm not sure that this will do it but in a way it sums down to this—a certain group of guys—I don't care where they come from —that have a heart feeling and a rhythm in their systems that you couldn't budge, a rhythm you couldn't take away from them even if they were in a symphony organization. Regardless of what type of music they decided to play, they could feel a beat from the conductor. They could feel the beat better than someone who has memorized the book. These are men whose way of playing you couldn't alter no matter where you put them or what you tried to teach them.

JO JONES

Jazz has to swing. The easiest way you can recognize whether a man is swinging or not is when the man gives his every note its full beat. Like a full note four beats, and a half note two beats, and a quarter note one beat. And there are four beats to a measure that really are as even as our breathing. A man doesn't swing when there's anticipation. A man might anticipate a whole note and give it less value than it's supposed to receive and do the same thing with the other notes. Swinging has to do with what could be called "projection," but I mean musically. It has nothing to do with visual projection. Once people get confused by the visual physical experience that they see in an individual's playing they say he's swinging. But he may not be.

I could go into chapters on swinging. There is the matter of the touch that's so important. It's a real simple thing, but there are some things you can't describe, some things that have never been described. And swinging is one of them. I certainly never heard a description of it in any of my classes. The best way you can say what swinging is, is you either play with a feeling or you don't. It's just like the difference between receiving a genuine handshake or a fishy one. Sometimes, a certain kind of musician receives written praise and he believes it, but it eventually does more harm than good because he knows within himself that he doesn't have the feeling for jazz. To play jazz you have to have more than a desire. It's like beauty—something you can't describe.

To play classical music you don't necessarily even have to have the desire, because that approach to music is scientific—the musician plays the music set before him. There are people in the classical field, of course, who are open-minded enough to cover the whole realm of music and who do have enough flexibility to understand and to diversify their approach for different programs. But the good jazz musician has to be flexible and open to begin with.

COLEMAN HAWKINS

What is jazz? The rhythm—the feeling. It can be taught. Or at least its mechanical aspects can be. I think that out of so many of these thousands of musicians, plenty are mechanical, rather than real jazz musicians. But today the public doesn't know the difference. But it certainly used to.

WALLY ROSE

The only way I can describe swinging is it's the kind of rhythmic movement where you can place a note where and when it's due. The only thing that keeps you together is when the whole band meets on this beat, meets on the split second you all think the beat is due. The slightest deviation from that causes tension and frustration. And the musicians will feel that tension immediately even where the audience wouldn't detect it. In a jazz band you have to listen to each other and feel together.

JO JONES

Another thing about rhythm is that when an artist is performing on his instrument he breathes in his normal fashion, and he has a listening audience that breathes along with him. When the artist is breathing improperly, it's like the audience is left with a little case of indigestion. It's like eating a meal in a hurry, not swinging is like that. It leads to a tension in the audience. It's a physical reaction which you give off.

TURK MURPHY

We have bad nights on which everybody feels sick musically. Other nights are good and we're all elated. It's not so much a matter of how the crowd reacts but rather of how it sounds to us. And it sounds good to us if it swings, if it moves.

When the music is running well, it swings to us. That's the common ground—the beat—that keeps us together. And what makes for those nights when we have a slump is when one guy is off on the beat. One guy can knock the whole band flat by not feeling the rhythm with us. You can play jazz easy or you can do it the hard way. It depends on whether the band has the swing or not. And it differs from night to night.

DAVE BRUBECK

What is jazz? When there is not complete freedom of the soloist, it ceases to be jazz. Jazz is about the only form of art existing today in which there is this freedom of the individual without the loss of group contact.

When we play arrangements, we try to get our freedom in the middle. We start with an arranged chorus, and then it's completely free for as long as the soloist feels like playing, and then it goes out with an arrangement. And when we're playing well, the out parts are ridiculous, usually, because the inner parts have come up to the level where you're truly improvising.

You're above what you can usually write in the jazz idiom. And that's what is so amazing about jazz. When you hear something that's really inspired, it projects to an audience, projects to all the musicians, more than anything you could write.

And all the gimmicks you hear being used in popular music lack inspiration. The best sound usually comes the first time you do something. If it's spontaneous, it's going to be rough, not clean, but it's going to have the spirit which is the essence of jazz.

The important thing about jazz right now is that it's keeping alive the feeling of the group getting together. Jazz, to make it, has got to be a group feeling and a group feeling for everyone concerned at the time.

In other words, when we're playing well, I consider the audience as important a factor as the guys on the stand. One deadhead in the front row can ruin the night. It's too bad they don't dance to jazz any more, so that it becomes a complete group expression.

I'm sincere in this audience participation thing. We made some experiments at an army mental institution. Those guys in the psychopathic wards were the best audience we ever had. We always played our best there, by far. These men were complete catatonics, hadn't moved for years, but started to beat their feet when we played.

One who hadn't talked for years started to sing. We got more through in half an hour than the doctors ever had. That's on record, too.

Also, in this experiment, the recorded music meant nothing to the patients. They needed the human warmth of the musicians there in the room with them.

409

So it isn't always the music; it's the trading back and forth of human emotion which you find in jazz that you rarely find in the concert hall.

MUTT CAREY

Hell, that music was swinging all the way back in Bolden's time, and before him in the Holy Roller churches he got it from.

JIM ROBINSON

I enjoy playing for people that are happy. I like to see people happy. If everyone is in a frisky spirit, the spirit gets to me and I can make my trombone sing. If my music makes people happy, I will try to do more. It is a challenge to me. I always want people around me. It gives me a warm heart and that gets into my music. When I play sweet music, I try to give my feelings to the other fellow. That's always in my mind. Everyone in the world should know this.

Index

Bold face: person speaking, actual page italic numerals
Italic text: musical compositions, publications, boats
CAPS AND SMALL CAPS: plays, movies

422

423

A CATALOG OF SELECTED
DOVER BOOKS
IN ALL FIELDS OF INTEREST

A CATALOG OF SELECTED DOVER
BOOKS IN ALL FIELDS OF INTEREST

DRAWINGS OF REMBRANDT, edited by Seymour Slive. Updated Lippmann, Hofstede de Groot edition, with definitive scholarly apparatus. All portraits, biblical sketches, landscapes, nudes. Oriental figures, classical studies, together with selection of work by followers. 550 illustrations. Total of 630pp. 9⅛ × 12¼.
21485-0, 21486-9 Pa., Two-vol. set $29.90

GHOST AND HORROR STORIES OF AMBROSE BIERCE, Ambrose Bierce. 24 tales vividly imagined, strangely prophetic, and decades ahead of their time in technical skill: "The Damned Thing," "An Inhabitant of Carcosa," "The Eyes of the Panther," "Moxon's Master," and 20 more. 199pp. 5⅜ × 8½. 20767-6 Pa. $4.95

ETHICAL WRITINGS OF MAIMONIDES, Maimonides. Most significant ethical works of great medieval sage, newly translated for utmost precision, readability. Laws Concerning Character Traits, Eight Chapters, more. 192pp. 5⅜ × 8½.
24522-5 Pa. $4.50

THE EXPLORATION OF THE COLORADO RIVER AND ITS CANYONS, J. W. Powell. Full text of Powell's 1,000-mile expedition down the fabled Colorado in 1869. Superb account of terrain, geology, vegetation, Indians, famine, mutiny, treacherous rapids, mighty canyons, during exploration of last unknown part of continental U.S. 400pp. 5⅜ × 8½. 20094-9 Pa. $7.95

HISTORY OF PHILOSOPHY, Julián Marías. Clearest one-volume history on the market. Every major philosopher and dozens of others, to Existentialism and later. 505pp. 5⅜ × 8½. 21739-6 Pa. $9.95

ALL ABOUT LIGHTNING, Martin A. Uman. Highly readable non-technical survey of nature and causes of lightning, thunderstorms, ball lightning, St. Elmo's Fire, much more. Illustrated. 192pp. 5⅜ × 8½. 25237-X Pa. $5.95

SAILING ALONE AROUND THE WORLD, Captain Joshua Slocum. First man to sail around the world, alone, in small boat. One of great feats of seamanship told in delightful manner. 67 illustrations. 294pp. 5⅜ × 8½. 20326-3 Pa. $4.95

LETTERS AND NOTES ON THE MANNERS, CUSTOMS AND CONDITIONS OF THE NORTH AMERICAN INDIANS, George Catlin. Classic account of life among Plains Indians: ceremonies, hunt, warfare, etc. 312 plates. 572pp. of text. 6⅛ × 9¼. 22118-0, 22119-9, Pa. Two-vol. set $17.90

ALASKA: The Harriman Expedition, 1899, John Burroughs, John Muir, et al. Informative, engrossing accounts of two-month, 9,000-mile expedition. Native peoples, wildlife, forests, geography, salmon industry, glaciers, more. Profusely illustrated. 240 black-and-white line drawings. 124 black-and-white photographs. 3 maps. Index. 576pp. 5⅜ × 8½. 25109-8 Pa. $11.95

THE BOOK OF BEASTS: Being a Translation from a Latin Bestiary of the Twelfth Century, T. H. White. Wonderful catalog real and fanciful beasts: manticore, griffin, phoenix, amphivius, jaculus, many more. White's witty erudite commentary on scientific, historical aspects. Fascinating glimpse of medieval mind. Illustrated. 296pp. 5⅜ × 8¼. (Available in U.S. only)   24609-4 Pa. $6.95

FRANK LLOYD WRIGHT: ARCHITECTURE AND NATURE With 160 Illustrations, Donald Hoffmann. Profusely illustrated study of influence of nature—especially prairie—on Wright's designs for Fallingwater, Robie House, Guggenheim Museum, other masterpieces. 96pp. 9¼ × 10¾.   25098-9 Pa. $8.95

FRANK LLOYD WRIGHT'S FALLINGWATER, Donald Hoffmann. Wright's famous waterfall house: planning and construction of organic idea. History of site, owners, Wright's personal involvement. Photographs of various stages of building. Preface by Edgar Kaufmann, Jr. 100 illustrations. 112pp. 9¼ × 10.
23671-4 Pa. $8.95

YEARS WITH FRANK LLOYD WRIGHT: Apprentice to Genius, Edgar Tafel. Insightful memoir by a former apprentice presents a revealing portrait of Wright the man, the inspired teacher, the greatest American architect. 372 black-and-white illustrations. Preface. Index. vi + 228pp. 8¼ × 11.   24801-1 Pa. $10.95

THE STORY OF KING ARTHUR AND HIS KNIGHTS, Howard Pyle. Enchanting version of King Arthur fable has delighted generations with imaginative narratives of exciting adventures and unforgettable illustrations by the author. 41 illustrations. xviii + 313pp. 6⅛ × 9¼.   21445-1 Pa. $6.95

THE GODS OF THE EGYPTIANS, E. A. Wallis Budge. Thorough coverage of numerous gods of ancient Egypt by foremost Egyptologist. Information on evolution of cults, rites and gods; the cult of Osiris; the Book of the Dead and its rites; the sacred animals and birds; Heaven and Hell; and more. 956pp. 6⅛ × 9¼.
22055-9, 22056-7 Pa., Two-vol. set $21.90

A THEOLOGICO-POLITICAL TREATISE, Benedict Spinoza. Also contains unfinished Political Treatise. Great classic on religious liberty, theory of government on common consent. R. Elwes translation. Total of 421pp. 5⅜ × 8½.
20249-6 Pa. $7.95

INCIDENTS OF TRAVEL IN CENTRAL AMERICA, CHIAPAS, AND YUCATAN, John L. Stephens. Almost single-handed discovery of Maya culture; exploration of ruined cities, monuments, temples; customs of Indians. 115 drawings. 892pp. 5⅜ × 8½.   22404-X, 22405-8 Pa., Two-vol. set $15.90

LOS CAPRICHOS, Francisco Goya. 80 plates of wild, grotesque monsters and caricatures. Prado manuscript included. 183pp. 6⅛ × 9⅜.   22384-1 Pa. $5.95

AUTOBIOGRAPHY: The Story of My Experiments with Truth, Mohandas K. Gandhi. Not hagiography, but Gandhi in his own words. Boyhood, legal studies, purification, the growth of the Satyagraha (nonviolent protest) movement. Critical, inspiring work of the man who freed India. 480pp. 5⅜ × 8½. (Available in U.S. only)
24593-4 Pa. $6.95

ILLUSTRATED DICTIONARY OF HISTORIC ARCHITECTURE, edited by Cyril M. Harris. Extraordinary compendium of clear, concise definitions for over 5,000 important architectural terms complemented by over 2,000 line drawings. Covers full spectrum of architecture from ancient ruins to 20th-century Modernism. Preface. 592pp. 7½ × 9⅝. 24444-X Pa. $15.95

THE NIGHT BEFORE CHRISTMAS, Clement Moore. Full text, and woodcuts from original 1848 book. Also critical, historical material. 19 illustrations. 40pp. 4⅝ × 6. 22797-9 Pa. $2.50

THE LESSON OF JAPANESE ARCHITECTURE: 165 Photographs, Jiro Harada. Memorable gallery of 165 photographs taken in the 1930's of exquisite Japanese homes of the well-to-do and historic buildings. 13 line diagrams. 192pp. 8⅜ × 11¼. 24778-3 Pa. $10.95

THE AUTOBIOGRAPHY OF CHARLES DARWIN AND SELECTED LETTERS, edited by Francis Darwin. The fascinating life of eccentric genius composed of an intimate memoir by Darwin (intended for his children); commentary by his son, Francis; hundreds of fragments from notebooks, journals, papers; and letters to and from Lyell, Hooker, Huxley, Wallace and Henslow. xi + 365pp. 5⅜ × 8. 20479-0 Pa. $6.95

WONDERS OF THE SKY: Observing Rainbows, Comets, Eclipses, the Stars and Other Phenomena, Fred Schaaf. Charming, easy-to-read poetic guide to all manner of celestial events visible to the naked eye. Mock suns, glories, Belt of Venus, more. Illustrated. 299pp. 5¼ × 8¼. 24402-4 Pa. $7.95

BURNHAM'S CELESTIAL HANDBOOK, Robert Burnham, Jr. Thorough guide to the stars beyond our solar system. Exhaustive treatment. Alphabetical by constellation: Andromeda to Cetus in Vol. 1; Chamaeleon to Orion in Vol. 2; and Pavo to Vulpecula in Vol. 3. Hundreds of illustrations. Index in Vol. 3. 2,000pp. 6⅛ × 9¼. 23567-X, 23568-8, 23673-0 Pa., Three-vol. set $41.85

STAR NAMES: Their Lore and Meaning, Richard Hinckley Allen. Fascinating history of names various cultures have given to constellations and literary and folkloristic uses that have been made of stars. Indexes to subjects. Arabic and Greek names. Biblical references. Bibliography. 563pp. 5⅜ × 8½. 21079-0 Pa. $8.95

THIRTY YEARS THAT SHOOK PHYSICS: The Story of Quantum Theory, George Gamow. Lucid, accessible introduction to influential theory of energy and matter. Careful explanations of Dirac's anti-particles, Bohr's model of the atom, much more. 12 plates. Numerous drawings. 240pp. 5⅜ × 8½. 24895-X Pa. $5.95

CHINESE DOMESTIC FURNITURE IN PHOTOGRAPHS AND MEASURED DRAWINGS, Gustav Ecke. A rare volume, now affordably priced for antique collectors, furniture buffs and art historians. Detailed review of styles ranging from early Shang to late Ming. Unabridged republication. 161 black-and-white drawings, photos. Total of 224pp. 8⅜ × 11¼. (Available in U.S. only) 25171-3 Pa. $13.95

VINCENT VAN GOGH: A Biography, Julius Meier-Graefe. Dynamic, penetrating study of artist's life, relationship with brother, Theo, painting techniques, travels, more. Readable, engrossing. 160pp. 5⅜ × 8½. (Available in U.S. only) 25253-1 Pa. $4.95

HOW TO WRITE, Gertrude Stein. Gertrude Stein claimed anyone could understand her unconventional writing—here are clues to help. Fascinating improvisations, language experiments, explanations illuminate Stein's craft and the art of writing. Total of 414pp. 4⅝ × 6⅜. 23144-5 Pa. $6.95

ADVENTURES AT SEA IN THE GREAT AGE OF SAIL: Five Firsthand Narratives, edited by Elliot Snow. Rare true accounts of exploration, whaling, shipwreck, fierce natives, trade, shipboard life, more. 33 illustrations. Introduction. 353pp. 5⅜ × 8½. 25177-2 Pa. $8.95

THE HERBAL OR GENERAL HISTORY OF PLANTS, John Gerard. Classic descriptions of about 2,850 plants—with over 2,700 illustrations—includes Latin and English names, physical descriptions, varieties, time and place of growth, more. 2,706 illustrations. xlv + 1,678pp. 8½ × 12¼. 23147-X Cloth. $75.00

DOROTHY AND THE WIZARD IN OZ, L. Frank Baum. Dorothy and the Wizard visit the center of the Earth, where people are vegetables, glass houses grow and Oz characters reappear. Classic sequel to *Wizard of Oz*. 256pp. 5⅜ × 8. 24714-7 Pa. $5.95

SONGS OF EXPERIENCE: Facsimile Reproduction with 26 Plates in Full Color, William Blake. This facsimile of Blake's original "Illuminated Book" reproduces 26 full-color plates from a rare 1826 edition. Includes "The Tyger," "London," "Holy Thursday," and other immortal poems. 26 color plates. Printed text of poems. 48pp. 5¼ × 7. 24636-1 Pa. $3.95

SONGS OF INNOCENCE, William Blake. The first and most popular of Blake's famous "Illuminated Books," in a facsimile edition reproducing all 31 brightly colored plates. Additional printed text of each poem. 64pp. 5¼ × 7. 22764-2 Pa. $3.95

PRECIOUS STONES, Max Bauer. Classic, thorough study of diamonds, rubies, emeralds, garnets, etc.: physical character, occurrence, properties, use, similar topics. 20 plates, 8 in color. 94 figures. 659pp. 6⅛ × 9¼. 21910-0, 21911-9 Pa., Two-vol. set $15.90

ENCYCLOPEDIA OF VICTORIAN NEEDLEWORK, S. F. A. Caulfeild and Blanche Saward. Full, precise descriptions of stitches, techniques for dozens of needlecrafts—most exhaustive reference of its kind. Over 800 figures. Total of 679pp. 8⅛ × 11. Two volumes. Vol. 1 22800-2 Pa. $11.95
Vol. 2 22801-0 Pa. $11.95

THE MARVELOUS LAND OF OZ, L. Frank Baum. Second Oz book, the Scarecrow and Tin Woodman are back with hero named Tip, Oz magic. 136 illustrations. 287pp. 5⅜ × 8½. 20692-0 Pa. $5.95

WILD FOWL DECOYS, Joel Barber. Basic book on the subject, by foremost authority and collector. Reveals history of decoy making and rigging, place in American culture, different kinds of decoys, how to make them, and how to use them. 140 plates. 156pp. 7⅞ × 10¾. 20011-6 Pa. $8.95

HISTORY OF LACE, Mrs. Bury Palliser. Definitive, profusely illustrated chronicle of lace from earliest times to late 19th century. Laces of Italy, Greece, England, France, Belgium, etc. Landmark of needlework scholarship. 266 illustrations. 672pp. 6⅛ × 9¼. 24742-2 Pa. $14.95

ILLUSTRATED GUIDE TO SHAKER FURNITURE, Robert Meader. All furniture and appurtenances, with much on unknown local styles. 235 photos. 146pp. 9 × 12. 22819-3 Pa. $8.95

WHALE SHIPS AND WHALING: A Pictorial Survey, George Francis Dow. Over 200 vintage engravings, drawings, photographs of barks, brigs, cutters, other vessels. Also harpoons, lances, whaling guns, many other artifacts. Comprehensive text by foremost authority. 207 black-and-white illustrations. 288pp. 6 × 9. 24808-9 Pa. $9.95

THE BERTRAMS, Anthony Trollope. Powerful portrayal of blind self-will and thwarted ambition includes one of Trollope's most heartrending love stories. 497pp. 5⅜ × 8½. 25119-5 Pa. $9.95

ADVENTURES WITH A HAND LENS, Richard Headstrom. Clearly written guide to observing and studying flowers and grasses, fish scales, moth and insect wings, egg cases, buds, feathers, seeds, leaf scars, moss, molds, ferns, common crystals, etc.—all with an ordinary, inexpensive magnifying glass. 209 exact line drawings aid in your discoveries. 220pp. 5⅜ × 8½. 23330-8 Pa. $4.95

RODIN ON ART AND ARTISTS, Auguste Rodin. Great sculptor's candid, wide-ranging comments on meaning of art; great artists; relation of sculpture to poetry, painting, music; philosophy of life, more. 76 superb black-and-white illustrations of Rodin's sculpture, drawings and prints. 119pp. 8⅜ × 11¼. 24487-3 Pa. $7.95

FIFTY CLASSIC FRENCH FILMS, 1912–1982: A Pictorial Record, Anthony Slide. Memorable stills from Grand Illusion, Beauty and the Beast, Hiroshima, Mon Amour, many more. Credits, plot synopses, reviews, etc. 160pp. 8¼ × 11. 25256-6 Pa. $11.95

THE PRINCIPLES OF PSYCHOLOGY, William James. Famous long course complete, unabridged. Stream of thought, time perception, memory, experimental methods; great work decades ahead of its time. 94 figures. 1,391pp. 5⅜ × 8½. 20381-6, 20382-4 Pa., Two-vol. set $23.90

BODIES IN A BOOKSHOP, R. T. Campbell. Challenging mystery of blackmail and murder with ingenious plot and superbly drawn characters. In the best tradition of British suspense fiction. 192pp. 5⅜ × 8½. 24720-1 Pa. $4.95

CALLAS: PORTRAIT OF A PRIMA DONNA, George Jellinek. Renowned commentator on the musical scene chronicles incredible career and life of the most controversial, fascinating, influential operatic personality of our time. 64 black-and-white photographs. 416pp. 5⅜ × 8¼. 25047-4 Pa. $8.95

GEOMETRY, RELATIVITY AND THE FOURTH DIMENSION, Rudolph Rucker. Exposition of fourth dimension, concepts of relativity as Flatland characters continue adventures. Popular, easily followed yet accurate, profound. 141 illustrations. 133pp. 5⅜ × 8½. 23400-2 Pa. $4.95

HOUSEHOLD STORIES BY THE BROTHERS GRIMM, with pictures by Walter Crane. 53 classic stories—Rumpelstiltskin, Rapunzel, Hansel and Gretel, the Fisherman and his Wife, Snow White, Tom Thumb, Sleeping Beauty, Cinderella, and so much more—lavishly illustrated with original 19th century drawings. 114 illustrations. x + 269pp. 5⅜ × 8½. 21080-4 Pa. $4.95

SUNDIALS, Albert Waugh. Far and away the best, most thorough coverage of ideas, mathematics concerned, types, construction, adjusting anywhere. Over 100 illustrations. 230pp. 5⅜ × 8½. 22947-5 Pa. $5.95

PICTURE HISTORY OF THE NORMANDIE: With 190 Illustrations, Frank O. Braynard. Full story of legendary French ocean liner: Art Deco interiors, design innovations, furnishings, celebrities, maiden voyage, tragic fire, much more. Extensive text. 144pp. 8⅞ × 11¾. 25257-4 Pa. $10.95

THE FIRST AMERICAN COOKBOOK: A Facsimile of "American Cookery," 1796, Amelia Simmons. Facsimile of the first American-written cookbook published in the United States contains authentic recipes for colonial favorites—pumpkin pudding, winter squash pudding, spruce beer, Indian slapjacks, and more. Introductory Essay and Glossary of colonial cooking terms. 80pp. 5⅜ × 8½. 24710-4 Pa. $3.50

101 PUZZLES IN THOUGHT AND LOGIC, C. R. Wylie, Jr. Solve murders and robberies, find out which fishermen are liars, how a blind man could possibly identify a color—purely by your own reasoning! 107pp. 5⅜ × 8½. 20367-0 Pa. $2.50

ANCIENT EGYPTIAN MYTHS AND LEGENDS, Lewis Spence. Examines animism, totemism, fetishism, creation myths, deities, alchemy, art and magic, other topics. Over 50 illustrations. 432pp. 5⅜ × 8½. 26525-0 Pa. $8.95

ANTHROPOLOGY AND MODERN LIFE, Franz Boas. Great anthropologist's classic treatise on race and culture. Introduction by Ruth Bunzel. Only inexpensive paperback edition. 255pp. 5⅜ × 8½. 25245-0 Pa. $6.95

THE TALE OF PETER RABBIT, Beatrix Potter. The inimitable Peter's terrifying adventure in Mr. McGregor's garden, with all 27 wonderful, full-color Potter illustrations. 55pp. 4¼ × 5½. (Available in U.S. only) 22827-4 Pa. $1.75

THREE PROPHETIC SCIENCE FICTION NOVELS, H. G. Wells. *When the Sleeper Wakes, A Story of the Days to Come* and *The Time Machine* (full version). 335pp. 5⅜ × 8½. (Available in U.S. only) 20605-X Pa. $6.95

APICIUS COOKERY AND DINING IN IMPERIAL ROME, edited and translated by Joseph Dommers Vehling. Oldest known cookbook in existence offers readers a clear picture of what foods Romans ate, how they prepared them, etc. 49 illustrations. 301pp. 6⅛ × 9¼. 23563-7 Pa. $7.95

SHAKESPEARE LEXICON AND QUOTATION DICTIONARY, Alexander Schmidt. Full definitions, locations, shades of meaning of every word in plays and poems. More than 50,000 exact quotations. 1,485pp. 6½ × 9¼.
22726-X, 22727-8 Pa., Two-vol. set $31.90

THE WORLD'S GREAT SPEECHES, edited by Lewis Copeland and Lawrence W. Lamm. Vast collection of 278 speeches from Greeks to 1970. Powerful and effective models; unique look at history. 842pp. 5⅜ × 8½. 20468-5 Pa. $12.95

THE BLUE FAIRY BOOK, Andrew Lang. The first, most famous collection, with many familiar tales: Little Red Riding Hood, Aladdin and the Wonderful Lamp, Puss in Boots, Sleeping Beauty, Hansel and Gretel, Rumpelstiltskin; 37 in all. 138 illustrations. 390pp. 5⅜ × 8½. 21437-0 Pa. $6.95

THE STORY OF THE CHAMPIONS OF THE ROUND TABLE, Howard Pyle. Sir Launcelot, Sir Tristram and Sir Percival in spirited adventures of love and triumph retold in Pyle's inimitable style. 50 drawings, 31 full-page. xviii + 329pp. 6½ × 9¼. 21883-X Pa. $7.95

THE MYTHS OF THE NORTH AMERICAN INDIANS, Lewis Spence. Myths and legends of the Algonquins, Iroquois, Pawnees and Sioux with comprehensive historical and ethnological commentary. 36 illustrations. 5⅜ × 8½.
25967-6 Pa. $8.95

GREAT DINOSAUR HUNTERS AND THEIR DISCOVERIES, Edwin H. Colbert. Fascinating, lavishly illustrated chronicle of dinosaur research, 1820's to 1960. Achievements of Cope, Marsh, Brown, Buckland, Mantell, Huxley, many others. 384pp. 5¼ × 8¼. 24701-5 Pa. $7.95

THE TASTEMAKERS, Russell Lynes. Informal, illustrated social history of American taste 1850's–1950's. First popularized categories Highbrow, Lowbrow, Middlebrow. 129 illustrations. New (1979) afterword. 384pp. 6 × 9.
23993-4 Pa. $8.95

DOUBLE CROSS PURPOSES, Ronald A. Knox. A treasure hunt in the Scottish Highlands, an old map, unidentified corpse, surprise discoveries keep reader guessing in this cleverly intricate tale of financial skullduggery. 2 black-and-white maps. 320pp. 5⅜ × 8½. (Available in U.S. only) 25032-6 Pa. $6.95

AUTHENTIC VICTORIAN DECORATION AND ORNAMENTATION IN FULL COLOR: 46 Plates from "Studies in Design," Christopher Dresser. Superb full-color lithographs reproduced from rare original portfolio of a major Victorian designer. 48pp. 9¼ × 12¼. 25083-0 Pa. $7.95

PRIMITIVE ART, Franz Boas. Remains the best text ever prepared on subject, thoroughly discussing Indian, African, Asian, Australian, and, especially, Northern American primitive art. Over 950 illustrations show ceramics, masks, totem poles, weapons, textiles, paintings, much more. 376pp. 5⅜ × 8. 20025-6 Pa. $7.95

SIDELIGHTS ON RELATIVITY, Albert Einstein. Unabridged republication of two lectures delivered by the great physicist in 1920–21. *Ether and Relativity* and *Geometry and Experience*. Elegant ideas in non-mathematical form, accessible to intelligent layman. vi + 56pp. 5⅜ × 8½. 24511-X Pa. $2.95

THE WIT AND HUMOR OF OSCAR WILDE, edited by Alvin Redman. More than 1,000 ripostes, paradoxes, wisecracks: Work is the curse of the drinking classes, I can resist everything except temptation, etc. 258pp. 5⅜ × 8½. 20602-5 Pa. $4.95

ADVENTURES WITH A MICROSCOPE, Richard Headstrom. 59 adventures with clothing fibers, protozoa, ferns and lichens, roots and leaves, much more. 142 illustrations. 232pp. 5⅜ × 8½. 23471-1 Pa. $3.95

PLANTS OF THE BIBLE, Harold N. Moldenke and Alma L. Moldenke. Standard reference to all 230 plants mentioned in Scriptures. Latin name, biblical reference, uses, modern identity, much more. Unsurpassed encyclopedic resource for scholars, botanists, nature lovers, students of Bible. Bibliography. Indexes. 123 black-and-white illustrations. 384pp. 6 × 9. 25069-5 Pa. $8.95

FAMOUS AMERICAN WOMEN: A Biographical Dictionary from Colonial Times to the Present, Robert McHenry, ed. From Pocahontas to Rosa Parks, 1,035 distinguished American women documented in separate biographical entries. Accurate, up-to-date data, numerous categories, spans 400 years. Indices. 493pp. 6½ × 9¼. 24523-3 Pa. $10.95

THE FABULOUS INTERIORS OF THE GREAT OCEAN LINERS IN HISTORIC PHOTOGRAPHS, William H. Miller, Jr. Some 200 superb photographs capture exquisite interiors of world's great "floating palaces"—1890's to 1980's: Titanic, Ile de France, Queen Elizabeth, United States, Europa, more. Approx. 200 black-and-white photographs. Captions. Text. Introduction. 160pp. 8⅜ × 11¼. 24756-2 Pa. $9.95

THE GREAT LUXURY LINERS, 1927–1954: A Photographic Record, William H. Miller, Jr. Nostalgic tribute to heyday of ocean liners. 186 photos of Ile de France, Normandie, Leviathan, Queen Elizabeth, United States, many others. Interior and exterior views. Introduction. Captions. 160pp. 9 × 12. 24056-8 Pa. $10.95

A NATURAL HISTORY OF THE DUCKS, John Charles Phillips. Great landmark of ornithology offers complete detailed coverage of nearly 200 species and subspecies of ducks: gadwall, sheldrake, merganser, pintail, many more. 74 full-color plates, 102 black-and-white. Bibliography. Total of 1,920pp. 8⅜ × 11¼. 25141-1, 25142-X Cloth. Two-vol. set $100.00

THE SEAWEED HANDBOOK: An Illustrated Guide to Seaweeds from North Carolina to Canada, Thomas F. Lee. Concise reference covers 78 species. Scientific and common names, habitat, distribution, more. Finding keys for easy identification. 224pp. 5⅜ × 8½. 25215-9 Pa. $6.95

THE TEN BOOKS OF ARCHITECTURE: The 1755 Leoni Edition, Leon Battista Alberti. Rare classic helped introduce the glories of ancient architecture to the Renaissance. 68 black-and-white plates. 336pp. 8⅜ × 11¼. 25239-6 Pa. $14.95

MISS MACKENZIE, Anthony Trollope. Minor masterpieces by Victorian master unmasks many truths about life in 19th-century England. First inexpensive edition in years. 392pp. 5⅜ × 8½. 25201-9 Pa. $8.95

THE RIME OF THE ANCIENT MARINER, Gustave Doré, Samuel Taylor Coleridge. Dramatic engravings considered by many to be his greatest work. The terrifying space of the open sea, the storms and whirlpools of an unknown ocean, the ice of Antarctica, more—all rendered in a powerful, chilling manner. Full text. 38 plates. 77pp. 9¼ × 12. 22305-1 Pa. $4.95

THE EXPEDITIONS OF ZEBULON MONTGOMERY PIKE, Zebulon Montgomery Pike. Fascinating first-hand accounts (1805–6) of exploration of Mississippi River, Indian wars, capture by Spanish dragoons, much more. 1,088pp. 5⅜ × 8½. 25254-X, 25255-8 Pa. Two-vol. set $25.90

A CONCISE HISTORY OF PHOTOGRAPHY: Third Revised Edition, Helmut Gernsheim. Best one-volume history—camera obscura, photochemistry, daguerreotypes, evolution of cameras, film, more. Also artistic aspects—landscape, portraits, fine art, etc. 281 black-and-white photographs. 26 in color. 176pp. 8⅜ × 11¼. 25128-4 Pa. $13.95

THE DORÉ BIBLE ILLUSTRATIONS, Gustave Doré. 241 detailed plates from the Bible: the Creation scenes, Adam and Eve, Flood, Babylon, battle sequences, life of Jesus, etc. Each plate is accompanied by the verses from the King James version of the Bible. 241pp. 9 × 12. 23004-X Pa. $9.95

WANDERINGS IN WEST AFRICA, Richard F. Burton. Great Victorian scholar/adventurer's invaluable descriptions of African tribal rituals, fetishism, culture, art, much more. Fascinating 19th-century account. 624pp. 5⅜ × 8½. 26890-X Pa. $12.95

FLATLAND, E. A. Abbott. Intriguing and enormously popular science-fiction classic explores the complexities of trying to survive as a two-dimensional being in a three-dimensional world. Amusingly illustrated by the author. 16 illustrations. 103pp. 5⅜ × 8½. 20001-9 Pa. $2.50

THE HISTORY OF THE LEWIS AND CLARK EXPEDITION, Meriwether Lewis and William Clark, edited by Elliott Coues. Classic edition of Lewis and Clark's day-by-day journals that later became the basis for U.S. claims to Oregon and the West. Accurate and invaluable geographical, botanical, biological, meteorological and anthropological material. Total of 1,508pp. 5⅜ × 8½.
21268-8, 21269-6, 21270-X Pa. Three-vol. set $26.85

LANGUAGE, TRUTH AND LOGIC, Alfred J. Ayer. Famous, clear introduction to Vienna, Cambridge schools of Logical Positivism. Role of philosophy, elimination of metaphysics, nature of analysis, etc. 160pp. 5⅜ × 8½. (Available in U.S. and Canada only) 20010-8 Pa. $3.95

MATHEMATICS FOR THE NONMATHEMATICIAN, Morris Kline. Detailed, college-level treatment of mathematics in cultural and historical context, with numerous exercises. For liberal arts students. Preface. Recommended Reading Lists. Tables. Index. Numerous black-and-white figures. xvi + 641pp. 5⅜ × 8½.
24823-2 Pa. $11.95

HANDBOOK OF PICTORIAL SYMBOLS, Rudolph Modley. 3,250 signs and symbols, many systems in full; official or heavy commercial use. Arranged by subject. Most in Pictorial Archive series. 143pp. 8⅛ × 11. 23357-X Pa. $6.95

INCIDENTS OF TRAVEL IN YUCATAN, John L. Stephens. Classic (1843) exploration of jungles of Yucatan, looking for evidences of Maya civilization. Travel adventures, Mexican and Indian culture, etc. Total of 669pp. 5⅜ × 8½.
20926-1, 20927-X Pa., Two-vol. set $11.90

CATALOG OF DOVER BOOKS

DEGAS: An Intimate Portrait, Ambroise Vollard. Charming, anecdotal memoir by famous art dealer of one of the greatest 19th-century French painters. 14 black-and-white illustrations. Introduction by Harold L. Van Doren. 96pp. 5⅜ × 8½.
25131-4 Pa. $4.95

PERSONAL NARRATIVE OF A PILGRIMAGE TO ALMANDINAH AND MECCAH, Richard Burton. Great travel classic by remarkably colorful personality. Burton, disguised as a Moroccan, visited sacred shrines of Islam, narrowly escaping death. 47 illustrations. 959pp. 5⅜ × 8½.   21217-3, 21218-1 Pa., Two-vol. set $19.90

PHRASE AND WORD ORIGINS, A. H. Holt. Entertaining, reliable, modern study of more than 1,200 colorful words, phrases, origins and histories. Much unexpected information. 254pp. 5⅜ × 8½.   20758-7 Pa. $5.95

THE RED THUMB MARK, R. Austin Freeman. In this first Dr. Thorndyke case, the great scientific detective draws fascinating conclusions from the nature of a single fingerprint. Exciting story, authentic science. 320pp. 5⅜ × 8½. (Available in U.S. only)   25210-8 Pa. $6.95

AN EGYPTIAN HIEROGLYPHIC DICTIONARY, E. A. Wallis Budge. Monumental work containing about 25,000 words or terms that occur in texts ranging from 3000 B.C. to 600 A.D. Each entry consists of a transliteration of the word, the word in hieroglyphs, and the meaning in English. 1,314pp. 6⅝ × 10.
23615-3, 23616-1 Pa., Two-vol. set $35.90

THE COMPLEAT STRATEGYST: Being a Primer on the Theory of Games of Strategy, J. D. Williams. Highly entertaining classic describes, with many illustrated examples, how to select best strategies in conflict situations. Prefaces. Appendices. xvi + 268pp. 5⅜ × 8½.   25101-2 Pa. $6.95

THE ROAD TO OZ, L. Frank Baum. Dorothy meets the Shaggy Man, little Button-Bright and the Rainbow's beautiful daughter in this delightful trip to the magical Land of Oz. 272pp. 5⅜ × 8.   25208-6 Pa. $5.95

POINT AND LINE TO PLANE, Wassily Kandinsky. Seminal exposition of role of point, line, other elements in non-objective painting. Essential to understanding 20th-century art. 127 illustrations. 192pp. 6½ × 9¼.   23808-3 Pa. $5.95

LADY ANNA, Anthony Trollope. Moving chronicle of Countess Lovel's bitter struggle to win for herself and daughter Anna their rightful rank and fortune—perhaps at cost of sanity itself. 384pp. 5⅜ × 8½.   24669-8 Pa. $8.95

EGYPTIAN MAGIC, E. A. Wallis Budge. Sums up all that is known about magic in Ancient Egypt: the role of magic in controlling the gods, powerful amulets that warded off evil spirits, scarabs of immortality, use of wax images, formulas and spells, the secret name, much more. 253pp. 5⅜ × 8½.   22681-6 Pa. $4.50

THE DANCE OF SIVA, Ananda Coomaraswamy. Preeminent authority unfolds the vast metaphysic of India: the revelation of her art, conception of the universe, social organization, etc. 27 reproductions of art masterpieces. 192pp. 5⅜ × 8½.
24817-8 Pa. $5.95

CHRISTMAS CUSTOMS AND TRADITIONS, Clement A. Miles. Origin, evolution, significance of religious, secular practices. Caroling, gifts, yule logs, much more. Full, scholarly yet fascinating; non-sectarian. 400pp. 5⅜ × 8½.
23354-5 Pa. $6.95

THE HUMAN FIGURE IN MOTION, Eadweard Muybridge. More than 4,500 stopped-action photos, in action series, showing undraped men, women, children jumping, lying down, throwing, sitting, wrestling, carrying, etc. 390pp. 7⅞ × 10⅝.
20204-6 Cloth. $24.95

THE MAN WHO WAS THURSDAY, Gilbert Keith Chesterton. Witty, fast-paced novel about a club of anarchists in turn-of-the-century London. Brilliant social, religious, philosophical speculations. 128pp. 5⅜ × 8½.
25121-7 Pa. $3.95

A CEZANNE SKETCHBOOK: Figures, Portraits, Landscapes and Still Lifes, Paul Cezanne. Great artist experiments with tonal effects, light, mass, other qualities in over 100 drawings. A revealing view of developing master painter, precursor of Cubism. 102 black-and-white illustrations. 144pp. 8¾ × 6⅝.
24790-2 Pa. $6.95

AN ENCYCLOPEDIA OF BATTLES: Accounts of Over 1,560 Battles from 1479 B.C. to the Present, David Eggenberger. Presents essential details of every major battle in recorded history, from the first battle of Megiddo in 1479 B.C. to Grenada in 1984. List of Battle Maps. New Appendix covering the years 1967–1984. Index. 99 illustrations. 544pp. 6½ × 9¼.
24913-1 Pa. $14.95

AN ETYMOLOGICAL DICTIONARY OF MODERN ENGLISH, Ernest Weekley. Richest, fullest work, by foremost British lexicographer. Detailed word histories. Inexhaustible. Total of 856pp. 6½ × 9¼.
21873-2, 21874-0 Pa., Two-vol. set $19.90

WEBSTER'S AMERICAN MILITARY BIOGRAPHIES, edited by Robert McHenry. Over 1,000 figures who shaped 3 centuries of American military history. Detailed biographies of Nathan Hale, Douglas MacArthur, Mary Hallaren, others. Chronologies of engagements, more. Introduction. Addenda. 1,033 entries in alphabetical order. xi + 548pp. 6½ × 9¼. (Available in U.S. only)
24758-9 Pa. $13.95

LIFE IN ANCIENT EGYPT, Adolf Erman. Detailed older account, with much not in more recent books: domestic life, religion, magic, medicine, commerce, and whatever else needed for complete picture. Many illustrations. 597pp. 5⅜ × 8½.
22632-8 Pa. $8.95

HISTORIC COSTUME IN PICTURES, Braun & Schneider. Over 1,450 costumed figures shown, covering a wide variety of peoples: kings, emperors, nobles, priests, servants, soldiers, scholars, townsfolk, peasants, merchants, courtiers, cavaliers, and more. 256pp. 8⅜ × 11¼.
23150-X Pa. $9.95

THE NOTEBOOKS OF LEONARDO DA VINCI, edited by J. P. Richter. Extracts from manuscripts reveal great genius; on painting, sculpture, anatomy, sciences, geography, etc. Both Italian and English. 186 ms. pages reproduced, plus 500 additional drawings, including studies for *Last Supper, Sforza* monument, etc. 860pp. 7⅞ × 10¾. (Available in U.S. only) 22572-0, 22573-9 Pa., Two-vol. set $31.90

THE ART NOUVEAU STYLE BOOK OF ALPHONSE MUCHA: All 72 Plates from "Documents Decoratifs" in Original Color, Alphonse Mucha. Rare copyright-free design portfolio by high priest of Art Nouveau. Jewelry, wallpaper, stained glass, furniture, figure studies, plant and animal motifs, etc. Only complete one-volume edition. 80pp. 9⅜ × 12¼. 24044-4 Pa. $9.95

ANIMALS: 1,419 COPYRIGHT-FREE ILLUSTRATIONS OF MAMMALS, BIRDS, FISH, INSECTS, ETC., edited by Jim Harter. Clear wood engravings present, in extremely lifelike poses, over 1,000 species of animals. One of the most extensive pictorial sourcebooks of its kind. Captions. Index. 284pp. 9 × 12. 23766-4 Pa. $9.95

OBELISTS FLY HIGH, C. Daly King. Masterpiece of American detective fiction, long out of print, involves murder on a 1935 transcontinental flight—"a very thrilling story"—NY Times. Unabridged and unaltered republication of the edition published by William Collins Sons & Co. Ltd., London, 1935. 288pp. 5⅜ × 8½. (Available in U.S. only) 25036-9 Pa. $5.95

VICTORIAN AND EDWARDIAN FASHION: A Photographic Survey, Alison Gernsheim. First fashion history completely illustrated by contemporary photographs. Full text plus 235 photos, 1840–1914, in which many celebrities appear. 240pp. 6½ × 9¼. 24205-6 Pa. $8.95

THE ART OF THE FRENCH ILLUSTRATED BOOK, 1700–1914, Gordon N. Ray. Over 630 superb book illustrations by Fragonard, Delacroix, Daumier, Doré, Grandville, Manet, Mucha, Steinlen, Toulouse-Lautrec and many others. Preface. Introduction. 633 halftones. Indices of artists, authors & titles, binders and provenances. Appendices. Bibliography. 608pp. 8⅜ × 11¼. 25086-5 Pa. $24.95

THE WONDERFUL WIZARD OF OZ, L. Frank Baum. Facsimile in full color of America's finest children's classic. 143 illustrations by W. W. Denslow. 267pp. 5⅜ × 8½. 20691-2 Pa. $7.95

FOLLOWING THE EQUATOR: A Journey Around the World, Mark Twain. Great writer's 1897 account of circumnavigating the globe by steamship. Ironic humor, keen observations, vivid and fascinating descriptions of exotic places. 197 illustrations. 720pp. 5⅜ × 8½. 26113-1 Pa. $15.95

THE FRIENDLY STARS, Martha Evans Martin & Donald Howard Menzel. Classic text marshalls the stars together in an engaging, non-technical survey, presenting them as sources of beauty in night sky. 23 illustrations. Foreword. 2 star charts. Index. 147pp. 5⅜ × 8½. 21099-5 Pa. $3.95

FADS AND FALLACIES IN THE NAME OF SCIENCE, Martin Gardner. Fair, witty appraisal of cranks, quacks, and quackeries of science and pseudoscience: hollow earth, Velikovsky, orgone energy, Dianetics, flying saucers, Bridey Murphy, food and medical fads, etc. Revised, expanded In the Name of Science. "A very able and even-tempered presentation."—The New Yorker. 363pp. 5⅜ × 8. 20394-8 Pa. $6.95

ANCIENT EGYPT: ITS CULTURE AND HISTORY, J. E Manchip White. From pre-dynastics through Ptolemies: society, history, political structure, religion, daily life, literature, cultural heritage. 48 plates. 217pp. 5⅜ × 8½. 22548-8 Pa. $5.95

SIR HARRY HOTSPUR OF HUMBLETHWAITE, Anthony Trollope. Incisive, unconventional psychological study of a conflict between a wealthy baronet, his idealistic daughter, and their scapegrace cousin. The 1870 novel in its first inexpensive edition in years. 250pp. 5⅜ × 8½.   24953-0 Pa. $6.95

LASERS AND HOLOGRAPHY, Winston E. Kock. Sound introduction to burgeoning field, expanded (1981) for second edition. Wave patterns, coherence, lasers, diffraction, zone plates, properties of holograms, recent advances. 84 illustrations. 160pp. 5⅜ × 8¼. (Except in United Kingdom)   24041-X Pa. $3.95

INTRODUCTION TO ARTIFICIAL INTELLIGENCE: SECOND, EN-LARGED EDITION, Philip C. Jackson, Jr. Comprehensive survey of artificial intelligence—the study of how machines (computers) can be made to act intelligently. Includes introductory and advanced material. Extensive notes updating the main text. 132 black-and-white illustrations. 512pp. 5⅜ × 8½.   24864-X Pa. $8.95

HISTORY OF INDIAN AND INDONESIAN ART, Ananda K. Coomaraswamy. Over 400 illustrations illuminate classic study of Indian art from earliest Harappa finds to early 20th century. Provides philosophical, religious and social insights. 304pp. 6⅜ × 9⅜.   25005-9 Pa. $11.95

THE GOLEM, Gustav Meyrink. Most famous supernatural novel in modern European literature, set in Ghetto of Old Prague around 1890. Compelling story of mystical experiences, strange transformations, profound terror. 13 black-and-white illustrations. 224pp. 5⅜ × 8½. (Available in U.S. only)   25025-3 Pa. $6.95

PICTORIAL ENCYCLOPEDIA OF HISTORIC ARCHITECTURAL PLANS, DETAILS AND ELEMENTS: With 1,880 Line Drawings of Arches, Domes, Doorways, Facades, Gables, Windows, etc., John Theodore Haneman. Sourcebook of inspiration for architects, designers, others. Bibliography. Captions. 141pp. 9 × 12.   24605-1 Pa. $7.95

BENCHLEY LOST AND FOUND, Robert Benchley. Finest humor from early 30's, about pet peeves, child psychologists, post office and others. Mostly unavailable elsewhere. 73 illustrations by Peter Arno and others. 183pp. 5⅜ × 8½.
                                                           22410-4 Pa. $4.95

ERTÉ GRAPHICS, Erté. Collection of striking color graphics: *Seasons, Alphabet, Numerals, Aces* and *Precious Stones*. 50 plates, including 4 on covers. 48pp. 9⅜ × 12¼.   23580-7 Pa. $7.95

THE JOURNAL OF HENRY D. THOREAU, edited by Bradford Torrey, F. H. Allen. Complete reprinting of 14 volumes, 1837–61, over two million words; the sourcebooks for *Walden*, etc. Definitive. All original sketches, plus 75 photographs. 1,804pp. 8½ × 12¼.   20312-3, 20313-1 Cloth., Two-vol. set $125.00

CASTLES: THEIR CONSTRUCTION AND HISTORY, Sidney Toy. Traces castle development from ancient roots. Nearly 200 photographs and drawings illustrate moats, keeps, baileys, many other features. Caernarvon, Dover Castles, Hadrian's Wall, Tower of London, dozens more. 256pp. 5⅜ × 8¼.
                                                           24898-4 Pa. $6.95

AMERICAN CLIPPER SHIPS: 1833–1858, Octavius T. Howe & Frederick C. Matthews. Fully-illustrated, encyclopedic review of 352 clipper ships from the period of America's greatest maritime supremacy. Introduction. 109 halftones. 5 black-and-white line illustrations. Index. Total of 928pp. 5⅜ × 8½.
25115-2, 25116-0 Pa., Two-vol. set $17.90

TOWARDS A NEW ARCHITECTURE, Le Corbusier. Pioneering manifesto by great architect, near legendary founder of "International School." Technical and aesthetic theories, views on industry, economics, relation of form to function, "mass-production spirit," much more. Profusely illustrated. Unabridged translation of 13th French edition. Introduction by Frederick Etchells. 320pp. 6⅛ × 9¼. (Available in U.S. only)
25023-7 Pa. $8.95

THE BOOK OF KELLS, edited by Blanche Cirker. Inexpensive collection of 32 full-color, full-page plates from the greatest illuminated manuscript of the Middle Ages, painstakingly reproduced from rare facsimile edition. Publisher's Note. Captions. 32pp. 9⅜ × 12¼.
24345-1 Pa. $4.95

BEST SCIENCE FICTION STORIES OF H. G. WELLS, H. G. Wells. Full novel *The Invisible Man*, plus 17 short stories: "The Crystal Egg," "Aepyornis Island," "The Strange Orchid," etc. 303pp. 5⅜ × 8½. (Available in U.S. only)
21531-8 Pa. $6.95

AMERICAN SAILING SHIPS: Their Plans and History, Charles G. Davis. Photos, construction details of schooners, frigates, clippers, other sailcraft of 18th to early 20th centuries—plus entertaining discourse on design, rigging, nautical lore, much more. 137 black-and-white illustrations. 240pp. 6⅛ × 9¼.
24658-2 Pa. $6.95

ENTERTAINING MATHEMATICAL PUZZLES, Martin Gardner. Selection of author's favorite conundrums involving arithmetic, money, speed, etc., with lively commentary. Complete solutions. 112pp. 5⅜ × 8½.
25211-6 Pa. $2.95

THE WILL TO BELIEVE, HUMAN IMMORTALITY, William James. Two books bound together. Effect of irrational on logical, and arguments for human immortality. 402pp. 5⅜ × 8½.
20291-7 Pa. $7.95

THE HAUNTED MONASTERY and THE CHINESE MAZE MURDERS, Robert Van Gulik. 2 full novels by Van Gulik continue adventures of Judge Dee and his companions. An evil Taoist monastery, seemingly supernatural events; overgrown topiary maze that hides strange crimes. Set in 7th-century China. 27 illustrations. 328pp. 5⅜ × 8½.
23502-5 Pa. $6.95

CELEBRATED CASES OF JUDGE DEE (DEE GOONG AN), translated by Robert Van Gulik. Authentic 18th-century Chinese detective novel; Dee and associates solve three interlocked cases. Led to Van Gulik's own stories with same characters. Extensive introduction. 9 illustrations. 237pp. 5⅜ × 8½.
23337-5 Pa. $5.95

Prices subject to change without notice.
Available at your book dealer or write for free catalog to Dept. GI, Dover Publications, Inc., 31 East 2nd St., Mineola, N.Y. 11501. Dover publishes more than 175 books each year on science, elementary and advanced mathematics, biology, music, art, literary history, social sciences and other areas.